1st Workshop on Natural Language Generation, Evaluation and Metrics (GEM 2021)

Held online due to COVID-19

5-6 August 2021
Bangkok, Thailand

ISBN: 978-1-7138-3375-8

Printed from e-media with permission by:

Curran Associates, Inc.
57 Morehouse Lane
Red Hook, NY 12571

CURRAN ASSOCIATES INC.
proceedings
.com

Some format issues inherent in the e-media version may also appear in this print version.

Association for Computational Linguistics
209 N. Eighth Street
Stroudsburg, Pennsylvania 18360

Phone: 1-570-476-8006
Fax: 1-570-476-0860

acl@aclweb.org

Additional copies of this publication are available from:

Curran Associates, Inc.
57 Morehouse Lane
Red Hook, NY 12571 USA
Phone: 845-758-0400
Fax: 845-758-2633
Email: curran@proceedings.com
Web: www.proceedings.com

GEM 2021

The 1st Workshop on Natural Language Generation, Evaluation, and Metrics

Proceedings of the Workshop

August 5 - 6, 2021
Bangkok, Thailand (online)

Message from the Organizing Committee

The first Workshop on Natural Language Generation, Evaluation, and Metrics (GEM) was held on August 6, colocated with ACL 2021. The GEM workshop is endorsed by SIGGEN. The organization of GEM was started following discussions during Bird-of-a-Feather sessions at ACL 2020 in which a large share of the attending generation researchers agreed that we need a community-driven project focused on combining advancements in data, models, and (automatic and human) evaluation to measure progress in natural language generation (NLG).

The focus of the GEM workshop was in the shared task for the associated benchmark which was created by the entire program committee. In addition to making an in-depth evaluation of generation models possible, GEM also aims to make generation research more inclusive of additional languages by being designed to be extended with newly created datasets and by prioritizing inclusion of datasets that target languages beyond English. Preliminary results of the shared task were announced at the workshop.

In addition to four reports of shared task participants, we also received 14 research papers of which 11 were accepted for presentation at the workshop. We further invited the authors of 12 Findings of the ACL papers to present, leading to a total of 27 presentations.

Asli Celikyilmaz gave an invited keynote and participated in one of the two panel discussions on responsible progress in NLG. The other panelists were Anya Belz, Hady Elsahar, Seraphina Goldfarb-Tarrant, He He, Mike Lewis, Lisa Li, Wang Lu, and Ehud Reiter.

We would like to thank the members of the Program Committee for their timely reviews. We also would like to thank the participants of the shared task and all volunteers who helped with the evaluations.

Antoine Bosselut, Esin Durmus, Varun Prashant Gangal, Sebastian Gehrmann, Yacine Jernite, Laura Perez-Beltrachini, Samira Shaikh, and Wei Xu

Organizers

Organizing Committee

Antoine Bosselut, Esin Durmus, Varun Prashant Gangal, Sebastian Gehrmann, Yacine Jernite, Laura Perez-Beltrachini, Samira Shaikh, and Wei Xu

Program Committee

Tosin Adewumi, Karmanya Aggarwal, Pawan Sasanka Ammanamanchi, Aremu Anuoluwapo, Antoine Bosselut, Khyathi Raghavi Chandu, Miruna Clinciu, Dipanjan Das, Kaustubh D. Dhole, Wanyu Du, Esin Durmus, Ondřej Dušek, Chris Emezue, Varun Gangal, Cristina Garbacea, Sebastian Gehrmann, Tatsunori Hashimoto, Yufang Hou, Yacine Jernite, Harsh Jhamtani, Yangfeng Ji, Shailza Jolly, Mihir Kale, Dhruv Kumar, Faisal Ladhak, Aman Madaan, Mounica Maddela, Khyati Mahajan, Saad Mahamood, Bodhisattwa Prasad Majumder, Pedro Henrique Martins, Angelina McMillan-Major, Simon Mille, Emiel van Miltenburg, Moin Nadeem, Shashi Narayan, Vitaly Nikolaev, Rubungo Andre Niyongabo, Salomey Osei, Ankur Parikh, Laura Perez-Beltrachini, Niranjan Ramesh Rao, Vikas Raunak, Juan Diego Rodriguez, Sashank Santhanam, João Sedoc, Thibault Sellam, Samira Shaikh, Anastasia Shimorina, Marco Antonio Sobrevilla Cabezudo, Hendrik Strobelt, Nishant Subramani, Wei Xu, Diyi Yang, Akhila Yerukola, Jiawei Zhou

Invited Speaker

Asli Celikyilmaz

Invited Panelists

Anya Belz, Asli Celikyilmaz, Hady Elsahar, Seraphina Goldfarb-Tarrant, He He, Mike Lewis, Lisa Li, Wang Lu, and Ehud Reiter

Table of Contents

Conference Program

Friday, August 6, 2021

11:30–12:00 Opening Remarks and Overview of the Virtual Platform

12:00–12:55 Poster Session

Flesch-Kincaid is Not a Text Simplification Evaluation Metric
Teerapaun Tanprasert and David Kauchak

Human Perception in Natural Language Generation
Lorenzo De Mattei, Huiyuan Lai, Felice Dell'Orletta and Malvina Nissim

Semantic Similarity Based Evaluation for Abstractive News Summarization
Figen Beken Fikri, Kemal Oflazer and Berrin Yanikoglu

Shades of BLEU, Flavours of Success: The Case of MultiWOZ
Tomáš Nekvinda and Ondřej Dušek

13:00–13:45 Panel Session

13:00–13:45 *Panel*

Friday, August 6, 2021 (continued)

14:00–15:00 Talk Session

14:00–14:15 *Personalized Response Generation with Tensor Factorization*
Zhenghui Wang, Lingxiao Luo and Diyi Yang

14:15–14:30 *A Review of Human Evaluation for Style Transfer*
Eleftheria Briakou, Sweta Agrawal, Ke Zhang, Joel Tetreault and Marine Carpuat

14:30–14:45 *GOT: Testing for Originality in Natural Language Generation*
Jennifer Brooks and Abdou Youssef

14:45–15:00 *Evaluating Text Generation from Discourse Representation Structures*
Chunliu Wang, Rik van Noord, Arianna Bisazza and Johan Bos

15:00–15:55 Poster Session

Human Evaluation of Creative NLG Systems: An Interdisciplinary Survey on Recent Papers
Mika Hämäläinen and Khalid Alnajjar

16:00–16:50 Keynote Session

16:00–16:50 *Keynote*
Asli Celikyilmaz

Friday, August 6, 2021 (continued)

17:00–17:45 Panel Session

17:00–17:45 *Panel*

18:00–19:00 GEM Overview Session

18:00–18:15 *The GEM Benchmark: Natural Language Generation, its Evaluation and Metrics*
Sebastian Gehrmann, Tosin Adewumi, Karmanya Aggarwal, Pawan Sasanka Ammanamanchi, Anuoluwapo Aremu, Antoine Bosselut, Khyathi Raghavi Chandu, Miruna-Adriana Clinciu, Dipanjan Das, Kaustubh Dhole, Wanyu Du, Esin Durmus, Ondřej Dušek, Chris Chinenye Emezue, Varun Gangal, Cristina Garbacea, Tatsunori Hashimoto, Yufang Hou, Yacine Jernite, Harsh Jhamtani, Yangfeng Ji, Shailza Jolly, Mihir Kale, Dhruv Kumar, Faisal Ladhak, Aman Madaan, Mounica Maddela, Khyati Mahajan, Saad Mahamood, Bodhisattwa Prasad Majumder, Pedro Henrique Martins, Angelina McMillan-Major, Simon Mille, Emiel van Miltenburg, Moin Nadeem, Shashi Narayan, Vitaly Nikolaev, Andre Niyongabo Rubungo, Salomey Osei, Ankur Parikh, Laura Perez-Beltrachini, Niranjan Ramesh Rao, Vikas Raunak, Juan Diego Rodriguez, Sashank Santhanam, João Sedoc, Thibault Sellam, Samira Shaikh, Anastasia Shimorina, Marco Antonio Sobrevilla Cabezudo, Hendrik Strobelt, Nishant Subramani, Wei Xu, Diyi Yang, Akhila Yerukola and Jiawei Zhou

18:15–18:30 *Reusable Templates and Guides For Documenting Datasets and Models for Natural Language Processing and Generation: A Case Study of the HuggingFace and GEM Data and Model Cards*
Angelina McMillan-Major, Salomey Osei, Juan Diego Rodriguez, Pawan Sasanka Ammanamanchi, Sebastian Gehrmann and Yacine Jernite

19:00–20:00 GEM Systems Session

19:00–19:15 *Structure-to-Text Generation with Self-Training, Acceptability Classifiers and Context-Conditioning for the GEM Shared Task*
Shreyan Bakshi, Soumya Batra, Peyman Heidari, Ankit Arun, Shashank Jain and Michael White

19:15–19:30 *NUIG-DSI's submission to The GEM Benchmark 2021*
Nivranshu Pasricha, Mihael Arcan and Paul Buitelaar

19:30–19:45 *SimpleNER Sentence Simplification System for GEM 2021*
K V Aditya Srivatsa, Monil Gokani and Manish Shrivastava

19:45–20:00 *System Description for the CommonGen task with the POINTER model*
Anna Shvets

Friday, August 6, 2021 (continued)

20:00–20:55 Poster Session

Decoding Methods for Neural Narrative Generation
Alexandra DeLucia, Aaron Mueller, Xiang Lisa Li and João Sedoc

Flesch-Kincaid is Not a Text Simplification Evaluation Metric

Teerapaun Tanprasert
Pomona College
Claremont, CA
teerapaun.tanprasert@pomona.edu

David Kauchak
Pomona College
Claremont, CA
david.kauchak@pomona.edu

Abstract

Sentence-level text simplification is evaluated using both automated metrics and human evaluation. For automatic evaluation, a combination of metrics is usually employed to evaluate different aspects of the simplification. Flesch-Kincaid Grade Level (FKGL) is one metric that has been regularly used to measure the readability of system output. In this paper, we argue that FKGL should not be used to evaluate text simplification systems. We provide experimental analyses on recent system output showing that the FKGL score can easily be manipulated to improve the score dramatically with only minor impact on other automated metrics (BLEU and SARI). Instead of using FKGL, we suggest that the component statistics, along with others, be used for posthoc analysis to understand system behavior.

1 Introduction

Critical to any application area is evaluation. Evaluation is often accomplished using one or more quantifiable evaluation metrics. Evaluation metrics are the main tool for comparing and analyzing approaches (Hossin and Sulaiman, 2015) and are often used to define whether progress is being made in a field. A good evaluation metric should be a proper measure of the quality of a particular algorithm and, importantly, should not be "gameable". Specifically, an approach should not be able to obtain a better score on the evaluation metric by manipulating the algorithm or output in ways that do not improve the actual quality of the output.

In this paper, we examine evaluation for text simplification, specifically, sentence-level text simplification. Text simplification aims to transform text into a variant that is easier to understand by a broader range of people while retaining as much of the original content as possible. A range of approaches for text simplification have been proposed ranging from lexical simplification (Shardlow, 2014), where only words and phrases are changed, to fully generative approaches that leverage models from machine translation (Coster and Kauchak, 2011a; Wubben et al., 2012) and recent sequential neural networks (Nisioi et al., 2017; Zhang and Lapata, 2017; Nishihara et al., 2019). Text simplification evaluation has been done with two general approaches: human evaluation and automated metrics.

Human evaluation relies on annotators to judge the quality of the simplifications on three dimensions: fluency/grammaticality, how well the sentence represents fluent, grammatical text; adequacy, how well the content is preserved; and, simplicity, how simple the text is (Woodsend and Lapata, 2011). The first two metrics were adapted from other text generation tasks (Knight and Marcu, 2002) with the addition of simplicity for text simplification. When human evaluation is used, these three metrics have been consistently employed. Human evaluations provide concrete analysis of texts simplification systems along important dimensions, however, human evaluation is costly and is not practical for development, tuning, and other real-time uses. As such, text simplification has also relied on automated metrics for evaluation.

Automatic evaluation of text simplification has varied more across papers, though three metrics are most commonly employed: BLEU, SARI, and Flesch-Kincaid. BLEU (Papineni et al., 2001) compares the n-gram overlap via precision of a system simplification with a human reference simplification and was borrowed from machine translation. BLEU was the first metric suggested for text simplification that utilized reference simplifications (Zhu et al., 2010), however, it focuses less on simplicity and more on fluency and content preservation. To counter this, SARI was proposed as an alternate metric (Xu et al., 2016). SARI also compares

Proceedings of the 1st Workshop on Natural Language Generation, Evaluation, and Metrics (GEM 2021), pages 1–14
August 5–6, 2021.

against human references, but also utilizes the input sentence allowing it to better capture addition and deletion of information.

Finally, a third automated metric that has been used to measure readability and fluency is Flesch-Kincaid Grade Level (FKGL). FKGL was initially proposed in the 1940s (Flesch, 1948) and since then has been used extensively in the medical domain, though it has never been shown to affect actual comprehension (Shardlow, 2014; Kauchak and Leroy, 2016). FKGL combines two text statistics to calculate the score: the average number of syllables per word and the average number of words per sentence:

$$FKGL = 0.39\frac{N_{words}}{N_{sentences}} + 11.8\frac{N_{syllables}}{N_{words}} - 15.59 \quad (1)$$

In recent text simplification papers, both BLEU and SARI are common evaluation metrics (Vu et al., 2018; Guo et al., 2018; Scarton and Specia, 2018; Qiang, 2018; Niklaus et al., 2019; Nishihara et al., 2019). FKGL is not as popular as it was before SARI was introduced, but it continues to be used as an evaluation metric in recent papers (Xu et al., 2016; Zhang and Lapata, 2017; Guo et al., 2018; Qiang, 2018; Scarton and Specia, 2018; Nassar et al., 2019; Nishihara et al., 2019).

In this paper, we argue that FKGL is not a proper evaluation metric for text simplification and should not be used to evaluate text simplification systems, i.e., alongside other metrics like BLEU and SARI. FKGL was one of the first metrics suggested for text simplification (Zhu et al., 2010) and has been used by many as an evaluation metric to compare systems. However, FKGL was not originally designed to evaluate system output (it was designed to measure human output) and, because of its simplistic nature, is very easy to game, either explicitly (as we do in this paper) or implicitly by certain model biases (e.g., text simplification algorithms that split sentences will tend to have better FKGL scores). Recent work has shown that systems with good FKGL scores are not necessarily correlated with high-quality simplifications (Martin et al., 2018; Alva-Manchego et al., 2020), however, this is the first in-depth analysis of the FKGL metric for evaluation and where specific system transformations are analyzed.

To explore how FKGL can be manipulated, we introduce six simple methods for modifying system output and examine the impact these modifications have on automated evaluation metrics. The modifications could be made explicitly by a system in an attempt to improve their score, or, more worrisome, implicitly. In addition to the FKGL scores, we also present and and discuss how BLEU and SARI respond to the modifications. We show that with some very minor modifications, FKGL can be improved dramatically with minimal effect on the other two evaluation metrics. We conclude with some recommendations on how to incorporate FKGL-like metrics into text simplification analysis.

2 History of Flesch-Kincaid

The earliest version of the Flesch-Kincaid readability formula appears in Flesch's doctoral dissertation (Flesch, 1943) and calculated based on the the average number of words per sentence, the number of affixes, and the number of references to people. The formula was derived based on the McCall-Crabbs Standard Test Lessons in Reading (McCall and Crabbs, 1926), a standardized test given to children in grades 3-7. The McCall-Crabbs tests contains 376 passages with 8 reading comprehensive questions per passage. Each lesson is labeled with its difficulty as a grade level. Based on these texts, Flesch developed the formula to predict the grade of children in grades 3-7 who answered at least 75% of the questions correctly about a given passage. The original goal of the formula was to help students track their progress.

Five years later, he published a new formula: the Reading Ease Score (Flesch, 1948). He adjusted the original formula by recomputing the coefficients and replacing previous text measurements with the ones used today, the average number of syllables and the average sentences length. Like the original study, this new formula was validated with children and was based on the same criterion, McCall-Crabbs Standard Test Lessons in Reading.

Flesch-Kincaid Grade Level is a variation of the Reading Ease formula with readjusted weights and is the formula that has been commonly used in text simplification evaluation. The formula was derived three decades later (Kincaid et al., 1975) specifically to evaluate the readability of technical materials for military personnel. 531 Navy personnel in four technical training schools at Navy bases were tested for their reading comprehension level according to the comprehension section of the Gates-McGinitie reading test as well as their comprehension of 18 passages from Rate Training

Manuals. Despite the fact that this formula was derived from Navy personnel, with military-based material, and specifically for Navy use, it has been broadly used in a range of settings to evaluate the readability of text, for example, it is commonly used to guide text generation by medical writers in the medical domain and even Microsoft Word includes both the Flesch Reading Ease and FKGL scores (Shedlosky-Shoemaker et al., 2009).

We provide this background to raise some concerns based on its origins for its application for text simplification evaluation. The inputs of the formula – sentence count, word count, and syllable count – were decided based on a study in the 1940s where modern text analysis tools were not available. Both the Flesch Reading Ease and FKGL scores were developed based on very specific corpora and very targeted populations, children grades 3-7 in the former case and Navy personnel in the latter case. Most importantly, the text passages used to collect data were always written by people and assumed to be mostly free of errors in terms of writing. These assumption cannot be made for text generated by automated systems.

3 Modifying Text Simplification Output

One of the main drawbacks of the FKGL metric is that the formula is based on fairly simplistic text statistics. Because of this, it is straightforward to manipulate the output of a text simplification to artificially improve the FKGL score. We suggest six approaches to modify the output of an automatically simplified text that aim to manipulate these statistics. We view the modifications as an explicit post-processing step, however, many of them could be incorporated into a text simplification system either explicitly as a way to improve the score, or implicitly as a side-effect of the algorithm used (e.g., sentence splitting). Each approach suggested modifies the output text on a sentence level. In the analyses we consider the effect of applying each approach to varying proportions of the sentences output by the system.

random-period: Randomly insert a period into the sentence. Adding a period to the sentence splits the sentence into two sentences which reduces the average number of words per sentence.

random-the: Randomly insert the word "the" into the sentence. This adds a short and very common word to reduce the average syllable count per word while minimizing the impact on the meaning.

replace-longest: Replace the longest word in the sentence (by character count) with the word "the". Assuming that the number of characters in a word positively correlates with the number of syllables, replacing the longest word with "the" should reduce the average syllable count per word.

replace-rand-period: Replace a random word with a period in the sentence. This is similar to *random-period*, but additionally removes a random word to reduce the number of words per sentence.

replace-rand-the: Replace a random word with "the": imitates *random-the.*, but additionally removes a random word to reduce the number of words per sentence.

rand-period+ repl-longest: combine *random-period* and *replace-longest* to magnify the effects on FKGL.

4 Data

To understand the problems with FKGL, we analyzed the output from the five text simplification systems examined by Zhang and Lapata (2017), a number of which are state-of-the-art: PBMT-R (Wubben et al., 2012), a phrase-based approach based on statistical MT; Hybrid (Narayan and Gardent, 2014), a model that combines sentence splitting and deletion with PBMT-R; EncDecA, a basic neural encoder-decoder model with attention; and two deep reinforcement learning models, Dress and Dress-Ls (Zhang and Lapata, 2017).

There are two main corpora that are used to train and evaluate text simplification systems: Wikipedia (Zhu et al., 2010; Coster and Kauchak, 2011b), which consists of automatically aligned sentences between English Wikipedia and Simple English Wikipedia, and Newsela (Xu et al., 2015), which consists of news articles manually simplified at varying levels of simplicity. We present the results for the Newsela corpus since it involves explicit human simplification and has been shown to be less noisy than the Wikipedia corpus (Xu et al., 2015). We also conducted the experimental analysis on the Wikipedia corpus and saw similar results.

5 Experimental Analysis

We applied each of the modification techniques to a varied percentage of output sentences, from 10% to 100% in increments of 10%, for the five text simplification systems. The sentences to be modified were randomly selected from the system output.

We calculated FKGL[1] as well as BLEU (Papineni et al., 2001) and SARI[2] (Xu et al., 2016) to observe how the modifications affect other common text simplification evaluation metrics. To account for per-sentence variation and randomness in some of the modification approaches, we repeated the experiments 100 times and averaged the results.

5.1 Results

Figure 1 shows the trends of the effect that the modification approaches have on FKGL for Dress-Ls, and Table 1 presents more detailed experimental results for the three best performing systems (Dress-Ls, EncDecA, and Hybrid). The three methods that involve sentence splitting result in aggressive improvements in the FKGL score; replacing the longest word shows some improvement; and the other two approaches involving "the" have minimal effect. In the most extreme case, *rand-period+ repl-longest* reduces the FKGL score to almost zero when applied to all of the sentences. *With simple post-processing applied to the output, a text simplification approach can achieve an arbitrarily low FKGL score.*

Figures 2 and 3 show the effect that the modification approaches have on the BLEU and SARI scores for Dress-Ls. There is virtually no effect on the SARI scores by any of the modification techniques and none of the approaches change the score by more than 0.004, regardless of percentage of sentences modified. BLEU, on the other hand, does register some differences for the modified output. *rand-period+ repl-longest* has the most drastic effect and, in the most extreme case, for Dress-Ls it reduces the BLEU score from 0.2374 to 0.1710 when it is applied to all sentences. The other five modification techniques have more minor effects, e.g., *random-period* drops the score to 0.1953, when applied to all sentences.

Using multiple evaluation metrics partially mitigates the gameability of FKGL since BLEU is affected. However, the effect on BLEU is significantly smaller than the effect on FKGL. While the Dress-Ls system did originally have the highest BLEU and SARI scores, it did not have the highest FKGL score. However, if we randomly inserted a period into just 10% of the sentences of the Dress-Ls output, the FKGL score would improve to 4.543, the BLEU score would drop slightly to

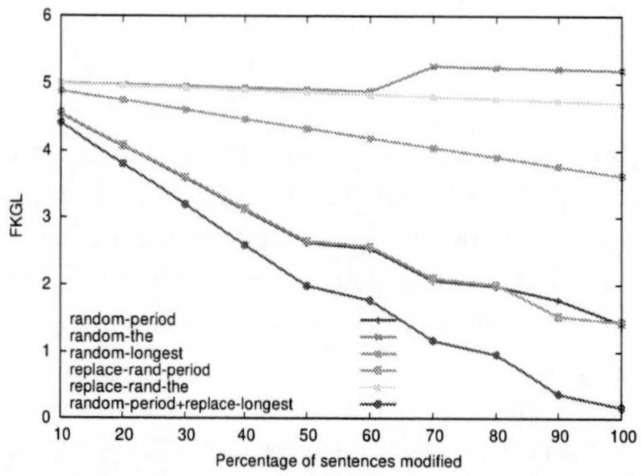

Figure 1: FKGL scores (smaller is better) from the experiments on the Dress-Ls test output, averaged over 100 runs.

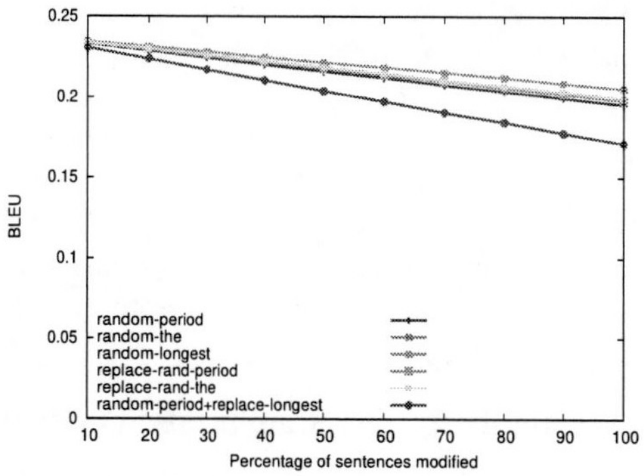

Figure 2: BLEU scores (larger is better) from the experiments on the Dress-Ls test output, averaged over 100 runs.

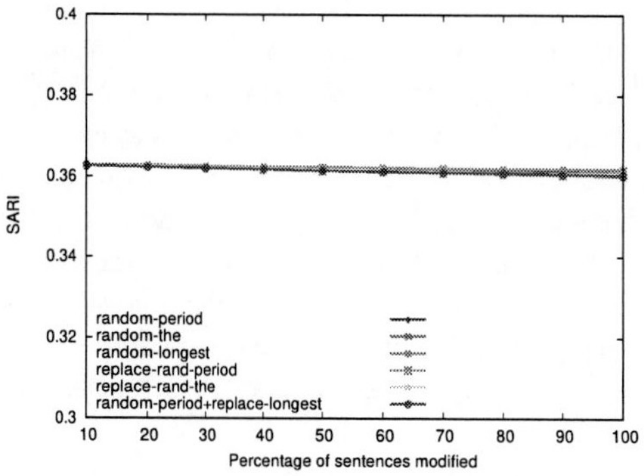

Figure 3: SARI scores (larger is better) from the experiments on the Dress-Ls test output, averaged over 100 runs.

0.233 and there is no significant change in SARI score. After the transformation, the system would still be the best performing model with respect to BLEU and SARI, but now it would also be the best performing model with respect to FKGL. *With a*

[1] https://github.com/mmautner/readability

[2] We used the implementation for BLEU and SARI from the Joshua Simplification System.

FKGL	Dress-Ls				EncDecA				Hybrid			
Approach	**0%**	**10%**	**50%**	**100%**	**0%**	**10%**	**50%**	**100%**	**0%**	**10%**	**50%**	**100%**
random-period		4.5426	2.6223	1.4154		5.2902	3.4309	1.9016		4.2706	2.6543	1.3512
random-the		5.0006	4.9095	5.1919		6.1273	6.0509	5.9596		4.7434	4.6204	4.8678
replace-longest	5.024	4.8837	4.3242	3.6244	5.757	5.6408	5.1763	4.5984	4.775	4.6108	3.9492	3.1241
replace-rand-period		4.5510	2.6494	1.4359		5.2959	3.4474	1.9173		4.2884	2.7283	1.4524
replace-rand-the		4.9915	4.8636	4.7003		5.8014	5.8058	5.8001		4.7282	4.5449	4.3104
rand-period+ repl-longest		4.4098	1.9831	0.1643		5.1806	2.8913	0.8477		4.1234	1.9268	-0.0665

BLEU	Dress-Ls				EncDecA				Hybrid			
Approach	**0%**	**10%**	**50%**	**100%**	**0%**	**10%**	**50%**	**100%**	**0%**	**10%**	**50%**	**100%**
random-period		0.2330	0.2158	0.1953		0.2086	0.1954	0.1794		0.1069	0.1004	0.0898
random-the		0.2334	0.2174	0.1985		0.2088	0.1963	0.1814		0.1071	0.1015	0.0919
replace-longest	0.237	0.2343	0.2215	0.2052	0.212	0.2097	0.2008	0.1895	0.108	0.1069	0.1016	0.0948
replace-rand-period		0.2336	0.2176	0.1977		0.2088	0.1965	0.1808		0.1063	0.0984	0.0883
replace-rand-the		0.2337	0.2184	0.1991		0.2088	0.1965	0.1808		0.1063	0.0984	0.0879
rand-period+ repl-longest		0.2306	0.2036	0.1710		0.2067	0.1871	0.1621		0.1059	0.0957	0.0806

SARI	Dress-Ls				EncDecA				Hybrid			
Approach	**0%**	**10%**	**50%**	**100%**	**0%**	**10%**	**50%**	**100%**	**0%**	**10%**	**50%**	**100%**
random-period		0.3626	0.3618	0.3608		0.3598	0.3593	0.3586		0.3470	0.3468	0.3465
random-the		0.3627	0.3621	0.3616		0.3599	0.3596	0.3593		0.3471	0.3471	0.3473
replace-longest	0.363	0.3627	0.3622	0.3618	0.360	0.3600	0.3598	0.3597	0.347	0.3471	0.3472	0.3474
replace-rand-period		0.3626	0.3614	0.3601		0.3598	0.3590	0.3579		0.3470	0.3466	0.3462
replace-rand-the		0.3626	0.3617	0.3607		0.3599	0.3593	0.3586		0.3470	0.3469	0.3468
rand-period+ repl-longest		0.3625	0.3614	0.3604		0.3598	0.3591	0.3587		0.3470	0.3471	0.3471

Table 1: Experimental results (FKGL, BLEU and SARI scores) for 10%, 50% and 100% of the sentences being modified on three systems: Dress-Ls, EncDecA and Hybrid.

simple modification to the system output, the best performing model could be changed with respect to FKGL without affecting the other two metrics significantly.

For the sake of brevity, we only include detailed experimental analysis of the output of Dress-Ls, however, the results were similar across all systems[3]. To provide some additional examples, Table 1 shows the FKGL, BLEU, and SARI scores for Dress-Ls, EncDecA, and Hybrid where 10%, 50%, and 100% of the sentences were modified. We chose EncDecA and Hybrid as additional systems to include since they performed well on at least one of the automated metrics and represent fairly different approaches to the text simplification problem. The trends seen for Dress-Ls are also seen with the other two systems: FKGL can be aggressively improved, BLEU is slightly impacted, and SARI is not affected. Regardless of the type of system, because of the simplicity of FKGL, the results can be arbitrarily improved.

[3]Complete experimental results are included in the appendix.

5.2 Understanding BLEU and SARI

Although the focus of this paper was on FKGL, we also analyzed BLEU and SARI further to understand why the modification approaches affected those metrics. The BLEU score is calculated as the average of the n-gram precisions of size 1 to 4, where precision is the proportion of n-grams in the system output that are found in the corresponding reference simplification. The SARI score is an average of F1 scores based on three operations relative to the reference text: added n-grams, kept n-grams, and deleted n-grams.

Table 2 shows each of the individual component calculations for the Dress-Ls system when the six modifications are applied to 100% of the sentences. Since the approaches rely on randomization, the results shown are an average of 100 trials. For conciseness, we only include the results for Dress-Ls, though all systems showed very similar trends. Full results, including 2-gram and 3-gram F1 and precision scores for SARI, for all systems are provided in the appendix.

For BLEU, all levels of precision drop for all three modification approaches. The 1-gram precision is the least affected, while larger n-gram

Percent Modified	0	100					
Approach	**none**	**random-period**	**random-the**	**replace-longest**	**replace-rand-period**	**replace-rand-the**	**rand-period+repl-longest**
BLEU							
1-gram	0.4590	0.4300	0.4394	0.4468	0.4340	0.4428	0.4186
2-gram	0.2638	0.2289	0.2301	0.2339	0.2289	0.2276	0.2026
3-gram	0.1896	0.1496	0.1509	0.1581	0.1511	0.1497	0.1249
4-gram	0.1384	0.0997	0.1003	0.1074	0.1016	0.1003	0.0763
SARI							
1-gram							
Add F1	0.0382	0.0382	0.0518	0.0505	0.0371	0.0504	0.0505
Keep F1	0.1181	0.1181	0.1169	0.1181	0.1186	0.1174	0.1181
Delete P	0.9740	0.9740	0.9741	0.9722	0.9718	0.9717	0.9722
4-gram							
Add F1	0.0189	0.0155	0.0145	0.0150	0.0154	0.0143	0.0112
Keep F1	0.0450	0.0446	0.0450	0.0463	0.0448	0.0447	0.0455
Delete P	0.9885	0.9876	0.9879	0.9878	0.9874	0.9874	0.9869

Table 2: Breakdown of the components making up BLEU and SARI scores for the original Dress-Ls output and the modified texts.

precisions show increasingly larger effects. This intuitively makes sense since randomly inserting/replacing a word in an originally correct sequence of words should affect multiple n-grams of larger size. None of the decreases are large in magnitude, but they are all in the same direction and contribute to the slight drop in BLEU scores.

For SARI, at the 1-gram level, the Add F1 score actually improves for both *random-the* and *replace-longest* since they add a common word ("the") that has a high likelihood of matching with a word in the reference simplification. However, for longer n-grams the Add F1 score drops for similar reasons to the BLEU score precisions drop. Besides the Add F1 score, however, the other scores remain virtually unchanged. In aggregate, the Add effect tends to balance out between increases in smaller n-grams and decreases in larger n-grams and because the other components do not change much, the overall SARI score remains unaffected.

The effects of the modifications on BLEU and SARI are minimal, especially compared to the effects on FKGL. While this helps illustrate how a manipulation of FKGL could be done, it does not necessarily imply that BLEU and SARI are sufficiently reliable. Even though both metrics are relatively resilient against our modification approaches, these approaches were designed specifically to manipulate the FKGL score and, thus, do not serve as evidence against the concerns that have been raised about their robustness (Callison-Burch et al., 2006; Sulem et al., 2018).

System	Average length	Average syllables	% split
Original	23.08	1.346	0
Reference	12.741	1.263	1.857
Dress-Ls	14.392	1.284	1.207
EncDecA	16.986	1.280	0.557
Hybrid	12.382	1.329	0.000
Dress	14.222	1.276	1.207
PBMT-R	22.933	1.304	1.300

Table 3: Post-hoc statistics for original and reference data from the test corpus and five system outputs.

6 A Better Approach

FKGL should not be used as an evaluation metric. Instead, it can be used for post-hoc analysis to understand the behavior of the systems. Even better, rather than reporting the FKGL score, which can be affected by multiple types of changes in the system, papers can report the individual components of FGKL, i.e., the average sentence length and the average number of syllables. This demystifies the readability score and provides concrete information about the types of changes that are being made by the systems. A comparative analysis of 30 metrics showed that these features are better correlated with human judgement than FKGL (Martin et al., 2018), and some recent papers have reported the average sentence length statistic already (Kriz et al., 2019; Kumar et al., 2020; Maddela et al., 2021). These two metrics can be supplemented with other corpus statistics that also help understand what changes the systems are making, e.g., the proportion of sentences that are split.

Table 3 shows these three statistics for the five

text simplification approaches. These statistics allow for a concrete analysis of what the different approaches are doing. All the models reduce the sentence length, except for PBMT-R. Hybrid is the most aggressive at creating short sentences, though it does not do any sentence splitting, so it accomplishes this through deletion, which may explain the low BLEU score. All of the models are selecting words with less syllables, except for Hybrid. Finally, all models except Hybrid are doing sentence splitting, with the EncDecA doing the least splitting. These statistics paint a much more vivid picture of what the different approach are doing than a single readability score.

7 Conclusions

In this paper, we have provided an experimental analysis of the FKGL score on state-of-the-art text simplification systems. We find that very basic post-processing techniques can drastically improve the FKGL score of a system with negligible effects on two other metrics, BLEU and SARI. Based on these findings, we argue that FKGL should no longer be used as a text simplification evaluation metric. Instead, the components of FKGL and other related statistics should be used to help understand what different systems are doing. If this analysis is not compelling enough and FKGL continues to be used, then we propose concrete methods for improving FKGL, with minimal work and only minor effects on the other automated metrics.

References

Fernando Alva-Manchego, Carolina Scarton, and Lucia Specia. 2020. Data-driven sentence simplification: Survey and benchmark. *Computational Linguistics*, 46(1):135–187.

Chris Callison-Burch, Miles Osborne, and Philipp Koehn. 2006. Re-evaluation the role of bleu in machine translation research. In *Proceedings of European Association for Computational Linguistics*.

William Coster and David Kauchak. 2011a. Learning to simplify sentences using wikipedia. In *Proceedings of the workshop on monolingual text-to-text generation*.

William Coster and David Kauchak. 2011b. Simple english wikipedia: a new text simplification task. In *Proceedings of Assication for Computational Linguistics*.

Rudolf Flesch. 1943. Marks of readable style; a study in adult education. *Teachers College Contributions to Education*.

Rudolph Flesch. 1948. A new readability yardstick. *Journal of applied psychology*, 32(3):221.

Han Guo, Ramakanth Pasunuru, and Mohit Bansal. 2018. Dynamic multi-level multi-task learning for sentence simplification. In *Proceedings of International Conference on Computational Linguistics*, pages 462–476.

Mohammad Hossin and MN Sulaiman. 2015. A review on evaluation metrics for data classification evaluations. *International Journal of Data Mining & Knowledge Management Process*.

David Kauchak and Gondy Leroy. 2016. Moving beyond readability metrics for health-related text simplification. *IT professional*, 18(3):45–51.

J Peter Kincaid, Robert P Fishburne Jr, Richard L Rogers, and Brad S Chissom. 1975. Derivation of new readability formulas (automated readability index, fog count and flesch reading ease formula) for navy enlisted personnel.

Kevin Knight and Daniel Marcu. 2002. Summarization beyond sentence extraction: A probabilistic approach to sentence compression. *Artificial Intelligence*, 139(1):91–107.

Reno Kriz, Joao Sedoc, Marianna Apidianaki, Carolina Zheng, Gaurav Kumar, Eleni Miltsakaki, and Chris Callison-Burch. 2019. Complexity-weighted loss and diverse reranking for sentence simplification. In *Proceedings of NAACL-HLT*, pages 3137–3147.

Dhruv Kumar, Lili Mou, Lukasz Golab, and Olga Vechtomova. 2020. Iterative edit-based unsupervised sentence simplification. In *Proceedings of Association for Computational Linguistics*, pages 7918–7928.

Mounica Maddela, Fernando Alva-Manchego, and Wei Xu. 2021. Controllable text simplification with explicit paraphrasing. In *NAACL-HLT*, Online. Association for Computational Linguistics.

Louis Martin, Samuel Humeau, Pierre-Emmanuel Mazare, Éric Villemonte de la Clergerie, Antoine Bordes, and Benoît Sagot. 2018. Reference-less quality estimation of text simplification systems. In *Proceedings of the Workshop on Automatic Text Adaptation*, pages 29–38.

William Anderson McCall and Lelah Mae Crabbs. 1926. *Standard Test Lessons in Reading...* 5. Teachers College, Columbia University, Bureau of Publications.

Shashi Narayan and Claire Gardent. 2014. Hybrid simplification using deep semantics and machine translation. In *Proceedings Association for Computational Linguistics*.

Islam Nassar, Michelle Ananda-Rajah, and Gholamreza Haffari. 2019. Neural versus non-neural text simplification: A case study. In *Proceedings of the Workshop of the Australasian Language Technology Association*, pages 172–177.

Christina Niklaus, Matthias Cetto, André Freitas, and Siegfried Handschuh. 2019. Transforming complex sentences into a semantic hierarchy. In *Proceedings of Association for Computational Linguistics*, pages 3415–3427.

Daiki Nishihara, Tomoyuki Kajiwara, and Yuki Arase. 2019. Controllable text simplification with lexical constraint loss. In *Proceedings of Association for Computational Linguistics: Student Research Workshop*, pages 260–266.

Sergiu Nisioi, Sanja Štajner, Simone Paolo Ponzetto, and Liviu P Dinu. 2017. Exploring neural text simplification models. In *Proceedings of Association for Computational Linguistics*, pages 85–91.

Kishore Papineni, Salim Roukos, Todd Ward, and Wei-Jing Zhu. 2001. BLEU. In *Proceedings of the 40th Annual Meeting on Association for Computational Linguistics - ACL*. Association for Computational Linguistics.

Jipeng Qiang. 2018. Improving neural text simplification model with simplified corpora. *CoRR*, abs/1810.04428.

Carolina Scarton and Lucia Specia. 2018. Learning simplifications for specific target audiences. In *Proceedings of Association for Computational Linguistics*, pages 712–718.

Matthew Shardlow. 2014. A survey of automated text simplification. *International Journal of Advanced Computer Science and Applications*.

Randi Shedlosky-Shoemaker, Amy Curry Sturm, Muniba Saleem, and Kimberly M Kelly. 2009. Tools for assessing readability and quality of health-related web sites. *Journal of genetic counseling*, 18(1):49.

Elior Sulem, Omri Abend, and Ari Rappoport. 2018. Bleu is not suitable for the evaluation of text simplification. In *Proceedings of Empirical Methods in Natural Language Processing*, pages 738–744.

Tu Vu, Baotian Hu, Tsendsuren Munkhdalai, and Hong Yu. 2018. Sentence simplification with memory-augmented neural networks. In *Proceedings of North American Chapter of the Association for Computational Linguistics: Human Language Technologies*, pages 79–85.

Kristian Woodsend and Mirella Lapata. 2011. Learning to simplify sentences with quasi-synchronous grammar and integer programming. In *Proceedings of Empirical Methods in Natural Language Processing*, pages 409–420.

Sander Wubben, Antal van den Bosch, and Emiel Krahmer. 2012. Sentence simplification by monolingual machine translation. In *Proceedings of the 50th Annual Meeting of the Association for Computational Linguistics (Volume 1: Long Papers)*, pages 1015–1024.

Wei Xu, Chris Callison-Burch, and Courtney Napoles. 2015. Problems in current text simplification research: New data can help. *Transactions of the Association of Computational Linguistics*.

Wei Xu, Courtney Napoles, Ellie Pavlick, Quanze Chen, and Chris Callison-Burch. 2016. Optimizing statistical machine translation for text simplification. *Transactions of the Association for Computational Linguistics*, 4:401–415.

Xingxing Zhang and Mirella Lapata. 2017. Sentence simplification with deep reinforcement learning. In *Proceedings of Empirical Methods in Natural Language Processing*, pages 584–594.

Zhemin Zhu, Delphine Bernhard, and Iryna Gurevych. 2010. A monolingual tree-based translation model for sentence simplification. In *Proceedings of ICCL*.

Appendix

A Experimental Results for All Systems

Tables 4-8 show the complete FKGL, BLEU and SARI scores for the modified outputs of all five systems: Dress-Ls, EncDecA, Hybrid, Dress and PBMT-R.

B BLEU n-gram Score Breakdown

Table 9 shows the precision scores for the individual n-grams (1-4) of the unmodified system output and output with all sentences modified (100%) for each of the six modification approaches on outputs of all five systems.

C SARI n-gram Score Breakdown

Table 10 shows the SARI component scores for the unmodified system output and with all sentences modified (100%) for each of the six modification approaches on all five systems.

	Dress-Ls									
Approach/ % modified	10	20	30	40	50	60	70	80	90	100
FKGL										
random-period	4.5426	4.0609	3.5802	3.1014	2.6223	2.5358	2.0595	1.9742	1.7763	1.4154
random-the	5.0006	4.9772	4.9543	4.9319	4.9095	4.8870	5.2557	5.2346	5.2130	5.1919
replace-longest	4.8837	4.7464	4.6050	4.4644	4.3242	4.1857	4.0442	3.9038	3.7647	3.6244
replace-rand-period	4.5510	4.0765	3.6007	3.1251	2.6494	2.5670	2.0910	2.0005	1.5256	1.4359
replace-rand-the	4.9915	4.9607	4.9259	4.8955	4.8636	4.8288	4.7985	4.7638	4.7324	4.7003
random-period +replace-longest	4.4098	3.8000	3.1911	2.5864	1.9831	1.7665	1.1681	0.9604	0.3671	0.1643
SARI										
random-period	0.3626	0.3624	0.3622	0.3619	0.3618	0.3616	0.3613	0.3612	0.3610	0.3608
random-the	0.3627	0.3626	0.3624	0.3623	0.3621	0.3620	0.3619	0.3618	0.3617	0.3616
replace-longest	0.3627	0.3626	0.3625	0.3623	0.3622	0.3622	0.3620	0.3620	0.3619	0.3618
replace-rand-period	0.3626	0.3623	0.3620	0.3617	0.3614	0.3612	0.3609	0.3606	0.3604	0.3601
replace-rand-the	0.3626	0.3624	0.3622	0.3619	0.3617	0.3615	0.3612	0.3611	0.3609	0.3607
random-period +replace-longest	0.3625	0.3622	0.3619	0.3617	0.3614	0.3612	0.3609	0.3608	0.3606	0.3604
BLEU										
random-period	0.2330	0.2287	0.2243	0.2200	0.2158	0.2119	0.2075	0.2033	0.1994	0.1953
random-the	0.2334	0.2293	0.2253	0.2216	0.2174	0.2136	0.2097	0.2059	0.2022	0.1985
replace-longest	0.2343	0.2312	0.2281	0.2247	0.2215	0.2184	0.2151	0.2120	0.2086	0.2052
replace-rand-period	0.2336	0.2297	0.2258	0.2218	0.2176	0.2138	0.2099	0.2057	0.2017	0.1977
replace-rand-the	0.2337	0.2300	0.2261	0.2224	0.2184	0.2148	0.2104	0.2068	0.2032	0.1991
random-period +replace-longest	0.2306	0.2237	0.2170	0.2104	0.2036	0.1972	0.1903	0.1843	0.1775	0.1710

Table 4: Metric scores of 10-100% modified outputs of Dress-LS

EncDecA										
Approach/ % modified	10	20	30	40	50	60	70	80	90	100
FKGL										
random-period	5.2905	4.8237	4.3576	3.8938	3.4304	2.9668	2.8942	2.4334	2.3618	1.9012
random-the	6.1272	6.1077	6.0884	6.0696	6.0507	6.0319	6.0138	5.9956	5.9777	5.9600
replace-longest	5.6413	5.5258	5.4092	5.2943	5.1792	5.0623	4.9459	4.8306	4.7143	4.5984
replace-rand-period	5.2958	4.8351	4.3718	3.9104	3.4496	2.9878	2.9127	2.4525	2.3804	1.9200
replace-rand-the	5.8045	5.8418	5.7950	5.7942	5.8163	5.8146	5.8060	5.7801	5.7838	5.7498
random-period +replace-longest	5.1811	4.6057	4.0323	3.4621	2.8906	2.3232	2.1496	1.5827	1.4098	0.8463
SARI										
random-period	0.3598	0.3597	0.3595	0.3594	0.3592	0.3591	0.3590	0.3588	0.3587	0.3586
random-the	0.3599	0.3598	0.3597	0.3596	0.3596	0.3595	0.3595	0.3594	0.3593	0.3593
replace-longest	0.3600	0.3599	0.3599	0.3598	0.3598	0.3597	0.3598	0.3597	0.3597	0.3597
replace-rand-period	0.3598	0.3596	0.3593	0.3591	0.3590	0.3587	0.3585	0.3583	0.3582	0.3580
replace-rand-the	0.3599	0.3597	0.3596	0.3594	0.3593	0.3591	0.3589	0.3588	0.3587	0.3585
random-period +replace-longest	0.3598	0.3597	0.3595	0.3593	0.3592	0.3590	0.3590	0.3589	0.3588	0.3587
BLEU										
random-period	0.2085	0.2052	0.2019	0.1987	0.1954	0.1921	0.1891	0.1858	0.1827	0.1796
random-the	0.2087	0.2056	0.2024	0.1994	0.1964	0.1935	0.1905	0.1875	0.1844	0.1815
replace-longest	0.2098	0.2075	0.2053	0.2031	0.2007	0.1986	0.1964	0.1941	0.1918	0.1895
replace-rand-period	0.2088	0.2058	0.2025	0.1994	0.1966	0.1932	0.1903	0.1871	0.1841	0.1808
replace-rand-the	0.2089	0.2057	0.2027	0.1995	0.1965	0.1933	0.1900	0.1870	0.1837	0.1805
random-period +replace-longest	0.2068	0.2019	0.1967	0.1917	0.1869	0.1817	0.1768	0.1721	0.1670	0.1621

Table 5: Metric scores of 10-100% modified outputs of EncDecA

Hybrid										
Approach/ % modified	10	20	30	40	50	60	70	80	90	100
FKGL										
random-period	4.2706	3.7659	3.2634	3.1522	2.6543	2.5450	2.0501	1.9458	1.4523	1.3512
random-the	4.7434	4.7118	4.6808	4.6503	4.6204	4.5907	4.9520	4.9236	4.8950	4.8678
replace-longest	4.6108	4.4474	4.2792	4.1167	3.9492	3.7866	3.6211	3.4546	3.2903	3.1241
replace-rand-period	4.2884	3.7986	3.3114	3.2161	2.7283	2.5598	2.1379	2.0364	1.5465	1.4524
replace-rand-the	4.7282	4.6833	4.6363	4.5903	4.5449	4.4997	4.4539	4.4070	4.3613	4.3104
random-period +replace-longest	4.1234	3.4704	2.8198	2.5699	1.9268	1.6807	1.0422	0.7992	0.1686	-0.0665
SARI										
random-period	0.3470	0.3469	0.3469	0.3468	0.3468	0.3467	0.3467	0.3466	0.3466	0.3465
random-the	0.3471	0.3471	0.3471	0.3471	0.3471	0.3472	0.3472	0.3472	0.3472	0.3473
replace-longest	0.3471	0.3471	0.3472	0.3472	0.3472	0.3473	0.3473	0.3473	0.3474	0.3474
replace-rand-period	0.3470	0.3469	0.3468	0.3467	0.3466	0.3466	0.3465	0.3464	0.3463	0.3462
replace-rand-the	0.3470	0.3470	0.3470	0.3470	0.3469	0.3469	0.3469	0.3469	0.3468	0.3468
random-period +replace-longest	0.3470	0.3470	0.3471	0.3471	0.3471	0.3471	0.3471	0.3471	0.3471	0.3471
BLEU										
random-period	0.1069	0.1054	0.1042	0.1026	0.1004	0.0981	0.0959	0.0939	0.0917	0.0898
random-the	0.1071	0.1059	0.1047	0.1033	0.1015	0.0994	0.0975	0.0956	0.0938	0.0919
replace-longest	0.1069	0.1055	0.1043	0.1028	0.1016	0.1002	0.0989	0.0975	0.0962	0.0948
replace-rand-period	0.1063	0.1043	0.1025	0.1006	0.0984	0.0965	0.0944	0.0926	0.0904	0.0883
replace-rand-the	0.1063	0.1042	0.1022	0.1004	0.0984	0.0962	0.0941	0.0921	0.0898	0.0879
random-period +replace-longest	0.1059	0.1036	0.1012	0.0986	0.0957	0.0924	0.0895	0.0866	0.0836	0.0806

Table 6: Metric scores of 10-100% modified outputs of Hybrid

Dress										
Approach/ % modified	10	20	30	40	50	60	70	80	90	100
FKGL										
random-period	4.4416	3.9367	3.4778	2.9987	2.5223	2.4322	1.9566	1.8709	1.3976	1.3138
random-the	4.9011	4.8782	4.8557	4.8336	4.8115	4.7899	4.7686	5.1378	5.1166	5.0966
replace-longest	4.7838	4.6432	4.5021	4.3628	4.2182	4.0781	3.9378	3.7971	3.6582	3.5147
replace-rand-period	4.3679	3.7817	3.4981	3.0221	2.5450	2.4596	1.9872	1.8958	1.4210	1.3311
replace-rand-the	4.8922	4.8580	4.8276	4.7936	4.7614	4.7301	4.6980	4.6648	4.6344	4.5964
random-period +replace-longest	4.3096	3.3390	3.0860	2.4810	1.8723	1.6601	1.0603	0.8498	0.2588	0.0536
SARI										
random-period	0.3621	0.3618	0.3616	0.3614	0.3612	0.3610	0.3608	0.3607	0.3605	0.3603
random-the	0.3622	0.3620	0.3619	0.3617	0.3616	0.3615	0.3614	0.3613	0.3612	0.3611
replace-longest	0.3622	0.3621	0.3620	0.3620	0.3619	0.3618	0.3618	0.3617	0.3617	0.3617
replace-rand-period	0.3620	0.3617	0.3614	0.3612	0.3609	0.3607	0.3605	0.3601	0.3599	0.3597
replace-rand-the	0.3621	0.3619	0.3617	0.3615	0.3613	0.3612	0.3609	0.3608	0.3607	0.3605
random-period +replace-longest	0.3620	0.3618	0.3615	0.3613	0.3612	0.3609	0.3608	0.3606	0.3604	0.3603
BLEU										
random-period	0.2230	0.2187	0.2145	0.2104	0.2062	0.2021	0.1979	0.1941	0.1902	0.1864
random-the	0.2233	0.2193	0.2156	0.2116	0.2078	0.2041	0.2005	0.1969	0.1931	0.1895
replace-longest	0.2243	0.2214	0.2183	0.2156	0.2124	0.2095	0.2066	0.2034	0.2004	0.1974
replace-rand-period	0.2234	0.2196	0.2156	0.2121	0.2080	0.2041	0.2005	0.1964	0.1925	0.1889
replace-rand-the	0.2234	0.2198	0.2158	0.2120	0.2080	0.2043	0.2003	0.1964	0.1926	0.1886
random-period +replace-longest	0.2208	0.2142	0.2078	0.2015	0.1954	0.1887	0.1826	0.1761	0.1700	0.1638

Table 7: Metric scores of 10-100% modified outputs of Dress

PBMT-R										
Approach/ % modified	10	20	30	40	50	60	70	80	90	100
FKGL										
random-period	7.5360	7.0897	6.2541	5.8091	5.3639	4.9187	4.4746	4.4210	3.9773	3.5354
random-the	8.7462	8.7303	8.7147	8.6992	8.6838	8.6684	8.6535	8.6384	8.6233	8.6087
replace-longest	8.2773	8.1807	8.0855	7.9908	7.8946	7.7988	7.7028	7.6075	7.5115	7.4150
replace-rand-period	7.6177	7.0975	6.2632	5.8203	5.3775	4.9330	4.4944	4.3366	3.9970	3.5487
replace-rand-the	8.3526	8.3343	8.3227	8.3330	8.3251	8.2865	8.3119	8.3015	8.3143	8.3201
random-period +replace-longest	7.4441	6.9062	5.9773	5.4449	4.9073	4.3749	3.8442	3.7010	3.1695	2.6411
SARI										
random-period	0.3568	0.3566	0.3565	0.3563	0.3562	0.3560	0.3559	0.3557	0.3556	0.3555
random-the	0.3568	0.3568	0.3567	0.3566	0.3565	0.3565	0.3564	0.3564	0.3563	0.3562
replace-longest	0.3568	0.3566	0.3564	0.3563	0.3562	0.3560	0.3559	0.3558	0.3557	0.3556
replace-rand-period	0.3566	0.3564	0.3561	0.3559	0.3556	0.3554	0.3553	0.3550	0.3548	0.3546
replace-rand-the	0.3567	0.3565	0.3564	0.3561	0.3560	0.3558	0.3557	0.3555	0.3554	0.3553
random-period +replace-longest	0.3566	0.3564	0.3561	0.3558	0.3556	0.3554	0.3552	0.3549	0.3549	0.3546
BLEU										
random-period	0.1751	0.1730	0.1709	0.1689	0.1668	0.1647	0.1628	0.1608	0.1588	0.1567
random-the	0.1752	0.1732	0.1711	0.1692	0.1674	0.1655	0.1637	0.1617	0.1598	0.1580
replace-longest	0.1754	0.1736	0.1718	0.1700	0.1682	0.1664	0.1647	0.1628	0.1611	0.1592
replace-rand-period	0.1751	0.1732	0.1710	0.1691	0.1670	0.1650	0.1631	0.1610	0.1590	0.1571
replace-rand-the	0.1752	0.1732	0.1713	0.1691	0.1673	0.1651	0.1632	0.1611	0.1590	0.1571
random-period +replace-longest	0.1736	0.1701	0.1664	0.1628	0.1593	0.1559	0.1523	0.1487	0.1454	0.1418

Table 8: Metric scores of 10-100% modified outputs of PBMT-R

Percent Modified	0	100					
Approach		random-period	random-the	replace-longest	replace-rand-period	replace-rand-the	random-period +replace-longest
Dress-Ls							
1-gram	0.4590	0.4300	0.4394	0.4468	0.4340	0.4428	0.4186
2-gram	0.2638	0.2289	0.2301	0.2339	0.2289	0.2276	0.2026
3-gram	0.1896	0.1496	0.1509	0.1581	0.1511	0.1497	0.1249
4-gram	0.1384	0.0997	0.1003	0.1074	0.1016	0.1003	0.0763
EncDecA							
1-gram	0.4156	0.4300	0.4394	0.4468	0.4340	0.4428	0.4186
2-gram	0.2373	0.2281	0.2300	0.2339	0.2291	0.2275	0.2037
3-gram	0.1686	0.1495	0.1518	0.1581	0.1516	0.1501	0.1265
4-gram	0.1212	0.0990	0.1014	0.1074	0.1019	0.1005	0.0787
Hybrid							
1-gram	0.3708	0.4300	0.4394	0.4468	0.4339	0.4432	0.4186
2-gram	0.1328	0.2281	0.2298	0.2339	0.2286	0.2275	0.2038
3-gram	0.0710	0.1494	0.1517	0.1581	0.1509	0.1501	0.1268
4-gram	0.0442	0.0991	0.1015	0.1074	0.1012	0.1007	0.0794
Dress							
1-gram	0.4517	0.4300	0.4394	0.4468	0.4336	0.4432	0.4186
2-gram	0.2537	0.2282	0.2299	0.2339	0.2286	0.2281	0.2038
3-gram	0.1800	0.1499	0.1516	0.1581	0.1507	0.1500	0.1266
4-gram	0.1292	0.0998	0.1016	0.1074	0.1010	0.1005	0.0790
PBMT-R							
1-gram	0.3577	0.4300	0.4394	0.4468	0.4340	0.4428	0.4186
2-gram	0.2020	0.2280	0.2299	0.2339	0.2289	0.2274	0.2039
3-gram	0.1392	0.1492	0.1518	0.1581	0.1514	0.1500	0.1270
4-gram	0.0979	0.0990	0.1014	0.1074	0.1016	0.1008	0.0796

Table 9: BLEU score breakdown (1-, 2-, 3- and 4-gram scores) for all combination of systems and modification approaches

Percent Modified	0	100					
Approach		random-period	random-the	replace-longest	replace-rand-period	replace-rand-the	random-period +replace-longest
Dress-Ls							
1-gram							
Add F1	0.0382	0.0382	0.0518	0.0505	0.0371	0.0504	0.0505
Keep F1	0.1181	0.1181	0.1169	0.1181	0.1186	0.1174	0.1181
Delete P	0.9740	0.9740	0.9741	0.9722	0.9718	0.9717	0.9722
2-gram							
Add F1	0.0370	0.0345	0.0322	0.0319	0.0323	0.0311	0.0285
Keep F1	0.0742	0.0739	0.0740	0.0751	0.0736	0.0735	0.0746
Delete P	0.9805	0.9798	0.9800	0.9794	0.9788	0.9787	0.9784
3-gram							
Add F1	0.0263	0.0229	0.0215	0.0215	0.0221	0.0211	0.0173
Keep F1	0.0573	0.0570	0.0573	0.0588	0.0569	0.0569	0.0582
Delete P	0.9850	0.9841	0.9844	0.9843	0.9837	0.9836	0.9832
4-gram							
Add F1	0.0189	0.0155	0.0145	0.0150	0.0154	0.0143	0.0112
Keep F1	0.0450	0.0446	0.0450	0.0463	0.0448	0.0447	0.0455
Delete P	0.9885	0.9876	0.9879	0.9878	0.9874	0.9874	0.9869
EncDecA							
1-gram							
Add F1	0.0382	0.0382	0.0518	0.0505	0.0372	0.0511	0.0505
Keep F1	0.1181	0.1181	0.1169	0.1181	0.1188	0.1174	0.1181
Delete P	0.9740	0.9740	0.9741	0.9722	0.9719	0.9718	0.9722
2-gram							
Add F1	0.0387	0.0343	0.0317	0.0319	0.0333	0.0316	0.0289
Keep F1	0.0744	0.0738	0.0739	0.0751	0.0736	0.0736	0.0748
Delete P	0.9812	0.9798	0.9800	0.9794	0.9788	0.9788	0.9785
3-gram							
Add F1	0.0293	0.0228	0.0217	0.0215	0.0223	0.0215	0.0174
Keep F1	0.0576	0.0570	0.0571	0.0588	0.0570	0.0568	0.0586
Delete P	0.9859	0.9841	0.9843	0.9843	0.9837	0.9836	0.9833
4-gram							
Add F1	0.0219	0.0154	0.0148	0.0150	0.0150	0.0147	0.0113
Keep F1	0.0454	0.0449	0.0450	0.0463	0.0448	0.0448	0.0459
Delete P	0.9893	0.9877	0.9879	0.9878	0.9874	0.9874	0.9870
Hybrid							
1-gram							
Add F1	0.0382	0.0382	0.0518	0.0505	0.0365	0.0511	0.0505
Keep F1	0.1181	0.1181	0.1169	0.1181	0.1186	0.1174	0.1181
Delete P	0.9740	0.9740	0.9741	0.9722	0.9718	0.9717	0.9722
2-gram							
Add F1	0.0387	0.0339	0.0319	0.0319	0.0324	0.0312	0.0286
Keep F1	0.0744	0.0739	0.0740	0.0751	0.0732	0.0734	0.0744
Delete P	0.9812	0.9798	0.9800	0.9794	0.9787	0.9787	0.9784
3-gram							
Add F1	0.0293	0.0225	0.0215	0.0215	0.0215	0.0210	0.0177
Keep F1	0.0576	0.0571	0.0571	0.0588	0.0563	0.0567	0.0579
Delete P	0.9859	0.9841	0.9843	0.9843	0.9835	0.9836	0.9832
4-gram							
Add F1	0.0219	0.0153	0.0145	0.0150	0.0144	0.0142	0.0116
Keep F1	0.0454	0.0451	0.0449	0.0463	0.0440	0.0446	0.0452
Delete P	0.9893	0.9877	0.9879	0.9878	0.9873	0.9874	0.9869

Percent Modified	0	100					
Approach		random-period	random-the	replace-longest	replace-rand-period	replace-rand-the	random-period +replace-longest
Dress							
1-gram							
Add F1	0.0382	0.0382	0.0518	0.0505	0.0369	0.0511	0.0505
Keep F1	0.1181	0.1181	0.1169	0.1181	0.1187	0.1174	0.1181
Delete P	0.9740	0.9740	0.9741	0.9722	0.9718	0.9717	0.9722
2-gram							
Add F1	0.0387	0.0340	0.0324	0.0319	0.0324	0.0317	0.0287
Keep F1	0.0744	0.0738	0.0739	0.0751	0.0735	0.0735	0.0745
Delete P	0.9812	0.9797	0.9800	0.9794	0.9788	0.9787	0.9784
3-gram							
Add F1	0.0293	0.0224	0.0215	0.0215	0.0218	0.0216	0.0173
Keep F1	0.0576	0.0568	0.0571	0.0588	0.0567	0.0568	0.0579
Delete P	0.9859	0.9841	0.9843	0.9843	0.9836	0.9836	0.9832
4-gram							
Add F1	0.0219	0.0151	0.0147	0.0150	0.0146	0.0147	0.0113
Keep F1	0.0454	0.0446	0.0450	0.0463	0.0445	0.0445	0.0452
Delete P	0.9893	0.9876	0.9878	0.9878	0.9874	0.9873	0.9869
PBMT-R							
1-gram							
Add F1	0.0382	0.0382	0.0518	0.0505	0.0368	0.0509	0.0505
Keep F1	0.1181	0.1181	0.1169	0.1181	0.1187	0.1172	0.1181
Delete P	0.9740	0.9740	0.9741	0.9722	0.9718	0.9716	0.9722
2-gram							
Add F1	0.0387	0.0337	0.0320	0.0319	0.0327	0.0311	0.0288
Keep F1	0.0744	0.0739	0.0740	0.0751	0.0736	0.0731	0.0746
Delete P	0.9812	0.9798	0.9800	0.9794	0.9788	0.9786	0.9784
3-gram							
Add F1	0.0293	0.0223	0.0216	0.0215	0.0220	0.0207	0.0177
Keep F1	0.0576	0.0571	0.0572	0.0588	0.0568	0.0564	0.0581
Delete P	0.9859	0.9842	0.9843	0.9843	0.9837	0.9835	0.9832
4-gram							
Add F1	0.0219	0.0148	0.0145	0.0150	0.0151	0.0137	0.0116
Keep F1	0.0454	0.0447	0.0449	0.0463	0.0447	0.0442	0.0454
Delete P	0.9893	0.9877	0.9878	0.9878	0.9874	0.9873	0.9869

Table 10: SARI score breakdown (F1 and precision scores used in the score calculation for 1-, 2-, 3- and 4-gram) for all combination of systems and modification approaches (long table spanning two pages)

Human Perception in Natural Language Generation

Lorenzo De Mattei[⋆◇♣‡], **Huiyuan Lai**[♣], **Felice Dell'Orletta**[◇], **Malvina Nissim**[♣]
⋆ Department of Computer Science, University of Pisa / Italy
◇ ItaliaNLP Lab, Istituto di Linguistica Computazionale "Antonio Zampolli", Pisa / Italy
♣ CLCG, University of Groningen / The Netherlands
‡ Aptus.AI / Pisa, Italy
lorenzo.demattei@di.unipi.it
{h.lai,m.nissim}@rug.nl
felice.dellorletta@ilc.cnr.it

Abstract

We take a collection of short texts, some of which are human-written, while others are automatically generated, and ask subjects, who are unaware of the texts' source, whether they perceive them as human-produced. We use this data to fine-tune a GPT-2 model to push it to generate more human-like texts, and observe that the production of this fine-tuned model is indeed perceived as more human-like than that of the original model. Contextually, we show that our automatic evaluation strategy correlates well with human judgements. We also run a linguistic analysis to unveil the characteristics of human- vs machine-perceived language.

1 Introduction

Pre-trained language models, such as the BERT (Devlin et al., 2019) and the GPT (Radford et al., 2018, 2019) families, are nowadays the core component of NLP systems. These models, based on the Transformer (Vaswani et al., 2017) and trained using huge amounts of crawl data (which can contain substantial noise), have been shown to produce high quality text, more often than not judged as human-written (Radford et al., 2019; De Mattei et al., 2020; Brown et al., 2020). Existing evaluations of GPT-2 models (Ippolito et al., 2020; De Mattei et al., 2020) have shown that while generated sentences were ranked lower in human perception than gold sentences, many gold sentences were also not perceived as human-like. To make the model produce more human-like texts one could train it only on gold data which is highly perceived as human, but such data is costly, and full model retraining is often a computationally non-viable option. As an alternative route, we explore whether and how an existing pre-trained model can be instead *fine-tuned* to produce more humanly-perceived texts, and how to evaluate this potentially shifted behaviour.

We see the advantage of this experiment at least in two ways. One is that the generation of more human-like texts is highly beneficial for specific applications, as for example human-machine interaction in dialogues; the other is that it opens the opportunity to investigate what linguistic aspects make a text more humanly-perceived. We run our experiments on Italian, using `GePpeTto` (De Mattei et al., 2020) as pre-trained model. First, we collect human judgements on gold texts and texts generated by `GePpeTto` in terms of how they are perceived (human or automatically produced). We then fine-tune `GePpeTto` with this perception-labelled data. In addition, inspired by the classifier-based reward used in style transfer tasks (Lample et al., 2019; Gong et al., 2019; Luo et al., 2019; Sancheti et al., 2020), we reward the model to push its classification confidence. We evaluate the new perception-enhanced models in comparison with the original `GePpeTto` by running both an automatic as well as a human evaluation on output generated by the various models. Lastly, we conduct a linguistic analysis to highlight which linguistic characteristics are more commonly found in human- and machine-perceived text.

Author contribution note: Lorenzo De Mattei and Huiyuan Lai contributed equally.

Proceedings of the 1st Workshop on Natural Language Generation, Evaluation, and Metrics (GEM 2021), pages 15–23
August 5–6, 2021.

Contributions We show that a GPT-2 pre-trained model can be fine-tuned to produce text that is perceived as more human, and we release this model for Italian. Second, we provide a stronger automatic evaluation method where training is done on perception labels rather than the actual source, which yields results that correlate with human judgments, providing a different angle for automatic evaluation of generated sentences. Lastly, we run a linguistic analysis of the humanly-perceived texts that can open up to new opportunities for understanding and model human-like perception.

2 Data

We collected human judgments over a series of gold and generated sentences in terms of how much a given text is *perceived* as human-like. The obtained labelled data is used to fine-tune our base model towards generating more humanly-perceived texts; it is also used to test the resulting models through an automatic evaluation strategy that we implement next to human judgements.

Training Data From the original `GePpeTto`'s training corpus (De Mattei et al., 2020), we collected 1400 random gold sentences in the following way. We sentence split all the documents and we picked the first sentence of each document. In order to allow for length variation, which has an impact on perception, we selected the first 200 sentences with length 10, 15, 20, 25, 30, 35 and 40 tokens.

We also let `GePpeTto` generate texts starting with the first word of randomly selected documents, we sentence-split the generated texts, and select the first 200 sentences with length 10, 15, 20, 25, 30, 35 and 40 tokens. This procedure creates a training set with perception labels containing a total of 2800 instances (1400 gold and 1400 generated).

We asked native Italian speakers if they felt the text they were seeing had been written, on a 1–5 Likert Scale, by a human (1) or a machine (5). Each texts was assessed by 7 different judges. The subjects for the task were laypeople recruited via the crowdsourcing platform Prolific[1]. We did not control for, and thus did not elicit, any demographic features. As a proxy for attention and quality control, we used completion time, and filtered out participants who took too little time to perform the task (we set a threshold of at least 5 minutes for 70 assessments as a reliable minimum effort).[2]

Mapping the average of human judgements to a binary classification (human if < 3), we obtain the matrix in Tab. 1 showing perception labels and the actual source labels. While human texts are more often perceived as human-like than machine-generated ones, the matrix shows that 44.2% of the texts are perceived as artificial, suggesting that a good portion of the training data might lead to generation that is not so much human-like. We train two classifiers on 80% of this data on the task of detecting human-like perception and that of detecting the actual source. The classifiers are built adding a dropout (Srivastava et al., 2014) and a dense layer on the top of UmBERTo[3], which is a Roberta (Liu et al., 2019) based Language Model trained on large Italian corpora. We train them using Adam (Kingma and Ba, 2015), initial learning rate 1e-5, and batch size 16. On the remaining 20% of the data we obtain F=0.97 for the source identification task, and F=0.92 for the perception task, showing the feasibility of the classification and thus the possibility of using these classifiers for evaluation (Section 4).

	AI-perceived	humanly-perceived
`GePpeTto`	62.3%	37.7%
Gold	44.2%	55.8%

Table 1: Source vs perception matrix (training data).

Test Data We use 1400 sentences: 350 are produced by humans, 1050 are generated (350 for each of the three models we use, see Section 3). As for training, human texts were selected picking the first 50 sentences with 10, 15, 20, 25, 30, 35 and 40 tokens. For each system, we also picked the first 50 generated sentences with length 10, 15, 20, 25, 30, 35 and 40 tokens. Each of the 1400 sentences was assessed by 5 users, on a 1–5 Likert scale, as human- or artificial-like.

3 Models

We use three models for text generation, all based on the GPT-2 architecture (Radford et al., 2019). The basic model is `GePpeTto`, a GPT-2-based model for Italian released by (De Mattei et al., 2020). The others are built on `GePpeTto` using

[1]https://www.prolific.co/

[2]Crowdworkers were compensated with a rate of £5.04 per estimated hour. In practice, tasks were completed in a shorter time than estimated, so the hourly rate was a bit higher.

[3]`https://huggingface.co/Musixmatch/umberto-commoncrawl-cased-v1`

the perception-labelled data in fine-tuning and in a reinforcement learning setting.

3.1 GePpeTto

GePpeTto is built using GPT-2 base architecture with 12 layers and 117M parameters. GePpeTto is trained on two main sources: a dump of Italian Wikipedia, consisting of 2.8GB of text; and the ItWac corpus (Baroni et al., 2009), which amounts to 11GB of web texts. De Mattei et al. (2020) show that GePpeTto is able to produce text which is much closer to human quality rather than to the text generated by other baseline models. Still, real human-produced text is recognised as such more often than GePpeTto's output.

3.2 GePpeTto fine-tuned

Using the original settings of GePpeTto, the model is fine-tuned on the training portion of the humanly-perceived sentences of the perception-labelled data (Tab. 1), using the Huggingface implementation (Wolf et al., 2020).[4]. We use the Adam optimiser (Kingma and Ba, 2015) with initial learning rate 2e-5. The mini-batch size is set to 8. During fine-tuning, we set an early stopping with patience 5 if the performance on validation does not improve.[5] The resulting model should produce text recognised more frequently as human-produced than the original GePpeTto.

3.3 GePpeTto rewarded

To further encourage GePpeTto-F to generate more humanly-perceived texts, we introduce a confidence reward based on the 'perception classifier' (PC) described in Section 2: the model gets rewarded for generating more human-like text. The PC's confidence is formulated as

$$R_{conf} = softmax_0(PC(y', \theta)) \tag{1}$$

where θ are the PC's parameters, fixed during fine-tuning GePpeTto . Formally, the confidence is used for policy learning that maximizes the expected reward $E[R]$ of the generated sequence; the corresponding policy gradient is formulated as

$$\nabla_\phi E(R) = \nabla_\phi \sum_k (P(y_t^s | y_{1:t-1}^s; \phi))R_k \tag{2}$$

where ϕ are the parameters of GePpeTto, and R_k is the reward of the k_{th} sequence y^s sampled from the distribution of model's outputs at each time step in decoding. The framework can be trained end-to-end by combining the policy gradient with the cross entropy loss of the base model.

4 Evaluation

We run both a human and an automatic evaluation, in line with Ippolito et al. (2020)'s and Hashimoto et al. (2019)'s suggestions in terms of evaluation's diversity and quality. For the automatic evaluation, we train a regressor on the perception-labelled data (with the original 1–5 values) adding a dropout (Srivastava et al., 2014) and a dense layer on the top of UmBERTo. We use Adam (Kingma and Ba, 2015) with initial learning rate is 1e-5, and set the batch size to 16. We calculate the correlation of the regressor's scores with human judgements over each single data point in the test set (N=1400), and observe good scores (Pearson=0.54 ($p < 10^{-4}$) and RMSE=0.75).

For the human evaluation, we assign to each sentence the average score computed over all human judgements. We then average all resulting scores over the seven length bins. Results are shown in two tables, as follows.

First, as we did for the training data (see Table 1), we mapped the average of human judgements to a binary classification (human if< 3), and obtain the matrix in Table 2. This shows perception labels and the actual source labels for the three models and gold data. We see that the human produced texts are the most humanly-perceived, but both the fine-tuned and the rewarded model produced texts that are more humanly-perceived than GePpeTto, with the fine-tuned model performing better than the rewarded one.

Second, Table 3 shows the average score over all length bins for the four models: GePpeTto, GePpeTto fine-tuned (GePpeTto-F), GePpeTto rewarded (GePpeTto-R) and the original human texts (Human). This table also reports the average scores over all lengths as assigned by the regressor.[6] The closer to 1, the more humanly-

[4]In preliminary experiments, we also fine-tuned GePpeTto on a larger silver data-set obtained by letting the perception classifier select what it deemed are human-perceived texts from GePpeTto's training set. The results of our automatic evaluation were however not encouraging, suggesting that the increased performance we obtain with the fine-tuned model is indeed ascribable to manually labelled gold data.

[5]Due to small training size, we validate against silver data obtained by labelling generated and gold text with our perception-classifier.

[6]Detailed results per length are Appendix Tables A.1-A.2.

perceived the sentence.

	AI-perceived	humanly-perceived
GePpeTto	61.1%	38.96%
GePpeTto-F	55.7%	44.3%
GePpeTto-R	59.1%	40.9%
Gold	37.4%	62.6%

Table 2: Source vs perception matrix (test data).

model	humans (std)	regressor (std)
GePpeTto	2.85 (0.83)	2.74 (0.71)
GePpeTto-F	2.74 (0.83)	2.49 (0.55)
GePpeTto-R	2.84 (0.87)	2.56 (0.57)
Human	2.41 (0.77)	2.47 (0.66)
avg	2.71 (0.85)	2.57 (0.63)

Table 3: Scores for each system as evaluated by humans and by the regressor, averaged over test set instances and thus over all sentence lengths.

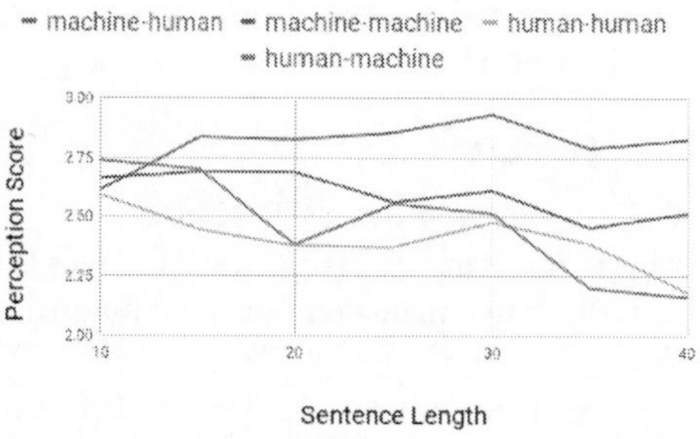

Figure 1: Average perception scores for human vs machine generated texts as assessed by humans and our regressor. In legend: <producer-assessor>. Machine scores are averaged across the three models.

As a first observation, in both the human and the automatic evaluations the final rank for the systems is the same, showing the reliability of the automatic evaluation. The gold texts are perceived as most human-like by humans (score: 2.41) and by the regressor (score: 2.47). Regarding systems, the fine-tuned model (GePpeTto-F) performs better than both the basic and the rewarded model.

To compare the overall performance of machine vs humans, in Fig 1 we plot the average performance of the three models per length as judged by humans (blue) and the regressor (red). These two lines are compared with gold texts, again assessed by humans (yellow) and the regressor (green).

Comparing the models and the humans as assessed by humans (lines blue and yellow) we see that while for short sentences humans perceive the generated and the natural texts equally human-like, this changes substantially for longer fragments. At length 40, we observe the largest gap in perception between the models and the natural texts, with the latter being perceived much more human-like.

In terms of machine-based evaluation (lines red and green), the behaviour of the BERT regressor on human data is very similar to the human judgements (line green vs yellow). Although the two curves are similar also for the texts generated by the models, the regressor here overestimates as human-produced texts that are actually machine generated (line red vs blue). This is potentially due to the fact that GePpeTto-F and GePpeTto-R use the same (human labelled) training data for fine-tuning which is used to train the regressor model. This phenomenon appears exacerbated with longer texts, as the blue and red lines are more distant after length 20.[7] This behaviour of the regressor is also reflected by its scores being more compressed towards the middle. Indeed, the average standard deviations in Table 3, show higher variability in human judgements than in the regressor's assessment. In Table 4 same examples of generated sentences together with their scores are reported.

5 Linguistic Analysis

We ran a linguistic analysis over the human and the generated text using Profiling-UD (Brunato et al., 2020), a tool that extracts linguistic features of varying complexity, ranging from raw text aspects, such as average length of words and sentences, to lexical, morpho-syntactic, and syntactic properties. In particular, we study (i) which features characterise the most humanly-perceived texts in the training data, independently of who generated them; (ii) the difference between human-produced texts and those generated by our best model (GePpeTto-F) in the test set when they are perceived as human.[8]

Regarding (i), the features that most correlate with a text being perceived as human have to do with sentence length and complexity. For example, the longer the sentence or the clauses therein, or the longer and deeper the syntactic links, the more humanly-perceived is the text. On the other side of the spectrum, linguistic features associated to texts

[7]The detailed tables in the Appendix further show this divergence with specific scores per model.

[8]Findings summarised; detailed correlations in Appendix.

model	output	human-score	regressor-score
Human	La ex Chiesa di Santa Caterina del Monte di Pietà era una chiesa cattolica che si trova ad Alcamo, in provincia di Trapani. (The former Church of Santa Caterina del Monte di Pietà was a Catholic church located in Alcamo, in the province of Trapani.)	1.71	1.88
GePpeTto-F	La nuova sede fu inaugurata il 19 luglio 1885 e inaugurata ufficialmente il 30 novembre 1889, giorno in cui fu completata la facciata. (The new headquarters were inaugurated on July 19, 1885 and officially inaugurated on November 30, 1889, the day the facade was completed.)	1.86	2.34
GePpeTto-R	La casa si trova in una posizione favorevole all'espansione del mercato e, in alcuni casi, alla costruzione di tende per bambini. (The house is in a favorable position for the expansion of the market and, in some cases, for the construction of children's tents.)	3.14	2.68
GePpeTto	La squadra era composta di due squadre, una delle quali era la "Rhodesliga" con il termine del "Propaganda Fiumana". (The team was made up of two teams, one of which was the "Rhodesliga" with the term of "Propaganda Fiumana".)	3.15	3.07

Table 4: Sample model outputs and their sentence-level score. Prompt: "La" ("The$_{[feminine]}$").

judged as machine-generated are heavy presence of punctuation and of interjections and symbols.

For (ii), we zoom in on humanly-perceived texts only, but looking at the source that generated them. For human texts, length and complexity are still the relevant features for being perceived as human; these are proxied by complex verbal structures charactersied by auxiliaries, use of past tense, number of main predicates in a sentence. For the generated texts, instead, we observe that both those characteristics that are similar to the human texts, such as the use of the indicative mood and finite tenses, as well as those more specific to machine-generated texts, such as a low density of subordinate clauses and shorter sentences, are simpler structures where it is more likely that the machine does not incur evident mistakes: it is easier for the model to produce human looking sentences if they are kept short and simple. With longer sentences the model struggles to ensure semantic and pragmatic coherence, two aspects that most likely require further and more complex modelling beyond simple fine-tuning.

6 Conclusions

We elicited judgements on the human-likeness of gold and generated Italian texts and used these judgements to fine-tune a pre-trained GPT-2 model to push it to produce more human-like texts. Our evaluation shows that people indeed find the output of the fine-tuned model more human-like than that of the basic one. Contextually, we show that our proposed automatic evaluation correlates well with human judgements, and it is therefore a reliable strategy that can be applied in absence of subjects.

An analysis of linguistic features reveals that while complexity is associated with human-likeness in gold data, simplicity is a key feature of artificial texts that are assessed as human-like, perhaps because simpler texts are less prone to expose machine behaviour.

Future work will include an expansion of the perception-labelled data to (i) assess training size in fine-tuning, and (ii) perform a finer-grained analysis correlating assessments to different text genres and subject demographics.

Impact Statement

All work that automatically generates text could unfortunately be used maliciously. While we cannot fully prevent such uses once our models are made public, we do hope that writing about risks explicitly and also raising awareness of this possibility in the general public are ways to contain the effects of potential harmful uses. We are open to any discussion and suggestions to minimise such risks. The contributors of human judgements elicited for this work have been fairly compensated.

Acknowledgements

We would like to thank the Center for Information Technology of the University of Groningen for their support and for providing access to the Peregrine high performance computing cluster. We are also grateful to the anonymous GEM reviewers whose comments contributed to improving this paper.

References

Marco Baroni, Silvia Bernardini, Adriano Ferraresi, and Eros Zanchetta. 2009. The wacky wide web: a collection of very large linguistically processed web-crawled corpora. *Language Resources and Evaluation*, 43(3):209–226.

Tom Brown, Benjamin Mann, Nick Ryder, Melanie Subbiah, Jared D Kaplan, Prafulla Dhariwal, Arvind Neelakantan, Pranav Shyam, Girish Sastry, Amanda Askell, Sandhini Agarwal, Ariel Herbert-Voss, Gretchen Krueger, Tom Henighan, Rewon Child, Aditya Ramesh, Daniel Ziegler, Jeffrey Wu, Clemens Winter, Chris Hesse, Mark Chen, Eric Sigler, Mateusz Litwin, Scott Gray, Benjamin Chess, Jack Clark, Christopher Berner, Sam McCandlish, Alec Radford, Ilya Sutskever, and Dario Amodei. 2020. Language models are few-shot learners. In *Advances in Neural Information Processing Systems*, volume 33, pages 1877–1901. Curran Associates, Inc.

Dominique Brunato, Andrea Cimino, Felice Dell'Orletta, Giulia Venturi, and Simonetta Montemagni. 2020. Profiling-ud: a tool for linguistic profiling of texts. In *Proceedings of The 12th Language Resources and Evaluation Conference*, pages 7145–7151.

Lorenzo De Mattei, Michele Cafagna, Felice Dell'Orletta, Malvina Nissim, and Marco Guerini. 2020. Geppetto carves italian into a language model. In *Proceedings of the Seventh Italian Conference on Computational Linguistics, CLiC-it 2020, Bologna, Italy, March 1-3, 2021*, volume 2769 of *CEUR Workshop Proceedings*. CEUR-WS.org.

Jacob Devlin, Ming-Wei Chang, Kenton Lee, and Kristina Toutanova. 2019. BERT: Pre-training of deep bidirectional transformers for language understanding. In *Proceedings of the 2019 Conference of the North American Chapter of the Association for Computational Linguistics: Human Language Technologies, Volume 1 (Long and Short Papers)*, pages 4171–4186, Minneapolis, Minnesota. Association for Computational Linguistics.

Hongyu Gong, Suma Bhat, Lingfei Wu, JinJun Xiong, and Wen-mei Hwu. 2019. Reinforcement learning based text style transfer without parallel training corpus. In *Proceedings of the 2019 Conference of the North American Chapter of the Association for Computational Linguistics: Human Language Technologies, Volume 1 (Long and Short Papers)*, pages 3168–3180.

Tatsunori B. Hashimoto, Hugh Zhang, and Percy Liang. 2019. Unifying human and statistical evaluation for natural language generation. *CoRR*, abs/1904.02792.

Daphne Ippolito, Daniel Duckworth, Chris Callison-Burch, and Douglas Eck. 2020. Automatic detection of generated text is easiest when humans are fooled. In *Proceedings of the 58th Annual Meeting of the Association for Computational Linguistics*, pages 1808–1822, Online. Association for Computational Linguistics.

Diederik P Kingma and Jimmy Ba. 2015. Adam: A method for stochastic optimization. In *Proceedings of the 3rd International Conference for Learning Representations*.

Guillaume Lample, Sandeep Subramanian, Eric Smith, Ludovic Denoyer, Marc'Aurelio Ranzato, and Y-Lan Boureau. 2019. Multiple-attribute text rewriting. In *International Conference on Learning Representations*.

Yinhan Liu, Myle Ott, Naman Goyal, Jingfei Du, Mandar Joshi, Danqi Chen, Omer Levy, Mike Lewis, Luke Zettlemoyer, and Veselin Stoyanov. 2019. Roberta: A robustly optimized BERT pretraining approach. *CoRR*, abs/1907.11692.

Fuli Luo, Peng Li, Jie Zhou, Pengcheng Yang, Baobao Chang, Zhifang Sui, and Xu Sun. 2019. A dual reinforcement learning framework for unsupervised text style transfer. In *Proceedings of the 28th International Joint Conference on Artificial Intelligence*, pages 5116–5122.

Alec Radford, Karthik Narasimhan, Tim Salimans, and Ilya Sutskever. 2018. Improving language understanding by generative pre-training.

Alec Radford, Jeff Wu, Rewon Child, David Luan, Dario Amodei, and Ilya Sutskever. 2019. Language models are unsupervised multitask learners.

Abhilasha Sancheti, Kundan Krishna, Balaji Vasan Srinivasan, and Anandhavelu Natarajan. 2020. Reinforced rewards framework for text style transfer. In *Advances in Information Retrieval*, pages 545–560.

Nitish Srivastava, Geoffrey Hinton, Alex Krizhevsky, Ilya Sutskever, and Ruslan Salakhutdinov. 2014. Dropout: A simple way to prevent neural networks from overfitting. *Journal of Machine Learning Research*, 15(56):1929–1958.

Ashish Vaswani, Noam Shazeer, Niki Parmar, Jakob Uszkoreit, Llion Jones, Aidan N Gomez, Łukasz Kaiser, and Illia Polosukhin. 2017. Attention is all you need. In *Proceedings of the 31st International Conference on Neural Information Processing Systems*, pages 6000–6010.

Thomas Wolf, Lysandre Debut, Victor Sanh, Julien Chaumond, Clement Delangue, Anthony Moi, Pierric Cistac, Tim Rault, Rémi Louf, Morgan Funtowicz, Joe Davison, Sam Shleifer, Patrick von Platen, Clara Ma, Yacine Jernite, Julien Plu, Canwen Xu, Teven Le Scao, Sylvain Gugger, Mariama Drame, Quentin Lhoest, and Alexander M. Rush. 2020. Transformers: State-of-the-art natural language processing. In *Proceedings of the 2020 Conference on Empirical Methods in Natural Language Processing: System Demonstrations*, pages 38–45, Online. Association for Computational Linguistics.

A Appendix

This Appendix contains:

- detailed results of human and machine evaluation for gold and all models' data (Tables A.1–A.2), expanding the compressed results shown in Table 2 in the main paper.
- details of linguistic features (correlated with human and machine perception, Tables A3–A4) which are discussed in Section 5 in the main paper.

	Length							
Tipo	10	15	20	25	30	35	40	AVG
`GePpeTto`	2.80	2.83	3.05	2.89	3.08	2.55	2.77	2.85 (0.83)
`GePpeTto-F`	2.44	2.68	2.57	2.85	2.74	2.97	2.93	2.74 (0.83)
`GePpeTto-R`	2.61	3.01	2.87	2.83	2.97	2.85	2.78	2.84 (0.87)
`Human`	2.59	2.45	2.38	2.37	2.48	2.39	2.18	2.41 (0.77)
avg	2.61	2.74	2.72	2.74	2.82	2.69	2.67	2.71 (0.85)

Table A.1: Average scores for each system grouped by sentence length as assigned by humans on the test set.

	Length							
Tipo	10	15	20	25	30	35	40	AVG
`GePpeTto`	2.79	2.78	2.88	2.80	2.76	2.53	2.68	2.74 (0.71)
`GePpeTto-F`	2.53	2.62	2.52	2.44	2.44	2.46	2.43	2.49 (0.55)
`GePpeTto-R`	2.68	2.67	2.67	2.45	2.63	2.38	2.44	2.56 (0.57)
`Human`	2.74	2.70	2.38	2.55	2.51	2.20	2.16	2.47 (0.66)
avg	2.68	2.69	2.61	2.56	2.59	2.39	2.43	2.57 (0.63)

Table A.2: Average scores for each system grouped by sentence length as assigned by the BERT based regressor on the test set.

Human Texts		Generated Texts	
Feature	Correlation (p-values)	Feature	Correlation (p-values)
n_tokens	-0.2 (7.34e-14)	upos_dist_NOUN	-0.15 (1.08e-08)
avg_max_links_len	-0.19 (1.85e-13)	dep_dist_compound	-0.13 (2.17e-06)
max_links_len	-0.18 (2.52e-11)	subj_pre	-0.1 (8.90e-05)
avg_max_depth	-0.17 (1.86e-10)	prep_dist_1	-0.09 (6.15e-04)
avg_links_len	-0.13 (2.43e-06)	avg_prepositional_chain_len	-0.09 (7.12e-04)
avg_token_per_clause	-0.12 (1.20e-05)	n_prepositional_chains	-0.09 (7.53e-04)
upos_dist_X	-0.1 (1.20e-04)	n_tokens	-0.09 (8.45e-04)
dep_dist_goeswith	-0.1 (1.43e-04)	dep_dist_amod	-0.08 (2.37e-03)
verbal_head_per_sent	-0.1 (3.50e-04)	upos_dist_ADJ	-0.08 (2.39e-03)
subj_pre	-0.09 (4.07e-04)	dep_dist_nsubj	-0.08 (4.03e-03)
verbal_root_perc	-0.09 (6.48e-04)	avg_max_depth	-0.08 (4.06e-03)
avg_verb_edges	-0.09 (1.03e-03)	avg_token_per_clause	-0.08 (4.19e-03)
obj_post	-0.09 (1.04e-03)	dep_dist_case	-0.07 (8.76e-03)
verbs_num_pers_dist_+	-0.08 (1.54e-03)	max_links_len	-0.07 (9.10e-03)
dep_dist_det	-0.08 (1.58e-03)	verbs_form_dist_Inf	-0.07 (9.78e-03)
...			
dep_dist_iobj	0.04 (9.89e-02)	dep_dist_nmod:tmod	0.04 (1.15e-01)
dep_dist_appos	0.05 (7.38e-02)	verb_edges_dist_1	0.04 (1.10e-01)
dep_dist_advcl	0.05 (7.29e-02)	dep_dist_advmod	0.04 (1.01e-01)
dep_dist_flat	0.06 (1.87e-02)	aux_mood_dist_Imp	0.05 (8.17e-02)
lexical_density	0.06 (1.84e-02)	upos_dist_CCONJ	0.06 (2.98e-02)
subordinate_dist_3	0.06 (1.56e-02)	upos_dist_PROPN	0.06 (2.35e-02)
dep_dist_nmod:tmod	0.07 (1.38e-02)	dep_dist_discourse	0.08 (4.42e-03)
aux_form_dist_Inf	0.07 (9.01e-03)	dep_dist_appos	0.08 (3.43e-03)
dep_dist_nummod	0.08 (2.63e-03)	upos_dist_INTJ	0.08 (2.43e-03)
upos_dist_PROPN	0.11 (4.98e-05)	dep_dist_conj	0.08 (1.61e-03)
upos_dist_NUM	0.12 (3.36e-06)	verbs_form_dist_Ger	0.09 (1.01e-03)
upos_dist_PUNCT	0.13 (2.08e-06)	upos_dist_SYM	0.11 (4.11e-05)
upos_dist_SYM	0.13 (1.26e-06)	dep_dist_root	0.11 (1.70e-05)
dep_dist_punct	0.14 (1.65e-07)	upos_dist_PUNCT	0.25 (1.31e-21)
dep_dist_root	0.26 (2.07e-22)	dep_dist_punct	0.25 (4.71e-22)

Table A.3: Linguistic features in training data. Generated = GePpeTto base

Human Texts		Generated Texts	
Feature	Correlation (p-values)	Feature	Correlation (p-values)
verbal_root_perc	-0.28 (9.25e-08)	principal_proposition_dist	-0.2 (1.33e-04)
verbs_tense_dist_Past	-0.21 (6.34e-05)	dep_dist_nsubj:pass	-0.19 (3.55e-04)
upos_dist_DET	-0.18 (8.41e-04)	dep_dist_aux:pass	-0.18 (5.71e-04)
dep_dist_det	-0.17 (1.19e-03)	dep_dist_root	-0.18 (7.22e-04)
aux_form_dist_Fin	-0.17 (1.33e-03)	aux_mood_dist_Ind	-0.18 (7.45e-04)
upos_dist_AUX	-0.17 (1.51e-03)	aux_form_dist_Fin	-0.17 (1.94e-03)
aux_num_pers_dist_Sing+3	-0.17 (1.65e-03)	aux_tense_dist_Past	-0.16 (1.97e-03)
verbal_head_per_sent	-0.17 (1.79e-03)	aux_num_pers_dist_Sing+3	-0.16 (2.87e-03)
aux_mood_dist_Ind	-0.16 (2.11e-03)	dep_dist_obl:agent	-0.16 (3.25e-03)
dep_dist_obl	-0.16 (2.31e-03)	verbal_root_perc	-0.14 (7.63e-03)
dep_dist_expl	-0.16 (2.45e-03)	dep_dist_flat	-0.13 (1.20e-02)
dep_dist_case	-0.14 (6.99e-03)	dep_dist_det	-0.13 (1.57e-02)
aux_tense_dist_Past	-0.14 (7.98e-03)	lexical_density	-0.12 (2.06e-02)
dep_dist_cop	-0.13 (1.22e-02)	upos_dist_AUX	-0.12 (2.74e-02)
upos_dist_ADP	-0.13 (1.55e-02)	verb_edges_dist_5	-0.11 (4.33e-02)
...			
dep_dist_flat:name	0.1 (5.16e-02)	n_prepositional_chains	0.12 (2.02e-02)
verbs_tense_dist_Pres	0.11 (3.77e-02)	verbs_num_pers_dist_Plur+3	0.13 (1.59e-02)
verbs_form_dist_Inf	0.11 (3.54e-02)	dep_dist_punct	0.13 (1.48e-02)
char_per_tok	0.12 (2.98e-02)	upos_dist_PUNCT	0.13 (1.40e-02)
dep_dist_compound	0.12 (2.40e-02)	dep_dist_nummod	0.15 (4.12e-03)
dep_dist_root	0.14 (1.08e-02)	dep_dist_conj	0.15 (3.76e-03)
upos_dist_PUNCT	0.14 (9.63e-03)	upos_dist_PRON	0.16 (3.56e-03)
dep_dist_punct	0.14 (9.63e-03)	upos_dist_SYM	0.16 (2.19e-03)
upos_dist_PROPN	0.15 (6.28e-03)	dep_dist_acl:relcl	0.17 (1.36e-03)
dep_dist_nmod	0.17 (1.81e-03)	dep_dist_appos	0.17 (1.29e-03)
upos_dist_SYM	0.17 (1.63e-03)	n_tokens	0.19 (4.73e-04)
dep_dist_nummod	0.17 (1.17e-03)	tokens_per_sent	0.19 (4.73e-04)
lexical_density	0.17 (1.12e-03)	avg_links_len	0.25 (1.94e-06)
dep_dist_flat	0.22 (2.46e-05)	avg_max_links_len	0.26 (1.02e-06)
upos_dist_NUM	0.25 (2.08e-06)	max_links_len	0.26 (1.02e-06)

Table A.4: Linguistic features on test data. Generated = GePpeTto-F.

Semantic Similarity Based Evaluation for Abstractive News Summarization

Figen Beken Fikri[1], Kemal Oflazer[2], Berrin Yanıkoğlu[1]

[1]Department of Computer Science and Engineering, Sabancı University, Istanbul, Turkey
[2]Department of Computer Science, Carnegie Mellon University - Qatar, Doha, Qatar
[1]*{fbekenfikri,berrin}@sabanciuniv.edu*, [2]*ko@andrew.cmu.edu*

Abstract

ROUGE is a widely used evaluation metric in text summarization. However, it is not suitable for the evaluation of abstractive summarization systems as it relies on lexical overlap between the gold standard and the generated summaries. This limitation becomes more apparent for agglutinative languages with very large vocabularies and high type/token ratios. In this paper, we present semantic similarity models for Turkish and apply them as evaluation metrics for an abstractive summarization task. To achieve this, we translated the English STSb dataset into Turkish and presented the first semantic textual similarity dataset for Turkish. We showed that our best similarity models have better alignment with average human judgments compared to ROUGE in both Pearson and Spearman correlations.

1 Introduction

Automatic document summarization aims to produce a summary that conveys the salient information in the given text(s). Automatic summarizers provide reduction in the size of the text, as well as, combine and cluster different sources of information, while preserving the informational content. There are two approaches to summarization: extractive and abstractive. Extractive summarization yields a summary by extracting important phrases or sentences from the document. In contrast, abstractive summarization provides a much more human-like summary by capturing the internal semantic meaning and generating new sentences.

ROUGE is a widely used evaluation metric in text summarization. It compares the system summary with the human generated summary or summaries, by considering the overlapping units such as n-gram, word sequences and word pairs (Lin, 2004). However, in abstractive summarization systems, the generated summary does not necessarily contain the same words in the gold standard summary. On the contrary, an abstractive summarization model is expected to generate new words that may not even appear in the source. For agglutinative languages, the ineffectiveness of ROUGE metric becomes more apparent. For instance, both of the following sentences has the meaning "I want to call the embassy":

Büyükelçiliği aramak istiyorum.

Büyükelçiliğe telefon etmek istiyorum.

While, "aramak" is a verb that takes an object in accusative case, "telefon etmek" is a compound verb in Turkish and the equivalent of the accusative object in the first sentence is realized with a noun in dative case (as highlighted with underlines). Although, these sentences are semantically equivalent, ROUGE-1, ROUGE-2 and ROUGE-3 scores of these sentences are 0.25, 0, and 0.25 respectively.

In this paper, we present a semantic similarity model which can be applied to abstractive summarization as a semantic evaluation metric. To this end, we translated the English Semantic Textual Similarity benchmark (STSb) dataset (Cer et al., 2017) into Turkish and presented the first semantic textual similarity dataset for Turkish as well. STSb dataset is a selection of data from English STS shared tasks between 2012 and 2017. These datasets have been widely used for sentence level similarity and semantic representations research (Cer et al., 2017).

We also leveraged the NLI-TR dataset that has been presented recently for Turkish natural language inference task (Budur et al., 2020). The NLI-TR dataset combines the translated Stanford Natural Language Inference (SNLI) (Bowman et al., 2015) and MultiGenre Natural Language Inference (MultiNLI) (Williams et al., 2018) datasets.

Proceedings of the 1st Workshop on Natural Language Generation, Evaluation, and Metrics (GEM 2021), pages 24–33
August 5–6, 2021. ©2021 Association for Computational Linguistics

Our paper is structured in the following way: In section 2, we explain recent studies and evaluation metrics. In section 3, we explain natural language inference and semantic textual similarity. We present our STSb Turkish dataset and translation quality. In section 4, we present our experiments for semantic textual similarity. In section 5, we present the experiments for summarization. We applied our best performing four semantic similarity models as evaluation metrics to the summarization results. In section 6, we present our results both qualitatively and quantitatively by comparing the semantic similarity and ROUGE scores with human judgments in Pearson and Spearman correlations.

2 Related Work

The most widely used evaluation metric for summarization is ROUGE which compares the system summary with the human generated summary or summaries by considering the overlapping units such as n-gram, word sequences and word pairs (Lin, 2004). Recently, there has been a range of studies focusing on the evaluation of factual correctness in the generated summaries. Falke et al. (2019) has studied whether textual entailment can be used to detect factual errors in generated summaries based on the idea that the source document should entail the information in a summary. The authors investigated whether factual errors can be reduced by reranking the alternative summaries using models trained on NLI datasets. They found that out-of-the-box NLI models do not perform well on the task of factual correctness. Kryscinski et al. (2020) proposed a model-based approach on the document-sentence level for verifying factual consistency in generated summaries. Zhao et al. (2020) addressed the problem of unsupported information in the generated summaries known as factual hallucination. Durmus et al. (2020) and Wang et al. (2020) suggested question answering based methods to evaluate the faithfullness of the generated summaries.

In addition to the studies focusing on summarization evaluation, there are some recently proposed metrics to evaluate generated text with the gold standard. Zhang et al. (2019) proposed BERTScore that uses BERT (Devlin et al., 2019) to compute a similarity score between the generated and reference text. Several recent works proposed new evaluaiton metrics for machine translation (BLEURT (Sellam et al., 2020), COMET (Rei et al., 2020), YiSi (Lo, 2019), Prism (Thompson and Post, 2020)).

3 Methodology

3.1 Natural Language Inference

Natural language inference is the study of determining whether there is an entailment, a contradiction or a neutral relationship between a hypothesis and a given premise. There are two major corpora in literature for natural language inference in English. These are Stanford Natural Language Inference (SNLI) (Bowman et al., 2015) and MultiGenre Natural Language Inference (MultiNLI) (Williams et al., 2018) datasets. The SNLI corpus is about 570k sentence pairs while the MultiNLI corpus is about 433k sentence pairs. The MultiNLI corpus is in the same format as SNLI, but with more varied text genres. Recently, these corpora have been translated into Turkish (Budur et al., 2020). In this study, we used the NLI-TR dataset.[1]

3.2 Semantic Textual Similarity

Semantic textual similarity aims to determine how similar two pieces of texts are. There are many application areas such as machine translation, summarization, text generation, question answering, dialogue and speech systems. It has become a remarkable area with the competitions organized by SemEval since 2012.

Semantic textual similarity studies are very common in English, and are based on datasets that are annotated and given similarity scores by human annotators. However, annotation is costly and time consuming. Recently, with the increase of success in machine translation and the development of multi-language models, it has become possible to use datasets by translating them from one language to another, e.g., Isbister and Sahlgren (2020), Budur et al. (2020).

In this study, we use the English STS Benchmark (STSb) dataset (Cer et al., 2017) that we translated into Turkish using the Google Cloud Translation API.[2,3] The STSb dataset consists of all the English datasets used in SemEval STS studies between 2012 and 2017. It consists of 8628 sentence pairs (5749 train, 1500 dev, 1379 test), (see Table 3

[1] NLI-TR dataset consists of the translations of SNLI and MultiNLI data sets available on GitHub: https://github.com/boun-tabi/NLI-TR

[2] https://cloud.google.com/translate/docs/basic/translating-text

[3] https://github.com/verimsu/STSb-TR

Sentence 1	Sentence 2	Similarity Score
Adam ata biniyor. (The man is riding a horse.)	Bir adam ata biniyor. (A man is riding on a horse.)	5.0
Bir kız uçurtma uçuruyor. (A girl is flying a kite.)	Koşan bir kız uçurtma uçuruyor. (A girl running is flying a kite.)	4.0
Bir adam gitar çalıyor. (A man is playing a guitar.)	Bir adam şarkı söylüyor ve gitar çalıyor. (A man is singing and playing a guitar.)	3.6
Bir adam gitar çalıyor. (A man is playing a guitar.)	Bir kız gitar çalıyor. (A girl is playing a guitar.)	2.8
Bir bebek kaplan bir topla oynuyor. (A baby tiger is playing with a ball.)	Bir bebek bir oyuncak bebekle oynuyor. (A baby is playing with a doll.)	1.6
Bir kadın dans ediyor. (A woman is dancing.)	Bir adam konuşuyor. (A man is talking.)	0.0

Table 1: Sample translations from STSb-TR dataset and the corresponding labels taken from the English dataset. Original English sentences are given in parenthesis.

for details). In this dataset, each sentence pair was annotated by crowdsourcing and assigned a semantic similarity score. Five scores were collected for each pair and gold scores were generated by taking the median value of these scores (Agirre et al., 2016). Scores range from 0 (no semantic similarity) to 5 (semantically equivalent) on a continuous scale. Some examples from the STS dataset and their translations are given in Table 1.

Here, we apply various state-of-the-art models on the translated dataset, and the best performing four models are used for semantic similarity based evaluation metric for the task of abstractive summarization.

3.3 Translation Quality

It is possible to encounter some translation errors in the translated texts. The most striking mistakes are related to expressions that are not used in Turkish. For instance, the sentence in S1 is translated as T1; however, a more appropriate translation would be C1, as "sitting" is translated differently for inanimate subjects.

S1: Old green bottle sitting on a table.

T1: Bir masada <u>oturan</u> eski yeşil şişe.

C1: Bir masada <u>duran</u> eski yeşil şişe.

Another typical error is possessive agreement mismatch. For example, the sentence S2 is translated as T2 but the correct translation would be C2.

S2: Group of people sitting at table of restaurant.

T2: Bir grup insan restoran <u>masada</u> oturuyor.

C2: Bir grup insan restoran <u>masasında</u> oturuyor.

In this paper, we assumed that such translation errors will not cause a major problem in our similarity models. In order to verify our assumption, we tested the quality of translations by selecting 50 sentence pairs (100 sentences) randomly, considering the percentage of the categories in the dataset. So, 6, 19 and 25 pairs chosen from forum, caption and news categories respectively. These sentences were translated by three native Turkish speakers who are fluent in English. We evaluated quality of the system translations with the three references using BLEU (Papineni et al., 2002) score. We used the SacreBLEU[4] tool (Post, 2018) version 1.5.1 and found BLEU score as 60.21 which shows that our system translations can be considered as very high quality translations (Google). Therefore, no changes have been made to the translations.

Table 2 shows vocabulary size (cased and uncased), type/token ratio, average word length and average sentence length values for English and Turkish datasets.[5]

[4]https://github.com/mjpost/sacrebleu

[5]Only the punctuation marks around the word and at the end of sentences were deleted.

Language	Vocab Size (Cased)	Vocab Size (Uncased)	Type/Token Ratio	Avg Word Length	Avg Sentence Length
English	18,736	16,225	0.09	4.62	10.15
Turkish	29,461	26,649	0.19	6.20	8.26

Table 2: English and Turkish STSb dataset statistics. Vocab size is the word count and type/token ratio is the number of different words divided by the total number of words. Word length is the amount of characters in the word and sentence length is the number of words in a sentence.

	Train	Dev	Test	Total
News	3,299	500	500	4,299
Caption	2,000	625	625	3,250
Forum	450	375	254	1,079
Total	5,749	1,500	1,379	8,628

Table 3: STSb dataset statistics in terms of number of sentence pairs.

4 Experiments for Semantic Textual Similarity

In order to assess the semantic similarity between a pair of texts, there are two main model structures: 1) Sentence representation models that try to map a sentence to a fixed-sized real-value vectors called sentence embeddings. 2) Cross-encoders that directly compute the semantic similarity score of a sentence pair.

In this paper, we experimented with state-of-the-art sentence representation models that are applicable to Turkish (language-specific and multilingual models) and BERT cross-encoders. In sentence representation models, we obtained the semantic similarity scores using cosine similarity. All models were tested on the STSb-TR test dataset.

4.1 Sentence Representation Models

We experimented with LASER, LaBSE, MUSE, BERT, XLM-R and Sentence-BERT models as explained below.

LASER Language-Agnostic SEntence Representations (LASER) is a language model based on the BiLSTM encoder trained on parallel data targeting translation. The model has been trained in 93 languages, including Turkish.[6] In this study, Turkish sentence embeddings were computed using a pre-trained LASER model.

LaBSE Language-agnostic BERT Sentence Embedding (LaBSE) is a BERT variant masked and trained on multilingual data for translation language modeling. The model produces language-independent sentence embeddings for 109 languages, including Turkish (Feng et al., 2020). Similar to the LASER model, Turkish sentence embeddings were computed using a pre-trained LaBSE model.

MUSE Multilingual Universal Sentence Encoder (MUSE) model is a sentence embedding model trained on multiple languages at the same time. The model creates a common semantic embedding area for a total of 16 languages, including Turkish (Yang et al., 2020). In this study, CNN[7] and Transformer[8] models that are shared publicly in TensorFlow Hub are used.

BERT Bidirectional Encoder Representations from Transformers (BERT) is designed to pre-train deep bi-directional representations from unlabeled text by conditioning together in both left and right context on all layers (Devlin et al., 2019). In this study, BERTurk[9] and M-BERT[10] (Pires et al., 2019) models were used. Sentence embeddings were obtained by averaging the BERT embeddings.[11] In addition, the models were integrated into the Siamese network that we explained in section 4.1.

XLM-R RoBERTa Transformer model[12] has been trained on a large multilingual data using a multilingual masked language modeling goal (Conneau et al., 2020). In this study, we used the model to compute sentence embeddings similar to BERT models. We also integrated it into the Siamese network used in Sentence-BERT.

[6]https://github.com/facebookresearch/LASER

[7]https://tfhub.dev/google/universal-sentence-encoder-multilingual/3

[8]https://tfhub.dev/google/universal-sentence-encoder-multilingual-large/3

[9]https://huggingface.co/dbmdz/bert-base-turkish-cased

[10]https://huggingface.co/bert-base-multilingual-cased

[11]The output of the CLS vectors yields significantly lower results compared to the results obtained.

[12]https://huggingface.co/xlm-roberta-base

Sentence-BERT Sentence-BERT (SBERT) (also called Bi-Encoder BERT) is a modification of pre-trained BERT network (or other transformer models) using Siamese and ternary network structures (Reimers and Gurevych, 2019). The model derives close fixed-size sentence embedding in vector space for semantically similar sentences. The training loss function differs depending on the dataset the model was trained on. During the training on the NLI dataset, the classification objective function was used; whereas during the training on the STSb dataset, the regression objective function was used (Reimers and Gurevych, 2019).

The classification objective function concatenates the sentence embeddings by element-wise difference and multiplies by a trainable weight. The model optimizes the cross entropy loss:

$$\text{o} = \text{softmax}(W_t(u, v, |u - v|)), W_t \epsilon R^{3n \times k}$$

where n is the size of the sentence embedding, and k is the number of labels.

In the regression objective function, the cosine similarity between two sentence embeddings, optimize the models for mean square error loss.

4.2 Cross-Encoders

We adopted cross-encoder architecture as explained in Reimers and Gurevych (2019). In the cross-encoder, both sentences are passed to the network and a similarity score between 0 and 1 obtained; no sentence embeddings are produced.[13] We experimented with BERTurk, M-BERT, and XLM-R with training on NLI-TR and STSb-TR datasets.

4.3 Results for Semantic Textual Similarity

All models were individually trained on NLI-TR and STSb-TR training datasets. Also, the models trained on the NLI-TR dataset were fine-tuned on the STSb-TR dataset. All models were then tested on the STSb-TR test dataset.

We trained/fine-tuned the models on STSb-TR dataset with 4 epochs and 10 random seeds[14] as suggested by Reimers and Gurevych (2018; 2019). Then, we reported the average test results of 5 successful models that perform best on the validation set. The models were evaluated by calculating the Spearman and Pearson correlations between the estimated similarity scores and the gold labels. Table 4 shows the results as ρ x 100. According to the results, training the models first on the NLI-TR dataset increases the model performance. This is particularly noticeable for the XLM-R models. The BERTurk model also gives very good results when trained directly on the STSb-TR dataset. Here, we observe that the existing multilingual LASER, LaBSE, MUSE models without any training for semantic textual similarity, give very good results. Compared to these models, the performance of BERT models without training are quite low. The best results were obtained by training the BERTurk model on the NLI-TR dataset first, and then on the STSb-TR dataset.

Model	Pearson	Spearman
Not trained for STS		
Avg. BERTurk embeddings	54.48	55.23
Avg. M-BERT embeddings	50.44	50.43
Avg. XLM-R embeddings	20.22	41.81
LASER	69.86	70.18
LaBSE	72.24	71.74
MUSE-CNN	71.09	69.91
MUSE-Transformer	**76.32**	**74.84**
Trained on STS		
BERTurk + STS	**83.32**	**82.22**
M-BERT + STS	79.08	78.15
XLM-R + STS	79.18	78.56
S-BERTurk + STS	81.97	81.43
S-M-BERT + STS	73.28	72.84
S-XLM-R + STS	71.89	71.02
Trained on NLI + STS		
BERTurk + NLI + STS	**85.36**	**84.59**
M-BERT + NLI + STS	79.30	78.39
XLM-R + NLI + STS	81.94	81.21
S-BERTurk + NLI + STS	82.85	83.31
S-M-BERT + NLI + STS	75.74	75.41
S-XLM-R + NLI + STS	77.26	77.32

Table 4: Experiment results for semantic textual similarity. BERTurk, M-BERT and XLM-R are cross-encoder models. S-BERTurk, S-M-BERT and S-XLM-R are bi-encoder models. Pearson and Spearman correlations were reported as ρ x 100.

5 Experiments for Summarization

To investigate the effectiveness of our semantic similarity models for summarization evaluation, we computed the correlations of ROUGE scores and our best performing four similarity models with human judgments for a state-of-the-art abstractive model. We reported semantic similarity scores for extractive baselines as well in order to observe their alignmnet with the ROUGE scores.

[13] https://www.sbert.net/examples/applications/cross-encoder/README.html

[14] Only S-XLM-R + STS was trained with 20 random seeds to have at least 5 successful models.

	Cross-Encoder		Bi-Encoder		ROUGE			Other Metrics
Model	NLI+STS	STS	NLI+STS	STS	ROUGE-1	ROUGE-2	ROUGE-L	BERTScore
Lead-1	52.11	55.71	59.18	61.67	26.56	17.31	25.31	73.72
Lead-3	**60.78**	**61.86**	**69.72**	**71.01**	30.04	18.90	28.83	74.15
mT5	59.00	61.03	66.43	68.29	**33.22**	**22.44**	**31.90**	**75.90**

Table 5: Results of the summarization models on MLSUM dataset. The values under Cross-Encoder are the average similarity scores predicted by the models; whereas, the values under Bi-Encoder are the average cosine similarities of sentence embeddings computed by these models. All the values were scaled to 100.

	Relevance		Consistency		Fluency		Human Average	
Metric	Pearson	Spearman	Pearson	Spearman	Pearson	Spearman	Pearson	Spearman
Rouge-1	42.79	43.87	28.18	32.36	21.40	20.30	36.79	37.51
Rouge-2	38.26	41.63	27.39	**35.78**	16.43	20.83	32.76	38.02
Rouge-L	41.83	41.95	26.29	28.85	20.17	18.63	35.15	35.11
BERTScore	45.49	45.75	25.14	22.47	24.74	19.85	37.88	38.07
S-BERTurk+STS	55.44	52.82	30.25	30.04	25.63	26.70	44.26	45.86
S-BERTurk+NLI+STS	58.77	58.72	32.80	32.67	31.24	**30.17**	48.80	51.85
BERTurk+STS	56.87	53.54	38.02	32.46	34.10	27.88	51.32	48.59
BERTurk+NLI+STS	**59.98**	**59.17**	**39.95**	34.24	**34.62**	29.31	**53.54**	**52.10**

Table 6: Pearson and Spearman correlations of ROUGE, BERTScore and proposed evaluation metrics with human judgments.

5.1 Dataset

MLSUM is the first large-scale MultiLingual SUMmarization dataset which contains 1.5M+ article/summary pairs including Turkish (Scialom et al., 2020). The authors compiled the dataset following the same methodology of CNN/DailyMail dataset. They considered news articles as the text input and their paired highlights/description as the summary. Turkish dataset was created from Internet Haber[15] by crawling archived articles between 2010 and 2019. All the articles shorter than 50 words or summaries shorter than 10 words were discarded. The data was split into train, validation and test sets, with respect to the publication dates. The data from 2010 to 2018 was used for training; data between January-April 2019 was used for validation; and data up to December 2019 was used for test (Scialom et al., 2020). In this study, we obtained the Turkish dataset from HuggingFace collection.[16] The dataset consists of 249,277 train, 11,565 validation, and 12,775 test samples.

5.2 Models

We experimented on MLSUM Turkish dataset with extractive baselines Lead-1 and Lead-3 and a state-of-the-art abstractive model mT5 described below.

Lead-1 We selected the first sentence of the source text as a summary.

Lead-3 We selected the first three sentences of the source text as a summary, based on the observation that the leading three sentences are a strong baseline for summarization (Nallapati et al., 2017; Sharma et al., 2019).

mT5 Multilingual T5 (mT5) (Xue et al., 2020) is a variant of T5 model (Raffel et al., 2020) that was pre-trained for 101 languages including Turkish on a new Common Crawl-based dataset. For Turkish summarization, we used mT5 model fine-tuned on MLSUM dataset available on HuggingFace.[17] The model was trained with 10 epochs, 8 batch size and 10e-4 learning rate. The max news length was 784 and max summary length was determined as 64.[18]

5.3 Evaluations

We evaluated the summarization models using semantic similarity-based evaluation, ROUGE scores, and human judgments. All the values were scaled to 100.

Semantic Similarity Evaluations We used the best performing four semantic similarity models to evaluate the summarization models. The values under Cross-Encoder are the average similarity scores predicted by the models; whereas, the values under Bi-Encoder are the average cosine similarities of sentence embeddings computed by these models.

[15] www.internethaber.com

[16] https://github.com/huggingface/datasets/tree/master/datasets/mlsum

[17] https://huggingface.co/ozcangundes/mt5-small-turkish-summarization

[18] During inference, we set max summary length to 120.

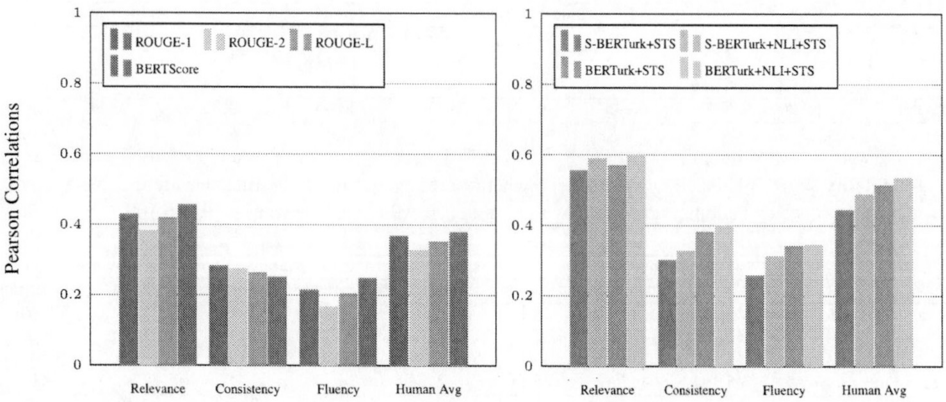

Figure 1: Pearson correlations between different evaluation metrics and human evaluations.

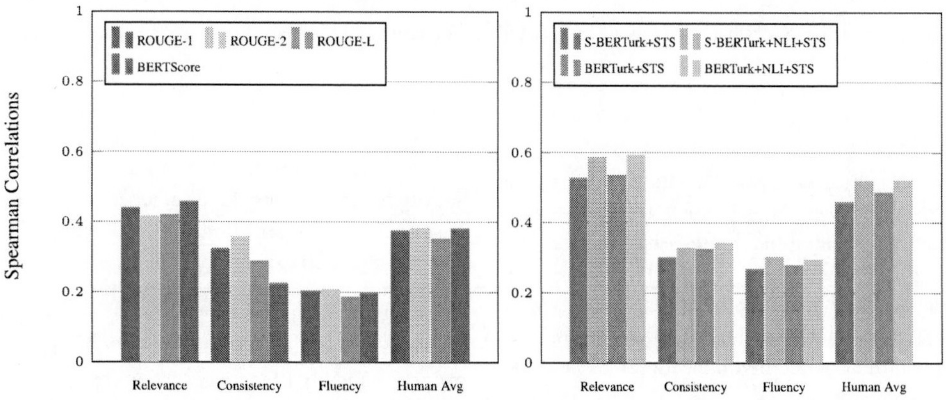

Figure 2: Spearman correlations between different evaluation metrics and human evaluations.

ROUGE We reported F1 scores for ROUGE-1, ROUGE-2 and ROUGE-L. ROUGE scores were computed using rouge package version 0.3.1.[19]

BERTScore We reported F1 score for BERTScore (Zhang et al., 2019).

Human Evaluations Human evaluations were conducted to show the effectiveness of our semantic similarity based evaluation metric. We randomly selected 50 articles from the test set with their predicted summaries via mT5 model. Following the work of Fabbri et al. (2021), we asked native Turkish annotators to rate each predicted summary in terms of relevance (selection of important content from the source), consistency (the factual alignment between the summary and the summarized source) and fluency (the quality of individual sentences) in the range of 1 (very bad) to 5 (very good). Overall, 5 annotators (3 university students, 1 Ph.D. student, and 1 professor) evaluated the summaries. Average relevance was 3.50 ± 0.78, average consistency was 4.45 ± 0.83, and average fluency was 4.34 ± 0.77.

6 Results

Quantitative Analysis We computed Pearson and Spearman correlations of human judgments with semantic similarity and ROUGE scores. Correlation values can be seen in Table 6 and are visualized in Figure 1 and Figure 2.[20] The results show that, our cross-encoder models have significantly better correlations with relevance, consistency, fluency, and human average. The correlations are higher compared to the bi-encoder models. This

[19]This is the package and version that the authors of MLSUM reported: https://github.com/recitalAI/MLSUM.

[20]All the correlations were significant ($p<.05$) except for the correlations between Fluency and S-BERTurk+STS, BERTScore, ROUGE-L as well as correlations between BERTScore and Consistency.

Article-1
Seattle şehrinin merkezinde meydana gelen olayda, Kanadalı olduğu belirtilen adam, *bir otomobilden söktüğü sunroof camıyla bölgede bulunan araçların ön camlarını* parçaladı. Araçların kaputlarına da çıkan adam, çevredeki birçok araca maddi hasar verdi. Sonrasında, çevrede bulunan otopark görevlisi adama müdahale etmek istedi. Elindeki cam tavanla bu sefer görevliye saldıran adam, *çevredeki diğer insanların müdahalesiyle etkisiz hale getirildi.* Olay yerine gelen polis, adamı gözaltına alırken; adamın uyuşturucu etkisi altında olduğu bildirildi.
Reference Summary
ABD'de bir adam, elindeki sunroof camıyla otomobillerin ön camlarını parçaladı. Adama müdahale etmek isteyen park görevlisi de adamın saldırısına uğradı.
Generated Summary
ABD'de bir otomobilden söktüğü sunroof camıyla bölgede bulunan araçların ön camlarını parçalayan adam, çevredeki diğer insanların müdahalesiyle etkisiz hale getirildi.
ROUGE-(1/2/L): 30.00, 10.53, 25.00
Semantic Similarity Scores BERTurk+NLI+STS (Cross Encoder / Bi-Encoder): 73.67 / 74.35
Human Evaluations (relevance / consistency / fluency / avg): 3.81 / 4.36 / 4.36 / 4.18

Article-2
Yangın, Salihli-Köprübaşı yolu Taytan Mahallesi Çaldırlık mevkisinde meydana geldi. Edinilen bilgiye göre, *seyir* halinde ilerleyen Servet Durmuş idaresindeki 43 HE 737 plakalı *otomobilin motor bölümünde yangın çıktı.* Alevlerin büyümesiyle birlikte otomobil ateş topuna döndü. Sürücü Durmuş hemen itfaiye ekiplerine haber verirken olay yerine gelen Manisa Büyükşehir Belediyesi Salihli İtfaiye Amirliği ekipleri yangına müdahale etti. Söndürülen otomobil kullanılamaz hale geldi. Yangınla ilgili soruşturma başlatıldı.
Reference Summary
Manisa'nın Salihli ilçesinde seyir halinde ilerleyen otomobil alevlere teslim oldu.
Generated Summary
Manisa'da seyir halindeki otomobilin motor bölümünde yangın çıktı.
ROUGE-(1/2/L): 11.11 / 0 / 11.11
Semantic Similarity Scores BERTurk+NLI+STS (Cross Encoder / Bi-Encoder): 76.16 / 81.75
Human Evaluations (relevance / consistency / fluency / avg): 4.0 / 4.8 / 5.0 / 4.6

Table 7: Example articles from MLSUM Turkish test dataset with their reference and generated summaries. The words that appear in both reference and generated summary are in blue, while the semantically similar words are in red. The italic text pieces in the article appear in the generated summary.

also shows that predicted similarity scores are more reliable than computed cosine similarities.

While the main idea of this paper is to evaluate abstractive summarization, we also showed that an extractive Lead-3 baseline yields better semantic similarity scores compared to the abstractive mT5 although it outperforms the extractive baselines in terms of BERTScore and ROUGE scores.

Qualitative Analysis We analyzed the effectiveness of our proposed metrics qualitatively as well. In Table 7, we show two example articles. In the first one, there are some overlapping words between two sentences and they share semantically similar information in the following parts: "*ABD'de bir adam, elindeki sunroof camıyla otomobillerin ön camlarını parçaladı*" and "*ABD'de bir otomobilden söktüğü sunroof camıyla bölgede bulunan araçların ön camlarını parçalayan adam*". So, we can say that both ROUGE and semantic similarity scores can be acceptable for this example. On the other hand, the second example is more critical as it has only one overlapping word between the reference and generated summary; however, there is a high semantic similarity between them and the predicted summary has high human evaluation scores. Our proposed metrics can capture this but apparently ROUGE cannot.

7 Conclusion

In this study, we presented the first Turkish semantic textual similarity corpus, called STSb-TR, by translating the original English STSb dataset via machine translation. We showed that the dataset has high quality translations and does not require costly human annotation. We applied state-of-the-art models to the STSb-TR dataset, and used the best performing four models as evaluation metrics for the text summarization task. We used natural language inference (NLI) models and observed that we can improve our semantic similarity models. We found high correlations between human judgments and our models, compared to BERTScore and ROUGE scores. Our qualitative analyses showed that the proposed models can capture the semantic similarity of reference and predicted summaries which cannot be caught by ROUGE scores. We conclude that our models can be applied as evaluation metric to abstractive summarization in Turkish.

References

Eneko Agirre, Carmen Banea, Daniel Cer, Mona Diab, Aitor Gonzalez Agirre, Rada Mihalcea, German Rigau Claramunt, and Janyce Wiebe. 2016. SemEval-2016 task 1: Semantic textual similarity, monolingual and cross-lingual evaluation. In *SemEval-2016. 10th International Workshop on Semantic Evaluation; 2016 Jun 16-17; San Diego, CA. Stroudsburg (PA): ACL; 2016. p. 497-511*. ACL (Association for Computational Linguistics).

Samuel Bowman, Gabor Angeli, Christopher Potts, and Christopher D Manning. 2015. A large annotated corpus for learning natural language inference. In *Proceedings of the 2015 Conference on Empirical Methods in Natural Language Processing*, pages 632–642.

Emrah Budur, Rıza Özçelik, Tunga Güngör, and Christopher Potts. 2020. Data and representation for Turkish natural language inference. In *Proceedings of the 2020 Conference on Empirical Methods in Natural Language Processing (EMNLP)*, pages 8253–8267.

Daniel Cer, Mona Diab, Eneko Agirre, Iñigo Lopez-Gazpio, and Lucia Specia. 2017. SemEval-2017 task 1: Semantic textual similarity multilingual and crosslingual focused evaluation. In *Proceedings of the 11th International Workshop on Semantic Evaluation (SemEval-2017)*, pages 1–14.

Alexis Conneau, Kartikay Khandelwal, Naman Goyal, Vishrav Chaudhary, Guillaume Wenzek, Francisco Guzmán, Édouard Grave, Myle Ott, Luke Zettlemoyer, and Veselin Stoyanov. 2020. Unsupervised cross-lingual representation learning at scale. In *Proceedings of the 58th Annual Meeting of the Association for Computational Linguistics*, pages 8440–8451.

Jacob Devlin, Ming-Wei Chang, Kenton Lee, and Kristina Toutanova. 2019. BERT: Pre-training of deep bidirectional transformers for language understanding. In *Proceedings of the 2019 Conference of the North American Chapter of the Association for Computational Linguistics: Human Language Technologies, Volume 1 (Long and Short Papers)*, pages 4171–4186.

Esin Durmus, He He, and Mona Diab. 2020. FEQA: A question answering evaluation framework for faithfulness assessment in abstractive summarization. In *Proceedings of the 58th Annual Meeting of the Association for Computational Linguistics*, pages 5055–5070.

Alexander R Fabbri, Wojciech Kryściński, Bryan McCann, Caiming Xiong, Richard Socher, and Dragomir Radev. 2021. SummEval: Re-evaluating summarization evaluation. *Transactions of the Association for Computational Linguistics*, 9:391–409.

Tobias Falke, Leonardo FR Ribeiro, Prasetya Ajie Utama, Ido Dagan, and Iryna Gurevych. 2019. Ranking generated summaries by correctness: An interesting but challenging application for natural language inference. In *Proceedings of the 57th Annual Meeting of the Association for Computational Linguistics*, pages 2214–2220.

Fangxiaoyu Feng, Yinfei Yang, Daniel Cer, Naveen Arivazhagan, and Wei Wang. 2020. Language-agnostic BERT sentence embedding. *arXiv preprint arXiv:2007.01852*.

Google. Evaluating models — automl translation documentation — google cloud.

Tim Isbister and Magnus Sahlgren. 2020. Why not simply translate? a first Swedish evaluation benchmark for semantic similarity. *arXiv preprint arXiv:2009.03116*.

Wojciech Kryscinski, Bryan McCann, Caiming Xiong, and Richard Socher. 2020. Evaluating the factual consistency of abstractive text summarization. In *Proceedings of the 2020 Conference on Empirical Methods in Natural Language Processing (EMNLP)*, pages 9332–9346.

Chin-Yew Lin. 2004. ROUGE: A package for automatic evaluation of summaries. In *Text summarization branches out*, pages 74–81.

Chi-kiu Lo. 2019. Yisi-a unified semantic MT quality evaluation and estimation metric for languages with different levels of available resources. In *Proceedings of the Fourth Conference on Machine Translation (Volume 2: Shared Task Papers, Day 1)*, pages 507–513.

Ramesh Nallapati, Feifei Zhai, and Bowen Zhou. 2017. Summarunner: A recurrent neural network based sequence model for extractive summarization of documents. In *Proceedings of the AAAI Conference on Artificial Intelligence*, volume 31.

Kishore Papineni, Salim Roukos, Todd Ward, and Wei-Jing Zhu. 2002. Bleu: a method for automatic evaluation of machine translation. In *Proceedings of the 40th annual meeting of the Association for Computational Linguistics*, pages 311–318.

Telmo Pires, Eva Schlinger, and Dan Garrette. 2019. How multilingual is multilingual BERT? In *Proceedings of the 57th Annual Meeting of the Association for Computational Linguistics*, pages 4996–5001.

Matt Post. 2018. A call for clarity in reporting bleu scores. In *Proceedings of the Third Conference on Machine Translation: Research Papers*, pages 186–191.

Colin Raffel, Noam Shazeer, Adam Roberts, Katherine Lee, Sharan Narang, Michael Matena, Yanqi Zhou, Wei Li, and Peter J Liu. 2020. Exploring the limits of transfer learning with a unified text-to-text transformer. *Journal of Machine Learning Research*, 21:1–67.

Ricardo Rei, Craig Stewart, Ana C Farinha, and Alon Lavie. 2020. COMET: A neural framework for MT evaluation. In *Proceedings of the 2020 Conference on Empirical Methods in Natural Language Processing (EMNLP)*, pages 2685–2702.

Nils Reimers and Iryna Gurevych. 2018. Why comparing single performance scores does not allow to draw conclusions about machine learning approaches. *arXiv preprint arXiv:1803.09578*.

Nils Reimers and Iryna Gurevych. 2019. Sentence-BERT: Sentence embeddings using Siamese BERT-networks. In *Proceedings of the 2019 Conference on Empirical Methods in Natural Language Processing and the 9th International Joint Conference on Natural Language Processing (EMNLP-IJCNLP)*, pages 3973–3983.

Thomas Scialom, Paul-Alexis Dray, Sylvain Lamprier, Benjamin Piwowarski, and Jacopo Staiano. 2020. MLSUM: The multilingual summarization corpus. In *Proceedings of the 2020 Conference on Empirical Methods in Natural Language Processing (EMNLP)*, pages 8051–8067.

Thibault Sellam, Dipanjan Das, and Ankur Parikh. 2020. BLEURT: Learning robust metrics for text generation. In *Proceedings of the 58th Annual Meeting of the Association for Computational Linguistics*, pages 7881–7892.

Eva Sharma, Chen Li, and Lu Wang. 2019. BIG-PATENT: A large-scale dataset for abstractive and coherent summarization. In *Proceedings of the 57th Annual Meeting of the Association for Computational Linguistics*, pages 2204–2213.

Brian Thompson and Matt Post. 2020. Automatic machine translation evaluation in many languages via zero-shot paraphrasing. In *Proceedings of the 2020 Conference on Empirical Methods in Natural Language Processing (EMNLP)*, pages 90–121.

Alex Wang, Kyunghyun Cho, and Mike Lewis. 2020. Asking and answering questions to evaluate the factual consistency of summaries. In *Proceedings of the 58th Annual Meeting of the Association for Computational Linguistics*, pages 5008–5020.

Adina Williams, Nikita Nangia, and Samuel Bowman. 2018. A broad-coverage challenge corpus for sentence understanding through inference. In *Proceedings of the 2018 Conference of the North American Chapter of the Association for Computational Linguistics: Human Language Technologies, Volume 1 (Long Papers)*, pages 1112–1122.

Linting Xue, Noah Constant, Adam Roberts, Mihir Kale, Rami Al-Rfou, Aditya Siddhant, Aditya Barua, and Colin Raffel. 2020. mT5: A massively multilingual pre-trained text-to-text transformer. *arXiv preprint arXiv:2010.11934*.

Yinfei Yang, Daniel Cer, Amin Ahmad, Mandy Guo, Jax Law, Noah Constant, Gustavo Hernandez Abrego, Steve Yuan, Chris Tar, Yun-hsuan Sung, et al. 2020. Multilingual universal sentence encoder for semantic retrieval. In *Proceedings of the 58th Annual Meeting of the Association for Computational Linguistics: System Demonstrations*, pages 87–94.

Tianyi Zhang, Varsha Kishore, Felix Wu, Kilian Q Weinberger, and Yoav Artzi. 2019. BERTScore: Evaluating text generation with BERT. In *International Conference on Learning Representations*.

Zheng Zhao, Shay B Cohen, and Bonnie Webber. 2020. Reducing quantity hallucinations in abstractive summarization. *arXiv preprint arXiv:2009.13312*.

Shades of BLEU, Flavours of Success: The Case of MultiWOZ

Tomáš Nekvinda and **Ondřej Dušek**
Charles University, Faculty of Mathematics and Physics
Institute of Formal and Applied Linguistics
Prague, Czech Republic
{nekvinda,odusek}@ufal.mff.cuni.cz

Abstract

The MultiWOZ dataset (Budzianowski et al., 2018) is frequently used for benchmarking context-to-response abilities of task-oriented dialogue systems. In this work, we identify inconsistencies in data preprocessing and reporting of three corpus-based metrics used on this dataset, i.e., BLEU score and Inform & Success rates. We point out a few problems of the MultiWOZ benchmark such as unsatisfactory preprocessing, insufficient or under-specified evaluation metrics, or rigid database. We re-evaluate 7 end-to-end and 6 policy optimization models in as-fair-as-possible setups, and we show that their reported scores cannot be directly compared. To facilitate comparison of future systems, we release our stand-alone standardized evaluation scripts. We also give basic recommendations for corpus-based benchmarking in future works.

1 Introduction

While human judgements are irreplaceable in dialogue systems evaluation and using full dialogue evaluation instead of evaluating isolated responses given ground-truth contexts cannot fully measure system performance (Liu et al., 2016; Takanobu et al., 2020), corpus-based evaluation metrics, such as BLEU and corpus-based entity match and success rate (Wen et al., 2017), are still very important for model development and are often used to compare models and establish state-of-the-art. We show on the MultiWOZ benchmark (Budzianowski et al., 2018), one of the most frequently used and most challenging dialogue system datasets today, that these comparisons do not hold if several basic conditions are not met, and that these conditions are not met for most of the recent works using corpus-based evaluation on this dataset. This means the assessment of progress in terms of dialogue modeling is obscured by noise coming from differences in preprocessing or metrics implementation variants.

This paper is not a critique of the MultiWOZ benchmark or of systems evaluated on it. Instead, it is a call for consistency and increased rigor in automatic evaluation. In addition to providing the analysis and identifying problems with the benchmark and current state-of-the-art reporting, we include recommendations for consistency in corpus-based score comparisons. In particular, we advocate for: (1) using standardized implementations of metrics; (2) evaluating either on detokenized surface texts, or using standardized preprocessing and postprocessing; (3) reporting the exact scripts used for evaluation; (4) release of system outputs. We also show that there is room for additional metrics of output diversity, and we add an observation on the overlap between the dialogue goals and states in training and test sections of the MultiWOZ data.

Our work can be summarized as follows:

- We identify, list, and discuss consistency issues associated with the MultiWOZ benchmark;
- We compare and re-evaluate 13 end-to-end or policy optimization systems, using a single implementation of metrics and preprocessing;
- We release the outputs of all compared systems in a unified format and provide stand-alone standardized evaluation scripts that allow for consistent comparison of future works on this dataset;[1]
- In addition to standard MultiWOZ corpus-based metrics, we evaluate all systems in terms of the diversity of their outputs.

2 Related Work

Most works on evaluation methods in dialogue response generation (Deriu et al., 2021) focus on human evaluation (Walker et al., 1997), e.g., choosing the best methodology with respect to quality

[1] https://github.com/Tomiinek/MultiWOZ_Evaluation

Proceedings of the 1st Workshop on Natural Language Generation, Evaluation, and Metrics (GEM 2021), pages 34–46
August 5–6, 2021. ©2021 Association for Computational Linguistics

and consistency (Santhanam and Shaikh, 2019) or robustness (Dinan et al., 2019). Recent surveys in natural language generation reflect on divergence and inconsistency in human evaluation practice (Howcroft et al., 2020; Belz et al., 2020), in a similar spirit to our examination, but on a broader scale.

Despite the availability of simulator evaluation (Schatzmann et al., 2006; Young et al., 2010; Zhu et al., 2020), corpus-based metrics have been the go-to evaluation method in end-to-end neural dialogue systems since the first implementations (Wen et al., 2017; Eric and Manning, 2017) and are a de-facto standard until today (cf. Section 3.3). There are works showing problems of corpus-based metrics: limited correlation with human judgements (Novikova et al., 2017; Takanobu et al., 2020) and mixed performance depending on human reference texts used (Freitag et al., 2020) or evaluated systems (Mathur et al., 2020). Many works aim at creating more reliable metrics (Galley et al., 2015). Recent focus is on trained neural metrics (Dziri et al., 2019; Mehri and Eskenazi, 2020), but they are not yet in wide use.

Our work is probably the closest to Post (2018)'s assessment of inconsistencies in different implementations of BLEU (Papineni et al., 2002, see Section 3.2), calling for comparability and proposing a standard implementation. To our knowledge, we are the first to evaluate the use of corpus-based metrics in dialogue systems in this fashion.

3 Benchmark and Systems

3.1 The MultiWOZ dataset

The MultiWOZ 2.0 dataset (Budzianowski et al., 2018) includes about 10k task-oriented dialogues in 7 domains (restaurants, hotels, tourist attractions, trains, taxi, hospital, police) with dialogue state and system action annotation. Larger domains (restaurants, hotels, attractions, trains) have an associated database. The data was collected via human-to-human interaction on a crowdsourcing platform using the Wizard-Of-Oz approach (Wen et al., 2017). Crowd workers were instructed with goals such as booking or finding information about a restaurant or train (see Table 1). The dataset authors provided supporting code[2] and baselines for dialogue state tracking (DST), context-to-text (CTR), and action-to-text generation tasks.

[2] https://github.com/budzianowski/multiwoz/

Side	Utterance
User	Can you help me find a train that will arrive in birmingham new street by 16:15?
Sys.	What day would you like to travel?
User	I would like to leave Friday from Cambridge.
Sys.	TR2716 will leave cambridge at 13:01 and arrive at birmingham at 15:44. The trip will take 163 minutes and cost 75.10 pounds. Would you like to book?
User	Yes, I would like to book for 3 people.
Sys.	I booked the train. It was 225.3 and your reference is AS5SBC8P . Do you need help with anything else?
User	Yes I also need information on queens' college.
Sys.	It's located in west Cambridge on silver street. The postcode is cb39et. The phone number is 01223335511. The entrance fee is 2.50 pounds. Do you need anything else?
User	No, that's great. Thank you. Good-bye.
Sys.	Thank you for using the Cambridge TownInfo centre.

Table 1: Example multi-domain conversation from the MultiWOZ dataset (conversation ID: PMUL1266).

MultiWOZ 2.1: Eric et al. (2020) released an update with re-annotated dialogue states and added explicit system action annotation.

MultiWOZ 2.2 (Zang et al., 2020) has more fixes for state annotation in 17.3% of turns, a redefined ontology, and canonical forms for slot values (e.g. "13:00" for "1pm") for better DST evaluation. Additionally, it introduces slot span annotations allowing easy delexicalization, which was previously based only on string matching heuristics.

3.2 Corpus-based Metrics on MultiWOZ

All standard CTR metrics on MultiWOZ – BLEU, Inform & Success rate – are calculated on *delexicalized* texts, i.e., texts where dialogue slot values, such as venue names, are replaced by placeholders (Wen et al., 2015). While using delexicalized utterances prevents errors in venue names to affect the evaluation, it prevents the use of an interactive human evaluation, model-based evaluation metrics known from open-domain dialogue research (Gao et al., 2020), or end-to-end evaluation with user simulators such as ConvLab (Zhu et al., 2020).

BLEU (Papineni et al., 2002), originally designed for machine translation (MT) evaluation, is based on comparison of n-grams in human-written references and machine-generated hypotheses. Following Wen et al. (2017), BLEU is used to measure *fluency* of output responses where the human utterances are used as the reference. Using the metric for assessing fluency of the responses is not ideal, because as opposed to the intended use of BLEU, there is only a single reference available. Moreover, the set of valid responses is arguably larger for dialogue than for MT. Liu et al. (2016) show that metrics adopted from MT correlate very weakly with human judgements in dialogue responses.

Inform & Success rates: The Inform rate relates to *informable* slots, which are attributes that allow the user to constrain database searches, e.g., restaurant location or price range. The Success rate focuses on *requestable* slots, i.e., those that can be asked by the user, e.g., phone number. Both are calculated on the level of dialogues.

Su et al. (2015) consider a dialogue to be successful if the evaluated system provided all of the requested information for an entity satisfying the user's constraints. Following this definition, Wen et al. (2017) set aside the Match rate describing whether the entity found at the *end* of each dialogue matches the user's goal. However, MultiWOZ dialogues include multiple interleaving domains and calculating the rates only at the end is not sufficient.

Therefore, Budzianowski et al. (2018) mark a dialogue as successful if for each domain in the user's dialogue goal: (1) the last offered entity matches (satisfies the goal constraints), and (2) the system mentioned all requestable slots required by the user. The *Inform* rate then marks the proportion of dialogues complying to (1), *Success* rate is the proportion of fully successful dialogues.

The offered entities and mentions of requestable slots are tracked over the delexicalized responses for the whole dialogue, making use of slot placeholders. If an utterance contains a slot naming an entity, e.g., restaurant name or train ID, the current dialogue state for the corresponding domain is used to query the database and an entry is sampled from the search results. At the end of a dialogue, the recorded entities and requestable slots are compared to expected values from the dialogue goal (see Appendix A for an example). The dialogue can thus be considered unsuccessful if the system does not mention a venue name or train ID at the right turn,[3] does not track the user's search constraints, or ignores the user's requests.

[3]It must in practice hit the single suitable turn because responses are generated given ground-truth dialogue context.

3.3 Systems Evaluating on MultiWOZ

We discuss performance of 13 recent systems that use CTR evaluation on MultiWOZ – 7 end-to-end and 6 policy-optimization systems, which use ground-truth dialogue states during training and inference. We include models for which we got test set predictions and systems with public code for which we managed to replicate reported results.[4]

Out of the 13 compared works, 7 only report BLEU, Inform, and Success with no other evaluation; 4 use human ratings of individual outputs, and only 2 include human evaluation on full dialogues.[5]

An important representative of the end-to-end systems is DAMD (Zhang et al., 2020b). It uses a multi-action data augmentation and multiple GRU (Cho et al., 2014) decoders. Similarly, LABES (Zhang et al., 2020a) employs a few GRU-based decoders, but it represents the dialog state as a latent variable. DoTS (Jeon and Lee, 2021) also uses GRUs, but the model makes use of a BERT encoder (Devlin et al., 2019) to get a context representation. MinTL (Lin et al., 2020) applies a diff-based approach to state updates, with backbones based on the T5 and BART models (Raffel et al., 2020; Lewis et al., 2020). UBAR is based on a fine-tuned GPT-2 model (Radford et al., 2019), similarly to AuGPT (Kulhánek et al., 2021) which uses back-translations for response augmentation, and SOLOIST (Peng et al., 2020) which makes use of machine teaching (Shukla et al., 2020). We used author-provided outputs for SOLOIST and AuGPT, author-trained checkpoints for DoTS, LABES,[6] and UBAR, and we trained DAMD and MinTL[7] from scratch using publicly available code. DAMD, MinTL and SOLOIST use MultiWOZ 2.0; the remaining models trained on the 2.1 version. DAMD, LABES, MinTL, and UBAR are based on the same code base and use similar evaluation scripts.

We also compared 6 policy optimization models. SFN (Mehri et al., 2019), HDNO (Wang et al., 2021), and LAVA (Lubis et al., 2020) use reinforcement learning for training. HDSA (Chen et al., 2019) uses a BERT backbone and exploits the hierarchical structure of dialog acts. MarCo (Wang

[4]We were not successful in getting code, model weights, or original predictions for other systems, such as SimpleTOD (Hosseini-Asl et al., 2020), or ARDM (Wu et al., 2021).

[5]Note that full interaction is not possible with policy optimization models unless an external DST model is applied.

[6]We were able to generate outputs for 91.66% test utterances with this checkpoint. We note this in Tables 4, 5 and 6.

[7]We were only able to reproduce the T5-small model and use it in this comparison.

Delexical.	Utterance
Original	Cafe jello gallery has a free entrance fee. The address is cafe jello gallery, 13 magdalene street and the post code is cb30af. Can i help you with anything else?
MWZ 2.2	[address] has a [entrancefee] entrance fee. The address is [name], [address] and the post code is [postcode]. Can I help you with anything else?
HDSA	[attraction_name] has a free entrance fee. The address is [attraction_address] and the post code is [attraction_postcode]. Can i help you with anything else?
DAMD	[value_name] has a [value_price] entrance fee. The address is cafe jello gallery, [value_address] and the post code is [value_postcode]. Can i help you with anything else?
AuGPT	[address] has a free entrance fee. The address is cafe jello gallery, [address] and the post code is [postcode]. Can I help you with anything else?
UniConv	[attraction_name] has a [attraction_pricerange] entrance fee. The address is [attraction_name], 13 [attraction_address] and the post code is [attraction_postcode]. Can i help you with anything else?
LAVA	[attraction_name] has a free entrance fee. The address is [attraction_name], [value_count] [attraction_address] and the post code is [restaurant_postcode]. Can i help you with anything else?

Table 2: An example utterance from the MultiWOZ dataset with different styles of delexicalization. The first row shows the non-delexicalized source response. Other styles are paired with the systems that use or introduced them.

et al., 2020) and UniConv (Le et al., 2020) generate explicit system actions in parallel with the response. We use the public predictions for LAVA and the provided pretrained models for other models. UniConv and HDNO are trained on MultiWOZ 2.1, other systems use the 2.0 version. As opposed to end-to-end models, the version affects the evaluation because the ground-truth state is supplied to the model. The comparison of these systems is thus not completely fair, but we believe that the differences are small in comparison with the differences in evaluation scripts and setups (see Section 5.2).

4 Benchmark Caveats

While MultiWOZ and the associated metrics described in Section 3 represent the state-of-the-art in corpus-based dialogue evaluation practice, the benchmark has the following limitations that researchers need to be aware of: (1) delexicalization problems – imprecise delexicalization based on string matching and varying implementations thereof (Section 4.1), (2) lack of standardized postprocessing (i.e., lexicalization methods, Section 4.2), (3) database problems, i.e., multiple surface forms of database values and no information about booking availability (Section 4.3), (4) atypical metric implementations (Section 4.4), (5) lack of diversity evaluation (Section 4.5), (6) similarity between training and test data (Section 4.6).

4.1 Preprocessing

CTR evaluation metrics used in the benchmark work with *delexicalized* texts (see Section 3.2). However, the implementation of delexicalization provided with the dataset is limited; it only applies to some expressions, leaving other slot values lexicalized. That is why most systems use their own delexicalization methods. The original delexicalization uses placeholders consisting of the domain name and the slot name, e.g. *taxi_phone*. Recent works following DAMD (Zhang et al., 2020b) remove domain names from the placeholders and determine the active domain from changes in the predicted dialogue state or model it directly.

We identified five different delexicalization styles among the 13 systems described in Section 3.3. Table 2 shows a sample system turn for which the outputs of all the delexicalization approaches are different. This is a problem since all works use their own preprocessed data as references for BLEU computation. We checked the test set for slot placeholders and found that 70.61% of the utterances contain a slot in at least one delexicalized variant and only 17.52% responses with slots exactly match for all the systems.[8]

Moreover, preprocessing scripts of some works remove contracted verb forms or keep suffixes such as "-s", "-ly" when delexicalizing nouns or adverbs, e.g., "moderately" becomes "[pricerange]-ly".

4.2 Postprocessing

The MultiWOZ code base does not implement backward lexicalization of texts. Out of 12 systems for which we have the source code available, only four offer scripts for lexicalizing slot values and thus allow further in-depth evaluation.

[8] 8 utterances (including the example in Table 2) are pairwise different between all 5 delexicalizations.

4.3 Database: Surface Forms and Booking

The original MultiWOZ implementation of the database performs only subtle normalization of the database search constraints, such as replacing "&" with "and". However, the slot values can have multiple valid surface forms; e.g., "4pm" and "16:00" or "the botanical gardens at cambridge university" and "cambridge university botanic gardens" correspond to the same database entities. Database query normalization is crucial for end-to-end systems, as opposed to the policy optimization models, which use ground-truth dialogue states with normalized values. The flexibility of the database might affect the Inform & Success rates, because they are based on information about database entries *complying* with the current dialogue state.

The original database does not contain any information about booking availability, because during the data collection, crowd workers were sometimes instructed to refuse a booking at a specific time, ask for another place, etc., and accept the booking with new constraints. This brings a problem into the evaluation, because some works use the ground-truth booking information (mined from the dialogue state and system action annotations) even during evaluation, whereas other ignore it and let their systems behave randomly.

4.4 Evaluation

BLEU: The original MultiWOZ BLEU implementation internally uses a trivial tokenization splitting on whitespace. However, current models often use subword tokenization and complex detokenization to remove any redundant whitespace (Sennrich et al., 2016; Kudo and Richardson, 2018). This new-style detokenization might produce words with leading or trailing punctuation. Some works ignore this fact completely, or use an alternative BLEU implementation, including tokenization, from NLTK (Bird and Loper, 2004).

Inform & Success rate: We found two main problems here. The first one comes from random database entry sampling – if multiple entities match the dialogue state, one of them is sampled at random from the database results. The set of entries complying with the dialogue state does not have to be a subset of the ground-truth set of entries complying with a given prescribed user goal from the test set. If the database results and the ground-truth set have an imperfect overlap, the sampling may choose an entry from the difference of the two sets, which is counted as a failure. However, if an entry from the intersection of the two sets is chosen, it counts as a match, which may lead to overestimating the system performance. Some systems bypass this by comparing the sets and accepting a dialogue as matching if the sets are intersecting, or if the offered set is a non-empty subset of the ground-truth set. However, these differences result in large variances in the rates (see Section 5).

Another problem is related to the domain-oblivious delexicalization proposed by Zhang et al. (2020b). MultiWOZ responses contain slots from multiple domains at the same time very rarely, so it is sufficient to consider a single active domain for each turn. However, some works that adopt this new delexicalization use the ground-truth active domain during evaluation. Note that true domains have to be inferred from changes in ground-truth dialogue states and system actions.

4.5 Output Diversity Metrics

The standard MultiWOZ metrics do not cover the diversity of the outputs, which can show the formulaic or repetitive nature of a system's responses (Holtzman et al., 2020). While diversity is typically measured for non-task-oriented dialogue (Li et al., 2016), we argue that it can serve as an indicator of the naturalness of using a system over longer periods of time even in task-oriented dialogue such as MultiWOZ (Oraby et al., 2018).

4.6 Dataset folds

MultiWOZ authors split the data into train, validation, and test folds randomly. Following Lampouras and Vlachos (2016)'s analysis of train-test overlap on other datasets, we inspected the goals of all 1000 test dialogues; 174 of them are also present in the train or validation folds. The test fold does not contain any unseen slot-value pairs, and has only 12 new domain-slot-value triplets. This means that the evaluation does not really check the generalization capabilities of the systems' state tracking, and it theoretically allows the systems to memorize the whole database and bypass it during operation, which is a rather unrealistic assumption.

5 Experiments

In this section, we work with outputs produced by all systems described in Section 3.3. We: (1) unify their responses in terms of delexicalization styles, and then compare BLEU when different

System	BLEU score		Inform & Success rate			
	Delexical.	Tokenization	Venue comparison	Venue updates	Reduced search	Domain source
DAMD	DAMD	word	intersection	name, id	✓	state change
MinTL	DAMD	sub-word	intersection	name, id	✓	state change
UBAR	DAMD	sub-word	intersection	name, id	✓	state change
SOLOIST	HDSA	sub-word	-	-	-	slot names
AuGPT	AuGPT	sub-word, NLTK	first	end	✗	predicted
LABES	DAMD	word	intersection	name, id	✓	state change
DoTS	HDSA	word	sampling	name, id	✗	slot names
MarCo	HDSA	word, NLTK	subset	name, id	✗	slot names
HDSA	HDSA	word, NLTK	subset	name, id	✗	slot names
HDNO	HDSA	word	sampling	name, id	✗	slot names
SFN	HDSA	word	sampling	name, id	✗	slot names
UniConv	UniConv	word	sampling	name, id, ref.	✗	slot names
LAVA	LAVA	word	sampling	name, id	✗	slot names

Table 3: Setups of compared systems with respect to the used delexicalization method, tokenization, and Inform & Success implementation. The "Venue comparison" column describes the method of comparing offered and goal database entries, "Venue updates" indicates when the set of database entries complying to the current state is updated, "Reduced search" reflects the database implementation that ignores other search constraints if a venue name or train ID is present, and "Domain source" describes the source of information about the active turn domain.

delexicalizations are applied, (2) evaluate Inform & Success under identical conditions,[9] (3) evaluate diversity and discuss similarity of the responses.

5.1 Setup

We report BLEU scores for six different delexicalized references (see Table 2). Five of them are styles used in HDSA, DAMD, AuGPT, UniConv, and LAVA. The sixth is delexicalization obtained from the MultiWOZ 2.2 span annotations. To make the BLEU-based comparison as fair as possible, we normalized the raw models' outputs. First, we remove start-of-sequence tokens, all "-s" and "-ly" strings and all "s" or "es" attached to a slot placeholder. Subsequently, we lowercase the utterances, identify slots names and map them to a unified slot name ontology. The ontology contains only 18 slot names (the original domain-aware delexicalization uses around 40 slot names). It is possible to map all the slot names used in the 6 different delexicalization styles onto it. To make a single mapping possible, the result is not lossless and reduces the finer level of detail provided by some systems. For example, slots named *departure*, *destination*, and *taxi_destination* are all replaced with the *PLACE* placeholder. Finally, we pass the utterances through Moses tokenizer and detokenizer[10] (Koehn et al., 2007). To calculate BLEU, we use the SacreBLEU package[11] (Post, 2018), which provides an implementation compatible with the original and is now a de-facto standard in MT (cf. Section 2).

Inform & Success rates depend on the database. Our database uses fuzzy matching for the different surface forms (see Section 4.3) using the FuzzyWuzzy package[12] with a similarity threshold of 90%. We use several rules to transform time strings, venue names, food types, and venue types to canonical forms matching the entries in the database (e.g., "ten o'clock p.m." is replaced with "22:00").

Our implementation of the Inform & Success rates follows the definition in Section 3.2. The list of offered database entries, i.e. those complying to the current dialogue state, is updated only if a venue name or a train ID is mentioned (cf. Table 3). Following HDSA, we accept a dialogue as matching if the set of offered entries is a non-empty subset of the set of entries matching the particular dialogue goal. Active domains of turns are taken from the original slot names if possible. If slot placeholders do not include the domain name, we either use model predictions if available, or estimate the domain from changes of state predictions in subsequent turns.

To better explain differences in the reported and our scores, we provide an *optimistic* Inform & Success following differences from the original implementation found in some systems, which can potentially overestimate results. In this setting, we: (1) use the intersection entry matching instead of subset matching, (2) ignore other search constraints if a name or ID is provided, (3) use ground-truth

[9]Note that we work with original authors' predictions, published pre-trained weights, or models trained from scratch, and thus we are not able to carry out a statistical analysis for the reported numbers.

[10]See https://github.com/alvations/sacremoses

[11]See https://github.com/mjpost/sacrebleu

[12]See https://github.com/seatgeek/fuzzywuzzy

Delexical.	End-to-end models							Policy optimization models					
	DAMD	MinTL	UBAR	SOLOIST	AuGPT	LABES*	DoTS	MarCo	HDSA	HDNO	SFN	UniConv	LAVA
MWZ 2.2	16.4	19.4	17.6	13.6	16.8	**18.9**	**16.8**	17.3	20.7	17.8	14.1	18.1	10.8
HDSA	15.5	18.6	16.3	**15.1**	15.5	17.1	15.7	**19.0**	**22.5**	**19.4**	**15.6**	17.9	11.4
DAMD	**16.9**	**20.0**	**17.9**	14.1	16.5	18.7	16.7	17.8	21.4	18.3	14.6	18.3	11.0
AuGPT	15.8	18.6	16.7	13.2	**17.0**	17.9	16.6	17.1	20.4	17.7	13.5	18.0	10.5
UniConv	15.1	18.2	15.9	13.7	15.5	16.9	15.5	17.6	20.6	18.1	14.1	**18.8**	10.9
LAVA	15.4	18.6	16.3	15.1	15.5	17.1	15.7	19.0	22.5	19.4	15.6	17.9	**11.4**
Reported	16.6	19.1	17.0	16.5	17.2	18.1	15.9	19.5	23.6	19.0	16.3	19.8	12.0

Table 4: Comparison of BLEU scores. The first column denotes the delexicalization style used for creating references. The highest score is highlighted for each system separately. The last row shows BLEU scores reported by authors. "*" denotes that scores for this system are computed on a subset of 91.66% test utterances.

Metric	End-to-end models							Policy optimization models					
	DAMD	MinTL	UBAR	SOLOIST	AuGPT	LABES*	DoTS	MarCo	HDSA	HDNO	SFN	UniConv	LAVA
Inform	57.9	73.7	**83.4**	82.3	76.6	68.5	80.4	94.5	87.9	93.3	93.4	66.7	**95.9**
Inform (rep.)	76.3	80.0	95.7	85.5	91.4	78.1	86.7	92.5	82.9	92.8	82.7	84.7	97.5
Inform (opt.)	73.7	79.3	**88.6**	86.1	78.1	75.8	84.4	96.9	91.6	97.7	96.7	67.5	**97.5**
Success	47.6	65.4	70.3	**72.4**	60.5	58.1	68.7	87.2	79.4	83.4	82.3	58.7	**93.5**
Success (rep.)	60.4	72.7	81.8	72.9	72.9	67.1	74.2	77.8	68.9	83.0	72.1	76.3	94.8
Success (opt.)	63.0	71.1	75.0	**76.2**	62.4	65.5	74.4	89.9	83.2	90.2	87.0	60.1	**95.9**

Table 5: Comparison of Inform & Success. "rep." marks authors' reported results, "opt." denotes results for the optimistic setting (see Section 5.1). "*" for LABES marks that scores were computed on 91.66% of the test set.

active domains.[13] Note that (2) is more permissive with respect to the system's state tracking as the ground-truth context used during response prediction often contains ground-truth names or IDs. These are then used for the database search even if user constraints are not predicted correctly.

5.2 Results

BLEU: Table 4 summarizes BLEU evaluation using different reference texts. We notice that using a different delexicalization might substantially change the score (up to 2% BLEU absolute). Most systems perform best on the references produced by their native delexicalization used for training. We can also see that different delexicalization styles result not only in different absolute values, but also in a different relative ordering of the systems. This shows that having a single standard delexicalization (which should always be used for model evaluation and score comparison, and preferably also during model development) is very important for any fair comparison between the models. Unlike in the case of end-to-end systems, the reported scores of the policy optimization models are higher then ours.

[13]We adopt the scripts for getting ground-truth active domains from DAMD's code base.

Inform & Success rate: Table 5 shows our and reported numbers for Inform & Success. The corpus data, i.e. ground-truth responses and dialogue states, yield Inform 93.7% and Success of 90.9%. When evaluating in the optimistic setup, these numbers grow to 97.9% and 96.6%, respectively.

Our numbers differ from the reported scores of end-to-end models to a large degree, e.g., DAMD's reported performance is around 20% higher for both rates. However, the optimistic setting results in much lower differences. This shows that DAMD has problems with DST, which is hidden in the optimistic setup. The original UBAR numbers are very high because some ground-truth data were used during evaluation. AuGPT reports higher rates caused by a different Inform rate computation, where the set of offered venues is obtained only at the end of the dialogue. Our scores are similar to the reported ones for SOLOIST and DoTS. UniConv has the most different rates among the policy optimization models (ca. 17% for both metrics). LAVA reports higher rates similar to ours in the optimistic setting, but the difference is small and may be caused by MultiWOZ version differences. Our rates for SFN are much higher than the reported. MarCo's and HDSA's difference in rates can be accounted to our more flexible database.

Measure	Ref.	End-to-end models							Policy optimization models					
		DAMD	MinTL	UBAR	SOLO.	AuGPT	LAB.*	DoTS	MarCo	HDSA	HDNO	SFN	UC	LAVA
Unique tokens	1407	212	297	478	**615**	608	374	411	**319**	259	103	188	338	176
Unique trigrams	25212	1755	2525	5238	**7923**	5843	3228	5162	**3002**	2019	315	1218	2932	708
Entropy tokens	7.21	6.12	6.19	6.40	6.45	**6.62**	6.22	6.48	**6.27**	6.16	5.46	6.03	6.46	5.50
Con. ent. bigram	3.37	1.65	1.81	2.10	**2.41**	2.15	1.83	2.10	**1.94**	1.64	0.84	1.63	1.79	1.27
MSTTR-50	0.75	0.62	0.66	0.68	0.66	**0.70**	0.67	0.66	0.67	0.67	0.59	0.62	**0.69**	0.54
Avg. turn length	14.07	14.27	14.78	13.54	18.45	12.90	14.20	14.66	16.01	14.42	14.96	14.93	14.17	13.28

Table 6: Comparison of lexical diversity measures. "Ref." shows values for delexicalized MultiWOZ 2.2 references (see Section 3). Each system has its own column. "*" denotes that scores for this system are computed on a subset of 91.66% test utterances. SOLO., LAB., UC stand for SOLOIST, LABES, and UniConv, respectively.

5.3 Evaluating Diversity

While the scores and rates differ between the evaluated systems, the generated utterances are similar and uniform (cf. Appendix B). To further understand differences between the systems, we analyzed the diversity of their responses (see Table 6).

We compare the texts on several diversity measures, following van Miltenburg et al. (2018) and Dušek et al. (2020): number of unique output tokens and trigrams, Shannon entropy and bigram conditional entropy, mean segmental type-token ratio (MSTTR-50),[14] and average output length. We used the normalized texts with unified slot ontology (see Section 5.2) for the comparison. The ground-truth responses with MultiWOZ 2.2 delexicalization were used as reference. Even though the systems use different delexicalization schemes, we can draw some conclusions from the analysis. First, all the systems use rather small vocabularies. The number of used trigrams is orders of magnitude lower compared to human-produced texts. The bigram conditional entropy is also much lower for all systems. Models which employ reinforcement-learning, i.e. HDNO, SFN, and LAVA, produce the least diverse outputs. HDNO uses only 315 trigrams, which is around 1.2% of the distinct trigrams seen in reference texts. On the other hand, AuGPT, UBAR, and DoTS seem to use a broader range of expressions. Extraordinarily diverse and long are the outputs of SOLOIST. However, they are still much more closer to other models then to the human reference.

[14]MSTTR measures the average type-token ratio over the output text cut into segments of equal length (50 in our case). This reduces dependency on the overall text length, which is very strong in regular type-token ratio.

6 Conclusion

The MultiWOZ benchmark is unique for its size and the inclusion of a complete database, making it possible to build end-to-end task-oriented dialogue systems. Because of its naturalness and thanks to multiple fixes and revisions of state annotations, it became very popular for dialogue state tracking. However, it still has limitations for context-to-response generation, partially because of lack of standardized preprocessing and postprocessing. Since standard, easy-to-use evaluation scripts are not available, researches are motivated to include their own modifications. This may appear unimportant, but as we showed in our analysis of 13 systems' outputs, it results in large differences in scores and makes any comparison or tracking of progress in this area problematic.

We contribute to the solution of this problem by releasing evaluation scripts, which allow consistent evaluation of future work. We further include the evaluation of output diversity, which adds an important aspect missing from corpus-based MultiWOZ evaluation so far.

Future work should include a manual revision of MultiWOZ 2.2 span annotation to reduce training noise and to enable fair evaluation on lexicalized outputs. More important, however, is the use of human evaluation and evaluation of full dialogues in addition to corpus-based metrics (Liu et al., 2016; Takanobu et al., 2020), which is still not standard for end-to-end dialogue systems (cf. Section 3.3).

Acknowledgements

We thank the reviewers for their kind feedback. This work was supported by the Charles University grants PRIMUS/19/SCI/10, GAUK 373921, and SVV 260 575.

References

Anya Belz, Simon Mille, and David M. Howcroft. 2020. Disentangling the Properties of Human Evaluation Methods: A Classification System to Support Comparability, Meta-Evaluation and Reproducibility Testing. In *Proceedings of the 13th International Conference on Natural Language Generation*, pages 183–194, Dublin, Ireland.

Steven Bird and Edward Loper. 2004. NLTK: The natural language toolkit. In *Proceedings of the ACL Interactive Poster and Demonstration Sessions*, pages 214–217, Barcelona, Spain.

Paweł Budzianowski, Tsung-Hsien Wen, Bo-Hsiang Tseng, Iñigo Casanueva, Stefan Ultes, Osman Ramadan, and Milica Gašić. 2018. MultiWOZ - a large-scale multi-domain Wizard-of-Oz dataset for task-oriented dialogue modelling. In *Proceedings of the 2018 Conference on Empirical Methods in Natural Language Processing*, pages 5016–5026.

Wenhu Chen, Jianshu Chen, Pengda Qin, Xifeng Yan, and William Yang Wang. 2019. Semantically conditioned dialog response generation via hierarchical disentangled self-attention. In *Proceedings of the 57th Annual Meeting of the Association for Computational Linguistics*, pages 3696–3709.

Kyunghyun Cho, Bart van Merriënboer, Caglar Gulcehre, Dzmitry Bahdanau, Fethi Bougares, Holger Schwenk, and Yoshua Bengio. 2014. Learning phrase representations using RNN encoder–decoder for statistical machine translation. In *Proceedings of the 2014 Conference on Empirical Methods in Natural Language Processing (EMNLP)*, pages 1724–1734, Doha, Qatar.

Jan Deriu, Alvaro Rodrigo, Arantxa Otegi, Guillermo Echegoyen, Sophie Rosset, Eneko Agirre, and Mark Cieliebak. 2021. Survey on Evaluation Methods for Dialogue Systems. *Artificial Intelligence Review*, 54:755–810.

Jacob Devlin, Ming-Wei Chang, Kenton Lee, and Kristina Toutanova. 2019. BERT: Pre-training of deep bidirectional transformers for language understanding. In *Proceedings of the 2019 Conference of the North American Chapter of the Association for Computational Linguistics: Human Language Technologies, Volume 1 (Long and Short Papers)*, pages 4171–4186, Minneapolis, Minnesota.

Emily Dinan, Samuel Humeau, Bharath Chintagunta, and Jason Weston. 2019. Build it Break it Fix it for Dialogue Safety: Robustness from Adversarial Human Attack. In *Proceedings of the 2019 Conference on Empirical Methods in Natural Language Processing and the 9th International Joint Conference on Natural Language Processing (EMNLP-IJCNLP)*, Hong Kong.

Ondřej Dušek, Jekaterina Novikova, and Verena Rieser. 2020. Evaluating the State-of-the-Art of End-to-End Natural Language Generation: The E2E NLG Challenge. *Computer Speech & Language*, 59:123–156.

Nouha Dziri, Ehsan Kamalloo, Kory Mathewson, and Osmar Zaiane. 2019. Evaluating Coherence in Dialogue Systems using Entailment. In *Proceedings of the 2019 Conference of the North American Chapter of the Association for Computational Linguistics: Human Language Technologies, Volume 1 (Long and Short Papers)*, pages 3806–3812.

Mihail Eric, Rahul Goel, Shachi Paul, Abhishek Sethi, Sanchit Agarwal, Shuyang Gao, Adarsh Kumar, Anuj Kumar Goyal, Peter Ku, and Dilek Hakkani-Tür. 2020. Multiwoz 2.1: A consolidated multi-domain dialogue dataset with state corrections and state tracking baselines. In *LREC*, pages 422–428.

Mihail Eric and Christopher D. Manning. 2017. A Copy-Augmented Sequence-to-Sequence Architecture Gives Good Performance on Task-Oriented Dialogue. In *Proceedings of the 15th Conference of the European Chapter of the Association for Computational Linguistics: Volume 2, Short Papers*, pages 468–473, Valencia, Spain.

Markus Freitag, David Grangier, and Isaac Caswell. 2020. BLEU might be Guilty but References are not Innocent. In *Proceedings of EMNLP*, pages 61–71, Online.

Michel Galley, Chris Brockett, Alessandro Sordoni, Yangfeng Ji, Michael Auli, Chris Quirk, Margaret Mitchell, Jianfeng Gao, and Bill Dolan. 2015. deltaBLEU: A discriminative metric for generation tasks with intrinsically diverse targets. In *Proceedings of ACL-IJCNLP*, pages 445–450.

Xiang Gao, Yizhe Zhang, Michel Galley, Chris Brockett, and Bill Dolan. 2020. Dialogue response ranking training with large-scale human feedback data. In *Proceedings of the 2020 Conference on Empirical Methods in Natural Language Processing (EMNLP)*, pages 386–395, Online.

Ari Holtzman, Jan Buys, Leo Du, Maxwell Forbes, and Yejin Choi. 2020. The Curious Case of Neural Text Degeneration. In *Proceedings of ICLR*, Online.

Ehsan Hosseini-Asl, Bryan McCann, Chien-Sheng Wu, Semih Yavuz, and Richard Socher. 2020. A simple language model for task-oriented dialogue. In *Advances in Neural Information Processing Systems*, volume 33, pages 20179–20191.

David M. Howcroft, Anya Belz, Miruna-Adriana Clinciu, Dimitra Gkatzia, Sadid A. Hasan, Saad Mahamood, Simon Mille, Emiel van Miltenburg, Sashank Santhanam, and Verena Rieser. 2020. Twenty Years of Confusion in Human Evaluation: NLG Needs Evaluation Sheets and Standardised Definitions. In *Proceedings of the 13th International Conference on Natural Language Generation*, pages 169–182, Dublin, Ireland.

Hyunmin Jeon and Gary Geunbae Lee. 2021. Domain state tracking for a simplified dialogue system.

Philipp Koehn, Hieu Hoang, Alexandra Birch, Chris Callison-Burch, Marcello Federico, Nicola Bertoldi, Brooke Cowan, Wade Shen, Christine Moran, Richard Zens, Chris Dyer, Ondřej Bojar, Alexandra Constantin, and Evan Herbst. 2007. Moses: Open source toolkit for statistical machine translation. In *Proceedings of the 45th Annual Meeting of the Association for Computational Linguistics Companion Volume Proceedings of the Demo and Poster Sessions*, pages 177–180, Prague, Czech Republic.

Taku Kudo and John Richardson. 2018. SentencePiece: A simple and language independent subword tokenizer and detokenizer for neural text processing. In *Proceedings of the 2018 Conference on Empirical Methods in Natural Language Processing: System Demonstrations*, pages 66–71, Brussels, Belgium.

Jonáš Kulhánek, Vojtěch Hudeček, Tomáš Nekvinda, and Ondřej Dušek. 2021. Augpt: Dialogue with pretrained language models and data augmentation.

Gerasimos Lampouras and Andreas Vlachos. 2016. Imitation learning for language generation from unaligned data. In *Proceedings of COLING 2016, the 26th International Conference on Computational Linguistics: Technical Papers*, pages 1101–1112.

Hung Le, Doyen Sahoo, Chenghao Liu, Nancy Chen, and Steven C.H. Hoi. 2020. UniConv: A unified conversational neural architecture for multi-domain task-oriented dialogues. In *Proceedings of the 2020 Conference on Empirical Methods in Natural Language Processing (EMNLP)*, pages 1860–1877.

Mike Lewis, Yinhan Liu, Naman Goyal, Marjan Ghazvininejad, Abdelrahman Mohamed, Omer Levy, Veselin Stoyanov, and Luke Zettlemoyer. 2020. BART: Denoising sequence-to-sequence pretraining for natural language generation, translation, and comprehension. In *Proceedings of the 58th Annual Meeting of the Association for Computational Linguistics*, pages 7871–7880, Online.

Jiwei Li, Michel Galley, Chris Brockett, Jianfeng Gao, and Bill Dolan. 2016. A Diversity-Promoting Objective Function for Neural Conversation Models. In *Proceedings of the 15th Annual Conference of the North American Chapter of the Association for Computational Linguistics: Human Language Technologies*, pages 110–119, San Diego, CA, USA.

Zhaojiang Lin, Andrea Madotto, Genta Indra Winata, and Pascale Fung. 2020. MinTL: Minimalist transfer learning for task-oriented dialogue systems. In *Proceedings of the 2020 Conference on Empirical Methods in Natural Language Processing (EMNLP)*, pages 3391–3405, Online.

Chia-Wei Liu, Ryan Lowe, Iulian Serban, Mike Noseworthy, Laurent Charlin, and Joelle Pineau. 2016. How NOT to evaluate your dialogue system: An empirical study of unsupervised evaluation metrics for dialogue response generation. In *Proceedings of the 2016 Conference on Empirical Methods in Natural Language Processing*, pages 2122–2132.

Nurul Lubis, Christian Geishauser, Michael Heck, Hsien-chin Lin, Marco Moresi, Carel van Niekerk, and Milica Gasic. 2020. LAVA: Latent action spaces via variational auto-encoding for dialogue policy optimization. In *Proceedings of the 28th International Conference on Computational Linguistics*, pages 465–479, Barcelona, Spain (Online).

Nitika Mathur, Timothy Baldwin, and Trevor Cohn. 2020. Tangled up in BLEU: Reevaluating the Evaluation of Automatic Machine Translation Evaluation Metrics. In *ACL*, Seattle, WA, USA.

Shikib Mehri and Maxine Eskenazi. 2020. USR: An Unsupervised and Reference Free Evaluation Metric for Dialog Generation. In *Proceedings of the 58th Annual Meeting of the Association for Computational Linguistics*.

Shikib Mehri, Tejas Srinivasan, and Maxine Eskenazi. 2019. Structured fusion networks for dialog. In *Proceedings of the 20th Annual SIGdial Meeting on Discourse and Dialogue*, pages 165–177.

Emiel van Miltenburg, Desmond Elliott, and Piek Vossen. 2018. Measuring the Diversity of Automatic Image Descriptions. In *Proceedings of the 27th International Conference on Computational Linguistics*, pages 1730–1741.

Jekaterina Novikova, Ondřej Dušek, Amanda Cercas Curry, and Verena Rieser. 2017. Why We Need New Evaluation Metrics for NLG. In *Proceedings of the 2017 Conference on Empirical Methods in Natural Language Processing*, pages 2243–2253, Copenhagen, Denmark.

Shereen Oraby, Lena Reed, Shubhangi Tandon, Sharath T.S., Stephanie Lukin, and Marilyn Walker. 2018. Controlling Personality-Based Stylistic Variation with Neural Natural Language Generators. In *Proceedings of the 19th Annual SIGdial Meeting on Discourse and Dialogue*, pages 180–190.

Kishore Papineni, Salim Roukos, Todd Ward, and Wei-Jing Zhu. 2002. Bleu: a method for automatic evaluation of machine translation. In *Proceedings of the 40th Annual Meeting of the Association for Computational Linguistics*, pages 311–318.

Baolin Peng, Chenguang Zhu, Chunyuan Li, Xiujun Li, Jinchao Li, Michael Zeng, and Jianfeng Gao. 2020. Few-shot natural language generation for task-oriented dialog. In *Findings of the Association for Computational Linguistics: EMNLP 2020*, pages 172–182, Online.

Matt Post. 2018. A call for clarity in reporting BLEU scores. In *Proceedings of the Third Conference on Machine Translation: Research Papers*, pages 186–191, Belgium, Brussels.

Alec Radford, Jeffrey Wu, Rewon Child, David Luan, Dario Amodei, and Ilya Sutskever. 2019. Language Models are Unsupervised Multitask Learners. Technical report, OpenAI.

Colin Raffel, Noam Shazeer, Adam Roberts, Katherine Lee, Sharan Narang, Michael Matena, Yanqi Zhou, Wei Li, and Peter J. Liu. 2020. Exploring the limits of transfer learning with a unified text-to-text transformer. *Journal of Machine Learning Research*, 21(140):1–67.

Sashank Santhanam and Samira Shaikh. 2019. Towards Best Experiment Design for Evaluating Dialogue System Output. In *Proceedings of INLG*, pages 88–94, Tokyo, Japan.

Jost Schatzmann, Karl Weilhammer, Matt Stuttle, and Steve Young. 2006. A survey of statistical user simulation techniques for reinforcement-learning of dialogue management strategies. *The Knowledge Engineering Review*, 21(2):97–126.

Rico Sennrich, Barry Haddow, and Alexandra Birch. 2016. Neural machine translation of rare words with subword units. In *Proceedings of the 54th Annual Meeting of the Association for Computational Linguistics (Volume 1: Long Papers)*, pages 1715–1725, Berlin, Germany.

Swadheen Shukla, Lars Liden, Shahin Shayandeh, Eslam Kamal, Jinchao Li, Matt Mazzola, Thomas Park, Baolin Peng, and Jianfeng Gao. 2020. Conversation Learner - a machine teaching tool for building dialog managers for task-oriented dialog systems. In *Proceedings of the 58th Annual Meeting of the Association for Computational Linguistics: System Demonstrations*, pages 343–349, Online.

Pei-Hao Su, David Vandyke, Milica Gašić, Dongho Kim, Nikola Mrkšić, Tsung-Hsien Wen, and Steve Young. 2015. Learning from real users: rating dialogue success with neural networks for reinforcement learning in spoken dialogue systems. In *Proceedings of Interspeech 2015*, pages 2007–2011.

Ryuichi Takanobu, Qi Zhu, Jinchao Li, Baolin Peng, Jianfeng Gao, and Minlie Huang. 2020. Is Your Goal-Oriented Dialog Model Performing Really Well? Empirical Analysis of System-wise Evaluation. In *SIGdial*, pages 297–310, Online.

Marilyn A. Walker, Diane J. Litman, Candace A. Kamm, and Alicia Abella. 1997. PARADISE: A Framework for Evaluating Spoken Dialogue Agents. In *Proceedings of the 35th Annual Meeting of the Association for Computational Linguistics*, pages 271–280, Madrid, Spain.

Jianhong Wang, Yuan Zhang, Tae-Kyun Kim, and Yunjie Gu. 2021. Modelling hierarchical structure between dialogue policy and natural language generator with option framework for task-oriented dialogue system. In *Proceedings of ICLR*.

Kai Wang, Junfeng Tian, Rui Wang, Xiaojun Quan, and Jianxing Yu. 2020. Multi-domain dialogue acts and response co-generation. In *Proceedings of the 58th Annual Meeting of the Association for Computational Linguistics*, pages 7125–7134, Online.

Tsung-Hsien Wen, Milica Gasic, Nikola Mrkšić, Pei-Hao Su, David Vandyke, and Steve Young. 2015. Semantically Conditioned LSTM-based Natural Language Generation for Spoken Dialogue Systems. In *Proceedings of the 2015 Conference on Empirical Methods in Natural Language Processing*, pages 1711–1721, Lisbon, Portugal.

Tsung-Hsien Wen, David Vandyke, Nikola Mrkšić, Milica Gašić, Lina M. Rojas-Barahona, Pei-Hao Su, Stefan Ultes, and Steve Young. 2017. A network-based end-to-end trainable task-oriented dialogue system. In *Proceedings of EACL*, pages 438–449, Valencia, Spain.

Qingyang Wu, Yichi Zhang, Yu Li, and Zhou Yu. 2021. Alternating recurrent dialog model with large-scale pre-trained language models. In *Proceedings of the 16th Conference of the European Chapter of the Association for Computational Linguistics: Main Volume*, pages 1292–1301, Online.

Steve Young, Milica Gašić, Simon Keizer, François Mairesse, Jost Schatzmann, Blaise Thomson, and Kai Yu. 2010. The Hidden Information State model: A practical framework for POMDP-based spoken dialogue management. *Computer Speech & Language*, 24(2):150–174.

Xiaoxue Zang, Abhinav Rastogi, Srinivas Sunkara, Raghav Gupta, Jianguo Zhang, and Jindong Chen. 2020. MultiWOZ 2.2 : A dialogue dataset with additional annotation corrections and state tracking baselines. In *Proceedings of the 2nd Workshop on Natural Language Processing for Conversational AI*, pages 109–117, Online.

Yichi Zhang, Zhijian Ou, Min Hu, and Junlan Feng. 2020a. A probabilistic end-to-end task-oriented dialog model with latent belief states towards semi-supervised learning. In *Proceedings of the 2020 Conference on Empirical Methods in Natural Language Processing (EMNLP)*, pages 9207–9219.

Yichi Zhang, Zhijian Ou, and Zhou Yu. 2020b. Task-oriented dialog systems that consider multiple appropriate responses under the same context. *Proceedings of the AAAI Conference on Artificial Intelligence*, 34(05):9604–9611.

Qi Zhu, Zheng Zhang, Yan Fang, Xiang Li, Ryuichi Takanobu, Jinchao Li, Baolin Peng, Jianfeng Gao, Xiaoyan Zhu, and Minlie Huang. 2020. ConvLab-2: An open-source toolkit for building, evaluating, and diagnosing dialogue systems. In *Proceedings of the 58th Annual Meeting of the Association for Computational Linguistics: System Demonstrations*, pages 142–149, Online.

Goal database entries (ID):	19212, 19185, 19197, 19219 (cheap and Chinese search constraints)			
Goal requested information:	ADDRESS, POST			
Turn utterances	**Dialogue state**	**Offered Entries**	**Active Domain**	**Provided Info**
User: I'd like to find a resturant that serves cheap Chinese food! *Ground-truth system:* Charlie Chan is located in the centre and it is cheap! Would you like me to book it for you? *System:* there are COUNT PRICE FOOD restaurant. do you have a preference of area?	food: chinese, pricerange: cheap	no update	restaurant	∅
User: Yes, go ahead and book it and please send me the address. *Ground-truth system:* The address is Regent Street City Centre. What day and time would you like to book? How many people? *System:* okay, i have booked NAME, which is located at ADDRESS. is there anything else i can do for you today?	food: chinese, pricerange: cheap, area: centre	19212, 19185, 19219	restaurant	ADDRESS
User: I do not need to book it. What is the postcode and the area please? *Ground-truth system:* The postcode is cb21db *System:* NAME is in the AREA and the postcode is POST. is there anything else i can help you with today?	food: chinese, pricerange: cheap, area: centre	19212, 19185, 19219	restaurant	POST, ADDRESS
User: Thanks very much! *Ground-truth system:* You're welcome! Have a great day! Goodbye. *System:* thank you for using our services.	food: chinese, pricerange: cheap, area: centre	no update	-	POST, ADDRESS

Table 7: Inform & Success calculation on the predictions of the UBAR model (conversation ID: SNG0805).

A Inform & Success Calculation Details

Table 7 walks through the process of Inform & Success calculation. Rows group conversation turns. The first column shows the last user utterance, the corresponding ground-truth system response and the delexicalized and normalized generated response. The second column shows the current dialogue state. The "Offered entities" column shows the changes of the set of matching venue or train IDs. Note that the set is updated only if the generated response contains the NAME or TRAINID placeholder. The "Active domain" column shows the currently active domain. The "Provided Info" column lists requestable slots mentioned until the given point.

This sample conversation is (1) matching, i.e. contributes positively to the Inform rate, because the set of offered entities or database entries at the end of the dialogue is a non-empty subset of the set of goal database entries, and also (2) successful because it is matching and all requested information defined by the dialogue goal, i.e., the restaurant address and post code, were provided. Note that the ground-truth context is used to generate system utterances during the evaluation, and thus the dialogue state might contain information from past ground-truth system utterances (such as the area slot in our example, which was never mentioned in the generated system or user utterances).

B Generated Texts Comparison

Tables 8 and 9 give a comparison of delexicalized utterances generated by all examined systems for two different contexts. Slot placeholders are shown in capital letters. While there are some differences in the systems' behavior, the outputs often contain very similar phrasing.

Context	User: Hello, I am doing research on plant life in England, and visiting cambridge as part of that, can you give me more info on the cambridge university botanic gardens.
System	**Normalized utterance**
Corpus	that sounds like an exciting trip! NAME is located in the AREA on ADDRESS. its admission fee is PRICE.
DAMD	the address is ADDRESS and the postcode is POST. is there anything else i can help you with?
MinTL	NAME is a TYPE in the AREA. it is located at ADDRESS. their phone number is PHONE.
UBAR	NAME is a TYPE located in the AREA at ADDRESS. it is PRICE to enter and is located on ADDRESS. is there anything else i can help you with?
SOLOIST	certainly! NAME is located at ADDRESS. their phone number is PHONE. is there anything else i can help you with?
AuGPT	NAME is a TYPE located in the AREA of town. the entrance fee is 4 pounds. the address is ADDRESS.
LABES	NAME is located in the AREA area of town
DoTS	NAME is a TYPE in the AREA. it's free to enter. do you need any other information?
MarCO	NAME is a nightclub in the AREA of town. the address is ADDRESS and the postcode is POST.
HDSA	it is a museum in the AREA of town. the entrance fee is free. would you like the address?
HDNO	NAME is a museum in the AREA. the address is ADDRESS. the phone number is PHONE. is there anything else i can help you with?
SFN	NAME is located at ADDRESS. the postcode is POST. the phone number is PHONE. can i help you with anything else?
UniConv	sure! it is a TYPE in the AREA part of town. would you like the address?
LAVA	the NAME is located at ADDRESS, postcode POST. the phone number is PHONE.

Table 8: Side-by-side comparison of system outputs for the 1st system turn of the conversation PMUL3012.

Context	User: I'm looking for a nice place to eat. System: There are many fine places to eat. What type of cuisine would you prefer? User: I don't care about the cuisine type, but I want it to be somewhere expensive and in the centre please.
System	**Normalized utterance**
Corpus	there are COUNT PRICE eateries in the AREA. how about one of my favorites - NAME? they serve FOOD food and it's delicious!
DAMD	how about NAME? it is an FOOD restaurant that is in the AREA of town and is in the PRICE price range .
MinTL	there are COUNT restaurant that meet your criteria. do you have a preference for type of food?
UBAR	there are COUNT PRICE restaurant in the AREA. do you have a cuisine preference?
SOLOIST	how about NAME? it is an FOOD restaurant that is in the AREA of town and is in the PRICE price range .
AuGPT	there are 33 PRICE restaurants in the AREA. What type of food would you like?
LABES	i have COUNT restaurants that meet your criteria.
DoTS	i would recommend NAME. would you like to make a reservation?
MarCO	there are COUNT restaurant that meet your criteria. i recommend NAME.
HDSA	i recommend NAME. would you like a reservation?
HDNO	NAME is a FOOD restaurant in the AREA. would you like me to book a table for you?
SFN	there are COUNT PRICE restaurant in the AREA. what type of cuisine would you like?
UniConv	there are 33 PRICE TYPE in the AREA. what type of food are you looking for?
LAVA	NAME is located at ADDRESS, postcode POST. the phone number is PHONE.

Table 9: Side-by-side comparison of system outputs for the 2nd system turn of the conversation PMUL2489.

Personalized Response Generation with Tensor Factorization

Zhenghui Wang[†], **Lingxiao Luo**[‡], **Diyi Yang**[†]
[†]Georgia Institute of Technology, [‡]Tsinghua University
luolx17@mails.tsinghua.edu.cn
{zhwang,dyang888}@gatech.edu

Abstract

Personalized response generation is essential for more human-like conversations. However, how to model user personalization information with no explicit user persona descriptions or demographics still remains under-investigated. To tackle the data sparsity problem and the huge number of users, we utilize tensor factorization to model users' personalization information with their posting histories. Specifically, we introduce the personalized response embedding for all question-user pairs and form them into a three-mode tensor, decomposed by Tucker decomposition. The personalized response embedding is fed to either the decoder of an LSTM-based Seq2Seq model or a transformer language model to help generate more personalized responses. To evaluate how personalized the generated responses are, we further propose a novel ranking-based metric called Per-Hits@k which measures how likely are the generated responses come from the corresponding users. Results on a large-scale English conversation dataset show that our proposed tensor factorization based models generate more personalized and higher quality responses compared to baselines. We have publicly released our code at https://github.com/GT-SALT/personalized_response_generation.

1 Introduction

Building human-like conversational systems has received much attention in artificial intelligence communities, and personalized response generation is one essential step towards this goal, as more personalized responses are often associated with increased user engagement (Shum et al., 2018; Huang et al., 2020). To this end, we focus on the task of personalized response generation in this work, and argue that incorporating personalization into text generation can benefit many downstream applications such as social chit-chat chatbots (Zhang et al., 2018) and auto-complete responses like Smart Replies (Kannan et al., 2016).

Prior text generation work on modeling personalization mainly relied on explicitly given persona or demographic information. For instance, (Zhang et al., 2018; Wolf et al., 2019; Xu et al., 2020) utilized a set of persona sentences to profile users, and other line of research leveraged demographics to model user personalization (Zheng et al., 2019, 2020). Despite its effectiveness, such approaches are limited when it comes to real world scenarios. First, explicit persona or demographic information is often not available. Second, collecting such personalization information is usually costly and time-consuming, which also suffers from either artificially designed persona descriptions from third-party annotators or subjective and unreliable self-reports from users themselves (Stone et al., 1999). Although such explicit personalization information is often unavailable, content that users produce is generally ubiquitous and can indicate their preferences, personal information, styles, and knowledge in a relatively implicit but objective manner. Our work thus utilizes these posts and comments users made to learn latent representations of their personalization information.

Different generation models have been designed to learn user personalization information and further impose such representation on text generation. For instance, Li et al. 2016 proposed the Speaker model based on Seq2Seq framework by introducing trainable *speaker embedding* for each user and feeding it to decoder at each step of decoding. However, there are always a large number of distinct users and users often participate in only a few conversations; as a result, the speaker embedding may be under-fitted given the limited data points associated with a user. Another line of research uses generative memory network (Zhang et al., 2018),

Proceedings of the 1st Workshop on Natural Language Generation, Evaluation, and Metrics (GEM 2021), pages 47–57

which first retrieves some most relevant responses to a user's input as the memory and then encodes them into an embedding. The difference between the embedding from memory network and speaker embedding is that the former encodes both information of question and user, while the latter represents only users. Nevertheless, the set of observable question-user pairs and their responses is still a small subset of the whole user and question sets, leading to the sparsity issue.

Matrix Factorization (MF) has been widely used to infer latent relationships between users and items in recommender systems, especially for data sparsity issues (kumar Bokde et al., 2015). Motivated by this, we propose to model latent interactions between questions and users by looking at who participated in which conversations, and infer user personalization information from data automatically, for personalized response generation tasks. Differently, as the score or rating used in recommender system usually denotes users' preferences towards items, such scalar is not enough to represent the semantic meaning of a response. Thus, we introduce a response vector to indicate the response content that a user will make for a given conversation, i.e., *personalized response embedding*, resulting in a tensor form representation for all question-user pairs. Decomposing this tensor (tensor factorization, TF) will lead to the factorized representations for each user, question, and dimension of the response embedding. We propose to augment response generation models with such TF-induced modules, which are model-agnostic and can be applied to many different generation models. Specifically, we introduce a TF module based framework on top of LSTM-based Seq2Seq model and transformer language model for personalized response generation, and further train them together in an end-to-end fashion. Evaluating response generation usually considers content relatedness and language quality to ensure that generated text is grammatically correct and fluent, using BLEU and Perplexity. However, evaluating personalization in personalized response generation is relatively challenging as there lacks effective metrics.

To this end, we propose a novel evaluation metric **Per-Hits@k** to model personalization , which for the response of a user first calculates its perplexity values via language models of all users, and then ranks the perplexity via this user's language model to examine whether it is ranked as top-k, based on a pre-trained GPT-2 language model (Radford et al., 2019) for each user. Our contributions are:

- propose a tensor factorization based framework to model personalization for response generation task;
- introduce a metric Per-Hits@k, to evaluate the personalization of the generated responses;
- experimental results on a large-scale personalized Reddit dataset show that our TF-based framework outperforms previous methods significantly in terms of both content generation quality and personalization.

2 Related Work

Personalized Response Generation Personalization has received much attention in the natural language processing community, such as personalized image captioning (Chunseong Park et al., 2017), personalized machine translation (Rabinovich et al., 2017), personalized response generation (Li et al., 2016), personalized intent classification and personalized slot tagging (Liu et al., 2016). Prior studies formulate the task of response generation as generating an output given an input text, mainly based on either the sequence-to-sequence (Seq2Seq) models (Vinyals and Le, 2015) or the pretrained models like GPT-2 (Radford et al., 2019) and BART (Lewis et al., 2019). When it comes to personalized response generation, Speaker model (Li et al., 2016) extended traditional response generation models by assigning each user with a trainable speaker ID embedding. Another line of research focuses on leveraging persona descriptions or demographic attributes (Zheng et al., 2020; Qian et al.; Wolf et al., 2019; Luo et al., 2019), building on recent personalized dialogue datasets such as PERSONA-CHAT (Zhang et al., 2018) and PersonalDialog (Zheng et al., 2019). For instance, Xu et al. (2020) utilized the predefined user persona description together with their semantically correlated content for generating personalized responses in dialogue systems.

Different learning paradigms have also been introduced for personalized response generation such as reinforcement learning (Mo et al., 2016; Yang et al., 2018; Xu et al., 2020) and transfer learning to benefit from a source domain with sufficient training data (Yang et al., 2017). However, most aforementioned approaches require explicit persona or demographic information which is often unavailable in real world scenarios. To fill this gap, we propose to learn latent representation of personalized user information from users' posts and model personalization jointly together with traditional generation methods for personalized response generation.

Evaluation Metrics for Personalized Response Generation Current automatic evaluation metrics for response generation can be broadly categorized into three classes. (1) Content relatedness measures how related a generated response is with its corresponding ground-truth, with representative metrics such as BLEU (Papineni et al., 2002), NIST (Doddington, 2002), and METEOR (Lavie and Agarwal, 2007). Speaker sensitive responses evaluation model (SSREM) (Bak and Oh, 2020) enhances the relatedness score with a context-response classifier. (2) Language quality mainly refers to the fluency and diversity, where the former is measured via perplexity (Chen et al., 1998) and the latter is assessed via distinct diversity (Li et al., 2015; Yang et al., 2020) that indicates how diverse the generated responses are. (3) Style adherence aims to evaluate the adherence of the generated responses' language style to the user's own language style; example metrics include the average negative log-likelihood (NLL) of one poet's generated lyrics on it's poet specific language model (Vechtomova et al., 2018), stylistic alignment (Syed et al., 2020) that looks at the language style alignment at the surface, lexical and syntactic level, and Hits@1/N (Dinan et al., 2019) that measures how accurate the generated response can be classified to its corresponding user by a classifier. Our proposed Per-Hits@k metric thus belongs to the style adherence class, a more fine-grained metric compared to the average NLL metric (Vechtomova et al., 2018).

3 Preliminaries

3.1 Tucker Decomposition

To learn latent association between users, questions and responses for personalized response generation, we choose Tucker decomposition, one widely used tensor factorization algorithm. Tucker decomposition (Tucker, 1966) decomposes a given 3-mode tensor $\mathcal{X} \in \mathbb{R}^{I\times J\times K}$ into a core tensor $\mathcal{G} \in \mathbb{R}^{R_1\times R_2\times R_3}$ and three factor matrices $\mathbf{A} \in \mathbb{R}^{I\times R_1}, \mathbf{B} \in \mathbb{R}^{J\times R_2}, \mathbf{C} \in \mathbb{R}^{K\times R_3}$:

$$\mathcal{X} \approx \mathcal{G} \times_1 \mathbf{A} \times_2 \mathbf{B} \times_3 \mathbf{C}$$

Here, $\times_i$ denotes the mode-i product of a tensor by a matrix ($i \in \{1,2,3\}$). Any element $\mathcal{X}_{(i,j,k)}$ in $\mathcal{X}$ can be approximated by:

$$\sum_{r_1=1}^{R_1}\sum_{r_2=1}^{R_2}\sum_{r_3=1}^{R_3} \mathcal{G}_{(r_1,r_2,r_3)}\mathbf{A}_{(i,r_1)}\mathbf{B}_{(j,r_2)}\mathbf{C}_{(k,r_3)}$$

3.2 LSTM-based Seq2Seq Model

LSTM-based Seq2Seq model consists of an encoder LSTM, a decoder LSTM, and attention mechanism (Yao et al., 2015). Suppose the source text is $S = (x_1, x_2, \ldots, x_m)$ and the target text is $T = (x_{m+1}, x_{m+2}, \ldots, x_N)$, the encoder LSTM first encodes S into hidden vector $\boldsymbol{h}_m^e$ and cell vector $\boldsymbol{c}_m^e$, then the decoder LSTM has its initial hidden vector $\boldsymbol{h}_0^d$ and cell vector $\boldsymbol{c}_0^d$ as:

$$\boldsymbol{h}_0^d = \boldsymbol{h}_m^e$$
$$\boldsymbol{c}_0^d = \boldsymbol{c}_m^e$$

The hidden vector of decoder at time step t is:

$$\boldsymbol{h}_t^d = g(\boldsymbol{h}_{t-1}^d, \boldsymbol{c}_{t-1}^d, \boldsymbol{y}_t^*),$$

where g is the LSTM cell operation and $\boldsymbol{y}_t^*$ is the embedding of the input token at time step t.

Standard Seq2Seq models are not personalized, because there is no mechanism to incorporate user-specific information into their input. Speaker Model (Li et al., 2016) alleviates this by explicitly concatenating a trainable *speaker embedding* $\boldsymbol{v}_j$ to $\boldsymbol{y}_t^*$ for user j. Therefore, the hidden vector of decoder of Speaker model at time step t is:

$$\boldsymbol{h}_t^d = g(\boldsymbol{h}_{t-1}^d, \boldsymbol{c}_{t-1}^d, [\boldsymbol{y}_t^*; \boldsymbol{v}_j]),$$

3.3 Transformer Language Model

DialoGPT (Zhang et al., 2020) is a pre-trained conversational response generation model. Based on the architecture of GPT-2 (Radford et al., 2019), DialoGPT is trained on 147M Reddit discussions. For a question-user pair (i, j) with source input S and target response T, DialogGPT generates responses by modeling the conditional probability:

$$P(T \mid S) = \prod_{n=m+1}^{N} P(x_n \mid x_1, x_2, \ldots, x_{n-1})$$

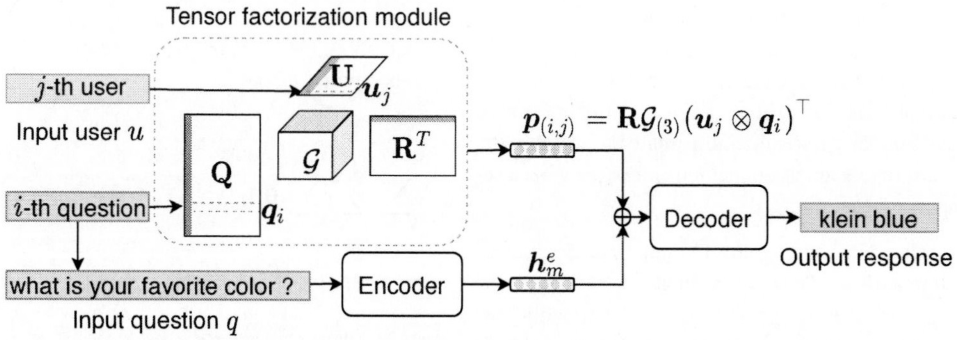

Figure 1: LSTM-based Seq2Seq model with our proposed tensor factorization module. The cell vector $\boldsymbol{c}_m^e$ from the encoder and the attention mechanism are omitted for brevity.

4 Method

We formulate the task of personalized response generation as follows: given a set of question-user pair $(q, u) \in S_{\text{q}} \times S_{\text{u}}$ where S_{q} and S_{u} refer to the question set and user set respectively, generate a response r for this question-user pair (q, u), i.e., posted by user u for question q. The overall model architecture is described in Figure 1.

4.1 Tensor Factorization Module

To enable personalized response generation, we first need to automatically infer personalized signals that users demonstrate in their participation such as questions that they might interact with, as such signatures are often not explicitly available. To this end, we introduce *personalized response embedding* $\boldsymbol{p}_{i,j}$, a K-dimensional vector, to represent the latent relationship between a question i and a user j. We then form a tensor using all $\boldsymbol{p}_{i,j}$ over all question-user pairs and factorize this tensor, to learn latent interactions between questions, users, and their responses.

Formally, for a dataset with $I = |S_{\text{q}}|$ questions and $J = |S_{\text{u}}|$ users, we have a tensor $\mathcal{P} \in \mathbb{R}^{I \times J \times K}$ where $\mathcal{P}_{(i,j,:)} = \boldsymbol{p}_{i,j}$ denotes each (i, j) pair. The notation $P_{(i,j,:)}$ refers to the mode-3 fiber (or tube) of the tensor $\mathcal{P}$. $\mathcal{P}$ can be further formulated via Tucker Decomposition as follows:

$$\mathcal{P} = \mathcal{G} \times_1 \mathbf{Q} \times_2 \mathbf{U} \times_3 \mathbf{R}$$

Here $\mathbf{Q} \in \mathbb{R}^{I \times R_1}$, $\mathbf{U} \in \mathbb{R}^{K \times R_2}$, $\mathbf{R} \in \mathbb{R}^{K \times R_3}$ are the factor matrices, and $\mathcal{G} \in \mathbb{R}^{R_1 \times R_2 \times R_3}$ is a core tensor. Once these factor matrices and core tensor are determined, the personalized response embedding $\boldsymbol{p}_{i,j}$ for any question-user pair (i, j) can be calculated as:

$$\boldsymbol{p}_{i,j} = \mathcal{P}_{(i,j,:)} = \mathbf{R}\mathcal{G}_{(3)} \left(\boldsymbol{u}_j \otimes \boldsymbol{q}_i\right)^\top$$

where $\boldsymbol{q}_i$ and $\boldsymbol{u}_j$ denote i-th and j-th row vector of $\mathbf{Q}$ and $\mathbf{U}$ respectively. $\otimes$ is the Kronecker product of two matrices.

Next, we introduce different mechanisms to incorporate TF modules especially $\boldsymbol{p}_{i,j}$ into traditional LSTM-based models and Transformer Language Models. This is essential to train better TF modules since it is impossible to directly supervise $\boldsymbol{p}_{i,j}$ as no ground truth is available.

4.2 LSTM-based Model with TF Module

To utilize TF module for standard LSTM-based Seq2Seq models, we propose to incorporate $\boldsymbol{p}_{i,j}$ into the initial hidden vector and cell vector of the LSTM decoder to help generate more personalized response, as personalized response embedding $\boldsymbol{p}_{i,j}$ is expected to also encode the target response:

$$\begin{aligned} \boldsymbol{h}_0^d &= (1-\lambda) \cdot \boldsymbol{h}_m^e + \lambda \cdot \boldsymbol{p}_{i,j} \\ \boldsymbol{c}_0^d &= (1-\lambda) \cdot \boldsymbol{c}_m^e + \lambda \cdot \boldsymbol{p}_{i,j}, \end{aligned} \tag{1}$$

Here λ is a coefficient to balance the information from the LSTM encoder and the personalized response embedding. Note that our TF module is agnostic to encoder-decoder frameworks, and can be applied to any Seq2Seq model similarly, including but not limited to Seq2Seq, Speaker model (Li et al., 2016), Seq2Seq with memory network (Zhang et al., 2018), and Speaker model with memory network. Figure 1 describes how the TF module is integrated with an LSTM-based Seq2Seq model. The TF module is randomly initialized and trained together with the Seq2Seq model. This allows TF module to access the supervision from the output response, thus learn the latent interaction between users and questions and produce personalized response embedding for the decoder.

4.3 Transformer with TF Module

Recent success of DialoGPT (Zhang et al., 2020) on conversational response generation shows the potential of (pre-trained) transformer language model for the task of response generation. Thus we propose to incorporate TF module with transformer language model, (DialoGPT in specific) for personalized response generation. Since DialoGPT is a language model rather than a Seq2Seq model, it does not have a encoder-decoder architecture but only one transformer model. Thus we cannot utilize $\boldsymbol{p}_{i,j}$ as the initial hidden vector for decoder like that in Eq. 1. Instead, we propose to add personalized response embedding $\boldsymbol{p}_{i,j}$ with the input token embedding, token type embedding and positional embedding together as the input embedding to DialoGPT model. As shown in Figure 2, the personalized response embedding $\boldsymbol{p}_{i,j}$ is added to token "<EOS>", "klein" and "bleu" in the input to decode the j-th user's response for the i-th question. The TF module that produces $\boldsymbol{p}_{i,j}$ is also trained together with the DialoGPT model in an end-to-end fashion.

5 Experiments

5.1 Dataset

To study the task of personalized response generation with no explicit personalization information, we used a personalized Reddit dataset **PERCHAT**, consisting of 200,156 responses that users posted to different questions, from r/AskReddit[1] (Wu et al., 2021). Building upon Wu et al. (2021), we used active users who joined more than average discussions, and popular questions that received more comments. This led to 4724 users under 39,187 questions. These users and questions were sampled because they were active users who joined more discussions or popular questions that received more comments. We filtered all forms of url links, emails and digits into unique tokens "url", "email" and "digit". Replicated words and punctuation were processed to their standard forms. We sampled 3 responses for each user for users in the validation and test set, and the rest are used for training. The proportion of split size of train, validation, test is 171812 : 14172 : 14172.

[1]https://www.reddit.com/r/AskReddit/

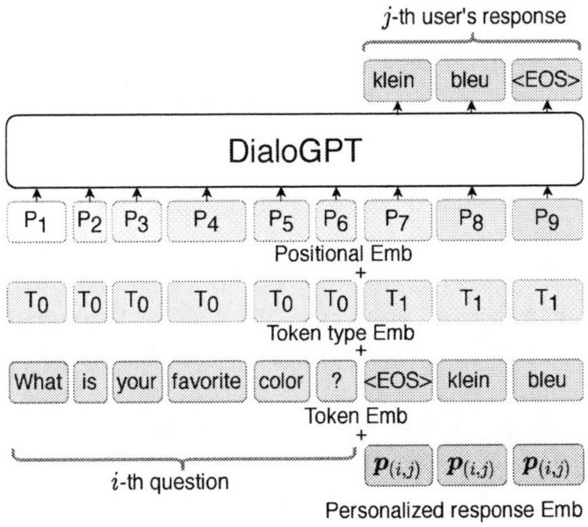

Figure 2: Input representation for DialoGPT model with TF module. TF module's personalized response embedding $\boldsymbol{p}_{i,j}$ is added with response token's word embedding, token type embedding and positional embedding.

5.2 Baselines and Our Models

We introduced several baselines for comparison with our proposed models. We introduced several baselines for comparison with our proposed models. (1) **DialoGPT**: A response generation model based on DialoGPT-medium provided in Zhang et al. 2019; (2) **Seq2Seq**: A standard Seq2Seq model with attention mechanisms with no personalization information; (3) **Speaker** model: Our implementation of the speaker model (Li et al., 2016). Following (Kottur et al., 2017), the Speaker embeddings were not initialized randomly but set as the average sentence embeddings from a user's all historical responses via sentence-BERT (Reimers and Gurevych, 2020); the dimension was reduced to 30 by principal component analysis. (4) **Memory** network: Our implementation of the generative memory network (Zhang et al., 2018) based on our Seq2Seq model with attention. We retrieved top-10 most relevant responses from a user for each question as the memory in the memory network; (5) **Memory+Speaker**: The generative memory network (Zhang et al., 2018), together with the use of the speaker embedding (Li et al., 2016).

Our models were based on the aforementioned baseline models by further incorporating our proposed TF module, i.e., the personalized response embedding from the TF module. **DialoGPT+TF** is a DialoGPT model with personalized response embedding added to each time step at the decoding stage shown in Figure 2. **Seq2Seq+TF, Speaker+TF, Memory+TF, Mem-**

ory+Speaker+TF are constructed on top of our baseline models with personalized response embedding added to the decoder as Eq. 1.

5.3 Evaluation Metrics

We evaluated different models with F1, BLEU, Distinct-N, perplexity (PPL), and our proposed Per-Hits@k. Here, F1 (Dinan et al., 2019) refers to the harmonic mean of precision and recall computed based on the tokens between generated and ground truth response. BLEU (Papineni et al., 2002) was first proposed for machine translation but is also widely used for evaluating response generation. Distinct-N (Li et al., 2015) aims to evaluate lexical diversity and we tested distinct unigrams (Distinct-1) and bigrams (Distinct-2). We used perplexity to evaluate the fluency of the generation model.

Per-Hits@k for Personalization Evaluation To evaluate the personalization in generated responses for a user, one needs to have a good understanding of that particular user who might sometimes have a very long posting history (500 responses per user on average in our dataset), making it hard for annotators to evaluate how personalized the generated response is for a user. Besides, not every response from a user will reveal their personalization information. Thus, we propose an automatic evaluation metric to evaluate the personalization degree of different generation models called Per-Hits@k. Suppose we have N users and there are M_i responses generated for user i to be evaluated. We firstly train a user-specific language model LM_i for each user i on all their responses in training set. We then test the j-th response's perplexity of user i on all users' language models, and denote its perplexity on user-n's language model as $\text{ppl}^n_{i,j}$. We rank the perplexity of user i's j-th response over N user language models (the lower the perplexity, the higher rank), and denote the ranking of the perplexity on user i's language model LM_i with $\text{rank}(\text{ppl}^i_{i,j})$. We define the value of Per-Hits@k in Per-Hits@k metric as:

$$\text{Per-Hits@}k = \frac{1}{\sum_{i=1}^{N} M_i} \sum_{i=1}^{N} \sum_{j=1}^{M_i} \mathbf{1}_{x \le k}(\text{rank}(\text{ppl}^i_{i,j}))$$

This measures how likely the generated response will be ranked as top-k with its corresponding user language model among N users. In our implementation, we fine-tuned GPT-2 (small) (Radford et al., 2019) for each user i to instantiate this user i's language model LM_i. To ensure the quality of LM_i, we only consider a subset of users ($N = 500$) and choose these users who have the most responses.

5.4 Implementation Details

We implemented our models with PyTorch (Paszke et al., 2019). For TF module, the core tensor is of size $50 \times 50 \times 50$, dimension of personalized response embedding is 512 for all Seq2Seq-based models with TF module (denote as Seq2Seq-based+TF), while it is 1024 for the DialoGPT+TF model. For any Seq2Seq-based+TF model, both encoder and decoder have 2 LSTM layers with hidden size of 512, while DialoGPT+TF model is based on the pre-trained medium DialoGPT model with hidden size of 1024. Any word appears more than three times were included in the vocabulary of Seq2Seq-based+TF models, and the size of the vocabulary is 30K. DialoGPT+TF model uses the pre-trained Byte-Pair-Encoding (BPE) tokenizer of size 50,257. The λ coefficient in Eq. 1 is set to 0.2. Adam (Kingma and Ba, 2014) is used as the optimizer and the learning rate was set to 1e-3 for TF-Speaker model and 1e-5 for TF-DialoGPT by grid search. Top-k ($k = 2$) sampling (Fan et al., 2018) was used without any re-scoring techniques to generate response at test stage. We selected models with the highest average Per-Hits@k ($k = 1, 2, 3, 4, 5$) on validation set.

5.5 Results

As shown in Table 1, we reported F1, BLEU, Distinct-N and Per-Hits@k on test data. Distinct-N and Per-Hits@k on ground truth test data and Per-Hits@k on random ranking were also reported. Overall, we found that TF based models significantly improved the personalization metric Per-Hits@k compared to all baselines, with comparable and even better performances in terms of other metrics. Specifically, our proposed Seq2Seq+TF model had an average hist@k score 4 times higher than the Seq2Seq baseline and the Memory+Speaker+TF model had the highest personalization score. This demonstrates that our proposed TF module can model users' personalization well using users' posting history. Furthermore, **1)** Per-Hits@k on ground truth data was far below its upper bound 100% but still much higher than Per-Hits@k of generation models, showing the effectiveness of our Per-Hits@k metric to evaluate user personalization. For example, a Per-Hits@1 score of 9.47% indicated that 9.47% of the ground truth responses were ranked as top-1 by its users' language model over

Method	F1 %	BLEU %	Distinct-N % D-1	D-2	PPL	Per-Hits@k % 1	2	3	4	5	Avg.
Random ranking	-	-	-	-	-	0.20	0.40	0.60	0.80	1.00	0.60
Ground truth	-	-	7.25	45.51	-	9.47	15.73	19.93	23.00	25.40	18.71
DialoGPT	13.64	0.86	3.24	18.68	27.20	0.40	0.67	1.00	1.27	1.60	0.99
Seq2Seq	14.42	1.22	0.66	4.01	92.24	0.60	0.87	1.00	1.20	1.53	1.04
Speaker	15.34	1.41	2.79	14.27	98.75	1.00	1.93	2.93	3.40	3.80	2.61
Memory	14.42	1.28	3.34	16.36	108.27	1.27	2.20	2.73	3.20	3.67	2.61
Memory+Speaker	14.60	1.11	3.52	17.64	110.31	1.53	2.73	3.47	4.33	5.00	3.41
DialoGPT+TF	13.61	0.80	**3.61**	**20.40**	**27.01**	0.53	1.00	1.27	1.67	1.73	1.24*
Seq2Seq+TF	**15.40***	1.58*	3.20*	15.95*	105.21	2.07*	3.20*	4.53*	5.40*	5.80*	4.20*
Speaker+TF	15.33	**1.59**	3.35*	17.19*	107.88	2.07*	3.33*	3.80	4.67	5.40*	3.85*
Memory+TF	14.99*	1.38*	3.52	16.69	107.46	2.40*	3.33*	4.00*	5.00*	5.60*	4.07*
Memory+Speaker+TF	14.99*	1.40*	3.34	16.29	107.55	**2.60***	**4.00***	**4.93***	**6.00***	**6.53***	**4.81***

Table 1: Performance comparison with baselines. A Wilcoxon signed-rank test was performed for Per-Hits@k and paired t-test was performed for other metrics, the significant ones ($p < 0.05$) over its baseline are marked as *.

Method	F1 %	BLEU %	Distinct-N % D-1	D-2	PPL	Per-Hits@k % 1	2	3	4	5	Avg.
Ground truth	-	-	26.51	73.31	-	100	100	100	100	100	100
DialoGPT	15.67	0.11	28.33	65.18	**20.96**	1.41	2.11	2.82	2.82	2.82	2.39
Seq2Seq	16.05	0.47	21.69	52.29	60.10	2.11	2.11	2.82	4.93	4.93	3.38
Speaker	19.69	4.40	19.42	48.47	55.81	3.52	6.34	9.15	9.86	9.86	7.75
Memory	19.02	4.33	23.08	54.56	60.44	4.23	7.04	8.45	9.15	9.86	7.75
Memory+Speaker	19.89	3.18	22.98	58.51	59.03	4.93	7.75	11.97	14.79	16.20	11.13
DialoGPT+TF	15.11	0.17	**30.29**	**65.19**	21.30	2.11	2.82	2.82	3.52	3.52	2.96*
Seq2Seq+TF	**22.98***	**5.77**	20.43	49.75	57.38	9.86*	13.38*	**16.90***	**16.90***	17.61*	14.93*
Speaker+TF	20.70	4.16	22.72*	53.02*	56.50	10.56*	13.38*	14.08	15.49	15.49	13.80*
Memory+TF	21.31*	3.10	23.45	55.10	57.65	**11.27***	12.68	13.38	15.49	16.20	13.80*
Memory+Speaker+TF	20.79	2.31	23.67	58.58	57.64	10.56*	**14.08***	15.49*	**16.90***	**18.31***	**15.07***

Table 2: Performance comparison with baselines on top-1 focused test set. A Wilcoxon signed-rank test was performed for Per-Hits@k and paired t-test was performed for other metrics, the significant ones ($p < 0.05$) over its baseline are marked as *.

the 500 users. One explanation why Per-Hits@1 on ground truth data was far below 100% might be that these responses from a user do not necessarily always reveal their persona. **2)** Although both Seq2Seq and DialoGPT did not model user personalization explicitly, they had higher than random Per-Hist@k. **3)** Compared to Seq2Seq, both Speaker and Memory model had about double Per-Hits@k and some degree of improvements over BLEU, F1, and Distinct-N. Combining the Memory and Speaker models led to further improvement on Per-Hits@k. Seq2Seq model with personalized response embedding form TF module (Seq2Seq+TF) achieved higher Per-Hits@k than all baselines, and our Memory+Speaker+TF model showed the highest Per-Hits@k score, demonstrating the effectiveness of our proposed TF module in capturing user personalization by learning the latent interactions between questions, users, and their responses. **4)** Compared to Seq2Seq model, DialoGPT performed worse on content relatedness measures like BLEU and F1 and personalization measure Per-Hits@k. But our TF module still improved the personalization on top of DialoGPT model, as well as the diversity measure Distinct-N. Note that the perplexity could not be compared between DialoGPT and LSTM-based models since they have different vocabulary sets. **5)** Memory+Speaker model had better Per-Hits@k but lower BLEU than Seq2Seq model, while our TF module improved Memory+Speaker model's BLEU and Per-Hits@k at the same time. Due to the open-ended nature of these discussions, we observed relatively low BLEUs across different models, in line with prior work on personalized generation (Zheng et al., 2020; Li et al., 2016).

Since we have relatively high Per-Hits@k on the ground truth test set, we hypothesize that those top ranked responses in the ground truth test set by Per-Hits@k might be more likely to contain user personalization information. In other words, for certain question-user pairs, a user is more likely to respond with some personalized content that could be better recognized by their language model. We

Method	F1 %	BLEU %	Distinct-N % D-1	D-2	PPL	Per-Hits@k % 1	2	3	4	5	Average
Random	15.45	1.36	**3.09**	14.90	**97.05**	**1.33**	1.73	1.87	2.53	2.93	2.08
History	15.34	1.41*	2.79	14.27	98.75	1.00	1.93	2.93*	3.40	3.80	2.61
TF-u	15.24	1.48*	2.48	12.52	101.77	1.07	1.60	2.40	2.73	2.93	2.15
History+TF-u	**15.60***	**1.59***	3.02	**15.42***	101.30	**1.33**	**2.67**	**3.67***	**4.20***	**4.93***	**3.36***

Table 3: Speaker model with different speaker embedding initialization methods. A Wilcoxon signed-rank test was performed for Per-Hits@k and paired t-test was performed for other metrics, the significant ones ($p < 0.05$) over Random are marked as *

top-m	Per-Hits@k from Seq2Seq+TF 1	2	3	4	5	Avg.
1	9.86	13.38	16.90	16.90	17.61	14.93
2	6.78	9.32	11.86	11.86	12.71	10.51
3	6.35	8.36	11.04	11.37	12.04	9.83
4	5.51	7.54	9.86	11.01	11.59	9.10
5	4.99	6.82	8.92	9.97	10.50	8.24
500	2.07	3.20	4.53	5.40	5.80	4.20

Table 4: Per-Hits@k on different top-m focused test sets.

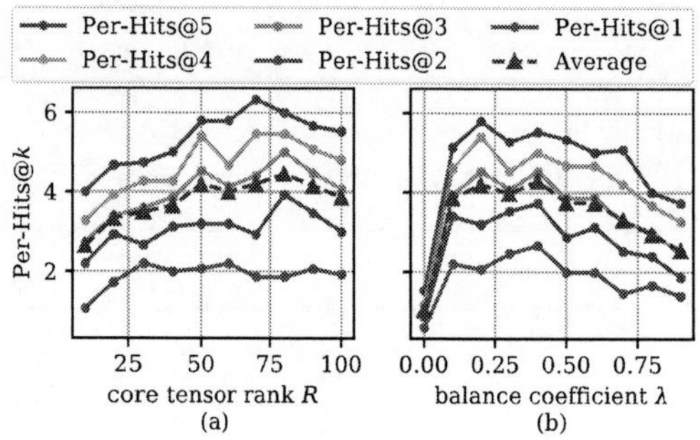

Figure 3: Per-Hits@k of Seq2Seq+TF model with (a): different Tucker's rank; (b): different balancer λ.

denote these question-user pairs that are ranked top-k by the Per-Hits@k from the test set as the top-m focused set. We evaluated Per-Hits@k of Seq2Seq+TF on different top-m ($m = 1, 2, 3, 4, 5$) test set in Table 4. Note that top-500 is the full test set we used for Per-Hits@k in Table 1. Per-Hits@k was higher on smaller top-m test set, showing the effectiveness of our Per-Hits@k measure, because Per-Hits@k of the same Seq2Seq+TF model was higher on the focused question-user subset when m is small, while lower on the larger and general test set. We then evaluated the baselines and our proposed models on top-1 focused test set in Table 2. Compared to the results on the full test set (Table 1), the gaps between our models and baselines on BLEU, F1, and Per-Hits@k are larger on this top-1 test set. This suggests that our TF module can help generate more personalized response for a user, especially in a context where a user is more likely to write personalized response.

5.6 Analysis and Ablation Studies

The Rank of Tucker Decomposition We first studied the influence of the rank of Tucker decomposition used in our TF module, i.e. the shape of the core tenser $\mathcal{G}$. We trained Seq2Seq+TF model with core tensor of shape $R \times R \times R, R \in \{10, 20, 30, 40, 50, 60, 70, 80, 90, 100\}$. From Figure 3(a), we found that Per-Hits@k first increased along with the rank, indicating that TF module with higher rank might better model latent user-questioninteractions. When the rank reaches around 50, there seems to be limited averaged gains on Per-Hits@k. Thus, we chose core tensor of shape $50 \times 50 \times 50$ for our TF module.

The Balancer λ We then studied the influence of the λ coefficient in Eq 1 which is used to balance the question information from the encoder and personalized response embedding from the TF module. We varied Seq2Seq+TF model's λ from 0 to 1, as shown in Figure 3(b). Note that Seq2Seq+TF with $\lambda = 0$ is the Seq2Seq baseline. We observed that Per-Hits@k increased a lot when λ changed from 0 to 0.1, confirming the effectiveness of our proposed TF module in modeling user personalization. Moreover, TF module was not sensitive to the hyper-parameter λ as Per-Hits@k were stable for $\lambda \in [0.1, 0.4]$. Per-Hits@k decreased when λ was larger than 0.4, suggesting the importance to balance the encoder and TF module.

User Factor Matrix To examine whether the TF module has learned user personalization information in user factor matrix $\mathbf{U}$, we trained a Speaker model that initialized the speaker embeddings with user embeddings in $\mathbf{U}$ and other initialization methods. Specifically we studied the user factor matrix (**TF-u**) from the Seq2Seq+TF model in Table 1 and compared it with: 1) random speaker embeddings

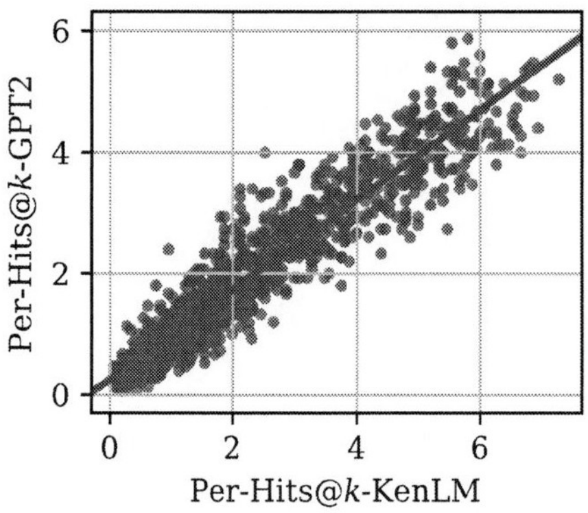

Figure 4: Per-Hits@k calculated by GPT2 and KenLM for different models. Pearson correlation r=0.941, with $p < .001$.

(**Random**) and 2) average sentence embeddings of each user's historical responses (**History**) which is used in our Speaker model baseline; 3) we further concatenated the history embeddings and our user embeddings in **U** to be the initial Speaker embeddings (**History+TF-u**). The results of the four variants of Speaker model are shown in Table 3. We found that both History and TF-u initialization improved Per-Hits@k over Random to some extent, suggesting that our TF module has learned some degree of user personalization in its user factor matrix **U**. Although TF-u had smaller Per-Hits@k improvement over Random, History+TF-u has the best Per-Hits@k, indicating that the personalization information learned by TF module is different to that from users' posting history.

Robustness of Personalization Metric To test the robustness of our Per-Hits@k metric, we trained trigram language models with the **KenLM** toolkit (Heafield et al., 2013) for the user specific language models used in Per-Hits@k. While GPT-2 is a transformer-based language model pretrained on large corpus and can be fine-tuned on each user's corpus, KenLM is impossible to follow this approach because it can only be trained in an end-to-end way, i.e. language models of KenLM is directly trained on each user's corpus. Thus we had two Per-Hits@k variants: Per-Hits@k-GPT2 (the one we used in previous sections) and Per-Hits@k-KenLM. We evaluated Per-Hits@k-GPT2 and Per-Hits@k-KenLM for all the models we trained with different settings and plot all (Per-Hits@k-KenLM, Per-Hits@k-GPT2) pairs for $k \in \{1, 2, 3, 4, 5\}$ in Figure 4. With a correlation of 0.941 between two variants, we conclude that Per-Hits@k is robust because it produces consistent and similar judgements regardless of which language model it uses.

6 Conclusion and Discussion

This work proposed a tensor factorization module to model user personalization from users' posting history for the task of personalized response generation, where explicit persona or demographic information is unavailable. To automatically evaluate the personalization of generated response, we proposed a new evaluation metric called Per-Hits@k. Extensive experiments on a large-scale dataset show that our proposed TF module outperforms previous methods significantly in terms of its content generation quality and also the personalization of generated responses. Our ablation studies further demonstrated the effectiveness and robustness of our TF based generation framework.

One limitation to note for our work is that our tensor factorization based framework to model personalization has only been tested on a corpus derived from Reddit (Wu et al., 2021). We acknowledge that potential user population bias might be introduced in this process. Another limitation of our results lies in dealing with new users, i.e., the cold start problem. Future research could further examine these issues, build upon our work to examine how different types of implicit information such as social knowledge and commonsense might be learned together with these user profiles in this tensor factorization manner, and model personalization in multi-turn dialogue systems.

Acknowledgment

We would like to thank the anonymous reviewers, and the members of Georgia Tech SALT group for their feedback. This work is supported in part by grants from Amazon, Salesforce, and the Institute for Data Engineering and Science (IDEaS).

References

JinYeong Bak and Alice Oh. 2020. Speaker sensitive response evaluation model. In *Proceedings of the 58th Annual Meeting of the Association for Computational Linguistics*, pages 6376–6385, Online. Association for Computational Linguistics.

Dheeraj kumar Bokde, Sheetal Girase, and Debajyoti Mukhopadhyay. 2015. Role of matrix factorization model in collaborative filtering algorithm: A survey. *CoRR, abs/1503.07475*.

Stanley F Chen, Douglas Beeferman, and Roni Rosenfeld. 1998. Evaluation metrics for language models.

Cesc Chunseong Park, Byeongchang Kim, and Gunhee Kim. 2017. Attend to you: Personalized image captioning with context sequence memory networks. In *Proceedings of the IEEE conference on computer vision and pattern recognition*, pages 895–903.

Emily Dinan, Varvara Logacheva, Valentin Malykh, Alexander Miller, Kurt Shuster, Jack Urbanek, Douwe Kiela, Arthur Szlam, Iulian Serban, Ryan Lowe, et al. 2019. The second conversational intelligence challenge (convai2). *arXiv preprint arXiv:1902.00098*.

George Doddington. 2002. Automatic evaluation of machine translation quality using n-gram co-occurrence statistics. In *Proceedings of the second international conference on Human Language Technology Research*, pages 138–145.

Angela Fan, Mike Lewis, and Yann Dauphin. 2018. Hierarchical neural story generation. *arXiv preprint arXiv:1805.04833*.

Kenneth Heafield, Ivan Pouzyrevsky, Jonathan H Clark, and Philipp Koehn. 2013. Scalable modified kneser-ney language model estimation. In *Proceedings of the 51st Annual Meeting of the Association for Computational Linguistics (Volume 2: Short Papers)*, pages 690–696.

Minlie Huang, Xiaoyan Zhu, and Jianfeng Gao. 2020. Challenges in building intelligent open-domain dialog systems. *ACM Transactions on Information Systems (TOIS)*, 38(3):1–32.

Anjuli Kannan, Karol Kurach, Sujith Ravi, Tobias Kaufmann, Andrew Tomkins, Balint Miklos, Greg Corrado, László Lukács, Marina Ganea, Peter Young, et al. 2016. Smart reply: Automated response suggestion for email. In *KDD*.

Diederik P Kingma and Jimmy Ba. 2014. Adam: A method for stochastic optimization. *arXiv preprint arXiv:1412.6980*.

Satwik Kottur, Xiaoyu Wang, and Vítor Carvalho. 2017. Exploring personalized neural conversational models. In *IJCAI*, pages 3728–3734.

Alon Lavie and Abhaya Agarwal. 2007. Meteor: An automatic metric for mt evaluation with high levels of correlation with human judgments. In *Proceedings of the second workshop on statistical machine translation*, pages 228–231.

Mike Lewis, Yinhan Liu, Naman Goyal, Marjan Ghazvininejad, Abdelrahman Mohamed, Omer Levy, Ves Stoyanov, and Luke Zettlemoyer. 2019. Bart: Denoising sequence-to-sequence pre-training for natural language generation, translation, and comprehension. *arXiv preprint arXiv:1910.13461*.

Jiwei Li, Michel Galley, Chris Brockett, Jianfeng Gao, and Bill Dolan. 2015. A diversity-promoting objective function for neural conversation models. *arXiv preprint arXiv:1510.03055*.

Jiwei Li, Michel Galley, Chris Brockett, Georgios Spithourakis, Jianfeng Gao, and Bill Dolan. 2016. A persona-based neural conversation model. In *Proceedings of the 54th Annual Meeting of the Association for Computational Linguistics (Volume 1: Long Papers)*, pages 994–1003.

Xiaohu Liu, Ruhi Sarikaya, Liang Zhao, Yong Ni, and Yi-Cheng Pan. 2016. Personalized natural language understanding. In *INTERSPEECH*, pages 1146–1150.

Liangchen Luo, Wenhao Huang, Qi Zeng, Zaiqing Nie, and Xu Sun. 2019. Learning personalized end-to-end goal-oriented dialog. In *Proceedings of the AAAI Conference on Artificial Intelligence*, volume 33, pages 6794–6801.

Kaixiang Mo, Shuangyin Li, Yu Zhang, Jiajun Li, and Qiang Yang. 2016. Personalizing a dialogue system with transfer reinforcement learning. *arXiv preprint arXiv:1610.02891*.

Kishore Papineni, Salim Roukos, Todd Ward, and Wei-Jing Zhu. 2002. Bleu: a method for automatic evaluation of machine translation. In *Proceedings of the 40th annual meeting of the Association for Computational Linguistics*, pages 311–318.

Adam Paszke, Sam Gross, Francisco Massa, Adam Lerer, James Bradbury, Gregory Chanan, Trevor Killeen, Zeming Lin, Natalia Gimelshein, Luca Antiga, et al. 2019. Pytorch: An imperative style, high-performance deep learning library. In *Advances in neural information processing systems*, pages 8026–8037.

Qiao Qian, Minlie Huang, Haizhou Zhao, Jingfang Xu, and Xiaoyan Zhu. Assigning personality/profile to a chatting machine for coherent conversation generation.

Ella Rabinovich, Raj Nath Patel, Shachar Mirkin, Lucia Specia, and Shuly Wintner. 2017. Personalized machine translation: Preserving original author traits. In *Proceedings of the 15th Conference of the European Chapter of the Association for Computational Linguistics: Volume 1, Long Papers*, pages 1074–1084.

Alec Radford, Jeffrey Wu, Rewon Child, David Luan, Dario Amodei, and Ilya Sutskever. 2019. Language models are unsupervised multitask learners. *OpenAI Blog*, 1(8):9.

Nils Reimers and Iryna Gurevych. 2020. Making monolingual sentence embeddings multilingual using knowledge distillation. *arXiv preprint arXiv:2004.09813*.

Heung-Yeung Shum, Xiao-dong He, and Di Li. 2018. From eliza to xiaoice: challenges and opportunities with social chatbots. *Frontiers of Information Technology & Electronic Engineering*, 19(1):10–26.

Arthur A Stone, Christine A Bachrach, Jared B Jobe, Howard S Kurtzman, and Virginia S Cain. 1999. *The science of self-report: Implications for research and practice*. Psychology Press.

Bakhtiyar Syed, Gaurav Verma, Balaji Vasan Srinivasan, Anandhavelu Natarajan, and Vasudeva Varma. 2020. Adapting language models for non-parallel author-stylized rewriting. In *AAAI*, pages 9008–9015.

Ledyard R Tucker. 1966. Some mathematical notes on three-mode factor analysis. *Psychometrika*, 31(3):279–311.

Olga Vechtomova, Hareesh Bahuleyan, Amirpasha Ghabussi, and Vineet John. 2018. Generating lyrics with variational autoencoder and multi-modal artist embeddings. *arXiv preprint arXiv:1812.08318*.

Oriol Vinyals and Quoc Le. 2015. A neural conversational model. *arXiv preprint arXiv:1506.05869*.

Thomas Wolf, Victor Sanh, Julien Chaumond, and Clement Delangue. 2019. Transfertransfo: A transfer learning approach for neural network based conversational agents. *arXiv preprint arXiv:1901.08149*.

Yuwei Wu, Xuezhe Ma, and Diyi Yang. 2021. Personalized response generation via generative split memory network. In *North American Chapter of the Association for Computational Linguistics*.

Minghong Xu, Piji Li, Haoran Yang, Pengjie Ren, Zhaochun Ren, Zhumin Chen, and Jun Ma. 2020. A neural topical expansion framework for unstructured persona-oriented dialogue generation. *arXiv preprint arXiv:2002.02153*.

Jingfeng Yang, Diyi Yang, and Zhaoran Ma. 2020. Planning and generating natural and diverse disfluent texts as augmentation for disfluency detection. In *Proceedings of the 2020 Conference on Empirical Methods in Natural Language Processing (EMNLP)*, pages 1450–1460.

Min Yang, Qiang Qu, Kai Lei, Jia Zhu, Zhou Zhao, Xiaojun Chen, and Joshua Z Huang. 2018. Investigating deep reinforcement learning techniques in personalized dialogue generation. In *Proceedings of the 2018 SIAM International Conference on Data Mining*, pages 630–638. SIAM.

Min Yang, Zhou Zhao, Wei Zhao, Xiaojun Chen, Jia Zhu, Lianqiang Zhou, and Zigang Cao. 2017. Personalized response generation via domain adaptation. In *Proceedings of the 40th International ACM SIGIR Conference on Research and Development in Information Retrieval*, pages 1021–1024.

Kaisheng Yao, Geoffrey Zweig, and Baolin Peng. 2015. Attention with intention for a neural network conversation model. *arXiv preprint arXiv:1510.08565*.

Saizheng Zhang, Emily Dinan, Jack Urbanek, Arthur Szlam, Douwe Kiela, and Jason Weston. 2018. Personalizing dialogue agents: I have a dog, do you have pets too? *arXiv preprint arXiv:1801.07243*.

Yizhe Zhang, Siqi Sun, Michel Galley, Yen-Chun Chen, Chris Brockett, Xiang Gao, Jianfeng Gao, Jingjing Liu, and Bill Dolan. 2020. Dialogpt: Large-scale generative pre-training for conversational response generation. In *ACL, system demonstration*.

Yinhe Zheng, Guanyi Chen, Minlie Huang, Song Liu, and Xuan Zhu. 2019. Personalized dialogue generation with diversified traits. *arXiv preprint arXiv:1901.09672*.

Yinhe Zheng, Rongsheng Zhang, Minlie Huang, and Xiaoxi Mao. 2020. A pre-training based personalized dialogue generation model with persona-sparse data. In *AAAI*, pages 9693–9700.

A Review of Human Evaluation for Style Transfer

Eleftheria Briakou[1] Sweta Agrawal[1] Ke Zhang[2] Joel Tetreault[2] Marine Carpuat[1]
[1]University of Maryland, [2]Dataminr, Inc.
ebriakou@cs.umd.edu, sweagraw@cs.umd.edu, kzhang@dataminr.com,
jtetreault@dataminr.com, marine@cs.umd.edu

Abstract

This paper reviews and summarizes human evaluation practices described in 97 style transfer papers with respect to three main evaluation aspects: style transfer, meaning preservation, and fluency. In principle, evaluations by human raters should be the most reliable. However, in style transfer papers, we find that protocols for human evaluations are often underspecified and not standardized, which hampers the reproducibility of research in this field and progress toward better human and automatic evaluation methods.

1 Introduction

Style Transfer (ST) in NLP refers to a broad spectrum of text generation tasks that aim to rewrite a sentence to change a specific attribute of language use in context while preserving others (e.g., make an informal request formal, Table 1). With the success of deep sequence-to-sequence models and the relative ease of collecting data covering various stylistic attributes, neural ST is a popular generation task with more than 100 papers published in this area over the last 10 years.

Despite the growing interest that ST receives from the NLP community, progress is hampered by the lack of standardized evaluation practices. One practical aspect that contributes to this problem is the conceptualization and formalization of styles in natural language. According to a survey of neural style transfer by Jin et al. (2021), in the context of NLP, ST is used to refer to tasks where styles follow a linguistically motivated dimension of language variation (e.g., formality), and also to tasks where the distinction between style and content is implicitly defined by data (e.g., positive or negative sentiment). Across these tasks, ST quality is usually evaluated across three dimensions: style transfer (has the desired attributed been changed as intended?), meaning preservation (are the other attributes preserved?), and fluency (is the output well-formed?) (Pang and Gimpel, 2019; Mir et al., 2019). Given the large spectrum of stylistic attributes studied and the lack of naturally occurring references for the associated ST tasks, prior work emphasizes the limitations of automatic evaluation. As a result, progress in this growing field relies heavily on human evaluations to quantify progress among the three evaluation aspects.

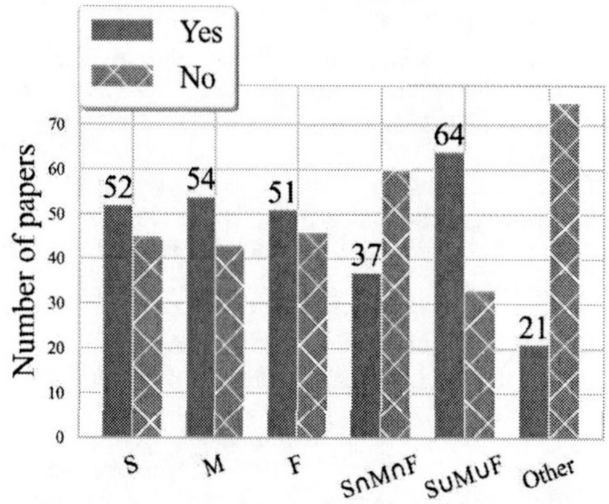

Figure 1: Number of papers employing human evaluations for style transfer (S), meaning preservation (M), fluency (F), all of them (S∪M∪F), at least one of them (S∩M∩F), or another aspect (OTHER).

FORMALITY
Gotta see both sides of the story. *(informal)*
You have to consider both sides of the story. *(formal)*
SENTIMENT
The screen is just the right size. *(positive)*
The screen is too small. *(negative)*
AUTHOR IMITATION
Bring her out to me. *(modern)*
Call her forth to me. *(shakespearean)*

Table 1: Examples of three ST attributes: formality, sentiment and Shakespearean transfer.

Proceedings of the 1st Workshop on Natural Language Generation, Evaluation, and Metrics (GEM 2021), pages 58–67
August 5–6, 2021. ©2021 Association for Computational Linguistics

Inspired by recent critiques of human evaluations of Natural Language Generation (NLG) systems (Howcroft et al., 2020; Lee, 2020; Belz et al., 2020, 2021; Shimorina and Belz, 2021), we conduct a structured review of human evaluation for neural style transfer systems as their evaluation is primarily based on human judgments. Concretely, out of the **97 papers we reviewed, 69 of them resort to human evaluation** (Figure 1), where it is treated either as a substitute for automatic metrics or as a more reliable evaluation.

This paper summarizes the findings of the review and raises the following concerns on current human evaluation practices:

1. **Underspecification** We find that many attributes of the human annotation design (e.g., annotation framework, annotators' details) are *underspecified* in paper descriptions, which hampers reproducibility and replicability;

2. **Availability & Reliability** The vast majority of papers do not release the human ratings and do not give details that can help assess their quality (e.g., agreement statistics, quality control), which hurts research on evaluation;

3. **Lack of standardization** The annotation protocols are inconsistent across papers which hampers comparisons across systems (e.g., due to possible bias in annotation frameworks).

The paper is organized as follows. In Section 2, we describe our procedure for analyzing the 97 papers and summarizing their evaluations. In Section 3, we present and analyze our findings. Finally, in Section 4, we conclude with a discussion of where the field of style transfer fares with respect to human evaluation today and outline improvements for future work in this area.

2 Reviewing ST Human Evaluation

Paper Selection We select papers for this study from the list compiled by Jin et al. (2021) who conduct a comprehensive review of ST that covers the task formulation; evaluation metrics; opinion papers and deep-learning based textual ST methods. The paper list contains more than 100 papers and is publicly available (`https://github.com/fuzhenxin/Style-Transfer-in-Text`). We reviewed all papers in this list to determine whether they conduct either human or automatic evaluation on system outputs for ST, and therefore should be included in our structured review. We did not review papers for text simplification, as it has been studied separately (Alva-Manchego et al., 2020; Sikka et al., 2020) and metrics for automatic evaluation have been widely adopted (Xu et al., 2016). Our final list consists of 97 papers: 86 of them are from top-tier NLP and AI venues: ACL, EACL, EMNLP, NAACL, TACL, IEEE, AAAI, NeurIPS, ICML, and ICLR, and the remaining 11 are pre-prints which have not been peer-reviewed.

Review Structure We review each paper based on a predefined set of criteria (Table 2). The rationale behind their choice is to collect information on the evaluation aspects that are underspecified in NLP in general as well as those specific to the ST task. For this work, we call the former *global criteria*. The latter is called *dimension-specific criteria* and is meant to illustrate issues with how each dimension (i.e., style transfer, meaning preservation, and fluency) is evaluated.

Global criteria can be split into three categories which describe: (1) the ST stylistic attribute, (2) four details about the annotators and their compensation, and (3) four general design choices of the human evaluation that are not tied to a specific evaluation dimension.

For the *dimension-specific criteria* we repurpose the following *operationalisation* attributes introduced by Howcroft et al. (2020): form of response elicitation (direct vs. relative), details on type of collected responses, size/scale of rating instrument, and statistics computed on response values. Finally, we also collect information on the quality criterion for each dimension (i.e., the wording used in the paper to refer to the specific evaluation dimension).

Process The review was conducted by the authors of this survey. We first went through each of the 97 papers and highlighted the sections which included mentions of human evaluation. Next, we developed our criteria by creating a draft based on prior work and issues we had observed in the first step. We then discussed and refined the criteria after testing it on a subset of the papers. Once the criteria were finalized, we split the papers evenly between all the authors. Annotations were spot-checked to resolve uncertainties or concerns that were found in reviewing dimension-specific criteria (e.g., scale of rating instrument is not explicitly

GLOBAL CRITERIA	
task(s)	ST *task(s) covered*
presence of human annotation	*presence of human evaluation*
annotators' details	*details on annotator's background/recruitment process*
annotators' compensation	*annotator's payment for annotating each instance*
quality control	*quality control methods followed to ensure reliability of collected judgments*
annotations' availability	*availability of collected judgments*
evaluated systems	*number of different systems present in human evaluation*
size of evaluated instance set	*number of instances evaluated for each system*
size of annotation set per instance	*number of collected annotations for each annotated instance*
agreement statistics	*presence of inter-annotator agreement statistics*
sampling method	*method for selecting instances for evaluation from the original test sets*

DIMENSION-SPECIFIC CRITERIA	
presence of human evaluation	*whether there exists human evaluation for a specific aspect*
quality criterion name	*quality criterion of evaluated attribute as mentioned in the paper*
direct response elicitation	*presence of direct assessment (i.e., each instance is evaluated on its own right)*
relative judgment type (if applicable)	*type of relative judgment (e.g., pairwise, ranking, best)*
direct rating scale (if applicable)	*list of possible response values*
presence of lineage reference	*whether the evaluation reuses an evaluation framework from prior work*
lineage source (if applicable)	*citation of prior evaluation framework*

Table 2: Descriptions of attributes studied in our structured review.

defined but inferred from the results discussion) and global criteria (e.g., number of systems not specified but inferred from tables). We release the spreadsheet used to conduct the review along with the reviewed PDFs that come with highlights on the human evaluation sections of each paper at `https://github.com/Elbria/ST-human-review`.

3 Findings

Based on our review, we first discuss trends of stylistic attributes as discussed in ST research through the years (§3.1), followed by global criteria of human evaluation (§3.2), and then turn to domain-specific criteria (§3.3).

3.1 Evolution of Stylistic Attributes

Table 3 presents statistics on the different style attributes considered in ST papers since 2011. First, we observe a significant increase in the number of ST papers starting in 2018 (in 2017 there were 8 ST papers; the following year there were 28). We believe this can be attributed to the creation of standardized training and evaluation datasets for various ST tasks. One example is the Yelp dataset, which consists of positive and negative reviews, and is used for unsupervised sentiment transfer (Shen et al., 2017). Another example is the GYAFC parallel corpus, consisting of informal-formal pairs that are generated using crowdsourced human rewrites (Rao and Tetreault, 2018). Second, we notice that new stylistic attributes are studied through time (21 over the last ten years), with sentiment and formality transfer being the most frequently studied.

3.2 Global Criteria

Annotators Table 4 summarizes statistics about how papers describe the background of their human judges. The majority of works (38%) rely on crowd workers mostly recruited using the Amazon Mechanical Turk crowdsourcing platform. Interestingly, for a substantial number of evaluations (45%), it is unclear who the annotators are and what their background is. In addition, we find that information about how much participants were compensated is missing from all but two papers. Finally, many papers collect 3 independent annotations, although this information is not specified in a significant percentage of evaluations (42%). In short, the ability to replicate a human evaluation from the bulk of current research is extremely challenging, and in many cases impossible, as so much is underspecified.

STYLE	2011	2012	2016	2017	2018	2019	2020	2021	TOTAL
anonymization					1				1
attractiveness				1			1		2
author imitation		1		2	2	1	5		11
debiasing							2		2
social register					1				1
expertise							1		1
formality	1				1	9	10	3	24
gender			1		2	3			6
political slant					2	1	1		4
sentiment				4	14	14	18	3	53
romantic/humorous					2	1	1		4
simile							1		1
excitement							1		1
profanity							1		1
prose				1	1				2
offensive language					1		1		2
multiple						1	1		2
persona			1			1	1		3
poeticness							1		1
politeness					1		1		2
emotion							1		1
TOTAL	**1**	**1**	**2**	**8**	**28**	**31**	**48**	**6**	**125**

Table 3: Number of ST papers per stylistic attribute across years. Some papers evalute multiple style attributes.

CROWD-SOURCING	PAPER'S DESCRIPTION OF ANNOTATORS	COUNT
YES	*"qualification test"*	6
	"number of approved HITs*'*	2
	"hire Amazon Mechanical Turk workers"	18
NO	*"bachelor or higher degree; independent of the authors' "research group", "annotators with linguistic background" "well-educated volunteers", "graduate students in computational linguistics" "major in linguistics" "linguistic background", "authors"*	12
UNCLEAR	*"individuals", "human judges", "human annotators" "unbiased human judges", "independent annotators"*	31

Table 4: Annotators' background for human evaluation as described in ST papers.

Annotations' Reliability Only 31% of evaluation methods that rely on crowd-sourcing employ quality control (QC) methods. The most common QC strategies are to require workers to pass a qualification test (Jin et al., 2019; Li et al., 2016; Ma et al., 2020; Pryzant et al., 2020) to hire the top-ranked workers based on pre-computed scores that reflect the number of their past approved tasks (Krishna et al., 2020; Li et al., 2019), to use location restrictions (Krishna et al., 2020), or to perform manual checks on the collected annotations (Rao and Tetreault, 2018; Briakou et al., 2021). Furthermore, only 20% of the papers report inter-annotator agreement statistics, and only 4 papers release the actual annotations to facilitate the reproducibility and further analysis of their results. Without this information, it is difficult to replicate the evaluation and compare different evaluation approaches.

Data Selection Human evaluation is typically performed on a sample of the test set used for automatic evaluation. Most works (62%) sample instances randomly from the entire set, with a few exceptions that employ stratified sampling according to the number of stylistic categories considered (e.g., random sampling from positive and negative classes for a binary definition of style). For 25% of ST papers information on the sampling method is not available. Furthermore, the sample size of instances evaluated per system varies from 50 to 1000, with most of them concentrated around 100.

3.3 Dimension-specific Criteria

Quality Criterion Names Table 5 summarizes the terms used to refer to the three main dimensions of style transfer, meaning preservation, and fluency. As Howcroft et al. (2020) found in the context of NLG evaluation, we see that the names of these dimensions are not standardized for the three ST evaluation dimensions. Each dimension has at least six different ways that past literature has referred to them. We should note that even with the same name, the nature of the evaluation is not necessarily the same across ST tasks: for instance, what constitutes content preservation differs in formality transfer and in sentiment transfer, since the latter arguably changes the semantics of the original text. While fluency is the aspect of evaluation that might be most generalizable across ST tasks, it is referred to in inconsistent ways across papers which could lead to different interpretations by annotators. For instance, the same text could be rated as natural but not grammatical. Overall, the variability in terminology makes it harder to understand exactly what is being evaluated and to compare evaluation methods across papers.

STYLE
attribute compatibility, formality, politeness level, sentiment, style transfer intensity, attractive captions, attribute change correctness, bias, creativity, highest agency, opposite sentiment, sentiment, sentiment strength, similarity to the target attribute, style correctness, style transfer accuracy, style transfer strength, stylistic similarity, target attribute match, transformed sentiment degree.
MEANING
content preservation, meaning preservation, semantic intent, semantic similarity, closer in meaning to the original sentence, content preservation degree, content retainment, content similarity, relevance, semantic adequacy.
FLUENCY
fluency, grammaticality, naturalness, gibberish language, language quality.

Table 5: Quality criterion names used in ST human evaluation descriptions for the three evaluation dimensions.

	2011	2012	2016	2017	2018	2019	2020	2021	Total
STYLE									
DIRECT	1	1		1	8	10	12	4	40
RELATIVE			1		4	7			12
NONE			2	6	11	11	15		45
MEANING									
DIRECT		1			12	10	18	4	45
RELATIVE				1		4	4		9
NONE	1		2	7	8	11	14		43
FLUENCY									
DIRECT		1		1	10	10	19	4	45
RELATIVE					4	2			6
NONE	1		1	2	8	6	7		46

Table 6: Number of papers using each rating type for the three evaluation dimensions across years.

Rating Type Table 6 presents statistics on the rating type (direct vs. relative) per dimension over time. *Direct rating* refers to evaluations where each system output is assessed in isolation for that dimension. *Relative rating* refers to evaluations where two or more system outputs are compared against each other. Rating types were more inconsistently used before 2020, with recent convergences toward direct assessment. Among papers that report rating type, direct assessment is the most frequent approach for all evaluation aspects over the years 2018 to 2021.

Possible Responses Tables 7, 8, and 9 summarize the range of responses elicited for direct and relative ratings. They cover diverse definitions of scales within each rating type. Across evaluation aspects, the dominant evaluation framework is **direct ratings** on a **5-point scale**. However, while that configuration is what the field tends to focus on, there is clearly a wide array of choices that the field also considers which, once again, makes comparing human evaluations head to head very difficult.

Direct (40)	Rating Scale	(1)	[-2,-1,0,1,2]
		(3)	[-3,-2, -1, 0, 1, 2, 3]
		(1)	[polite, slightly polite, neutral, slightly rude, rude]
		(4)	[positive, negative, neutral]
		(1)	[positive, negative, relaxed, annoyed]
		(1)	[more formal, more informal, neither]
		(2)	[0,1,2]
		(2)	[1,2,3]
		(1)	[0,1,2,3,4,5]
		(19)	**[1, 2, 3, 4, 5]**
		(2)	[1,2,3,4,5,6,7,8,9,10]
		(1)	binary
	Not available	(2)	
Relative (12)	Best selection	(5)	
	Pairwise	(7)	

Table 7: **Style** results. Numbers in parentheses denote paper counts per category. The most popular rating type across each dimension is highlighted.

Direct (45)	Rating Scale	(1)	[-2,-1,0,1,2]
		(6)	[0,1,2]
		(1)	[1,2,3]
		(1)	[1,2,3,4]
		(25)	**[1, 2, 3, 4, 5]**
		(1)	[0,1,2,3,4,5]
		(4)	[1,2,3,4,5,6]
		(3)	[1,2,3,4,5,6,7,8,9,10]
	Not available	(3)	
Relative (9)	Best selection	(3)	
	Pairwise	(3)	
	Ranking	(3)	

Table 8: **Meaning Preservation** results. Numbers in parentheses denote paper counts per category. The most popular rating type across each dimension is highlighted.

Direct (45)	Rating Scale	(1)	["easy to understand", "some grammar errors", "impossible to understand"]
		(1)	["incorrect", "partly correct", "correct"]
		(1)	[0,1]
		(3)	[0,1,2]
		(2)	[1,2,3]
		(4)	[1,2,3,4]
		(1)	[0,1,2,3,4]
		(26)	**[1, 2, 3, 4, 5]**
		(1)	[0,1,2,3,4,5]
		(1)	[1,2,3,4,5,6]
		(2)	[1,2,3,4,5,6,7,8,9,10]
	Not available	(2)	
Relative (6)	Best selection	(1)	
	Pairwise	(4)	
	Ranking	(1)	

Table 9: **Fluency** results. Numbers in parentheses denote paper counts per category. The most popular rating type across each dimension is highlighted.

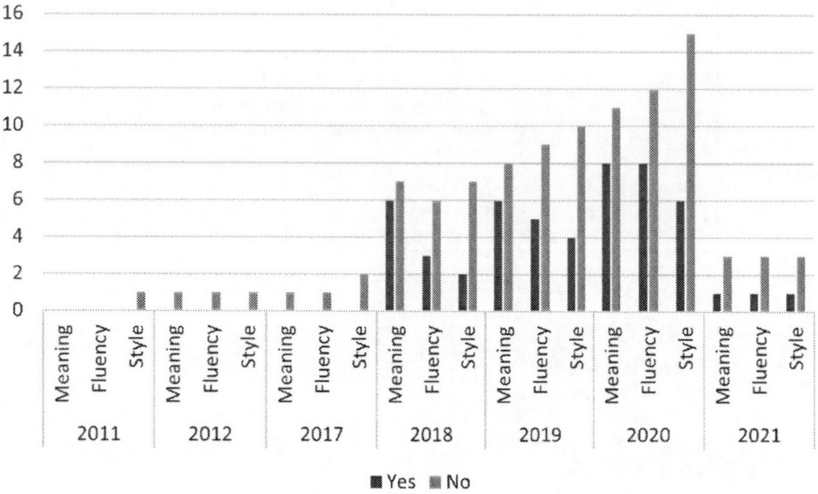

Figure 2: Lineage statistics (i.e., number of papers) for each ST evaluation aspect over years.

Lineage Figure 2 shows how often the human evaluation setup used in each reviewed paper is based on cited prior work, for each dimension over time. Only 19% of papers repurpose or reuse some prior work for the evaluation of style. Most of these papers target ST for formality or sentiment. Even when evaluating fluency or meaning preservation, more than 50% of the papers do not refer to any prior work. This is striking because it suggests that there is currently not a strong effort to replicate prior human evaluations.

For papers that mention lineage, the most common-set up for evaluating meaning preservation (24%) and fluency (28%) is Li et al. (2018). 43% of ST papers that work on sentiment also refer to Li et al. (2018). Some papers follow Agirre et al. (2016) for measuring textual similarity, Heilman et al. (2014) for grammaticality and Pavlick and Tetreault (2016) for formality.

4 Discussion & Recommendations

4.1 Describing Evaluation Protocols

Our structured review shows that human evaluation protocols for ST are mostly underspecified and lack standardization, which fundamentally hinders progress, as it is for other NLG tasks (Howcroft et al., 2020). The following attributes are commonly underspecified:

1. details on the procedures followed for recruiting annotators (i.e., linguistic background of expert annotators or quality control method employed when recruiting crowd-workers)

2. annotator's compensation to better understand their motivation for participating in the task,

3. inter-annotator agreement statistics,

4. number of annotations per instance (3-5 is the most popular choice of prior work),

5. number of systems evaluated,

6. number of instances annotated (minimum of 100 based on prior works),

7. selection method of the annotated instances (suggestion is same random sampled for all annotated systems).

8. detailed description of evaluated frameworks per evaluation aspect (e.g., rating type, response of elicitation).

Furthermore, we observe that annotated judgments are hardly ever made publicly available and that, when specified, evaluation frameworks are not standardized.

As a result, our first recommendation is simply to include all these details when describing a protocol for human evaluation of ST. We discuss further recommendations next.

4.2 Releasing Annotations

Making human-annotated judgments available would enable the development of better automatic metrics for ST. If all annotations had been released with the papers reviewed, we estimate that more than 10K human judgments per evaluation aspect would be available. Today this would suffice to train and evaluate dedicated evaluation models.

In addition, raw annotations can shed light on the difficulty of the task and nature of the data: they can be aggregated in multiple ways (Oortwijn et al., 2021), or used to account for annotator bias in model training (Beigman and Beigman Klebanov, 2009). Finally, releasing annotated judgments makes it possible to replicate and further analyze the evaluation outcome (Belz et al., 2021).

4.3 Standardizing Evaluation Protocols

Standardizing evaluation protocols is key to establishing fair comparisons across systems (Belz et al., 2020) and to improving evaluation itself.

Our survey sheds light on the most frequently used ST frameworks in prior work. Yet more research is needed to clarify how to evaluate, compare and replicate the protocols. For instance, Mir et al. (2019) point to evidence that relative judgments can be more reliable than absolute judgments (Stewart et al., 2005), as part of their work on designing automatic metrics for ST evaluation. However, research on human evaluation of machine translation shows that this can change depending on the specifics of the annotation task: relative judgments were replaced by direct assessment when Graham et al. (2013) showed that both intra and inter-annotator agreement could be improved by using a continuous rating scale instead of the previously common five or seven-point interval scale (Callison-Burch et al., 2007).

For ST, the lack of detail and clarity in describing evaluation protocols makes it difficult to improve them, as has been pointed out for other NLG tasks by Shimorina and Belz (2021) who propose evaluation datasheets for clear documentation of human evaluations, Lee (2020) and van der Lee et al. (2020) who propose best practices guidelines, and Belz et al. (2020, 2021) who raise concerns regarding reproducibility. This issue is particularly salient for ST tasks where stylistic changes are defined implicitly by data (Jin et al., 2021) and where the instructions given to human judges for style transfer might be the only explicit characterization of the style dimension targeted. Furthermore, since ST includes rewriting text according to pragmatic aspects of language use, who the human judgments are matters since differences in communication norms and expectations might result in different judgments for the same text.

Standardizing and describing protocols is also key to assessing the alignment of the evaluation with the models and task proposed (Hämäläinen and Alnajjar, 2021), and to understand potential biases and ethical issues that might arise from, e.g., compensation mechanisms (Vaughan, 2018; Schoch et al., 2020; Shmueli et al., 2021).

References

Eneko Agirre, Carmen Banea, Daniel Cer, Mona Diab, Aitor Gonzalez-Agirre, Rada Mihalcea, German Rigau, and Janyce Wiebe. 2016. SemEval-2016 task 1: Semantic textual similarity, monolingual and cross-lingual evaluation. In *Proceedings of the 10th International Workshop on Semantic Evaluation (SemEval-2016)*, pages 497–511, San Diego, California. Association for Computational Linguistics.

Fernando Alva-Manchego, Carolina Scarton, and Lucia Specia. 2020. Data-driven sentence simplification: Survey and benchmark. *Computational Linguistics*, 46(1):135–187.

Eyal Beigman and Beata Beigman Klebanov. 2009. Learning with annotation noise. In *Proceedings of the Joint Conference of the 47th Annual Meeting of the ACL and the 4th International Joint Conference on Natural Language Processing of the AFNLP*, pages 280–287, Suntec, Singapore. Association for Computational Linguistics.

Anya Belz, Shubham Agarwal, Anastasia Shimorina, and Ehud Reiter. 2021. A systematic review of reproducibility research in natural language processing. In *Proceedings of the 16th Conference of the European Chapter of the Association for Computational Linguistics: Main Volume*, pages 381–393, Online. Association for Computational Linguistics.

Anya Belz, Simon Mille, and David M. Howcroft. 2020. Disentangling the properties of human evaluation methods: A classification system to support comparability, meta-evaluation and reproducibility testing. In *Proceedings of the 13th International Conference on Natural Language Generation*, pages 183–194, Dublin, Ireland. Association for Computational Linguistics.

Eleftheria Briakou, Di Lu, Ke Zhang, and Joel Tetreault. 2021. Xformal: A benchmark for multilingual formality style transfer.

Chris Callison-Burch, Cameron Fordyce, Philipp Koehn, Christof Monz, and Josh Schroeder. 2007. (Meta-) Evaluation of Machine Translation. In *Proceedings of the Second Workshop on Statistical Machine Translation*, pages 136–158. Association for Computational Linguistics.

Yvette Graham, Timothy Baldwin, Alistair Moffat, and Justin Zobel. 2013. Continuous Measurement Scales in Human Evaluation of Machine Translation. In *Proceedings of the 7th Linguistic Annotation Workshop and Interoperability with Discourse*, pages 33–41, Sofia, Bulgaria. Association for Computational Linguistics.

Mika Hämäläinen and Khalid Alnajjar. 2021. The great misalignment problem in human evaluation of NLP methods. In *Proceedings of the Workshop on Human Evaluation of NLP Systems (HumEval)*, pages 69–74, Online. Association for Computational Linguistics.

Michael Heilman, Aoife Cahill, Nitin Madnani, Melissa Lopez, Matthew Mulholland, and Joel Tetreault. 2014. Predicting grammaticality on an ordinal scale. In *Proceedings of the 52nd Annual Meeting of the Association for Computational Linguistics (Volume 2: Short Papers)*, pages 174–180, Baltimore, Maryland. Association for Computational Linguistics.

David M. Howcroft, Anya Belz, Miruna-Adriana Clinciu, Dimitra Gkatzia, Sadid A. Hasan, Saad Mahamood, Simon Mille, Emiel van Miltenburg, Sashank Santhanam, and Verena Rieser. 2020. Twenty years of confusion in human evaluation: NLG needs evaluation sheets and standardised definitions. In *Proceedings of the 13th International Conference on Natural Language Generation*, pages 169–182, Dublin, Ireland. Association for Computational Linguistics.

Di Jin, Zhijing Jin, Zhiting Hu, Olga Vechtomova, and Rada Mihalcea. 2021. Deep learning for text style transfer: A survey.

Z. Jin, D. Jin, J. Mueller, N. Matthews, and E. Santus. 2019. Imat: Unsupervised text attribute transfer via iterative matching and translation. In *Proceedings of the 2019 Conference on Empirical Methods in Natural Language Processing and the 9th International Joint Conference on Natural Language Processing (EMNLP-IJCNLP)*, pages 3095–3107. Association for Computational Linguistics.

Kalpesh Krishna, John Wieting, and Mohit Iyyer. 2020. Reformulating unsupervised style transfer as paraphrase generation. In *Proceedings of the 2020 Conference on Empirical Methods in Natural Language Processing (EMNLP)*, pages 737–762, Online. Association for Computational Linguistics.

Chris van der Lee, Albert Gatt, Emiel van Miltenburg, and Emiel Krahmer. 2020. Human evaluation of automatically generated text: Current trends and best practice guidelines. *Computer Speech & Language*, page 101151.

Kiyong Lee. 2020. Annotation-based semantics. In *16th Joint ACL - ISO Workshop on Interoperable Semantic Annotation PROCEEDINGS*, pages 36–48, Marseille. European Language Resources Association.

Dianqi Li, Yizhe Zhang, Zhe Gan, Yu Cheng, Chris Brockett, Bill Dolan, and Ming-Ting Sun. 2019. Domain adaptive text style transfer. In *Proceedings of the 2019 Conference on Empirical Methods in Natural Language Processing and the 9th International Joint Conference on Natural Language Processing (EMNLP-IJCNLP)*, pages 3304–3313, Hong Kong, China. Association for Computational Linguistics.

Jiwei Li, Michel Galley, Chris Brockett, Georgios Spithourakis, Jianfeng Gao, and Bill Dolan. 2016. A persona-based neural conversation model. In *Proceedings of the 54th Annual Meeting of the Association for Computational Linguistics (Volume 1: Long Papers)*, pages 994–1003, Berlin, Germany. Association for Computational Linguistics.

Juncen Li, Robin Jia, He He, and Percy Liang. 2018. Delete, retrieve, generate: a simple approach to sentiment and style transfer. In *Proceedings of the 2018 Conference of the North American Chapter of the Association for Computational Linguistics: Human Language Technologies, Volume 1 (Long Papers)*, pages 1865–1874, New Orleans, Louisiana. Association for Computational Linguistics.

Xinyao Ma, Maarten Sap, Hannah Rashkin, and Yejin Choi. 2020. PowerTransformer: Unsupervised controllable revision for biased language correction. In *Proceedings of the 2020 Conference on Empirical Methods in Natural Language Processing (EMNLP)*, pages 7426–7441, Online. Association for Computational Linguistics.

Remi Mir, Bjarke Felbo, Nick Obradovich, and Iyad Rahwan. 2019. Evaluating style transfer for text. In *Proceedings of the 2019 Conference of the North American Chapter of the Association for Computational Linguistics: Human Language Technologies, Volume 1 (Long and Short Papers)*, pages 495–504, Minneapolis, Minnesota. Association for Computational Linguistics.

Yvette Oortwijn, Thijs Ossenkoppele, and Arianna Betti. 2021. Interrater disagreement resolution: A systematic procedure to reach consensus in annotation tasks. In *Proceedings of the Workshop on Human Evaluation of NLP Systems (HumEval)*, pages 131–141, Online. Association for Computational Linguistics.

Richard Yuanzhe Pang and Kevin Gimpel. 2019. Unsupervised evaluation metrics and learning criteria for non-parallel textual transfer. In *NGT@EMNLP-IJCNLP*.

Ellie Pavlick and Joel Tetreault. 2016. An empirical analysis of formality in online communication. *Transactions of the Association for Computational Linguistics*, 4:61–74.

Reid Pryzant, Richard Diehl Martinez, Nathan Dass, Sadao Kurohashi, Dan Jurafsky, and Diyi Yang. 2020. Automatically neutralizing subjective bias in text. *Proceedings of the AAAI Conference on Artificial Intelligence*, 34(01):480–489.

Sudha Rao and Joel Tetreault. 2018. Dear sir or madam, may I introduce the GYAFC dataset: Corpus, benchmarks and metrics for formality style transfer. In *Proceedings of the 2018 Conference of the North American Chapter of the Association for Computational Linguistics: Human Language Technologies, Volume 1 (Long Papers)*, pages 129–140, New Orleans, Louisiana. Association for Computational Linguistics.

Stephanie Schoch, Diyi Yang, and Yangfeng Ji. 2020. "This is a problem, don't you agree?" framing and bias in human evaluation for natural language generation. In *Proceedings of the 1st Workshop on Evaluating NLG Evaluation*, pages 10–16, Online (Dublin, Ireland). Association for Computational Linguistics.

Tianxiao Shen, Tao Lei, Regina Barzilay, and Tommi Jaakkola. 2017. Style transfer from non-parallel text by cross-alignment. In *Proceedings of the 31st International Conference on Neural Information Processing Systems*, NIPS'17, page 6833–6844, Red Hook, NY, USA. Curran Associates Inc.

Anastasia Shimorina and Anya Belz. 2021. The human evaluation datasheet 1.0: A template for recording details of human evaluation experiments in nlp. *arXiv preprint arXiv:2103.09710*.

Boaz Shmueli, Jan Fell, Soumya Ray, and Lun-Wei Ku. 2021. Beyond fair pay: Ethical implications of nlp crowdsourcing. *arXiv preprint arXiv:2104.10097*.

Punardeep Sikka, Manmeet Singh, Allen Pink, and Vijay Mago. 2020. A survey on text simplification. *arXiv preprint arXiv:2008.08612*.

Neil Stewart, Gordon D. A. Brown, and Nick Chater. 2005. Absolute identification by relative judgment. *Psychological Review*, 112(4):881–911.

Jennifer Wortman Vaughan. 2018. Making better use of the crowd: How crowdsourcing can advance machine learning research. *Journal of Machine Learning Research*, 18(193):1–46.

Wei Xu, Courtney Napoles, Ellie Pavlick, Quanze Chen, and Chris Callison-Burch. 2016. Optimizing statistical machine translation for text simplification. *Transactions of the Association for Computational Linguistics*, 4:401–415.

GOT: Testing for Originality in Natural Language Generation

Jennifer Brooks
Department of Computer Science
The George Washington University
Washington, DC
jtbrooks@gwu.edu

Abdou Youssef
Department of Computer Science
The George Washington University
Washington, DC
ayoussef@gwu.edu

Abstract

We propose an approach to automatically test for originality in generation tasks where no standard automatic measures exist. Our proposal addresses original uses of language, not necessarily original ideas. We provide an algorithm for our approach and a run-time analysis. The algorithm, which finds all of the original fragments in a ground-truth corpus and can reveal whether a generated fragment copies an original without attribution, has a run-time complexity of $\theta(n \log n)$ where n is the number of sentences in the ground truth.

1 Introduction

This research addresses an ethical consideration for Natural Language Generation, namely, plagiarism. The Oxford English Dictionary defines *original* (adjective) as "present or existing from the beginning; first or earliest" and "created directly and personally by a particular artist; not a copy or imitation". But, if we apply the definitions of "original" to *language*, then there are two ways in which a piece of generated text may be original. For one, the text may express an "original idea", such as Einstein did in 1905 with "$E = mc^2$". On the other hand, a non-original idea may be expressed in an original way, via, for example, figurative language. Our proposed approach addresses original uses of language. It does not necessarily address original ideas.

How do we protect intellectual property when it comes to language generators that are trained on a world-wide-web of data? Our language generators have to be held accountable. They should also be protected. What if a language generator generates an original analogy? What if it writes a poem that is so great that it ends up in the history books? Multiple language generators may be trained on the same ground truth (e.g., Wikipedia) with the same embedding vectors (e.g., BERT (Devlin et al., 2018) and GPT (Vaswani et al., 2017; Radford et al., 2018)) and the same technologies (deep neural networks, LSTM cells (Hochreiter and Schmidhuber, 1997), transformers (Vaswani et al., 2017)). It will become a question of "Whose generator said it first?" With automatic language generation, we need a way to automatically measure, store, and reference original ideas and language. We propose one possible solution to these originality-related problems.

For the purposes of our analyses, we define *ground truth* as the set of sentences that are compared with the generated sentences. The ground truth may be larger than the training set, but should include the training set. The gound truth would also, ideally, grow. For example, the ground truth could start out as the training set, but as new sentences are generated with a trained model, then the new sentences may be added to the ground truth. We also claim that generated sentences should only be added to the ground truth if they are original or include citations where appropriate.

2 Background

Our criteria and basis for evaluating measurements of originality are:

1. Can we tell whether a generated sentence is an original use of language?

2. Can we tell whether the sentence contains a fragment from the ground truth that is a candidate for protection as intellectual property?

Therefore, when measuring generation originality by comparing the generated sentence with the sentences in the ground truth, then the answers to numbers 1 and 2 above are binary. Either the generated sentence is an original use of language or it is not. Either the generation is at risk of plagiarism or

Proceedings of the 1st Workshop on Natural Language Generation, Evaluation, and Metrics (GEM 2021), pages 68–72
August 5–6, 2021. ©2021 Association for Computational Linguistics

it is not. However, if we consider that the ground truth may not be representative of all the sentences that have ever been generated, then there is a measure of uncertainty that may be added to the binary outcome.

There are no standard automatic measures for novelty and originality in stylized language generation (Mou and Vechtomova, 2020). High perplexity (PPL) and a low BLEU (Papineni et al., 2002) score may suggest novelty, but they are not sufficient for testing for originality. High PPL and a low BLEU score may be achieved when there is little overlap between the generated language and the ground truth, but nonesense and off-topic sentences are rewarded. While nonesense sentences may be novel, they may be grammatically incorrect, and sentences that are grammatically correct will likely have some overlap with fragments (n-grams) in the ground truth, such as using phrases like "she said that". So, we want a generation originality test that doesn't penalize n-gram overlap. (An original use of language may combine common n-grams in a new way.) We also want a generation originality test that flags potential plagiarism of original fragments in the ground truth, which neither BLEU nor PPL does.

We propose a generation originality test (GOT) that addresses original uses of language. It does not necessarily address original ideas. GOT is equally appropriate for stylized text generation, where novelty is desirable, and for other generation tasks where there is not an imposed style but the generation is open-ended, including summarization tasks.

3 Proposed Approach

Our proposed generation originality test (GOT) determines whether:

1. any fragment in a generated sentence equals an "original" fragment in the ground truth, in which case the generation may be in violation of a copyright law, if no citation of the original source is included; or,

2. the generated sentence is "original", per Definition 1, below.

Definition 1 (Original Sentence). *A sentence, whether generated or in the ground truth, of n tokens is original if there exists an original k-gram within the sentence for some k≤n. The originality of k-grams is defined next.*

The definition of originality of a fragment (or k-gram) depends on whether we are referring to a generated fragment or to a fragment in the ground truth. Generated fragments are tested against the ground truth. If the generated fragment does not appear in the ground truth, then the generated fragment is considered original. If it appears once in the ground truth, then it is considered not original and so a citation may be needed. See Table 1 for a summary of the criterion for each type of fragment to be true. In Table 1, C equals the number of times that fragment appears in the ground truth.

	Type	**Criterion**
Ground Truth Fragment	Original	$C = 1$
	Not Original	$C \geq 2$
Generated Fragment	Original	$C = 0$
	Not Original, Citation Needed	$C = 1$
	Not Original, No Citation Needed	$C \geq 2$

Table 1: Criterion per fragment type, where C is the number of times the fragment appears in the ground truth. Note, C is always with respect to counts in the ground truth, even when evaluating generated fragments.

Ground-truth fragments that appear once and only once in the ground truth are considered original.[1] Likewise, fragments that appear more than once in the ground truth are considered "not original". For example, "lengthened shadow" appeared twice in our ground truth and so it is not considered an original phrase in the ground truth. Combining non-original fragments to generate a new idea or analogy, however, could be considered an original use of language. For example, "the writer is the lengthened shadow of a man" contains the fragments "the writer is" and "the lengthened shadow" and "of a man" which are not original fragments in our ground truth. However, the way in which they are combined in this example creates an original use of language – in this case, a metaphor. (Examples of fragments that appeared many times in our

[1]For simplicity of explanation, we qualify a fragment as "original", and therefore a candidate for protection of intellectual property, if it appears "once and only once" in the ground truth. However, with very large datasets, it may be necessary to relax the criteria from "once and only once" to a relatively small number of occurrences, in order to consider a fragment a candidate for protection of intellectual property.

training set are "it is" and "human life".)

Here is one possible use of GOT. If a generated sentence contains a fragment that appears once and only once in the ground truth (after duplicate sentences are removed from the ground truth), then the generated sentence may be discarded because it contains a fragment from the ground truth that is a candidate for protection as intellectual property. In other words, the sentence may be in violation of a copyright law. Otherwise, the sentence could include a citation of the source for the original fragment.

The definition of ground-truth original fragments actually calls for more nuance, which we will elaborate and explain how to compute next. We maintain a count per fragment that is incremented each time the fragment appears in a new sentence in a new document or by a different author (if the author can be determined in both instances) in the ground truth. In other words, if a fragment in the ground truth is repeated in the same document, or by the same author across documents, then the count for that fragment is incremented only once. (Therefore, an author, if known, should also be stored for each fragment, at least until the count for that fragment is greater than 1. When the count for a fragment is greater than 1, then it has already been determined that the fragment was seen a second time in a different document by a different known, or unknown, author.) The count for a fragment will be 1 if it occurs just once in the ground truth, or if all of its occurrences are in the same document or by the same author; otherwise, the count will be greater than 1. Now, a ground-truth fragment is said to be original if and only if its count is 1.

See Algorithm 1 for psuedo-code to test for originality and find all original fragements in a dataset.

To examine fragments, we use a window length of wl varying between 2 and the sentence length, where wl is the number of words in the fragment. If the first or last word in the window is a determinant (e.g., 'a' or 'the'), any use of the verbs *to be* and *to have* ('is', 'are', 'am', 'was', 'were', 'has', 'had', 'have'), punctuation mark, or preposition/subordinating conjunction (e.g., 'to', 'of', or 'from'), the window is moved one step to the right. (Shortening the window to get rid of the determinant, special verb, special character, or preposition would result in a window size already covered in the previous step.) All words and characters are allowed in the other positions of the window, so, for example, a comma or preposition may appear in the middle of a window of size 3 or more.

3.1 Runtime Complexity

The following complexity analysis is with respect to Algorithm 1. We are representing F and O with balanced binary search trees (e.g., red-black tree (Guibas and Sedgewick, 1978; OKASAKI, 1999)) where the comparator is lexicographic ordering. Searching, insertion and deletion in such trees take $\theta(\log n)$ comparisons. Since the length of fragments is assumed to be constant on average, then each comparison takes constant time, implying that each search/insert/delete operation in O and F take $\theta(\log n)$ time.

Given our representation of F and O with balanced binary search trees, consider the following time complexity analysis:

- Let n = number of sentences in the dataset. The first for-loop (line 1) iterates n times.
- Let c = the average length (i.e., number of tokens) of a sentence in our ground truth. We found that $c = 25$, a fairly small constant. Therefore, the two for-loops in Steps 4 and 5 iterate on average a constant number of times.
- The binary search in F (line 10) has a runtime complexity of $\theta(\log n)$.
- Depending on the result of the binary search of F (line 10) there may be an insertion to F (line 14) which has a runtime complexity of $\theta(\log n)$.
- Then the number of calculations in lines 1-20 is the following function of n: $2c^2 n \log n$.
- The code segment of lines 21-26 takes $\theta(n)$ time because the number of wl-token fragments in the ground truth dataset (of n sentences where each sentence consists of c tokens on average) is at most cn.
- Therefore, the runtime complexity is: $\theta(n \log n)$.

This algorithm would be executed before generation tasks, but may also be executed whenever the

[2] If the first or last word in the window is a determinant (e.g., 'a' or 'the'), special verb ('is', 'are', 'am', 'was', 'were', 'has', 'had', 'have'), punctuation mark, or preposition/subordinating conjunction (e.g., 'to', 'of', or 'from'), the window is moved one step to the right.

Algorithm 1 Find Original Fragments in the Ground Truth

```
Require: Input S, the sentences in the ground truth to evaluate
Require: Input F, list of fragments already discovered, may be empty set;
Require: Input CountPerFrag(f), for all f ∈ 𝓕
Require: O, list of original fragments                    ▷ Count per o ∈ 𝓞 should always be 1
 1: for each s ∈ 𝓢 do
 2:     l = number of tokens in sentence s
 3:     sentParts = set of tokens in s
 4:     for each wl in range 2 to l do                     ▷ wl = length of window
 5:         for each i in range 0 to l − wl + 1 do         ▷ assume zero-based indexing
 6:             if sentParts[i] or sentParts[i + wl − 1] = special token[2] then
 7:                 Continue to next i
 8:             else
 9:                 frag = sentParts[i : i + wl]
10:                 if frag ∈ 𝓕 then                       ▷ binary search of F
11:                     CountPerFrag[frag] = CountPerFrag[frag] + 1
12:                     Break from for-loop in line 5
13:                 else                                   ▷ frag was not found in F
14:                     Add frag to F
15:                     CountPerFrag[frag] = 1
16:                 end if
17:             end if
18:         end for
19:     end for
20: end for
21: Set O to the empty set;
22: for each frag in F do
23:     if CountPerFrag[frag] == 1 then
24:         Add frag to O;
25:     end if
26: end for
```

reference set changes or is updated (for example, based on generated language).

4 Example: Results on One Application

To see how GOT performed on a generation task, we applied it to a metaphor generator that we built, based on an RNN (Elman, 1990) architecture with LSTM cells (Hochreiter and Schmidhuber, 1997) for training a language model on the language of metaphors, using only metaphors and their topics as input. (A topic was inserted at the beginning of each input sentence.)

The model was trained to predict the next word in the sentences from our ground truth—a set of 22,113 quotes, where each quote contains at least one metaphor and is labeled with a topic. There are 1,684 unique topics (e.g., "animals", "fear", "fishing", "grandparents", "happiness", "motives", "politics", and more examples listed in Table 2) and the dataset is currently available to the public online as part of "Dr. Mardy's Dictionary of Metaphorical Quotations" (Grothe, 2008).

To the trained language model, we apply an inference engine that uses weighted random choice with a "constraining factor" to encourage language coherence and originality in the output, and patterns of metaphors to encourage the generation of grammatically correct metaphors (Brooks and Youssef, 2020). The constraining factor, c (for $c \geq 1$), causes the inference engine to select—with a probability of $\frac{1}{c}$—the most likely word to appear next. Otherwise, and with a probability of $1 - \frac{1}{c}$, the inference engine will make a weighted random selection. Selecting the most likely next word encourages language coherencey in the output, while weighted random selection encourages originality. (We found that a constraining factor of 3 or 4 worked best with our model.)

A generated sentence failed the GOT if a fragment of at least 2 words appeared as an "original" fragment in the training set; that is, if the fragment appeared just once in the ground truth. Using our metaphor generator, we generated 500 metaphors from randomly chosen topics. Applying GOT on each of the 500 generated metaphors, we found that only 32 repeated an "original" fragment from the training set. From this experiment, we conclude that out of the 500 generated metaphors, 468 of them, or just over 93%, can be considered original. (Table 2 provides examples from our metaphor generator on randomly generated topics.)

Topic	Generated Metaphor
tears	The arrested waters shone and danced.
fathers	Expectations are premeditated resentments.
character	Today is the companion of genius.
friends	Assumptions are the termites of relationships.
writers	The writer is the lengthened shadow of a man.
world	This world is the rainbow of us.
truth	The brain is the eden of a star.
innocence	The cure for silence is the salt of speech.
imagination	Success is the only deadline.

Table 2: Examples of Generated Metaphors

5 Conclusion

Our approach to originality testing includes two contributions:

- An automatic test, where no standard existed, for originality in generated language
- An automatic test, where no standard existed, for identifying where generators are in violation of copying an original use of language without attribution

The first contribution tells us whether a generation is an original use of language. The second contribution tells us whether a generation is, at least, not at risk of committing plagiarism. For example, the sentence "A bird built a nest" is not an original use of language; however, it is at least probably not in violation of plagiarism since it does not contain a fragment that is so rare that it should be protected as an original use of language.

References

Jennifer Brooks and Abdou Youssef. 2020. Discriminative pattern mining for natural language metaphor generation. In *Proceedings of the Discriminative Pattern Mining Workshop*.

Jacob Devlin, Ming-Wei Chang, Kenton Lee, and Kristina Toutanova. 2018. BERT: pre-training of deep bidirectional transformers for language understanding. *CoRR*, abs/1810.04805.

Jeffrey L. Elman. 1990. Finding structure in time. *COGNITIVE SCIENCE*, 14(2):179–211.

Mardy Grothe. 2008. *I Never Metaphor I Didn't Like: A Comprehensive Compilation of History's Greatest Analogies, Metaphors, and Similes*. Harper Collins.

Leo J. Guibas and Robert Sedgewick. 1978. A dichromatic framework for balanced trees. In *19th Annual Symposium on Foundations of Computer Science (sfcs 1978)*, pages 8–21.

S. Hochreiter and J. Schmidhuber. 1997. Long short-term memory. *Neural Computation*, 9:1735–1780.

Lili Mou and Olga Vechtomova. 2020. Stylized text generation: Approaches and applications. In *Proceedings of the 58th Annual Meeting of the Association for Computational Linguistics: Tutorial Abstracts*, pages 19–22, Online. Association for Computational Linguistics.

CHRIS OKASAKI. 1999. Red-black trees in a functional setting. *Journal of Functional Programming*, 9(4):471–477.

Kishore Papineni, Salim Roukos, Todd Ward, and Wei jing Zhu. 2002. Bleu: a method for automatic evaluation of machine translation. pages 311–318.

Alec Radford, Karthik Narasimhan, Tim Salimans, and Ilya Sutskever. 2018. Improving language understanding by generative pre-training.

Ashish Vaswani, Noam Shazeer, Niki Parmar, Jakob Uszkoreit, Llion Jones, Aidan N Gomez, Ł ukasz Kaiser, and Illia Polosukhin. 2017. Attention is all you need. In I. Guyon, U. V. Luxburg, S. Bengio, H. Wallach, R. Fergus, S. Vishwanathan, and R. Garnett, editors, *Advances in Neural Information Processing Systems 30*, pages 5998–6008. Curran Associates, Inc.

Evaluating Text Generation from Discourse Representation Structures

Chunliu Wang
CLCG
Univ. of Groningen
chunliu.wang@rug.nl

Rik van Noord
CLCG
Univ. of Groningen
r.i.k.van.noord@rug.nl

Arianna Bisazza
CLCG
Univ. of Groningen
a.bisazza@rug.nl

Johan Bos
CLCG
Univ. of Groningen
johan.bos@rug.nl

Abstract

We present an end-to-end neural approach to generate English sentences from formal meaning representations, Discourse Representation Structures (DRSs). We use a rather standard bi-LSTM sequence-to-sequence model, work with a linearized DRS input representation, and evaluate character-level and word-level decoders. We obtain very encouraging results in terms of reference-based automatic metrics such as BLEU. But because such metrics only evaluate the surface level of generated output, we develop a new metric, ROSE, that targets specific semantic phenomena. We do this with five DRS generation challenge sets focusing on tense, grammatical number, polarity, named entities and quantities. The aim of these challenge sets is to assess the neural generator's systematicity and generalization to unseen inputs.

1 Introduction

Faithfully generating text from structured representations is an important task in NLP. Common tasks include generations from tables (Parikh et al., 2020), knowledge graphs (Gardent et al., 2017) and meaning representations (Horvat et al., 2015; Flanigan et al., 2016; Dušek and Jurčíček, 2019). Recently, many research efforts have focused on the graph-based semantic formalism Abstract Meaning Representation (AMR, Banarescu et al., 2013), with approaches based on machine translation (Pourdamghani et al., 2016; Konstas et al., 2017), specialized graph encoders (Song et al., 2018; Zhu et al., 2019; Cai and Lam, 2020; Zhao et al., 2020; Jin and Gildea, 2020) and pre-trained language models (Mager et al., 2020; Ribeiro et al., 2020).

However, far less attention has been given to generating text from formal meaning representation, such as Discourse Representation Structures (DRSs). DRSs are proposed in Discourse Representation Theory (Kamp and Reyle, 1993; Kadmon, 2001; Geurts et al., 2020), a well-studied semantic formalism, covering a wide range of linguistic phenomena. Differently from AMR, DRSs explicitly model scope, tense and definiteness. The lack of this information makes AMR-to-text challenging (Wang et al., 2020), but their inclusion presents a challenge for the generation methods as well, as they, for example, have to deal with a lot more variables in the representation (van Noord et al., 2018a). Another difference with AMR is that DRSs are in principle language neutral (at least the version of DRS that we use in this paper), with gold standard annotations publicly available in four languages (Abzianidze et al., 2017). For these reasons, developing portable and high-quality generation systems for DRSs is a promising research direction.

While there has been some initial work on DRS-to-text generation (Basile and Bos, 2011; Narayan and Gardent, 2014; Basile, 2015), most DRS-based work has focused on semantic parsing, that is mapping text to DRS (Liu et al., 2018; van Noord et al., 2018b, 2019; Liu et al., 2019b; Evang, 2019; van Noord et al., 2020; Fancellu et al., 2020). Our work has two main contributions. The first is on the modelling side, as we take the first step in DRS-to-text generation with neural networks.[1] Specifically, we use a bi-LSTM sequence-to-sequence model that processes linearized DRSs representations and produces English texts using a character-level decoder (see pipeline in Figure 1).

Our second contribution regards the evaluation of the produced text. Given the known limitations of reference-based automatic metrics for natural language generation (Reiter and Belz, 2009; Novikova et al., 2017a) and in particular for AMR-to-text (May and Priyadarshi, 2017; Manning et al., 2020), we design five DRS-specific challenge sets (Popović and Castilho, 2019) and use them to per-

[1]Concurrently to this work, Liu et al. (2021) published a DRS-to-text model that is based on tree-LSTMs.

Proceedings of the 1st Workshop on Natural Language Generation, Evaluation, and Metrics (GEM 2021), pages 73–83

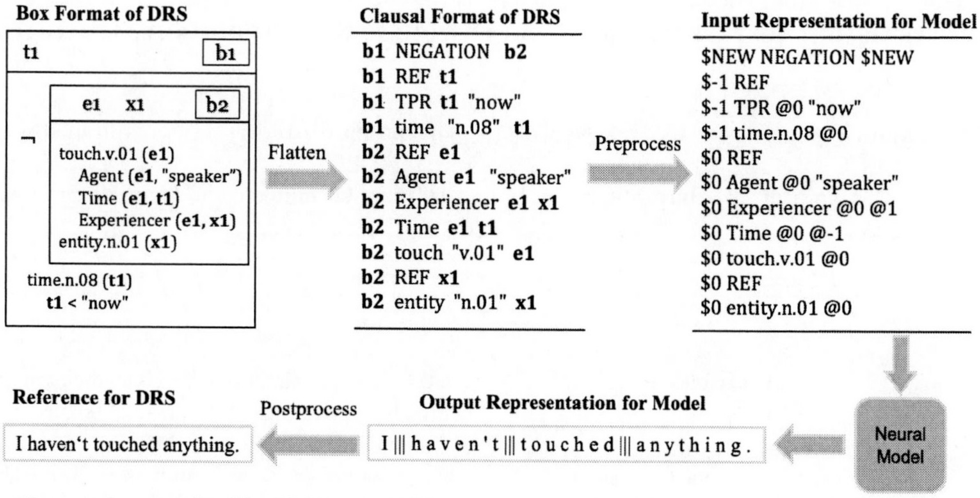

Figure 1: An example of the DRS data and a corresponding reference text with their processing procedures.

form a fine-grained manual evaluation. The general goal of these challenge sets is to assess the robustness of a DRS generator with respect to a number of linguistic phenomena. More specifically, we assess (i) generation systematicity with respect to three semantic phenomena (tense change, polarity change, singular↔plural switch), and (ii) generalization to unseen input literals (named entities and quantities). The idea is that by changing the meaning of a DRS in a controlled way, robustness of systems can be monitored in detail and assessed accordingly. Besides assessing the quality of a generator, these challenge sets also showcase the ease to which DRSs can be manipulated to express novel meaning combinations. All challenge sets are publicly available.[2]

2 Data and Methodology

In this section we describe the data and methodology we use for DRS generation. First we explain and motivate our representation of DRSs (input to the NLG system) and the generated text (see Figure 1 for a full overview of our source and target representations). Then we provide details of our NLG system, which is based on a recurrent neural network, and show how it is trained.

2.1 Input/Source Representation: DRSs

Discourse Representation Structures model the meaning of an entire text, ranging from isolated sentences to entire documents. A large repertoire of semantic phenomena is covered by DRSs, including quantification, negation, pronouns, comparatives, discourse relations, and presupposition. There are several variants of DRS; we use the fully interpretable version as employed in the Parallel Meaning Bank (Abzianidze et al., 2017), where concepts (triggered by nouns, verbs, adjectives and adverbs) are represented by WordNet synsets (Fellbaum, 1998), and semantic relations by Verbnet roles (Kipper et al., 2008).

DRS can be represented in box format or clause format (see Figure 1), where the letters *x*, *e*, *s*, and *t* are used for discourse referents denoting individuals, events, states, and time, respectively, and *b* is used for variables denoting DRSs. The clause format is a flat version of the standard box format, which represents DRS as a set of clauses. Due to its simple and flat structure, it has proven to be more suitable for machine learning tasks (van Noord et al., 2018a). The variables that occur in a DRS are rewritten using the relative naming method based on de Bruijn-indexing (Bruijn, de, 1972)).

We mostly follow van Noord et al. (2018b) in how to represent DRSs for neural processing, but make some important improvements. The idea is to represent meaningful units as atomic entites. These include the variable indices (`$0`, `@1`), the DRS operators (`REF`, `NOT`), the semantic relations (e.g., `Agent`, `Patient`, `Theme`), the deictic constants (`now`, `speaker`, `hearer`), and the concepts (e.g., `touch.v.01`).

The latter is a notable exception to van Noord et al. (2018b). By representing concepts, that correspond to WordNet-synsets, as single entities,

[2]`https://github.com/wangchunliu/DRS-generation`

we make sure that each concept is mapped to a language-independent embedding, even though its surface form may resemble the corresponding English word. This prevents the model from learning to predict target words (e.g., `touch`) by copying (part of) the characters that compose the Wordnet-synset (e.g., `touch.v.01`) in the input DRS.

The remaining parts of the DRSs are represented at the character-level. These include time/date expressions (e.g., `" 1 9 6 8 "`), value expressions such as scores (e.g., `" 2 - 0 "`), quantities (e.g., `" 2 6 0 0 "`), and proper names (e.g., `" b r a d ~ p i t t "`). They are all enclosed in quotation marks in the DRS representation. It would not make sense to represent these entities as words because times, dates, and quantities are clearly of compositional nature. Names are literal expressions, and therefore also are best represented by separate characters. Moreover, this representation reduces the size of the vocabulary, which in turn could reduce the learning difficulty of the model.

2.2 Output/Target Representation: Text

The spectrum to represent text ranges from single characters on one end till (tokenised) words or multi-word expressions on the other end, and there are many possibilities in between too, for instance using byte-pair encodings to combine characters into sub-words. As our aim is to get a relatively straightforward baseline NLG system, rather than exploring the full range of text representation possibilities, we considered just two ways to represent text: character-based, where raw characters are separate entities and spaces are indicated by a special symbol (three vertical bars); or (tokenised) word-based, where tokenised words form the basic entities. The character-based approach has the advantage that post-processing is straightforward. The use of word-level representations is the classical approach in natural language processing, but requires a de-tokenisation step after generating. Tokenisation and de-tokenisation is carried out with the Moses tokenizer (Koehn et al., 2007).

2.3 Neural Generation Model

We use a standard recurrent encoder-decoder architecture with attention as implemented in the Marian toolkit (Junczys-Dowmunt et al., 2018), using two bi-directional LSTM layers (Hochreiter and Schmidhuber, 1997). In particular, we use an embedding size of 300 for both the encoder and

Parameter	Value	Parameter	Value
dim-emb	300	dim-rnn	300
dec-cell	lstm	enc-depth	2
enc-cell	lstm	dec-depth	2
mini-batch	48	lr-decay	0.5
lr-decay-strategy	epoch	normalize	0.9
beam-size	10	learn-rate	0.002
dropout-rnn	0.2	cost-type	ce-mean
label-smoothing	0.1	optim	adam
early-stop	3	valid-metric	cross-entropy

Table 1: Hyperparameter settings of our experiments.

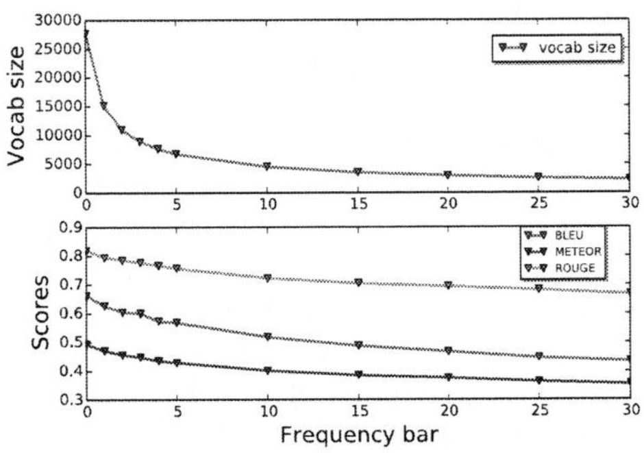

Figure 2: The correlation between the vocabulary size and the frequency threshold, along with the correlation between metric scores and the frequency threshold. Threshold set to 0 means using the full vocabulary.

decoder, a mini-batch size of 48 and the Adam optimizer (Kingma and Ba, 2015) with a learning rate of 0.002. All hyper-parameters are shown in Table1. We use the English gold standard training, dev and test data of PMB 3.0.0[3], containing 6,620, 885 and 898 instances, respectively. During training, we merge the gold standard with the only partially manually annotated silver standard of 97,598 instances. Differently from van Noord et al. (2018b), we do not fine-tune on the gold standard data in a second step, as this did not lead to improved performance.

Vocabulary For a word-level model, it can be beneficial to not include the full vocabulary. For example, it might learn to handle unknown words better if it was exposed to unknown word tokens during training. We experimented with the vocabulary size of the target representation on the development set, as is shown in Figure 2. We find that the we get best performance when including the full vocabulary, with decreasing performance as we decrease the vocabulary. We use this setting for our word-level experiments.

[3]https://pmb.let.rug.nl/data.php

3 Semantic Challenge Sets

Challenge sets are often used in Machine Translation to assess a model's ability to systematically deal with specific linguistic phenomena that may be infrequent in standard test sets (Popović and Castilho, 2019). Following this practice, we created five challenge sets for DRSs generation that focus on various semantic phenomena (see Table 2 and Figure 3). The variations are obtained by (manually) applying a minimal modification to a DRS and editing the corresponding text accordingly.

The resulting semantic challenge sets can be viewed as stress tests: if the generator performs well on these test suites it shows that it can deal with specific semantic phenomena adequately in unforeseen circumstances. We carry out these modifications on subsets of the PMB test data, and we group them into those that assess *systematic predictions* (tense, polarity, and grammatical number) and those that assess *generalisation to unseen input* (names and quantities). The specific challenge sets are described in detail below.

Original	Tom has three thousand books.
Tense	Tom had three thousand books.
Polarity	Tom does not have three thousand books.
Number	Tom has one book.
Names	Kirk has three thousand books.
Quantity	Tom has 3,200 books.

Table 2: Examples of how the challenge set DRSs are created. We show the reference texts of the modified DRSs here.

3.1 Tense Change

In English, tense is expressed by morphology and the use of auxiliary verbs. It is therefore a challenging phenomenon for NLG. There are three types of tense found in the DRSs of the Parallel Meaning Bank: past ($t < now$), present ($t = now$), and future tense ($t > now$). Aspect is not covered in detail in the Parallel Meaning Bank, and therefore we won't address it in the paper and as a result it won't be part of the current semantic challenge sets.

For creating the challenge set, we used the following procedure. For the first 200 examples in the test set that contained information about tense in their corresponding DRSs, we changed the tense in the DRS: past to present or future, present to past or future, and future to past or present. The corresponding text was changed to reflect the change in tense. Example: She bought a vacuum cleaner at the supermarket. → She will buy a vacuum cleaner at the supermarket.

3.2 Polarity Change

As negation plays a crucial role to determine the truth conditions of a sentence, there has been ample interest in recognizing negation in text (Morante and Blanco, 2012; Basile et al., 2012) and translating accurately (Sennrich, 2017; Tang, 2020). Here we focus on generation, that is expressing negation appropriately in a sentence given a meaning representation. Negation is expressed in a DRS with a unary operator, introducing an embedded DRS. For the first 100 instances of the test set we removed negation if it was already present, or, more frequently, added it if it was not. Again, the corresponding reference text was changed to reflect this change in meaning. Example: I cooked dinner. → I didn't cook dinner.

3.3 Grammatical Number Change

Concrete quantities are expressed in DRSs with the relation `Quantity` and a number. For the first 100 examples that permitted this, we changed the quantity from a number greater than one to one, or vice versa. This set can be used to check whether the model can recognize the number and generate the correct plural form of nouns to get the correct noun phrase (Sennrich, 2017). Example: It currently employs 180 people. → It currently employs one person. As many languages (including English) have a different surface realisation for singular and plural, an NLG system needs to handle this correctly.

3.4 Names Change

The goal of this challenge set is to assess the behaviour of NLG systems that find unexpected (not seen in training data) proper names in the meaning representation input. We took the first 50 instances of the test set with named entities (persons, locations, organisations, artifacts) and modified the DRSs in such a way that the names entities are replaced by alternative, but realistic names of the same type of entity and gender (in case of persons), that do not occur in the training data. Consider a sentence with the name "Howard Caine", with `Name(x, howard~caine)` in its corresponding DRS. We change this into a real name outside the coverage of the training data, e.g., `Name(x, howard~carpendale)`. This should generate

DRS: Original

```
b1 REF x1
b1 Name x1 "tom"
b1 PRESUPPOSITION b2
b1 male "n.02" x1
b2 REF e1
b2 REF t1
b2 EQU t1 "now"
b2 Pivot e1 x1
b2 Theme e1 x2
b2 Time e1 t1
b2 have "v.04" e1
b2 time "n.08" t1
b2 REF x2
b2 Quantity x2 "3000"
b2 book "n.02" x2
```

Reference: Tom has three thousand books.

DRS: Tense change

```
b1 REF x1
b1 Name x1 "tom"
b1 PRESUPPOSITION b2
b1 male "n.02" x1
b2 REF e1
b2 REF t1
b2 TPR t1 "now"
b2 Pivot e1 x1
b2 Theme e1 x2
b2 Time e1 t1
b2 have "v.04" e1
b2 time "n.08" t1
b2 REF x2
b2 Quantity x2 "3000"
b2 book "n.02" x2
```

Reference: Tom had three thousand books.

DRS: Polarity change

```
b1 REF x1
b1 Name x1 "tom"
b1 PRESUPPOSITION b2
b1 male "n.02" x1
b2 REF e1
b2 REF t1
b2 EQU t1 "now"
b2 NEGATION b3
b3 REF e1
b3 Pivot e1 x1
b3 Theme e1 x2
b3 Time e1 t1
b3 have "v.04" e1
b3 REF x2
b3 Quantity x2 "3000"
b3 book "n.02" x2
```

Reference: Tom does not have three thousand books..

DRS: Number change

```
b1 REF x1
b1 Name x1 "tom"
b1 PRESUPPOSITION b2
b1 male "n.02" x1
b2 REF e1
b2 REF t1
b2 EQU t1 "now"
b2 Pivot e1 x1
b2 Theme e1 x2
b2 Time e1 t1
b2 have "v.04" e1
b2 time "n.08" t1
b2 REF x2
b2 Quantity x2 "1"
b2 book "n.02" x2
```

Reference: Tom has one book.

DRS: Name change

```
b1 REF x1
b1 Name x1 "kirk"
b1 PRESUPPOSITION b2
b1 male "n.02" x1
b2 REF e1
b2 REF t1
b2 EQU t1 "now"
b2 Pivot e1 x1
b2 Theme e1 x2
b2 Time e1 t1
b2 have "v.04" e1
b2 time "n.08" t1
b2 REF x2
b2 Quantity x2 "3000"
b2 book "n.02" x2
```

Reference: Kirk has three thousand books.

DRS: Quantity change

```
b1 REF x1
b1 Name x1 "tom"
b1 PRESUPPOSITION b2
b1 male "n.02" x1
b2 REF e1
b2 REF t1
b2 EQU t1 "now"
b2 Pivot e1 x1
b2 Theme e1 x2
b2 Time e1 t1
b2 have "v.04" e1
b2 time "n.08" t1
b2 REF x2
b2 Quantity x2 "3200"
b2 book "n.02" x2
```

Reference: Tom has 3,200 books.

Figure 3: Examples of how the challenge set DRSs are created. Modified DRSs correspond to Table 2.

"Howard Carpendale", for which word-based systems would be expected to face more difficulties than character-based systems.

3.5 Quantities Change

In addition to named entities in meaning representation, the numeral expressions can also be changed to expressions that were never seen in the training data. We took the first 50 instances of the test set with numbers and then changed the numbers in the DRS representation to unknown quantity expressions, represented as a sequence of characters. For example, we changed `Quantity(x, 150)` to `Quantity(x, 152)`. This way, we test if the model can systematically generalize to generate the right numeral expression, even though it has not seen this particular sequence of characters before.

4 Assessment Methods

We consider two types of assessment for the generated English sentences. Our point of departure are the well-known automatic metrics based on word overlap. We complement these with manual metrics carried out by human experts.

4.1 Standard Automatic Metrics

We use three standard metrics measuring word-overlap between system output and references. They are BLEU (Papineni et al., 2002) used as standard in machine translation evaluation and very common in NLG, METEOR (Lavie and Agarwal, 2007), and ROUGE-L (Lin, 2004), which were applied in the COCO caption generation challenge as well as other NLG experiments (Novikova et al., 2017b; Dušek et al., 2020). As is well known, these standard metrics give a first, rough impression about the quality of the generated output, but often reveal only part of the story. This is why we also consider a further form of assessment.

4.2 Expert Assessment

Inspired by work of Jagfeld et al. (2018) and Belz et al. (2020), we believe that the manual evaluation method for our task should be simple in definition,

	BLEU	METEOR	ROUGE
Char-level (raw)	69.3	51.8	84.9
Word-level (tok)	64.7	47.8	81.8

Table 3: Performance of English DRS-to-text with two output representations, averaged over three runs.

easy to reproduce and high in generalization ability. The output of our NLG system was manually assessed by one expert. This was carried out by assigning three binary dimensions (either 0 or 1) to each generated text: (1) semantics; (2) grammaticality, and (3) phenomenon. As shown in Table 5: the first dimension, *semantics*, gets a score 1 if the meaning of the output reflects that of the underlying meaning representation, and 0 otherwise. The second dimension, *grammaticality*, receives a score 1 if the sentence is grammatical and free of spelling mistakes (but possibly gibberish), and 0 otherwise. The third dimension, *phenomenon*, gets a 1 if the phenomenon of control is generated at all, and 0 otherwise. We summarise these three dimensions into one score by taking the product of these numbers, and refer to this score as ROSE (Robust Overall Semantic Evaluation). Hence, a ROSE-score of 1 is given to output that is perfect (three ones); a ROSE-score of 0 is given if one of the three scores yields zero. Note that, usually, if the score for *phenomenon* is 0, then it follows that the score for *semantics* is 0, too.

5 Results and Analysis

Table 3 shows the performance of the models based on characters and words. The character-level model clearly outperforms the model based on word-tokenised text on all three automatic metric scores. This is in line with work on DRS parsing (van Noord et al., 2018b, 2019; Liu et al., 2019a) and other NLG tasks (Goyal et al., 2016; Agarwal and Dymetman, 2017; Jagfeld et al., 2018), where character-based models outperform word-based models. We will use the character-level model for the rest of the experiments in this paper.

5.1 Challenge Sets

Table 4 shows the overall results on the challenge sets for both the automatic evaluation results and manual evaluation. We can see that performance is hardly affected for the number, quantity and names challenge sets on the automatic evaluation metrics. It seems that our character-based model can indeed learn the shallow information contained in the input data and copy it to generate, even if these subsets (numbers, quantities and name entities) in the DRSs do not appear in the training set. However, for tense and polarity, all three automatic metrics are significantly lower in the challenge sentences than in the original sentences. Through the observation of the generated texts of the tense challenge set, we find that it is difficult for the model to generate future tense sentences, but past tense and present tense can be generated well. The original test set contained not so many DRSs in future tense, but in the challenge set we added relatively many of them, which likely caused the lower performance on the challenge set.

With regards to the polarity challenge set, inspection of the output shows that a common error is to confuse “never” with “not”. This difference in meaning is reflected in a DRS by the relative order of the reference time and the DRS negation operator. Interestingly, recent work in machine translation (Tang, 2020) and language modelling (Ettinger, 2020) has also shown that state-of-the-art neural models still struggle with handling negation.

Although the results of the automatic evaluation metrics in the last three challenge sets have no obvious changes compared with the original data sets, our manual evaluation results show that the performance of the model in all challenge sets is lower than the original data sets. This further shows that there is not always a positive correlation between automatic evaluation and manual evaluation, and it is still necessary to rely on manual evaluation.

5.2 Error Analysis

Table 5 shows a number of interesting outputs of our DRS-to-text model. Sometimes, the model outputs a combination of characters that is clearly wrong, such as in (a), though it still captured the phenomenon that the challenge set checks for (tense). Sentence (b) is a common mistake for the polarity challenge set: the model generates a negation in a grammatical way, but it is not the correct one. In (c) we show a mistake that occurs for the tense challenge set, in which the model was not able to capture the correct tense. Sentence (d) shows that the model sometimes has trouble with longer character-level sequences of numbers. Perhaps the model learned that the sequence "1 5" is generated as “fifteen” as text, which in this case resulted in the wrong output. In (e), the model

	#	BLEU Orig	BLEU Chal	METEOR Orig	METEOR Chal	ROUGE Orig	ROUGE Chal	Sem. Orig	Sem. Chal	Gram. Orig	Gram. Chal	Phen. Orig	Phen. Chal	ROSE Orig	ROSE Chal
Tense	200	68.4	55.8	50.9	44.8	85.0	76.1	80.0	71.0	92.0	87.5	99.5	86.5	78.0	64.0
Polarity	100	68.1	37.4	50.8	37.9	85.0	66.1	80.0	52.0	96.0	81.0	100.0	99.0	78.0	49.0
Number	100	72.5	69.2	53.7	53.4	85.7	86.4	80.0	79.0	95.0	84.0	100.0	95.0	77.0	69.0
Names	50	69.1	71.9	53.0	53.5	87.2	87.8	82.0	76.0	94.0	84.0	100.0	98.0	82.0	74.0
Quantity	50	69.7	68.0	56.4	50.6	86.0	83.4	88.0	72.0	98.0	90.0	92.0	84.0	86.0	70.0

Table 4: Performance of the character-level model for five different challenge sets. We report scores on both the original input (Orig) of the challenge sets and the actual challenge sets (Chal). The first three scores are automatic metrics, while the last four scores are accuracies based on human evaluation (see Section 4.2). **Sem.**, **Gram.**, and **Phen.** stand for *Semantics*, *Grammaticality* and *Phenomenon*, respectively.

	Reference text	Generated text	Sem.	Gram.	Phen.	ROSE
(a)	She liked short skirts.	She liked short tomical.	0	0	1	0
(b)	Tom does not have three thousand books.	Tom never has three thousand books.	0	1	1	0
(c)	The small skirt will be pink.	The small skirt was pink.	0	1	0	0
(d)	He left 157 minutes ago.	He left fifteen minutes ago.	0	1	0	0
(e)	I checked it nine times.	I checked it nine.	0	0	1	0
(f)	We are painting the house green.	I paint the house green.	1	1	1	1
(g)	That hat cost around fifty dollars.	This hat cost about 50 dollars.	1	1	1	1
(h)	When I painted this picture, I was 23 years old.	I painted the picture when I was twenty-three years old.	1	1	1	1

Table 5: Examples of generated texts from the challenge set DRSs, compared with reference texts. Note that the input for the model is a linearized DRS, not the reference text.

managed to capture the phenomenon (quantity), but did this in an non-grammatical way not preserving the meaning. Sentence (f) is interesting, because the DRS representation does not differentiate between "I" and "We", meaning the model can not be expected to (always) output the correct version. Therefore, such differences are not counted as a mistake during human evaluation. Finally, the output of (g) and (h) shows the necessity of human evaluation: the model produced sentences that captured the meaning perfectly, but used a different surface realization than in the reference text.

6 Conclusion and Future Work

We presented an end-to-end neural approach to generate natural language from Discourse Representation Structures. Our model is based on a bi-LSTM sequence-to-sequence architecture taking linearized DRSs as input. Comparing character level with word level for producing text, it achieves higher BLEU, METEOR and ROUGE scores on the former.

For a better understanding of our generator's robustness and its reliability, we designed several challenge sets focusing on specific semantic phenomena (tense, polarity, grammatical number) and types of unseen input (quantity and named entities). Automatic and manual evaluations on these challenge sets point out to negation as the most challenging phenomenon for DRS generation, followed by tense. By contrast, changes in grammatical number and generalizations to unseen quantities or names are well handled by the model.

Altogether, our results suggest that neural generation from DRSs is a very promising research direction, but more work is needed to ensure reliability in real-world applications. We hope that our challenge sets will foster future research on this topic and eventually lead to truly robust DRS generators. The challenge sets, as we have presented them, can be further refined, and other linguistic phenomena can be added as well. Possibilities that spring to mind are challenge sets for pronouns, definite descriptions, comparatives, aspect, and discourse particles. And obviously, we need to generate challenge sets for languages other than English, which might trigger language-specific phenomena as well that could be suitable for challenge sets for DRS generation.

Acknowledgements

This work was funded by the NWO-VICI grant "Lost in Translation—Found in Meaning" (288-89-003). The first author is supported by the China Scholarship Council (CSC201904890008). Arianna Bisazza was partly funded by the Netherlands Organization for Scientific Research (NWO) under project number 639.021.646. The Tesla K40 GPU used in this work was kindly donated to us by the NVIDIA Corporation. We would like to thank the Center for Information Technology of the University of Groningen for their support and for providing access to the Peregrine high performance computing cluster. Finally, we thank the anonymous reviewers for their insightful comments.

References

Lasha Abzianidze, Johannes Bjerva, Kilian Evang, Hessel Haagsma, Rik van Noord, Pierre Ludmann, Duc-Duy Nguyen, and Johan Bos. 2017. The Parallel Meaning Bank: Towards a multilingual corpus of translations annotated with compositional meaning representations. In *Proceedings of the 15th Conference of the European Chapter of the Association for Computational Linguistics: Volume 2, Short Papers*, pages 242–247, Valencia, Spain. Association for Computational Linguistics.

Shubham Agarwal and Marc Dymetman. 2017. A surprisingly effective out-of-the-box char2char model on the e2e nlg challenge dataset. In *SIGDIAL Conference*, pages 158–163.

Laura Banarescu, Claire Bonial, Shu Cai, Madalina Georgescu, Kira Griffitt, Ulf Hermjakob, Kevin Knight, Philipp Koehn, Martha Palmer, and Nathan Schneider. 2013. Abstract Meaning Representation for sembanking. In *Proceedings of the 7th Linguistic Annotation Workshop and Interoperability with Discourse*, pages 178–186, Sofia, Bulgaria. Association for Computational Linguistics.

Valerio Basile. 2015. *From logic to language: Natural language generation from logical forms*. Ph.D. thesis, University of Groningen.

Valerio Basile and Johan Bos. 2011. Towards generating text from discourse representation structures. In *Proceedings of the 13th European Workshop on Natural Language Generation*, pages 145–150, Nancy, France. Association for Computational Linguistics.

Valerio Basile, Johan Bos, Kilian Evang, and Noortje Venhuizen. 2012. UGroningen: Negation detection with discourse representation structures. In **SEM 2012: The First Joint Conference on Lexical and Computational Semantics – Volume 1: Proceedings of the main conference and the shared task, and Volume 2: Proceedings of the Sixth International Workshop on Semantic Evaluation (SemEval 2012)*, pages 301–309, Montréal, Canada. Association for Computational Linguistics.

Anya Belz, Simon Mille, and David M. Howcroft. 2020. Disentangling the properties of human evaluation methods: A classification system to support comparability, meta-evaluation and reproducibility testing. In *Proceedings of the 13th International Conference on Natural Language Generation*, pages 183–194, Dublin, Ireland. Association for Computational Linguistics.

N.G. Bruijn, de. 1972. Lambda calculus notation with nameless dummies, a tool for automatic formula manipulation, with application to the church-rosser theorem. *Indagationes Mathematicae (Proceedings)*, 75(5):381–392.

Deng Cai and Wai Lam. 2020. Graph transformer for graph-to-sequence learning. In *Proceedings of the AAAI Conference on Artificial Intelligence*, volume 34, pages 7464–7471.

Ondřej Dušek and Filip Jurčíček. 2019. Neural generation for Czech: Data and baselines. In *Proceedings of the 12th International Conference on Natural Language Generation*, pages 563–574, Tokyo, Japan. Association for Computational Linguistics.

Ondřej Dušek, Jekaterina Novikova, and Verena Rieser. 2020. Evaluating the state-of-the-art of end-to-end natural language generation: The e2e nlg challenge. *Computer Speech & Language*, 59:123 – 156.

Allyson Ettinger. 2020. What BERT is not: Lessons from a new suite of psycholinguistic diagnostics for language models. *Transactions of the Association for Computational Linguistics*, 8:34–48.

Kilian Evang. 2019. Transition-based DRS parsing using stack-LSTMs. In *Proceedings of the IWCS Shared Task on Semantic Parsing*, Gothenburg, Sweden. Association for Computational Linguistics.

Federico Fancellu, Ákos Kádár, Ran Zhang, and Afsaneh Fazly. 2020. Accurate polyglot semantic parsing with DAG grammars. In *Findings of the Association for Computational Linguistics: EMNLP 2020*, pages 3567–3580, Online. Association for Computational Linguistics.

Christiane Fellbaum. 1998. Wordnet: An electronic lexical database. *The MIT Press, Cambridge, Ma., USA*.

Jeffrey Flanigan, Chris Dyer, Noah A. Smith, and Jaime Carbonell. 2016. Generation from Abstract Meaning Representation using tree transducers. In *Proceedings of the 2016 Conference of the North American Chapter of the Association for Computational Linguistics: Human Language Technologies*, pages 731–739, San Diego, California. Association for Computational Linguistics.

Claire Gardent, Anastasia Shimorina, Shashi Narayan, and Laura Perez-Beltrachini. 2017. The WebNLG challenge: Generating text from RDF data. In *Proceedings of the 10th International Conference on Natural Language Generation*, pages 124–133, Santiago de Compostela, Spain. Association for Computational Linguistics.

Bart Geurts, David I. Beaver, and Emar Maier. 2020. Discourse Representation Theory. In Edward N. Zalta, editor, *The Stanford Encyclopedia of Philosophy*, spring 2020 edition. Metaphysics Research Lab, Stanford University.

Raghav Goyal, Marc Dymetman, and Eric Gaussier. 2016. Natural language generation through character-based RNNs with finite-state prior knowledge. In *Proceedings of COLING 2016, the 26th International Conference on Computational Linguistics: Technical Papers*, pages 1083–1092, Osaka, Japan. The COLING 2016 Organizing Committee.

Sepp Hochreiter and Jürgen Schmidhuber. 1997. Long short-term memory. *Neural computation*, 9(8):1735–1780.

Matic Horvat, Ann Copestake, and Bill Byrne. 2015. Hierarchical statistical semantic realization for Minimal Recursion Semantics. In *Proceedings of the 11th International Conference on Computational Semantics*, pages 107–117, London, UK. Association for Computational Linguistics.

Glorianna Jagfeld, Sabrina Jenne, and Ngoc Thang Vu. 2018. Sequence-to-sequence models for data-to-text natural language generation: Word- vs. character-based processing and output diversity. In *Proceedings of the 11th International Conference on Natural Language Generation*, pages 221–232, Tilburg University, The Netherlands. Association for Computational Linguistics.

Lisa Jin and Daniel Gildea. 2020. Generalized shortest-paths encoders for AMR-to-text generation. In *Proceedings of the 28th International Conference on Computational Linguistics*, pages 2004–2013, Barcelona, Spain (Online). International Committee on Computational Linguistics.

Marcin Junczys-Dowmunt, Kenneth Heafield, Hieu Hoang, Roman Grundkiewicz, and Anthony Aue. 2018. Marian: Cost-effective high-quality neural machine translation in C++. In *Proceedings of the 2nd Workshop on Neural Machine Translation and Generation*, pages 129–135, Melbourne, Australia. Association for Computational Linguistics.

Nirit Kadmon. 2001. *Formal Pragmatics*. Blackwell.

Hans Kamp and U. Reyle. 1993. From discourse to logic: Introduction to model theoretic semantics of natural language, formal logic and discourse representation theory. *Language*, 71(4).

Diederik P. Kingma and Jimmy Ba. 2015. Adam: A method for stochastic optimization. In *3rd International Conference on Learning Representations, ICLR 2015, San Diego, CA, USA, May 7-9, 2015, Conference Track Proceedings*.

Karin Kipper, Anna Korhonen, Neville Ryant, and Martha Palmer. 2008. A large-scale classification of english verbs. *Language Resources and Evaluation*, 42:21–40.

Philipp Koehn, Hieu Hoang, Alexandra Birch, Chris Callison-Burch, Marcello Federico, Nicola Bertoldi, Brooke Cowan, Wade Shen, Christine Moran, Richard Zens, Chris Dyer, Ondřej Bojar, Alexandra Constantin, and Evan Herbst. 2007. Moses: Open source toolkit for statistical machine translation. In *Proceedings of the 45th Annual Meeting of the Association for Computational Linguistics Companion Volume Proceedings of the Demo and Poster Sessions*, pages 177–180, Prague, Czech Republic. Association for Computational Linguistics.

Ioannis Konstas, Srinivasan Iyer, Mark Yatskar, Yejin Choi, and Luke Zettlemoyer. 2017. Neural AMR: Sequence-to-sequence models for parsing and generation. In *Proceedings of the 55th Annual Meeting of the Association for Computational Linguistics (Volume 1: Long Papers)*, pages 146–157, Vancouver, Canada. Association for Computational Linguistics.

Alon Lavie and Abhaya Agarwal. 2007. METEOR: An automatic metric for MT evaluation with high levels of correlation with human judgments. In *Proceedings of the Second Workshop on Statistical Machine Translation*, pages 228–231, Prague, Czech Republic. Association for Computational Linguistics.

Chin-Yew Lin. 2004. ROUGE: A package for automatic evaluation of summaries. In *Text Summarization Branches Out*, pages 74–81, Barcelona, Spain. Association for Computational Linguistics.

Jiangming Liu, Shay B. Cohen, and Mirella Lapata. 2018. Discourse representation structure parsing. In *Proceedings of the 56th Annual Meeting of the Association for Computational Linguistics (Volume 1: Long Papers)*, pages 429–439, Melbourne, Australia. Association for Computational Linguistics.

Jiangming Liu, Shay B. Cohen, and Mirella Lapata. 2019a. Discourse representation parsing for sentences and documents. In *Proceedings of the 57th Annual Meeting of the Association for Computational Linguistics*, pages 6248–6262, Florence, Italy. Association for Computational Linguistics.

Jiangming Liu, Shay B. Cohen, and Mirella Lapata. 2019b. Discourse representation structure parsing with recurrent neural networks and the transformer model. In *Proceedings of the IWCS Shared Task on Semantic Parsing*, Gothenburg, Sweden. Association for Computational Linguistics.

Jiangming Liu, Shay B. Cohen, and Mirella Lapata. 2021. Text generation from discourse representation structures. In *Proceedings of the 2021 Conference of the North American Chapter of the Association for Computational Linguistics: Human Language Technologies*, pages 397–415, Online. Association for Computational Linguistics.

Manuel Mager, Ramón Fernandez Astudillo, Tahira Naseem, Md Arafat Sultan, Young-Suk Lee, Radu Florian, and Salim Roukos. 2020. GPT-too: A language-model-first approach for AMR-to-text generation. In *Proceedings of the 58th Annual Meeting of the Association for Computational Linguistics*, pages 1846–1852, Online. Association for Computational Linguistics.

Emma Manning, Shira Wein, and Nathan Schneider. 2020. A human evaluation of AMR-to-English generation systems. In *Proceedings of the 28th International Conference on Computational Linguistics*, pages 4773–4786, Barcelona, Spain (Online). International Committee on Computational Linguistics.

Jonathan May and Jay Priyadarshi. 2017. SemEval-2017 task 9: Abstract Meaning Representation parsing and generation. In *Proceedings of the 11th International Workshop on Semantic Evaluation (SemEval-2017)*, pages 536–545, Vancouver, Canada. Association for Computational Linguistics.

Roser Morante and Eduardo Blanco. 2012. *SEM 2012 shared task: Resolving the scope and focus of negation. In **SEM 2012: The First Joint Conference on Lexical and Computational Semantics – Volume 1: Proceedings of the main conference and the shared task, and Volume 2: Proceedings of the Sixth International Workshop on Semantic Evaluation (SemEval 2012)*, pages 265–274, Montréal, Canada. Association for Computational Linguistics.

Shashi Narayan and Claire Gardent. 2014. Hybrid simplification using deep semantics and machine translation. In *Proceedings of the 52nd Annual Meeting of the Association for Computational Linguistics (Volume 1: Long Papers)*, pages 435–445, Baltimore, Maryland. Association for Computational Linguistics.

Rik van Noord, Lasha Abzianidze, Hessel Haagsma, and Johan Bos. 2018a. Evaluating scoped meaning representations. In *Proceedings of the Eleventh International Conference on Language Resources and Evaluation (LREC 2018)*, Miyazaki, Japan. European Language Resources Association (ELRA).

Rik van Noord, Lasha Abzianidze, Antonio Toral, and Johan Bos. 2018b. Exploring neural methods for parsing discourse representation structures. *Transactions of the Association for Computational Linguistics*, 6:619–633.

Rik van Noord, Antonio Toral, and Johan Bos. 2019. Linguistic information in neural semantic parsing with multiple encoders. In *Proceedings of the 13th International Conference on Computational Semantics - Short Papers*, Gothenburg, Sweden. Association for Computational Linguistics.

Rik van Noord, Antonio Toral, and Johan Bos. 2020. Character-level representations improve DRS-based semantic parsing Even in the age of BERT. In *Proceedings of the 2020 Conference on Empirical Methods in Natural Language Processing (EMNLP)*, pages 4587–4603, Online. Association for Computational Linguistics.

Jekaterina Novikova, Ondřej Dušek, Amanda Cercas Curry, and Verena Rieser. 2017a. Why we need new evaluation metrics for NLG. In *Proceedings of the 2017 Conference on Empirical Methods in Natural Language Processing*, pages 2241–2252, Copenhagen, Denmark. Association for Computational Linguistics.

Jekaterina Novikova, Ondřej Dušek, and Verena Rieser. 2017b. The E2E dataset: New challenges for end-to-end generation. In *Proceedings of the 18th Annual SIGdial Meeting on Discourse and Dialogue*, pages 201–206, Saarbrücken, Germany. Association for Computational Linguistics.

Kishore Papineni, Salim Roukos, Todd Ward, and Wei-Jing Zhu. 2002. Bleu: a method for automatic evaluation of machine translation. In *Proceedings of the 40th Annual Meeting of the Association for Computational Linguistics*, pages 311–318, Philadelphia, Pennsylvania, USA. Association for Computational Linguistics.

Ankur Parikh, Xuezhi Wang, Sebastian Gehrmann, Manaal Faruqui, Bhuwan Dhingra, Diyi Yang, and Dipanjan Das. 2020. ToTTo: A controlled table-to-text generation dataset. In *Proceedings of the 2020 Conference on Empirical Methods in Natural Language Processing (EMNLP)*, pages 1173–1186, Online. Association for Computational Linguistics.

Maja Popović and Sheila Castilho. 2019. Challenge test sets for MT evaluation. In *Proceedings of Machine Translation Summit XVII Volume 3: Tutorial Abstracts*, Dublin, Ireland. European Association for Machine Translation.

Nima Pourdamghani, Kevin Knight, and Ulf Hermjakob. 2016. Generating English from Abstract Meaning Representations. In *Proceedings of the 9th International Natural Language Generation conference*, pages 21–25, Edinburgh, UK. Association for Computational Linguistics.

Ehud Reiter and Anja Belz. 2009. An investigation into the validity of some metrics for automatically evaluating natural language generation systems. *Comput. Linguist.*, 35(4):529–558.

Leonardo FR Ribeiro, Martin Schmitt, Hinrich Schütze, and Iryna Gurevych. 2020. Investigating pretrained language models for graph-to-text generation. *arXiv preprint arXiv:2007.08426*.

Rico Sennrich. 2017. How grammatical is character-level neural machine translation? assessing MT quality with contrastive translation pairs. In *Proceedings of the 15th Conference of the European Chapter of the Association for Computational Linguistics: Volume 2, Short Papers*, pages 376–382, Valencia, Spain. Association for Computational Linguistics.

Linfeng Song, Yue Zhang, Zhiguo Wang, and Daniel Gildea. 2018. A graph-to-sequence model for AMR-to-text generation. In *Proceedings of the 56th Annual Meeting of the Association for Computational Linguistics (Volume 1: Long Papers)*, pages 1616–1626, Melbourne, Australia. Association for Computational Linguistics.

Gongbo Tang. 2020. *Understanding Neural Machine Translation: An investigation into linguistic phenomena and attention mechanisms*. Ph.D. thesis, Uppsala University, Department of Linguistics and Philology.

Tianming Wang, Xiaojun Wan, and Hanqi Jin. 2020. AMR-to-text generation with graph transformer. *Transactions of the Association for Computational Linguistics*, 8:19–33.

Chao Zhao, Marilyn Walker, and Snigdha Chaturvedi. 2020. Bridging the structural gap between encoding and decoding for data-to-text generation. In *Proceedings of the 58th Annual Meeting of the Association for Computational Linguistics*, pages 2481–2491, Online. Association for Computational Linguistics.

Jie Zhu, Junhui Li, Muhua Zhu, Longhua Qian, Min Zhang, and Guodong Zhou. 2019. Modeling graph structure in transformer for better AMR-to-text generation. In *Proceedings of the 2019 Conference on Empirical Methods in Natural Language Processing and the 9th International Joint Conference on Natural Language Processing (EMNLP-IJCNLP)*, pages 5459–5468, Hong Kong, China. Association for Computational Linguistics.

Human Evaluation of Creative NLG Systems: An Interdisciplinary Survey on Recent Papers

Mika Hämäläinen
Faculty of Arts
University of Helsinki
mika.hamalainen@helsinki.fi

Khalid Alnajjar
Faculty of Arts
University of Helsinki
khalid.alnajjar@helsinki.fi

Abstract

We survey human evaluation in papers presenting work on creative natural language generation that have been published in INLG 2020 and ICCC 2020. The most typical human evaluation method is a scaled survey, typically on a 5 point scale, while many other less common methods exist. The most commonly evaluated parameters are meaning, syntactic correctness, novelty, relevance and emotional value, among many others. Our guidelines for future evaluation include clearly defining the goal of the generative system, asking questions as concrete as possible, testing the evaluation setup, using multiple different evaluation setups, reporting the entire evaluation process and potential biases clearly, and finally analyzing the evaluation results in a more profound way than merely reporting the most typical statistics.

1 Introduction

Human evaluation in natural language generation (NLG) has become a hot topic lately, with the emergence of several survey papers on the topic that study how human evaluation has been conducted in the past in the field of NLG in general (Howcroft et al., 2020; Belz et al., 2020). This has led to several recent evaluation frameworks for evaluating the output of NLG systems (Liu et al., 2020; Gehrmann et al., 2021).

However, not all natural language generation tasks are of the nature that they are designed to convey factual information. Some of the NLG tasks deal with producing text of aesthetic nature such as poetry, stories, humor and so on. We call these creative NLG tasks. These types of tasks are simultaneously researched in two distinct fields of science: natural language processing (NLP) and computational creativity (CC). Existing survey papers have only focused on NLP research and they have not made a distinction between creative and non-creative NLG.

NLP and CC fields conduct work from very different starting points (Purver et al., 2016). NLP is often state-of-the-art driven whereas CC presents more of exploratory research without pursuing scores that outperform a baseline. In this paper, we want to study how human evaluation of creative NLG systems is conducted in the world of NLP and in the world of CC, what similarities there are and whether the two fields can learn something from each other.

We base our research on a literature review on the papers dealing with human evaluated creative NLG published in the 2020 editions of the International Conference on Computational Creativity (ICCC) and of the International Conference on Natural Language Generation (INLG). We picked these conferences as ICCC is the most important venue for CC research, and INLG the most important NLP focused venue for NLG research.

Our results show that there is no consensus at the moment on how evaluation should be conducted despite the many different efforts of establishing guidelines for evaluating computationally creative output (Pease and Colton, 2011; Jordanous, 2012; Lamb et al., 2018; Hämäläinen, 2020). We reflect on the results of our survey and propose a road-map for more sound future evaluation practices.

2 Surveying human evaluation methods

In this section, we go trough how human evaluation was conducted in the papers we selected for the survey. From the ICCC proceedings, we included all papers that dealt with NLG and had a human evaluation. We did not survey papers that presented work on generating something else than language such as music. From the INLG proceedings, we picked all papers that presented work on an open-ended NLG problem the output of which could exhibit some creativity ruling out papers that dealt

Proceedings of the 1st Workshop on Natural Language Generation, Evaluation, and Metrics (GEM 2021), pages 84–95
August 5–6, 2021.

Paper	NLG task	Evaluated parameters	Questions motivated	Evaluation type
1. Mathewson et al. 2020	Collaborative dialogue	engagement	Engagement measured the notions of revealing and concealing.	Ranking models
2. Cheatley et al. 2020	Song writing tool	Support of self-expression, therapeutic value and receptiveness to the tool and songs created	Not discussed	User study (qualitative)
3. Mirowski et al. 2020	Auxiliary tool for improv theater	Based on critics' previews and reviews	No questions	public performance
4. Spendlove and Ventura 2020	Generating six word stories	coherence, impactfulness	Not discussed	5 point scale
5. Ammanabrolu et al. 2020	Quest generation in text adventure games	coherence, originality (novelty), sense of acomplishment (value), unpredictability (surprise)	By Boden's theory on creativity	7 point scale
6. Mendes and Oliveira 2020b	Headline-proverb pair generation	relatedness, funniness	Not discussed	4 point scale
7. Tyler et al. 2020	Pun generation	funniness, surprise, cleverness, did the user laugh, wit, ingenuity, timelessness, and accessibility	Not discussed	5 point scale
8. Mendes and Oliveira 2020c	Contextual headline adaptation	syntax, relatedness, funniness	Not discussed	3 point scale
9. Hämäläinen et al. 2020 evaluation 1	Dialectal adaptation of generated poetry	poem (yes/no), typicality, understandability, quality of language, evoked imagery, evoked emotions, annotator's liking	Previous research	5 point scale
Hämäläinen et al. 2020 evaluation 2		emotivity, originality, creativity, poem-likeness, artificiality, fluency	Not discussed	Association
10. Savery et al. 2020	Real time human-machine rap battles	annotator's perception, coherence, rhythm, rhyme, quality, enjoyment, relation between the hip hop and metal dataset, and relationship between input and output	By research questions	open ended questions + automatic analysis, preference
11. Oliveira 2020	Song lyric transformation	familiarity, novelty, grammaticality, semantics, singability, overall appreciation and topicality	Not discussed	5 point scale and picking the most suitable topic
12. Shihadeh and Ackerman 2020	Emily Dickinson style poem generation	typicality, understandability, quality of language, evoked imagery, evoked emotions, annotator's liking	Previous research	5 point scale
13. Gong et al. 2020	Text style transfer	content preservation, transfer strength and fluency	Automated evaluation	picking the best
14. Obeid and Hoque 2020	Text generation from charts	informativeness, conciseness, coherence, fluency, factuality	Not discussed	5 point scale and yes/no/partially/can't decide for factuality
15. Lee 2020	Style transform	content, fluency, and style	Not discussed	5 point scale
16. Mendes and Oliveira 2020a	Enhancing headlines with creative expressions	relatedness, funniness	Not discussed	4 point scale
17. Langner 2020	Referring expression generation in a virtual environment	comprehension based on identification time, error rate and repetition counts	Not discussed	user study based on quantitative values
18. Scialom et al. 2020	Question generation from images	readability, caption relevance and image relevance	Not discussed	5 point scale
19. Ilinykh and Dobnik 2020	Multi-sentence image description generation	word choice, object salience, sentence structure and paragraph coherence	Not discussed	slider
20. Akermi et al. 2020	Question answering	relevance, errors	Not discussed	relevance (correct/not correct), error type checkboxes, open ended comment field
21. Nikolov et al. 2020 evaluation 1	Rap lyric generation	style, meaning, familiarity	Not discussed	5 point scale
Nikolov et al. 2020 evaluation 2		Turing test	Not discussed	picking which out of 2 is written by a human
Nikolov et al. 2020 evaluation 3		Turing test	Not discussed	human written (yes/no)
22. Wang et al. 2020	Paper review generation	constructiveness and validity	Not discussed	not stated
23. Hedayatnia et al. 2020	Response generation in a dialog system	appropriateness	Previous research	picking the best

Table 1: Evaluated parameters, their motivation and evaluation type in the surveyed papers

with purely factual data-to-text generation tasks.

In the ICCC 2020, there were 12 papers that presented human evaluated work on creative NLG, and in the INLG 2020, there were 11 such papers. We selected these papers for our survey. Fortunately, both of the venues had relatively the same amount of papers.

When surveying the papers, we only focused on human evaluation and we wanted to know what the NLG task was, what parameters were being evaluated (usually reflected by the evaluation questions), how these parameters (questions) were motivated and how the actual evaluation was conducted methodologically. We also paid attention to the evaluation setup: the number of evaluators and samples used and whether the evaluators were experts or laymen. Finally, we looked into the discussions and conclusions presented in the papers to see what role the human evaluation had there, especially in relation to concrete future directions in improving the system based on the evaluation results.

2.1 What is evaluated?

Table 1 shows the results of our survey in terms of what parameters were evaluated and how the evaluation was conducted. Papers 1-12 were published in ICCC and represent the CC field, whereas papers 13-23 were published in INLG representing the NLP side of the same coin.

When looking at the results, we can immediately see that there is quite a range of different NLG tasks. Even for papers that deal with very similar tasks such as papers 2, 10, 11 and 21, the framing of the problem is very different ranging from lyric transformation to full-blown human versus computer rap battles. The evaluated parameters were also very different.

Despite the parameters being very different from each other, several papers evaluated **meaning** in one way or another, for example, papers 4, 5, 10, 14 and 19 evaluated coherence, paper 11 semantics and paper 21 meaning. Papers 9 and 12 evaluated understandability, which is not directly the same as meaning.

Syntactic correctness of the language was also one of the commonly evaluated features. Papers 9, 13 and 14 measure fluency, paper 11 grammaticality, papers 9 and 12 quality of language and paper 8 syntax. In addition paper 18 evaluated readability, which is partially related to correctness and partially to meaning.

One of the parameters that was evaluated through multiple synonyms and even antonyms was **novelty**. Papers 5 and 9 evaluated originality, paper 11 novelty, paper 7 surprise and paper 5 unpredictability. Papers 9 and 12 evaluated the opposite of novelty, which is typicality.

Relevance was also commonly evaluated in papers 18 and 20. The parameter was evaluated as relatedness in papers 6, 8 an 16, although all of them are by the same authors.

Many papers also evaluated **emotional value**. Such as paper 9 through emotivity, paper 10 through enjoyment, paper 11 through engagement, papers 9 and 12 through evoked emotions and papers 7, 6, 8 and 16 through funniness, although three of these papers were by the same authors.

2.2 Why are the evaluation parameters chosen?

The aforementioned parameters do not cover all the parameters that were used in evaluation, however, they were the most typical ones. When we look into how the evaluation parameters were selected, we can notice that most of the papers do not present any reasoning as to why these are the relevant attributes to look at.

The few papers that did present a reasoning, had many different reasons for the evaluated parameters. Paper 1 motivates the evaluated parameter by stating that it evaluates revealing and concealing parameters that were defined important for the task. Paper 3 did not have any parameters at all for evaluation. Paper 5 motivated the evaluated parameters through an existing theory on computational creativity (Boden, 2007). Paper 10 had formulated the evaluated parameters based on the research questions established in the paper. Paper 13 formulated the evaluated parameters so that they would measure the same things as their automated evaluation.

Paper 9 and 12 used evaluation questions originally established by Toivanen et al. (2012). While basing evaluation on existing research makes the evaluation questions sound more well motivated, the original paper where these evaluation questions were first established did not present any reasoning as to why these should be the evaluation questions to be used with generated poetry. Also paper 23 stated they used "a similar setup" as proposed by Li et al. (2016). In practice this meant that whereas the original paper proposed 3 different evaluation setups, paper 23 only presented one of them. The reasoning for this evaluation was not discussed in the original paper.

2.3 How is the evaluation conducted?

Most of the papers present only one human evaluation method. The exceptions are paper 9 that presents two distinct evaluation setups and paper 21 that presents 3 distinct evaluation setups.

The most common way of conducting a human evaluation is to use a questionnaire that is rated on a **numerical scale**. Papers 4, 7, 9 (evaluation 1) 11, 12, 14, 15, 18 and 21 (evaluation 1) used a 5 point scale. Papers 6 and 16, written by the same authors, use a 4 point scale, and paper 8, also by the same authors, uses a 3 point scale. Paper 7 uses as big as a 7 point scale. The most deviant one of the papers using a numeric scale is paper 19. This paper presents a continuous slider the annotators can move freely. Some of the papers use a different scale for one of the questions.

The second most typical evaluation method is based on **preference**. Here the outputs are preferred or ranked in relation to each other. Paper 1 presents a ranking method where different models are ranked based on which one is the best. Paper 9 (evaluation 2) presents two poems side by side and asks annotators to associate the presented parameters with either one of them. Paper 10 uses preference of output as one of the evaluation criteria. Papers 13 and 23 ask the annotators to pick the best output candidate. Paper 21 (evaluation 2) asks the annotators to guess which output is human written and which AI written. Paper 11 asks the annotators to rank the most suitable topic. This is slightly different as here the annotators are not asked to rank the output per se. As we can see, there are a great number of different variations in how this type of an evaluation is conducted. As opposed to the most popular evaluation method, these methods only give relative results. This means that even if all of the output was bad, one of them is still picked as the best.

Two papers, 2 and 17, present a user-study. Paper 2 conducts this in a qualitative way with open ended questions where the discussion is directed towards the parameters that the authors wanted to measure. The discussions with the participants are not fully reported in the paper, instead the authors present some quotes relating to the parameters in study in a non-rigorous fashion. Paper 17 presents a quantitative user-study where the results are analyzed based on different values such as execution time that were gathered during the user-study.

Paper 3 presents something completely unique in terms of evaluation. The authors organize live improv theater sessions with the system and base the results on the reviews and previews by critics. However, these were not discussed in the paper in detail, but rather some cherry picked quotations were reported.

Paper 10 was another paper to conduct a qualitative evaluation. The annotators were asked to answer to open-ended questions. The input from the annotators was then automatically processed to reach to conclusions. An open-ended comments field was also provided in paper 20, however, the paper focused on discussing the results of the two other questions in the questionnaire. The annotators were asked to give a binary rating on whether the output was relevant or not, similarly, paper 9 (evaluation 1) presented one binary question about poeticity and Paper 21 (evaluation 3) presented a binary question whether the output was human authored. In addition, paper 20 asked the annotators to indicate which types of errors the output had by providing a set of check-boxes with predefined error types.

Unlike the rest of the papers, paper 22 did not explain how the evaluation was conducted in any detail. The results were percentages, which indicates that the evaluation might have been based on binary questions.

2.4 Sample sizes and annotators

Table 2 shows the number of annotators and sample sizes used in the different papers. We have tried to do our best in collecting the information from the papers, however, these parameters were not always expressed clearly. The worst example is paper 3 that stated that they got multiple reviews, previews and feedback from the audience and the actors without specifying the exact number.

Most of the papers relied on non-expert annotators for conducting the evaluation with the exception of paper 1, 21 and 22, and partially paper 3. The use of experts is understandable as not just about anyone is competent enough to tell whether, for example, generated reviews for scientific papers (as in paper 22) are good or bad. However, this leads to a small number of evaluators as experts are difficult to recruit. Papers that did not use experts to evaluate the output either did not report any special requirements or mostly ensured that the evaluators were proficient enough in the language of the output.

In terms of the sample size, that is how many generated artefacts were evaluated, the amount varies a lot from anything starting from 2 as in paper 5 up to 250 as in papers 15 and 19. The samples were mostly picked at random, however some papers like paper 7 evaluated manually picked output.

There was also a lot of divergence in the number of annotators. Some papers had all annotators go through all samples like paper 21 and 22 did, while some other papers had several annotators that annotated the outputs so that each individual output was evaluated at least by 3 annotators like paper 14 and 23. Usually, there wasn't any clear discussion on how many outputs a given annotator annotated with the exception of paper 19, which reported that a given annotator could only annotate up to 30 outputs.

2.5 Evaluation results

An interesting point we wanted to pay attention to was the use of the evaluation results. After conducting a costly and time consuming human evaluation, one would hope that the results give a direction to the future research. However, this was not the case. All papers were limited to writing out the evaluation results and stating which system was better if the papers evaluated multiple systems. None of the papers was able to identify any concrete future directions for improving the generative system based

Paper	Experts	Number of annotators	Number of samples
1. Mathewson et al. 2020	yes	4	3 conversations (5 utterance-response pairs in each)
2. Cheatley et al. 2020	no	3	Free engagement with the system
3. Mirowski et al. 2020	yes (reviews), no (audience)	multiple	Performance
4. Spendlove and Ventura 2020	no	14 per story	15 stories
5. Ammanabrolu et al. 2020	no	15 for each game	2 room layouts
6. Mendes and Oliveira 2020b	no	4 per headline	60 headlines
7. Tyler et al. 2020	no	10 in total	10 best manually selected puns
8. Mendes and Oliveira 2020c	no	2 in total	30 headlines
9. Hämäläinen et al. 2020 evaluation 1	no	5 per poem variant	10 poems
Hämäläinen et al. 2020 evaluation 2	no	5 per dialectal-standard Finnish poem pair	10 parallel poems
10. Savery et al. 2020	no	33	1 video clip, hand picked best output, 10 additional video clips and 10 generated tasks
11. Oliveira 2020	no	3 per lyric	120 lyics
12. Shihadeh and Ackerman 2020	no	17 in total	10 generated + 2 Emily Dickinson's poems
13. Gong et al. 2020	no	2 in total	outputs for 100 inputs
14. Obeid and Hoque 2020	no	3 per statistic	output for 40 charts
15. Lee 2020	no	6 people per sample	250 samples
16. Mendes and Oliveira 2020a	no	4 per headline	60 headlines
17. Langner 2020	no	34 participants	10 fixed sessions
18. Scialom et al. 2020	no	3 in total	50 images
19. Ilinykh and Dobnik 2020	no	154 in total (a participant could rate at most 30 images)	250 images
20. Akermi et al. 2020	no	20 in total	150 questions
21. Nikolov et al. 2020 evaluation 1	yes	3 in total	100 verses
Nikolov et al. 2020 evaluation 2	yes	3 in total	100 verses
Nikolov et al. 2020 evaluation 3	yes	3 in total	100 verses
22. Wang et al. 2020	yes	2 in total	50 papers
23. Hedayatnia et al. 2020	no	3 per snippet	200 snippets of 5 turn dialog

Table 2: Evaluators and samples in the surveyed papers

on the human evaluation results. Human evaluation was merely there to provide some convincing evidence on the quality of the systems.

The only exception to this was paper 9. The authors conducted two different evaluations and they reached to an insightful conclusion. The two evaluation methods contradicted each other; according to the first evaluation, standard Finnish was preferred over dialectal one in all the parameters. However, the second evaluation showed that a dialectal poem was more often associated with originality, creativity and poem-likeness than its standard Finnish variant. The authors note that the results are not only dependent on how you conduct your human evaluation, but also on familiarity bias. In the first evaluation, where dialect was a controlled variable, the further the dialect was from standard Finnish, the lower it scored as the annotators were less familiar with it.

3 Discussion

There are currently many different creative NLG tasks people work with, and it is understandable that each task calls for slightly different evaluation methods. However, even work on closely related topics prefers to use their own evaluation methods that are not based on any existing research. And most alarmingly, if the evaluation is based on existing research, the evaluation questions are not motivated in the earlier research either. This type of evaluation has become to be known as a symptom of the Great Misalignment Problem (Hämäläinen and Alnajjar, 2021). When the evaluation is not targeted towards evaluating exactly what has been modelled, any type of evaluation that seems remotely related to the task becomes seemingly valid.

However, when the evaluated parameters have only little to do with what was modelled, it is only evident that none of the surveyed papers was able to clearly identify the short-comings of their systems in such a way that they could propose some clear paths to follow for any future research. In fact, if you evaluate your system based on *relatedness* and *funniness* while neither is explicitly modelled, how can you know how to make your system more funny or produce more related output? The scores might have well been achieved by mere serendipity (the annotators happened to like the humor that happened to be in the small sample) (c.f. Gervás 2017) or by data the model was trained on.

Apart from the evaluation questions not aligning with the model, a much larger problem related to evaluation questions can be identified. Firstly, most of the papers were not clear about the actual evaluation questions used, instead they listed the evaluated parameters as though human evaluation was like an automated one where one can just score abstract notions such as *typicality* or *fluency* accurately on a 5 point scale. In other fields, it is known that even small changes in survey questions can lead to different survey results (Kalton and Schuman, 1982; de Bruin et al., 2011, 2012). Not revealing the actual questions only makes the situation worse. Another problem that rises from abstract evaluation questions is that it becomes less clear why the annotators gave certain answers.

Furthermore, people have a tendency on reading more into computer generated output than what the intention of the system was (Veale, 2016). If you train a generative neural model on jokes, it will surely learn to output jokes, while it does not necessarily have any internal representation of humor. In such a case, the humor is purely in the eyes of the beholder and in the data the model was trained on, not in the method itself[1]. For instance, Alnajjar et al. (2019) has shown that generated headlines were perceived more offensive by human annotators, while offensiveness was never modelled in the system.

While mostly every paper we surveyed opts for coming up with their own evaluation metrics, it is astonishing that these newly created evaluation settings are used as such. There are other fields dealing with human surveys that emphasize the need for conducting tests on your survey before conducting it in a larger scale to discover potential issues in your questionnaire (Collins, 2003; Presser et al., 2004; Thomas, 2004). None of the paper we surveyed discusses evaluation of evaluation. Instead, it is believed that any new evaluation metric the authors came up with just for a given paper will magically work as such and will yield scientifically valid results that will pass a peer review. All this while many of the papers ask questions using ambiguous terms such as *fluency* (is something grammatical fluent? is something that seems to make sense semantically fluent? is something that is close to the annotator's own idiolect more fluent than something further away from it? is text generated in American English more fluent to Americans than text generated in British English? and so on) and *coherence* (is something that repeats the same words coherent? can a complex figure of language be coherent if the annotator does not have time to think about it for more than a couple of seconds? does coherence have something to do with grammaticality as well? is a story that follows the same beliefs as the annotator seen as more coherent? and so on) that are reduced into a compact 1-5 scale that is later neatly averaged over all the annotators' opinions on all the samples. What does the average of 3.5 on a question all annotators might have interpreted differently even mean?

In other fields conducting online surveys, there are a lot of worries about selection bias of the human subjects (Bethlehem, 2010; Greenacre, 2016). This is hardly discussed in the fields of NLP and CC. Many of the papers we surveyed conducted their evaluation on a crowd-sourcing platform such as Amazon Mechanical Turk. None of the papers presented statistics on the demographics of the annotators. This might be a source of bias in the results. What makes such a bias even more problematic is the relatively small number of annotators that are usually recruited per individual output. Fields with more established human survey practices would not consider the typical 3-5 annotators of NLP and CC enough even for a *qualitative* survey, which requires 5-25 participants (Creswell, 1998) or at least 6 participants (Morse, 1994). However, human evaluation is usually conducted quantitatively, which means that the number of annotators depends heavily on multiple parameters and requires planning and justification on its own right (Bell, 1991; Lenth, 2001; Lavrakas, 2008).

It is also very well known that people do not perceive things in a vacuum but rather as a continuum of stimuli where previously perceived stimuli affect to the next one. This effect is called priming (see Henson 2009). To reduce the effect of priming

[1]See Colton (2008) for discussion on the roles of the programmer, program and perceiver in creative systems

or to have it consistent one should either shuffle the order in which the output is presented to the annotators or keep it always the same. Priming is especially in play in cases where annotators are to evaluate outputs produced by different systems. In such a case, output of a mediocre system might get greatly boosted when presented together with output by a bad systems. Nearly none of the papers we surveyed discussed this aspect of their evaluation setting.

Both CC and NLP have still a long way to go in order to reach to more sound human evaluation practices. However, INLG is still a step closer to scientific rigor as automated evaluation metrics were commonly used together with human evaluation, and sometimes as the only evaluation metric (such as Bień et al. 2020), whereas ICCC had several papers presenting work on creative NLG without any evaluation at all (such as Agafonova et al. 2020; Petac et al. 2020; Wright and Purver 2020).

The use of experts in evaluation is something that should be taken under rigorous inspection in the future. Currently, there are contradicting studies on the topic indicating that consulting expert does have an effect in machine translation (Toral et al., 2018) but not in poem generation (Lamb et al., 2017). However, this is a question that is very likely to depend on the output that is to be evaluated and also on how the evaluation is conducted.

Human computer interaction research has some more established methodologies for conducting human studies (see Jacko 2012; Lazar et al. 2017 such as cognitive walk-through (see Mahatody et al. 2010), human performance evaluation support system (Ha et al., 2007) and user studies (see MacKenzie 2015). These established methodologies could be taken into account when conducting evaluation of such an NLG system that calls for user interaction.

4 Advices for future evaluation

In this section, we outline how human evaluation of creative NLG systems should be conducted. We are not going to give an exact silver bullet framework to solve the problem, as the two fields are not at the state yet where enough would be known about human evaluation to state exactly how the evaluation needs to be conducted. Furthermore, we do not believe that a single fixed framework is enough to capture everything necessary in a topic as broad as creative text generation.

4.1 Define the goals

From the very early on, it is important to define what the goals of your system are (see Alnajjar and Hämäläinen 2018; Jordanous 2012). Try to be as concrete and precise as possible at this step. Once you have your goals clearly stated, it is easy to see the degree to which your implementation solution tries to achieve those goals and how much can be attributed to the method and how much to the training data. After this, the evaluation parameters will follow naturally from the goals you set for your system. This way, the evaluation questions do not appear seemingly from nowhere but are motivated by your research goals and implementation.

4.2 Go concrete

People have an inbuilt need to understand anything expressed in their language (see Veale 2016). This can lead easily into a situation, where annotators can read more into the evaluated output than what your system was aware of. By using evaluation questions that are as concrete as possible you can reduce the room for subjective interpretation (see Hämäläinen and Alnajjar 2019). For example, for a pun like *Becoming a vegetarian is a big missed steak* asking the annotators *Is this humorous?* and *Is this humorous because the pun "missed steak" sounds like "mistake"?* will result in different possible interpretations as the former question might let the annotators consider the generated joke funny for reasons other than those intended by the generative system.

4.3 Run some tests

As we have seen in this paper, the same concept can be evaluated through multiple different wordings and it is not always clear that the annotators understand the questions in the same way as the researchers intended. By running tests on your survey in real life, you can get more direct feedback than what you could get from annotators on Amazon Mechanical Turk. It is better to adjust your evaluation questions sooner than after running a costly crowd-sourcing.

Furthermore, the final number of annotators you need and how many samples you should evaluate depends on the evaluation task and setting. If you get high diversity in answers in the test run, you will probably need to have a larger number of annotators conducting the actual evaluation.

Testing is also a great way of seeing whether you are asking non-experts to evaluate things they consider too difficult or whether your questionnaire is too lengthy. You do not want your annotators to lose interest in the middle of the questionnaire and start annotating fast without paying too much attention.

4.4 Run multiple evaluations

Human evaluation does not need to be a one time thing conducted in a massive survey. You can run multiple different evaluations such as preference based ones, 5 point scale ones and true and false statements to better understand the limitations of your system and your human evaluation. The more evidence gathered by different evaluation methods you can show, the more confident you and other researchers can be of the quality of your method.

4.5 Report everything clearly

It is important to report the evaluation questions exactly as they were used, how the survey form was constructed including any instructions and wording used for the 5 point scale, and how the output was presented (always in the same order or shuffled). All these have an effect on the results. In software engineering, it is considered important to report any threats to the validity of the research (Feldt and Magazinius, 2010). The same should apply to NLP and CC. One of the important threats to the validity of human evaluation is bias in the results. Therefore, it is important to report and discuss what kind of people participated in the evaluation survey.

4.6 Analyze your results

It is also important to dig deeper into the human evaluation results. If you as a researcher put a considerable amount of money in getting your human evaluation results, you should probably make the most out of them too. Instead of merely reporting the typical stats (mean, mode, median, standard deviation), why not looking into the best and worst performing output by the system as well and let the human evaluation be a guide in a deeper error analysis? This can open up insightful directions for future research.

5 Conclusions

In this paper, we have surveyed papers presenting work on creative natural language generation that have been published in INLG 2020 and ICCC 2020. There have been many different evaluation methods including some unconventional ones such as critics' reviews and user testing. The most typical human evaluation method has been using a scaled survey, typically on a 5 point scale.

While most of the papers surveyed had come up with their own evaluation metrics, the most common parameters that have been evaluated were meaning, syntactic correctness, novelty, relevance and emotional value. Although, the terms used to refer to these notions have not been the same.

Most of the papers did not justify why they had evaluated certain parameters. Instead, the parameters were usually just stated as though they were an inarguable fact. It was more often than not the case that the actual evaluation questions were not revealed.

There was a lot of variation in the number of samples taken from the system output and how many annotators were used to conduct the evaluation. Typically the numbers were rather small. There was no discussion about the demographics of the annotators nor about what type of a bias it might have introduced.

Evaluation setups were never tested out beforehand, even though other fields dealing with human surveys recommend testing your questionnaires. This means that it is impossible to tell what the annotators really understood by the evaluation questions.

We established some advices for future evaluation, which include clearly defining the goal of the generative system, asking questions as concrete as possible, testing the evaluation setup, using multiple different evaluation setups, reporting the entire evaluation process and potential biases clearly, and finally analyzing the evaluation results in a more profound way than merely reporting the most typical statistics.

All in all, our fields, CC and NLP, have a lot to learn from other fields with longer traditions with human questionnaires in terms of conducting human evaluation. At the current stage, none of the papers we surveyed quite reached the same level of scientific rigor in their human evaluation as it is to be expected in other fields of science. However, this is not to say that the work of the authors of the papers we surveyed is inherently bad. This is just to highlight the fact that more attention needs to be paid in how human evaluation is conducted. Quite often with creative text generation, human judgment is the only viable metric to measure the performance of a system. Human evaluation of generated text has been conducted in the field of NLP already as early as in the 1960s (McDaniel et al., 1967) it is a pity it has not caught up with the rest of the development in the field.

References

Yana Agafonova, Alexey Tikhonov, and Ivan P Yamshchikov. 2020. Paranoid transformer: Reading narrative of madness as computational approach to creativity. In *Eleventh International Conference on Computational Creativity: ICCC'20*. Association for Computational Creativity.

Imen Akermi, Johannes Heinecke, and Frédéric Herledan. 2020. Tansformer based natural language generation for question-answering. In *Proceedings of the 13th International Conference on Natural Language Generation*, pages 349–359, Dublin, Ireland. Association for Computational Linguistics.

Khalid Alnajjar and Mika Hämäläinen. 2018. A master-apprentice approach to automatic creation of culturally satirical movie titles. In *Proceedings of the 11th International Conference on Natural Language Generation*, pages 274–283.

Khalid Alnajjar, Leo Leppänen, and Hannu Toivonen. 2019. No time like the present: methods for generating colourful and factual multilingual news headlines. In *Proceedings of the 10th International Conference on Computational Creativity*. Association for Computational Creativity.

Prithviraj Ammanabrolu, William Broniec, Alex Mueller, Jeremy Paul, and Mark Riedl. 2020. Toward automated quest generation in text-adventure games. In *Proceedings of the 11th International Conference on Computational Creativity*.

John F Bell. 1991. Big is not necessarily beautiful in survey design: Measurement error and the apu science survey. *Journal of the Royal Statistical Society: Series D (The Statistician)*, 40(3):291–300.

Anya Belz, Simon Mille, and David M. Howcroft. 2020. Disentangling the properties of human evaluation methods: A classification system to support comparability, meta-evaluation and reproducibility testing. In *Proceedings of the 13th International Conference on Natural Language Generation*, pages 183–194, Dublin, Ireland. Association for Computational Linguistics.

Jelke Bethlehem. 2010. Selection bias in web surveys. *International Statistical Review*, 78(2):161–188.

Michał Bień, Michał Gilski, Martyna Maciejewska, Wojciech Taisner, Dawid Wisniewski, and Agnieszka Lawrynowicz. 2020. RecipeNLG: A cooking recipes dataset for semi-structured text generation. In *Proceedings of the 13th International Conference on Natural Language Generation*, pages 22–28, Dublin, Ireland. Association for Computational Linguistics.

Margaret A Boden. 2007. Creativity in a nutshell. *Think*, 5(15):83–96.

Wändi Bruine de Bruin, Martine Baldassi, Bernd Figner, Baruch Fischhoff, Lauren Fleishman, David Hardisty, Eric Johnson, Gideon Keren, Maria Konnikova, and Irwin Levin. 2011. Framing effects in surveys: How respondents make sense of the questions we ask. In *Perspectives on Framing, edited by Gideon Keren, 303–325. New-York, NY. Taylor and Francis Group, Psychology Press*.

Wändi Bruine de Bruin, Wilbert Van der Klaauw, Giorgio Topa, Julie S Downs, Baruch Fischhoff, and Olivier Armantier. 2012. The effect of question wording on consumers' reported inflation expectations. *Journal of Economic Psychology*, 33(4):749–757.

Lee Cheatley, Margareta Ackerman, Alison Pease, and Wendy Moncur. 2020. Co-creative songwriting for bereavement support. In *Eleventh International Conference on Computational Creativity: ICCC'20*, pages 33–41. Association for Computational Creativity.

Debbie Collins. 2003. Pretesting survey instruments: an overview of cognitive methods. *Quality of life research*, 12(3):229–238.

Simon Colton. 2008. Creativity versus the perception of creativity in computational systems. In *AAAI spring symposium: creative intelligent systems*, volume 8.

John W Creswell. 1998. *Qualitative inquiry and research design: Choosing among five traditions.* Sage publications.

Robert Feldt and Ana Magazinius. 2010. Validity threats in empirical software engineering research-an initial survey. In *Seke*, pages 374–379.

Sebastian Gehrmann, Tosin Adewumi, Karmanya Aggarwal, Pawan Sasanka Ammanamanchi, Aremu Anuoluwapo, Antoine Bosselut, Khyathi Raghavi Chandu, Miruna Clinciu, Dipanjan Das, Kaustubh D. Dhole, Wanyu Du, Esin Durmus, Ondřej Dušek, Chris Emezue, Varun Gangal, Cristina Garbacea, Tatsunori Hashimoto, Yufang Hou, Yacine Jernite, Harsh Jhamtani, Yangfeng Ji, Shailza Jolly, Mihir Kale, Dhruv Kumar, Faisal Ladhak, Aman Madaan, Mounica Maddela, Khyati Mahajan, Saad Mahamood, Bodhisattwa Prasad Majumder, Pedro Henrique Martins, Angelina McMillan-Major, Simon Mille, Emiel van Miltenburg, Moin Nadeem, Shashi Narayan, Vitaly Nikolaev, Rubungo Andre Niyongabo, Salomey Osei, Ankur Parikh, Laura Perez-Beltrachini, Niranjan Ramesh Rao, Vikas Raunak, Juan Diego Rodriguez, Sashank Santhanam, João

Sedoc, Thibault Sellam, Samira Shaikh, Anastasia Shimorina, Marco Antonio Sobrevilla Cabezudo, Hendrik Strobelt, Nishant Subramani, Wei Xu, Diyi Yang, Akhila Yerukola, and Jiawei Zhou. 2021. The gem benchmark: Natural language generation, its evaluation and metrics. *arXiv preprint arXiv:2011.11928*.

Pablo Gervás. 2017. Template-free construction of rhyming poems with thematic cohesion. In *Proceedings of the Workshop on Computational Creativity in Natural Language Generation (CC-NLG 2017)*, pages 21–28, Santiago de Compostela, Spain. Association for Computational Linguistics.

Hongyu Gong, Linfeng Song, and Suma Bhat. 2020. Rich syntactic and semantic information helps unsupervised text style transfer. In *Proceedings of the 13th International Conference on Natural Language Generation*, pages 113–119, Dublin, Ireland. Association for Computational Linguistics.

Zerrin Asan Greenacre. 2016. The importance of selection bias in internet surveys. *Open Journal of Statistics*, 6(03):397.

Jun Su Ha, Poong Hyun Seong, Myeong Soo Lee, and Jin Hyuk Hong. 2007. Development of human performance measures for human factors validation in the advanced mcr of apr-1400. *IEEE Transactions on Nuclear Science*, 54(6):2687–2700.

Mika Hämäläinen. 2020. *Generating Creative Language-Theories, Practice and Evaluation*. University of Helsinki.

Mika Hämäläinen and Khalid Alnajjar. 2019. Let's face it. finnish poetry generation with aesthetics and framing. In *Proceedings of the 12th International Conference on Natural Language Generation*, pages 290–300.

Mika Hämäläinen and Khalid Alnajjar. 2021. The great misalignment problem in human evaluation of NLP methods. In *Proceedings of the Workshop on Human Evaluation of NLP Systems (HumEval)*, pages 69–74, Online. Association for Computational Linguistics.

Mika Hämäläinen, Niko Partanen, Khalid Alnajjar, Jack Rueter, and Thierry Poibeau. 2020. Automatic dialect adaptation in finnish and its effect on perceived creativity. In *11th International Conference on Computational Creativity (ICCC'20)*. Association for Computational Creativity.

Behnam Hedayatnia, Karthik Gopalakrishnan, Seokhwan Kim, Yang Liu, Mihail Eric, and Dilek Hakkani-Tur. 2020. Policy-driven neural response generation for knowledge-grounded dialog systems. In *Proceedings of the 13th International Conference on Natural Language Generation*, pages 412–421, Dublin, Ireland. Association for Computational Linguistics.

Rik Henson. 2009. Priming. In *Encyclopedia of Neuroscience*, volume 7. Academic Press.

David M. Howcroft, Anya Belz, Miruna-Adriana Clinciu, Dimitra Gkatzia, Sadid A. Hasan, Saad Mahamood, Simon Mille, Emiel van Miltenburg, Sashank Santhanam, and Verena Rieser. 2020. Twenty years of confusion in human evaluation: NLG needs evaluation sheets and standardised definitions. In *Proceedings of the 13th International Conference on Natural Language Generation*, pages 169–182, Dublin, Ireland. Association for Computational Linguistics.

Nikolai Ilinykh and Simon Dobnik. 2020. When an image tells a story: The role of visual and semantic information for generating paragraph descriptions. In *Proceedings of the 13th International Conference on Natural Language Generation*, pages 338–348, Dublin, Ireland. Association for Computational Linguistics.

Julie A Jacko. 2012. *Human computer interaction handbook: Fundamentals, evolving technologies, and emerging applications*. CRC press.

Anna Jordanous. 2012. A standardised procedure for evaluating creative systems: Computational creativity evaluation based on what it is to be creative. *Cognitive Computation*, 4(3):246–279.

Graham Kalton and Howard Schuman. 1982. The effect of the question on survey responses: A review. *Journal of the Royal Statistical Society: Series A (General)*, 145(1):42–57.

Carolyn Lamb, Daniel G Brown, and Charles LA Clarke. 2017. Incorporating novelty, meaning, reaction and craft into computational poetry: a negative experimental result. In *ICCC*, pages 183–188.

Carolyn Lamb, Daniel G Brown, and Charles LA Clarke. 2018. Evaluating computational creativity: An interdisciplinary tutorial. *ACM Computing Surveys (CSUR)*, 51(2):1–34.

Maurice Langner. 2020. OMEGA : A probabilistic approach to referring expression generation in a virtual environment. In *Proceedings of the 13th International Conference on Natural Language Generation*, pages 296–305, Dublin, Ireland. Association for Computational Linguistics.

Paul J Lavrakas. 2008. Sample size. In *Encyclopedia of survey research methods*. Sage publications.

Jonathan Lazar, Jinjuan Heidi Feng, and Harry Hochheiser. 2017. *Research methods in human-computer interaction*. Morgan Kaufmann.

Joosung Lee. 2020. Stable style transformer: Delete and generate approach with encoder-decoder for text style transfer. In *Proceedings of the 13th International Conference on Natural Language Generation*, pages 195–204, Dublin, Ireland. Association for Computational Linguistics.

Russell V Lenth. 2001. Some practical guidelines for effective sample size determination. *The American Statistician*, 55(3):187–193.

Jiwei Li, Will Monroe, Alan Ritter, Dan Jurafsky, Michel Galley, and Jianfeng Gao. 2016. Deep reinforcement learning for dialogue generation. In *Proceedings of the 2016 Conference on Empirical Methods in Natural Language Processing*, pages 1192–1202.

Dayiheng Liu, Yu Yan, Yeyun Gong, Weizhen Qi, Hang Zhang, Jian Jiao, Weizhu Chen, Jie Fu, Linjun Shou, Ming Gong, et al. 2020. Glge: A new general language generation evaluation benchmark. *arXiv preprint arXiv:2011.11928*.

I Scott MacKenzie. 2015. User studies and usability evaluations: from research to products. In *Graphics Interface*, pages 1–8.

Thomas Mahatody, Mouldi Sagar, and Christophe Kolski. 2010. State of the art on the cognitive walkthrough method, its variants and evolutions. *Intl. Journal of Human–Computer Interaction*, 26(8):741–785.

Kory Mathewson, Pablo Samuel Castro, Colin Cherry, George Foster, and Marc G Bellemare. 2020. Shaping the narrative arc: Information-theoretic collaborative dialogue.

J. McDaniel, W.L. Price, A.J.M. Szanser, and D.M. Yates. 1967. An evaluation of the usefulness of machine translations produced at the national physical laboratory, teddington, with a summary of the translation methods. In *COLING 1967 Volume 1: Conference Internationale Sur Le Traitement Automatique Des Langues*.

Rui Mendes and Hugo Gonçalo Oliveira. 2020a. Amplifying the range of news stories with creativity: Methods and their evaluation, in Portuguese. In *Proceedings of the 13th International Conference on Natural Language Generation*, pages 252–262, Dublin, Ireland. Association for Computational Linguistics.

Rui Mendes and Hugo Gonçalo Oliveira. 2020b. Comparing different methods for assigning portuguese proverbs to news headlines. In *Eleventh International Conference on Computational Creativity: ICCC'20*.

Rui Mendes and Hugo Gonçalo Oliveira. 2020c. Teco: Exploring word embeddings for text adaptation to a given context. *Eleventh International Conference on Computational Creativity: ICCC'20*.

Piotr Mirowski, Kory Mathewson, Boyd Branch, Thomas Winters, Ben Verhoeven, and Jenny Elfving. 2020. Rosetta code: Improv in any language. In *Proceedings of the 11th International Conference on Computational Creativity*, pages 115–122. Association for Computational Creativity.

Janice M Morse. 1994. *Designing funded qualitative research*. Sage Publications, Inc.

Nikola I. Nikolov, Eric Malmi, Curtis Northcutt, and Loreto Parisi. 2020. Rapformer: Conditional rap lyrics generation with denoising autoencoders. In *Proceedings of the 13th International Conference on Natural Language Generation*, pages 360–373, Dublin, Ireland. Association for Computational Linguistics.

Jason Obeid and Enamul Hoque. 2020. Chart-to-text: Generating natural language descriptions for charts by adapting the transformer model. In *Proceedings of the 13th International Conference on Natural Language Generation*, pages 138–147, Dublin, Ireland. Association for Computational Linguistics.

Hugo Gonçalo Oliveira. 2020. Weirdanalogymatic: Experimenting with analogy for lyrics transformation. In *Eleventh International Conference on Computational Creativity: ICCC'20*.

Alison Pease and Simon Colton. 2011. On impact and evaluation in computational creativity: A discussion of the turing test and an alternative proposal. In *Proceedings of the AISB symposium on AI and Philosophy*, volume 39.

Andreea-Oana Petac, Anne-Gwenn Bosser, Fred Charles, Pierre De Loor, and Marc Cavazza. 2020. A pragmatics-based model for narrative dialogue generation. In *Eleventh International Conference on Computational Creativity: ICCC'20*.

Stanley Presser, Mick P Couper, Judith T Lessler, Elizabeth Martin, Jean Martin, Jennifer M Rothgeb, and Eleanor Singer. 2004. Methods for testing and evaluating survey questions. *Public opinion quarterly*, 68(1):109–130.

Matthew Purver, Pablo Gervás, and Sascha Griffiths, editors. 2016. *Proceedings of the INLG 2016 Workshop on Computational Creativity in Natural Language Generation*. Association for Computational Linguistics, Edinburgh, UK.

Richard Savery, Lisa Zahray, and Gil Weinberg. 2020. Shimon the rapper: A real-time system for human-robot interactive rap battles. In *Eleventh International Conference on Computational Creativity: ICCC'20*.

Thomas Scialom, Patrick Bordes, Paul-Alexis Dray, Jacopo Staiano, and Patrick Gallinari. 2020. What BERT sees: Cross-modal transfer for visual question generation. In *Proceedings of the 13th International Conference on Natural Language Generation*, pages 327–337, Dublin, Ireland. Association for Computational Linguistics.

Juliana Shihadeh and Margareta Ackerman. 2020. Emily: An emily dickinson machine. In *Eleventh International Conference on Computational Creativity: ICCC'20*.

Brad Spendlove and Dan Ventura. 2020. Creating six-word stories via inferred linguistic and semantic formats. In *Proceedings of the 11th International Conference on Computational Creativity, under review*.

Susan J Thomas. 2004. Pilot testing the questionnaire. *Using web and paper questionnaires for Data-Based Decision Making*.

Jukka Toivanen, Hannu Toivonen, Alessandro Valitutti, and Oskar Gross. 2012. Corpus-based generation of content and form in poetry. In *Proceedings of the third international conference on computational creativity*. University College Dublin.

Antonio Toral, Sheila Castilho, Ke Hu, and Andy Way. 2018. Attaining the unattainable? reassessing claims of human parity in neural machine translation. In *Proceedings of the Third Conference on Machine Translation: Research Papers*, pages 113–123.

Bradley Tyler, Katherine Wilsdon, and Paul Bodily. 2020. Computational humor: Automated pun generation. In *Eleventh International Conference on Computational Creativity: ICCC'20*.

Tony Veale. 2016. *3. The shape of tweets to come: Automating language play in social networks*, pages 73–92. De Gruyter Mouton.

Qingyun Wang, Qi Zeng, Lifu Huang, Kevin Knight, Heng Ji, and Nazneen Fatema Rajani. 2020. ReviewRobot: Explainable paper review generation based on knowledge synthesis. In *Proceedings of the 13th International Conference on Natural Language Generation*, pages 384–397, Dublin, Ireland. Association for Computational Linguistics.

G Wright and Matthew Purver. 2020. Creative language generation in a society of engagement and reflection. In *Proceedings of the Eleventh International Conference on Computational Creativity*. Association for Computational Creativity (ACC).

The GEM Benchmark: Natural Language Generation, its Evaluation and Metrics

Sebastian Gehrmann,[9,*] Tosin Adewumi,[20,21] Karmanya Aggarwal,[14]
Pawan Sasanka Ammanamanchi,[15] Aremu Anuoluwapo,[21,38] Antoine Bosselut,[28]
Khyathi Raghavi Chandu,[2] Miruna Clinciu,[7,11,35] Dipanjan Das,[9] Kaustubh D. Dhole,[1]
Wanyu Du,[42] Esin Durmus,[5] Ondřej Dušek,[3] Chris Emezue,[21,30] Varun Gangal,[2]
Cristina Garbacea,[39] Tatsunori Hashimoto,[28] Yufang Hou,[13] Yacine Jernite,[12] Harsh Jhamtani,[2]
Yangfeng Ji,[42] Shailza Jolly,[6,29] Mihir Kale,[9] Dhruv Kumar,[44] Faisal Ladhak,[4] Aman Madaan,[2]
Mounica Maddela,[8] Khyati Mahajan,[34] Saad Mahamood,[32] Bodhisattwa Prasad Majumder,[37]
Pedro Henrique Martins,[16] Angelina McMillan-Major,[43] Simon Mille,[26] Emiel van Miltenburg,[31]
Moin Nadeem,[22] Shashi Narayan,[9] Vitaly Nikolaev,[9] Rubungo Andre Niyongabo,[21,36]
Salomey Osei,[19,21] Ankur Parikh,[9] Laura Perez-Beltrachini,[35] Niranjan Ramesh Rao,[24]
Vikas Raunak,[23] Juan Diego Rodriguez,[41] Sashank Santhanam,[34] João Sedoc,[25]
Thibault Sellam,[9] Samira Shaikh,[34] Anastasia Shimorina,[33] Marco
Antonio Sobrevilla Cabezudo,[40] Hendrik Strobelt,[13] Nishant Subramani,[17,21] Wei Xu,[8]
Diyi Yang,[8] Akhila Yerukola,[27] Jiawei Zhou[10]

[1]Amelia R&D, New York, [2]Carnegie Mellon University, [3]Charles University, Prague, [4]Columbia University, [5]Cornell University, [6]DFKI, Germany [7]Edinburgh Centre for Robotics, [8]Georgia Tech, [9]Google Research, [10]Harvard University, [11]Heriot-Watt University, [12]Hugging Face, [13]IBM Research, [14]IIIT Delhi, [15]IIIT Hyderabad, [16]Instituto de Telecomunicações, [17]Intelligent Systems Lab, Intel, [18]Johns-Hopkins University, [19]Kwame Nkrumah University of Science and Technology [20]Luleå University of Technology, [21]Masakhane, Africa, [22]Massachusetts Institute of Technology, [23]Microsoft, [24]National Institute of Technology Karnataka India, [25]New York University, [26]Pompeu Fabra University, [27]Samsung Research, [28]Stanford University, [29]Technical University of Kaiserslautern, [30]Technical University Munich, [31]Tilburg University, [32]trivago, [33]Université de Lorraine, [34]University of North Carolina Charlotte, [35]University of Edinburgh, [36]University of Electronic Science and Technology of China, [37]University of California San Diego, [38]University of Lagos, [39]University of Michigan Ann Arbor, [40]University of São Paulo, [41]University of Texas at Austin, [42]University of Virginia, [43]University of Washington, [44]University of Waterloo

Abstract

We introduce GEM, a living benchmark for natural language Generation (NLG), its Evaluation, and Metrics. Measuring progress in NLG relies on a constantly evolving ecosystem of automated metrics, datasets, and human evaluation standards. Due to this moving target, new models often still evaluate on divergent anglo-centric corpora with well-established, but flawed, metrics. This disconnect makes it challenging to identify the limitations of current models and opportunities for progress. Addressing this limitation, GEM provides an environment in which models can easily be applied to a wide set of tasks and in which evaluation strategies can be tested. Regular updates to the benchmark will help NLG research become more multilingual and evolve the challenge alongside models. This paper serves as the description of the data for which we are organizing a shared task at our ACL 2021 Workshop and to which we invite the entire NLG community to participate.

* Correspondence to gehrmann@google.com

1 Introduction

Natural language generation is the task to automatically generate understandable texts, typically using a non-linguistic or textual representation of information as input (Reiter and Dale, 2000). These texts aim to fulfill an underlying communicative goal (e.g., *to produce a summary of an article*) while remaining faithful to the input information, fluent, grammatical, and natural-looking. An NLG system needs to be robust to shifts in the data distribution and be able to produce text in many different languages. Finally, it is often desired that repeated interactions with the model produce diverse outputs, for example, to explain concepts in multiple ways or to become a more interesting conversational agent. These optimization objectives can often be conflicting (Hashimoto et al., 2019) and, as a result, evaluations that focus only on a single aspect may fail to recognize the drawbacks of a particular method. To demonstrate this trade-off, consider an improvement on the CNN-DM summarization dataset (Hermann et al., 2015; Nallapati et al., 2016) measured by the ROUGE-L met-

Proceedings of the 1st Workshop on Natural Language Generation, Evaluation, and Metrics (GEM 2021), pages 96–120
August 5–6, 2021. ©2021 Association for Computational Linguistics

ric (Lin, 2004). Since ROUGE only tests the extent to which a generated summary has a lexical overlap with a reference summary, it can erroneously produce high scores for fluent, yet meaningless and unfaithful outputs as long as many of the same words are used (Maynez et al., 2020; Gabriel et al., 2020). Moreover, ROUGE tends to favor systems that produce longer summaries (Sun et al., 2019). It is thus crucial to carefully assess the progress of NLG toward all of its goals at the same time in ways that evolve alongside the models. This is currently not the case; new models are evaluated on different datasets, most of which focus only on the English language (Bender, 2019), and using these flawed metrics. Moreover, while human evaluations of generated texts can provide complementary insights to automatic evaluation (Manning et al., 2020), it can also lead to contradicting results since studies often omit crucial replication details and assume different definitions of the measured quantities (Howcroft et al., 2020).

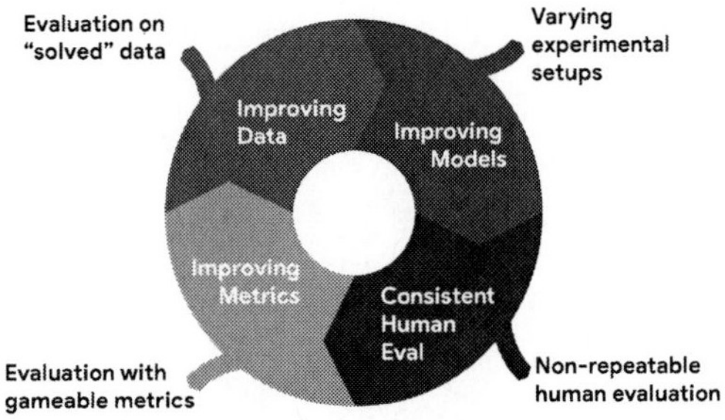

Figure 1: The opportunities of living benchmarks and pitfalls of evaluation. As models improve, we need consistent evaluations such that models can be compared to each other. This can only happen if we develop robust human evaluation standards and improve our automated metrics. Otherwise, results are challenging to interpret and compare to each other. Finally, as models improve and metrics saturate, we need to evaluate them on more challenging datasets instead of continuing to move sideways on old ones. GEM aims to provide this environment for natural language generation.

We propose a living benchmark called GEM (Generation, Evaluation, and Metrics) that aims to enable research on a wide range of NLG challenges. To avoid the fallacy of encouraging hill climbing on a leaderboard (Linzen, 2020), GEM focuses on an in-depth evaluation of model outputs across human and automatic evaluation that aims to uncover shortcomings and opportunities for progress. As datasets, metrics, and models improve, the benchmark environment will improve as well, replacing "solved" tasks with more challenging ones, incorporating newly developed metrics, and addressing discovered flaws in the experimental setup, as demonstrated in Figure 1. Making all model outputs available under an open-source license will support evaluation research and integrating new metrics will, in turn, help their adoption and increase the robustness of model evaluations.

The initial set of eleven included datasets is presented in Table 1. They measure specific generation challenges, such as the content selection and planning (*What to say?*), and the surface realization (*How to say it?*) (Reiter and Dale, 2000; Gatt and Krahmer, 2018). Models need to be capable of paraphrasing, simplification, and others. In addition to those challenges, GEM datasets also differ in their communicative goals, languages, the noisiness of data, and resource availability, to evaluate the consistency of evaluation schemes. About half of the datasets have multiple references and more than half were post-processed to improve data quality. The sizes range from 5k to 500k data points. GEM features 18 languages across all tasks and two of the datasets do not include English at all. To be able to properly assess the performance of models in a way robust to the shortcuts a model can take, we additionally introduce ten types of challenging test sets that probe for specific modeling aspects (Perez-Beltrachini and Gardent, 2017; Ribeiro et al., 2020). To ensure that research with GEM is conducted responsibly, all the datasets are documented in an NLG-specific version of data cards (Bender and Friedman, 2018; Gebru et al., 2018) we developed and for which we release a template and guide. Moreover, all submitted models will have an associated data card (Mitchell et al., 2019).

This paper describes the selection and construction of the GEM datasets in support of the announcement of the shared task at ACL 2021. More detailed information can be found on our website `https://gem-benchmark.com/`.

2 Benchmarks in NLG

In this section, we summarize common criticisms of benchmarks in NLP, discuss how they apply to NLG, and how we plan to address them. Then, we describe opportunities that GEM can provide. NLP benchmarks such as GLUE (Wang et al., 2019b) are common for natural language understanding

Dataset	Communicative Goal	Language(s)	Size	Input Type
CommonGEN (Lin et al., 2020)	Produce a likely sentence which mentions all of the source concepts.	en	67k	Concept Set
Czech Restaurant (Dušek and Jurčíček, 2019)	Produce a text expressing the given intent and covering the specified attributes.	cs	5k	Meaning Representation
DART (Radev et al., 2020)	Describe cells in a table, covering all information provided in triples.	en	82k	Triple Set
E2E clean (Novikova et al., 2017) (Dušek et al., 2019)	Describe a restaurant, given all and only the attributes specified on the input.	en	42k	Meaning Representation
MLSum (Scialom et al., 2020)	Summarize relevant points within a news article	*de/es	*520k	Articles
Schema-Guided Dialog (Rastogi et al., 2020)	Provide the surface realization for a virtual assistant	en	*165k	Dialog Act
ToTTo (Parikh et al., 2020)	Produce an English sentence that describes the highlighted cells in the context of the given table.	en	136k	Highlighted Table
XSum (Narayan et al., 2018)	Highlight relevant points in a news article	en	*25k	Articles
WebNLG (Gardent et al., 2017)	Produce a text that verbalises the input triples in a grammatical and natural way.	en/ru	50k	RDF triple
WikiAuto + Turk/ASSET (Jiang et al., 2020) (Xu et al., 2016) (Alva-Manchego et al., 2020)	Communicate the same information as the source sentence using simpler words and grammar.	en	594k	Sentence
WikiLingua (Ladhak et al., 2020)	Produce high quality summaries of an instructional article.	*ar/cs/de/en es/fr/hi/id/it ja/ko/nl/pt/ru th/tr/vi/zh	*550k	Article

Table 1: A description of all the datasets included in GEM. The tasks vary in communicative goal, data size, and input type. * indicates changes from the originally published dataset made for GEM.

(NLU) tasks. They aggregate multiple tasks under a unified evaluation framework, which enables researchers to fairly compare their models to others. Due to the improved model comparability, benchmarks are critical in measuring modeling progress.

However, they also pose a risk that progress is reduced to the single number shown in a benchmark's leaderboard and thus may encourage blindly optimizing it without regard to other considerations like model size or fairness (Ethayarajh and Jurafsky, 2020). This is especially challenging for benchmarks in NLG since, as discussed above, the performance cannot be described through a single metric and it is often not clear what metric to optimize for. This shortfall can be seen in benchmarks like DecaNLP (McCann et al., 2018) and GLGE (Liu et al., 2020a) which include NLG tasks but focus only on a single metric and, as a result, may mischaracterize a system's performance.

Moreover, an easy-to-use data infrastructure also disincentivizes researchers from interacting with and conducting in-depth analyses of the data sets that models are trained on. The limited analysis delegates the responsibility to ensure that all included datasets have been collected fairly to the creators of the benchmark (Denton et al., 2020). The dataset and benchmark creators thus must provide in-depth statements that describe the data characteristics and surface potential issues and consider these issues when selecting datasets for a benchmark (Gebru et al., 2018; Bender and Friedman, 2018).

These dangers emphasize selecting datasets for a benchmark needs to be carefully done, that the setup has to remain flexible to be able to address newly found limitations, and that the benchmark should focus on climbing a leaderboard. Instead, a living benchmark that can adjust its datasets and specific evaluation metrics can be much more powerful and long-lived. This can, for example, be seen in Dynabench,[1] (Potts et al., 2020) which has a static evaluation, but interactively adds more test

[1] https://dynabench.org/

data through a human-in-the-loop approach.

Increasing multilingualism of NLG research. Another potentially harmful choice by benchmark creators is the choice of the languages of the included datasets. It is often assumed that work on English transfers to other languages (Bender, 2011). However, this assumption does not consider differences between the languages that lead to higher modeling complexity, for example, a richer morphology or a flexible word-order. Still, the majority of work in NLP and almost all benchmarks exclusively focus on English (e.g., Wang et al., 2019b; Liu et al., 2020a; McCann et al., 2018). Even if multiple languages are considered, the availability of data in a language often does not represent the number of speakers of a language. This means that work on languages with little available data can potentially impact many more people than work on highly resourced languages (Joshi et al., 2020).

As a result, many recent benchmarking and dataset creation efforts in NLU develop and focus on tasks that are inherently multilingual or which explore cross-lingual transfer. For example, XTREME (Hu et al., 2020) introduces a benchmark covering 40 languages across multiple NLU and retrieval tasks, XCOPA (Ponti et al., 2020) is a commonsense reasoning dataset for eleven languages, and MLQA (Lewis et al., 2020b) is a dataset for extractive question answering across seven languages. We can observe a similar recent trend in natural language generation, where MLSum (Scialom et al., 2020) and WikiLingua (Ladhak et al., 2020) were created as multilingual summarization datasets. There also have been first steps toward including NLG tasks in multilingual NLU benchmarks. For example, XGLUE includes Question and News Title Generation (Liang et al., 2020). Unfortunately, XGLUE reduces the generation evaluation to BLEU-4, a metric that is inadequate for NLG (Reiter, 2018).

There have also been multiple shared tasks in NLG that focus on multilingualism, for instance, the shared task on multilingual surface realization which includes eleven languages (Mille et al., 2018, 2019, 2020). The shared task on document-level generation and translation featured German and English generation challenges (Heafield et al., 2020). The WebNLG+ shared task asked participants to contribute models that can realize text in Russian and English (Ferreira et al., 2020).

A benchmark that focuses only on NLG can enable much richer evaluation (as described in the next sections), and promote non-English datasets. In addition, it can ensure that the datasets created for those shared tasks continue being evaluated.

Providing a testbed for automated evaluation. Most traditional automated metrics, such as ROUGE (Lin, 2004) and BLEU (Papineni et al., 2002), measure the n-gram overlap between a reference and the generated text. However, in most cases, there is more than one correct way to generate a text, especially in tasks with a latent content planning or selection step (Reiter and Dale, 2000). That means that a correct solution may score low on a metric. While multiple references alleviate the issue somewhat, these metrics still have a low correlation with human judgments (Reiter, 2018; Fabbri et al., 2020). To address the issue, the machine translation community has been organizing yearly metrics shared tasks which produce metrics that achieve a high correlation (Stanojević et al., 2015; Bojar et al., 2016, 2017; Ma et al., 2018, 2019; Mathur et al., 2020b). The latest metrics focus on semantic equivalence instead of lexical similarity, which improves the correlations drastically. However, recent work by Fabbri et al. (2020) demonstrates that this may not hold in summarization, where the automated metric BERTScore (Zhang et al., 2020b) does not improve upon the correlation of ROUGE. Moreover, Mathur et al. (2020a) and Freitag et al. (2020) find that when comparing two high-quality systems, differences according to a metric may also stem from how references are written or flaws in the metric itself.[2]

Given that automated metrics perform differently across tasks, setups, and languages, a multi-task NLG benchmark has the opportunity to act as a testbed to evaluate how the latest advances in automated metrics perform on these different tasks. The benchmark can facilitate this research through the release of system outputs and associated human annotations, which is what we are planning to do with GEM. Moreover, we allow the integration of additional metrics into our living benchmark system, which enables a much faster adoption.

Developing reproducible human evaluation standards. In recent work, Howcroft et al. (2020) investigated NLG papers from the last

[2]For a more complete description of recent developments in NLG evaluation, we refer to the survey by Celikyilmaz et al. (2020).

twenty years and the evaluation methodologies differ drastically across papers. Moreover, in most cases, it is not even mentioned what the human evaluation aims to measure and that definitions of measures like "accuracy" or "fluency" are inconsistent. They thus suggest reporting standards for criteria and methods, following a classification system proposed by Belz et al. (2020). In addition, regularly scheduled shared tasks like WMT have lead to standardization of human evaluation setups and enabled controlled experimentation with them. GEM has the opportunity to develop reproducible standards for how human evaluation for NLG tasks beyond translation should be conducted while at the same time incorporating lessons from related work. Acting on the same need, the recently proposed GENIE (Khashabi et al., 2021) system aims to automate and standardize the human evaluation of different NLG systems, however with the contrasting goal of reducing the evaluating to a leaderboard-like score. To avoid further fragmentation of the field, GEM is developing its own human evaluation approaches, but uses the infrastructure provided by GENIE to run its human evaluation.

In addition to GENIE, multiple other related efforts exist that work toward the goal of reproducible and robust in-depth human and automatic evaluation for NLG tasks, and which focus on specific modeling- or task-aspects that are different from those in GEM. Among those are KILT (Petroni et al., 2020) which focuses on knowledge-intensive tasks and retrieval-based models, Storium (Akoury et al., 2020) which focuses on open-ended story generation, and BIG bench[3] which focuses on measuring few-shot and zero-shot capabilities of language models.

3 Dataset Selection

As highlighted in Figure 1, the selection of included datasets is an integral part of a benchmark. They should be challenging for models, but it should still be possible to evaluate models trained on them. Moreover, the datasets should cover a wide range of relevant generation challenges that allow for findings to be as general as possible. Finally, the datasets should cover tasks that are interesting for contributors to work on to facilitate the wide adoption of the benchmark.

To collect datasets with those desired properties, the selection methodology for GEM is composed of three steps. First, we elicited a set of proposals from everyone involved in the effort. Second, we identified criteria for the selection. Third, all GEM members voted on individual dataset and criteria utilities. The final selection maximizes the utility under constrained resources, similar to a knapsack solver.[4] This can be seen as an extension of the selection process of SuperGLUE (Wang et al., 2019a) that had similar first and second steps but made the final decision based on which were harder for a baseline model to solve after identifying a final set of candidate datasets. Since we are going to introduce challenge sets, the baseline performance of models on a dataset matters less.

Dataset Elicitation. In the first step, all GEM participants were asked to suggest datasets following the schema provided in Appendix A. The categories included multiple brief categorizations, such as a description of the challenge that this dataset provides, its high-level task, and the communicative goal of an agent trained on the data. Following our goal to focus on non-English languages, we further asked for the languages included in the dataset, as well as the language locale. This step yielded 35 proposed datasets, listed in Appendix B.

Estimating Task+Criterion Utility. The second step focused on the selection of criteria to inform the selection. The initial set of criteria was selected through open discussion involving all members. We split criteria into "hard" and "soft" ones – hard criteria would lead to the definite inclusion/exclusion of a task if (not) satisfied. Soft criteria inform the utility of the remaining tasks. All GEM members filled out a survey asking them to rate, on a 5-point Likert scale, how much they wanted to see a task included in GEM. Additionally, we posed yes/no questions for all considered hard criteria and various questions about the soft criteria (e.g., "what percentage of the tasks should feature non-English language?", or "do we prefer noisy or clean datasets?"). Finally, the survey included open text fields that asked for (1) comments on any of the tasks, (2) comments or suggestions on hard exclusion criteria, and (3) suggestions of additional criterion/criteria. The full list of questions is

[3]https://github.com/google/BIG-bench

[4]Consider the criterion "We need equal representation of large and small datasets" under the constraint that only two datasets can be selected. If we have two large datasets with utility 10, and one small one with utility 5, we may want to include the smaller dataset over the second large dataset to satisfy the criterion.

shown in Appendix C.

The survey received 28 responses, revealing that the initial version of GEM should include a median of 10 tasks or an average of 12. Of those tasks, about a third should feature non-English language.

Selected Criteria. For the hard criteria, there was an agreement to focus only on open-access datasets and that concurrent or past shared tasks for the same datasets are not an issue. Overall, the sentiment determined the following selection principles:

- We focus on diverse high-level tasks over a single high-level task evaluated in-depth. However, each high-level task should include multiple datasets.
- We focus on clean datasets to avoid conflating model mistakes and learned noise.
- We include a mix of high- and low-resource datasets.
- We focus on data with interesting test sets.
- We should not focus on the quality of current evaluation strategies for a given dataset.
- We prefer multi-reference datasets since those have been shown to lead to more robust automatic evaluation.

High-Level Tasks. Since these principles dictate that we should focus on a small set of high-level tasks, we used the free-text replies to evaluate the interest in different high-level tasks. Grouping the proposed tasks yielded the following candidates: Summarization, Dialog, Simplification/Compression, Question Answering, Creative Writing, Data-to-Text, and Question Generation.[5] There was a preference to exclude image inputs and question answering because those tasks add complexity to the evaluation beyond the generated text. Moreover, since creative generation tasks like story generation and poetry generation suffer even more from inadequate evaluation approaches, there was a consensus to not include them. There was, however, a strong preference for the high-level tasks Summarization, Data-to-text, and Dialog.[6]

Specific Datasets. The final selection is shown in Table 1. To arrive at the selection, we first ranked all datasets by their average rating. For this, we treated positive ratings as 1, negative ratings as -1, and neutral ratings as 0. The highest-ranked datasets were E2E with 0.577, XSum with 0.538, and ToTTo with 0.461. Unfortunately, non-English datasets were ranked lower, with only WebNLG and MLSum among the top 15 datasets. We grouped all datasets by their high-level tasks and selected a group that would not violate the selection principles (e.g., only high-resource tasks). If two datasets fit, we picked the one with a higher interest rating. Among the 11 datasets, we have 18different languages, and the dataset sizes range from 5,000 examples to 1.5M, with most datasets between 50-150k examples. Two of them do not include English at all, which we hope reduces the dependence of the modeling approaches on anglocentric pretraining (Anastasopoulos and Neubig, 2020). The high-level tasks include Dialog, Summarization, Data-to-Text, and Simplification. About half of the datasets have multiple references and more than half had post-processing steps applied to them to ensure high data quality.

3.1 GEMifying the data

We produce data cards (Bender and Friedman, 2018; Gebru et al., 2018) for all data sets in GEM, for which we developed an NLG-specific template.[7] In addition to describing the data itself, the cards acknowledge potential limitations of a dataset regarding its creation process and describe its real-world use cases to ensure that the research is conducted responsibly.

These datasets are the base selection, and as part of GEM, we may change datasets and how they are used. For example, we may improve the training sets, make the test sets more challenging, or probe for specific skills a model must exhibit with test-only datasets (Perez-Beltrachini and Gardent, 2017; Linzen, 2020; Ribeiro et al., 2020; Schlegel et al., 2020). We may also ask to evaluate a single model on multiple test sets, following the design by Dua et al. (2019).

We are including modifications to several of the datasets: (1) **MLSum**: We excluded all languages besides Spanish and German since the sources for other languages disallow scraping content. Addi-

[5]For a full overview of potential future expansions and challenges, we refer to the survey by Gatt and Krahmer (2018).

[6]One may question the absence of Translation from this list. While it is a generation task, we excluded it since Translation already has regular benchmarking efforts with WMT.

[7]Our template extends and restructures that from Hugging Face Datasets and along with a guide can be found at `https://gem-benchmark.com/data_cards`.

Challenge Set Type	Example	Tasks
Numerical Variation	53 ->79	WebNLG
Attribute Order	English Cheap ->Cheap English	All data-to-text tasks
Typographical Errors	English Cheap ->Enlish Chesp	Schema-Guided, WikiAuto, XSum
No Punctuation	... the dog. ->... the dog	Schema-Guided, WikiAuto, XSum
Backtranslation	fantastic ->toll ->great	Schema-Guided, WikiAuto, XSum
Train & Validation Samples		All tasks
Gender, Ethnicity, Nationality		ToTTo
Input Shape		WebNLG
Syntactic Complexity		WikiAuto
Covid Summaries		MLSUM (es+de), XSum

Table 2: An overview of the types of challenge sets for GEM. The first category are modifications to inputs of a model, the second category identifies contrast sets which are subsets of the original test set, and the third describes newly collected data.

tionally, we removed all duplicate items (i.e., items with the same input text) and we used langdetect[8] to filter out examples that were in the wrong language. In total, 147 examples were removed from the German portion (0.06%) and 7417 examples were removed from the Spanish portion (2.5%). (2) **XSum**: Summaries in this dataset often have divergence issues between the source and target texts since gold summaries are introductory sentences prefacing each article. Models agnostic to such noises are vulnerable to hallucinations (Wiseman et al., 2017; Dhingra et al., 2019). To combat this, we fine-tuned a BERT-based (Devlin et al., 2019) classifier on 500 document and gold summary pairs, manually annotated for faithfulness (Maynez et al., 2020) and excluded all document-summary pairs from the original XSum dataset where the classifier was not confident ($p(\text{faithful}) > 0.8$) whether the summary is faithful to the document or not. (3) **Schema-Guided Dialog**: We are focusing on the response-generation part of the dataset and thus reformatted the dataset to treat the service agent utterances as the targets to be generated and the previous customer utterance and the agent's dialog act as the input. We additionally reformat the dialog acts to directly conform to the format described in the paper (Kale and Rastogi, 2020). (4) **WikiLingua**: We focus on the same five languages that were benchmarked in its original release (en, es, ru, tr, vi) in a cross-lingual setup in which the inputs are in the respective language and the outputs are in English. However, we re-split the original data to avoid train-test overlaps between languages and provide training data in 13 additional languages (as shown in Table 1). For GEM, we allow submissions trained on any of the languages in isolation or as part of a multilingual model.

[8]https://pypi.org/project/langdetect/

3.2 Challenge Sets

In addition to applying consistent metrics to existing test sets, understanding specific model behavior, such as model generalization capabilities or performance under targeted cases, is also key for improvement. This is difficult to assess through evaluations on i.i.d. test splits. We thus release challenge sets to evaluate data-to-text and text-to-text models (overview in Table 2). In addition to enabling a more specific breakdown of how a model performs in the presence of challenging inputs, the set of system outputs on these test sets also constitutes a rich corpus that enables further error analysis and research. We apply multiple strategies to create the special test sets, in particular (I) alteration of the existing test sets (e.g., the introduction of distractors), (II) breaking down of the existing sets into subsets with certain properties (e.g., subsets with different complexity), and (III) the compilation of new test sets (e.g., out-of-vocabulary inputs). We restrict the size of each challenge set to about 500 examples to minimize computational overhead. On the WebNLG challenge sets, all subset items are selected proportionally from each category to ensure a similar distribution to the original set; on all other datasets the subset items are selected from the whole set. The results of the different systems on these subsets will be compared to the results obtained by the same systems on the same subsets of the original test data.

For case (I), altering existing test sets, the first challenge set adds **numerical variation** in WebNLG. This variation attempts to respect the format of the current cardinal value (e.g. alpha, integer, or floating-point) and replaces the existing value with a new random value as a means to challenge existing trained models. The generated number is lower-bounded between zero and upper bounded to be within to the highest power of 10 unit for the given value (e.g. replacing a value of 54 would result in a random value between 0-100). Floating values are also bounded to have the same degree of precision as the input value. For structure-to-text and dialog datasets, we produce a version of the test sets in which the **order of the components** of the input structures (triples, concepts, dialog acts, table rows, etc.) is randomly changed. For text-to-text datasets and Schema-guided Dialog, we introduce several types of perturbations: (a) **typographical errors**, using butter-fingers [9] with two thresholds 0.02 and 0.05, which respectively correspond to lower and higher error frequencies; (b) **removal of the final punctuation** sign (if any); (c) substitution of the input text by a **backtranslated version**, using the backtranslation implementation by Xie et al. (2020). We rejected backtranslation outputs based on a character length to ensure that the difference in character length between original and backtranslation does not exceed 35% of the original source character length. For XSum 99.8% of the backtranslations were accepted, for Wiki-Auto 94.42% (ASSET) and 87.18% (TURK), and for Schema-Guided Dialog 78%.

In case (II), the breaking down existing sets, we first provide for each dataset **random samples of training and validation data**, in order to assess to what extent the scores of the different systems drop when run on the test data. Then, specific splits are created for particular datasets, in order to assess possible biases of the models, and their robustness across inputs with different specifications. For ToTTo, test set splits are built according to several aspects that can be identified using WikiData: **gender, ethnicity and nationality grouped by continent**. For gender, we compare the performance between male and female people, but cannot compare other genders due to a lack of original data - only seven people in the original test set are marked as having a different gender. We compare across the continent of the underlying nationality to address the issue that data for each country can be very sparse – i.e., only 19 countries are represented by more than ten people and only one of these is located in Africa (Kenya). In case a person has citizenships across multiple continents, we may include the person in any of the included continents. Finally, we compare African Americans vs. all Americans. Ethnicity is very sparsely annotated in WikiData with fewer than 150 annotated test examples in total and 128 of these are African Americans. We thus are unable to compare the performance on, e.g., Yoruba or Punjabi people, both of which have fewer than five instances. Another caveat here is that only 21 of the 128 people are female. Our contrast subset that can include any US citizens matches these counts. Across all three challenge subsets, we additionally match the fraction of the existing non-overlap and overlap properties. For WebNLG, we propose subsets based on the **shape of the inputs** (number of triples, number of common subjects and/or objects, depth, etc.) For Turk/ASSET, splits are created in terms of the **syntactic complexity** of the sentences to be simplified. To characterise sentence complexity we use the developmental level scale proposed by Covington et al. (2006).[10] Although Turk and ASSET contain similar input sentences, the human references in Turk were created without allowing sentence splits and ASSET was created by encouraging annotators to split long sentences. For all datasets, we propose splits based on the frequency of the parts that compose the input in the training data; the resulting test sets range from being made of very common components to being made only from components unseen in the training data. For case (III), we collect time-shifted test data for news summarization in the form of articles with Covid19-related keywords. Since MLSum and XSum were collected before the pandemic, we can measure how a model responds to context not seen in the training data (outside of potential pretraining). The new set of articles covers existing article topics (economy, sports, etc.) but all in relation to the Covid19 pandemic. In addition, some new topics appear in the collected data derived from outlet sections that were not part of the original data collection.[11]

[9]`https://github.com/alexyorke/butter-fingers`

[10]We use the implementation provided by Lu (2010).

[11]To collect this data we use the scripts provided for the re-creation of MLSum and XSum datasets.

4 Experimental Setup

Since the GEM test sets and final metrics selection have not been released yet, we describe an experimental setup that will ensure that participating models are trained correctly and evaluated on publicly available data with available metrics that will give a sufficient indication of a model's performance. To do this, we are reporting the results of the baseline models on the validation sets.

4.1 Modeling Baselines

Much of the recent modeling progress in NLP can be attributed to the rise of the pretrain-then-finetune paradigm which has led to consistently better results. This finding is consistent with human judgments for summarization, as shown by Fabbri et al. (2020), among others. However, many of the tasks included in GEM may not benefit from a language model encoder since their input is not natural language. We thus apply a variety of different architectures that vary in size, complexity, and training schema. Our main baselines are T5 with 60M parameters (Raffel et al., 2020) and BART with 139M parameters (Lewis et al., 2020a). For non-English datasets, we use their multilingual counterparts mT5 in various sizes (Xue et al., 2020) and mBART (Liu et al., 2020b). We additionally train the following baselines on a subset of tasks: TGen (with added language model and lemma tags denoted as TGen+/++) (Dušek and Jurčíček, 2016b), an architecture for generation from dialog acts, an LSTM-based Sequence-to-sequence model with attention (Bahdanau et al., 2015), DialoGPT (Zhang et al., 2020c), a pretraining approach for conversational models, and PEGASUS (Zhang et al., 2020a), which uses a summarization-specific pretraining schema that masks and predicts entire sentences.For WikiLingua, we additionally report results on a setup proposed by Ladhak et al. (2020) which includes first training a monolingual model followed by finetuning with the correct source language, coupled with synthetic data generated through translation (mBART+).
Almost all baselines can be reproduced on a GPU-based colaboratory notebook within 2-3 hours.

4.2 Automated Evaluation

As mentioned above, GEM provides a testbed for automated metrics and can be used to popularize newly developed ones. Thus, models are evaluated via a constantly expanding list of metrics and, to avoid overfitting to known metrics, we will use metrics on the test submissions that are not included in this initial writeup. Consequentially, the baseline results are an incomplete list which will be expanded upon the announcement of the test metrics. The set of metrics can be computed via the framework described at `https://gem-benchmark.com/shared_task` which comprises metrics in the following categories:

Lexical Similarity. We include multiple "traditional" metrics as baseline metrics, notably BLEU (Papineni et al., 2002), ROUGE-1/2/L (Lin, 2004), and METEOR (Banerjee and Lavie, 2005). These metrics can often be gamed, for example, ROUGE can be improved by increased the output length of the model (Sun et al., 2019). Moreover, the reliability of these metrics depends on the quality and number of the references (Mathur et al., 2020a; Freitag et al., 2020). However, on a system-level, they still correlate well with human judgments for some tasks (Reiter, 2018).

Semantic Equivalence. More recently, metrics that rely on pretrained language models have shown improved correlations with human judgments on the segment-level. We thus include BERTScore (Zhang et al., 2020b), a metric based on the similarity of sentence embeddings, and BLEURT (Sellam et al., 2020), a metric that is fine-tuned on human ratings. The reported baseline results use RoBERTa-large (Liu et al., 2019) and mBERT (Devlin et al., 2019) for BERTScore and the English-only BLEURT-base-128 for BLEURT.

Probing for Faithfulness. Another approach that has shown promise in summarization. The approach relies on the insight that a reader of a reference and generated summary should be able to answer the same question, regardless of how the summary is phrased. There has been much development toward these QA-based approaches (Eyal et al., 2019; Scialom et al., 2019; Durmus et al., 2020; Wang et al., 2020, among others) and they can provide an alternative angle to model evaluation that does not highly correlate with other evaluation approaches (Fabbri et al., 2020). While most related work on these metrics is limited to summarization, we are evaluating systems using a QA-based method called QuestEval (Scialom et al., 2021) that supports all of our tasks.

In addition to QA-based evaluation, there have also been related efforts to develop more fine-

Dataset	Model	Metrics (Lexical Similarity and Semantic Equivalence)						
		METEOR	ROUGE-1	ROUGE-2	ROUGE-L	BLEU	BERTScore	BLEURT
CommonGen	BART	0.301	63.5	32.5	55.1	27.5	0.943	-0.400
	T5	0.291	64.0	29.4	54.5	26.4	0.942	-0.412
Czech Restaurant	mT5-small	0.229	47.3	28.6	43.0	17.9	0.895	–
	mT5-base	0.23	48.1	28.8	44.2	17.1	0.898	–
	mT5-large	0.233	51.3	30.0	46.4	17.5	0.902	–
	mT5-XL	0.229	52.1	31.3	47.3	17.0	0.905	–
	TGen	0.152	13.6	0.0	13.6	0.03	0.650	–
	TGen+	0.151	13.8	0.0	13.8	0.03	0.651	–
	TGen++	0.167	9.7	0.0	9.7	0.03	0.648	–
DART	BART	0.107	7.1	0.0	7.1	0.02	0.862	-0.261
	T5	0.115	8.4	0.0	8.4	0.02	0.901	-0.091
E2E clean	BART	0.373	73.6	48.5	57.8	43.5	0.948	0.190
	LSTM	0.394	75.0	50.3	58.9	46.9	0.950	0.252
	T5	0.369	72.6	47.5	56.4	43.0	0.945	0.384
	TGen	0.391	74.7	49.6	58.4	46.0	0.949	0.412
MLSum (de)	mBART	0.437	43.8	33.1	39.8	28.2	0.888	–
	mT5-small	0.098	11.8	3.4	10.0	5.0	0.826	–
	mT5-base	0.099	12.2	3.5	10.2	5.1	0.830	–
	mT5-large	0.101	12.4	3.6	10.4	5.2	0.832	–
	mT5-XL	0.102	12.6	3.7	10.5	5.3	0.832	–
MLSum (es)	mBART	0.210	28.4	10.9	22.4	7.4	0.836	–
	mT5-small	0.198	28.1	10.5	22.8	8.2	0.834	–
	mT5-base	0.214	29.5	11.7	23.9	9.6	0.839	–
	mT5-large	0.235	31.8	13.8	26.0	11.0	0.845	–
	mT5-XL	0.247	33.1	15.0	27.2	11.9	0.849	–
Schema-Guided	BART	0.089	13.6	4.4	11.3	2.7	0.691	-1.355
	T5	0.331	58.2	36.8	52.6	33.4	0.874	0.009
ToTTo	T5	0.363	70.1	48.3	60.1	42.2	0.914	0.179
XSum	PEGASUS	0.216	46.5	23.2	38.1	17.0	0.918	-0.186
WebNLG (en)	mBART	0.462	83.4	63.1	70.3	66.1	0.967	0.458
	mT5-small	0.442	78.8	59.2	67.2	60.2	0.948	0.416
	mT5-base	0.461	82.3	62.1	69.7	65.2	0.955	0.451
	mT5-large	0.473	83.8	64.4	71.6	68.0	0.959	0.479
	mT5-XL	0.472	83.5	63.6	71.0	67.6	0.958	0.47
WebNLG (ru)	mBART	0.613	34.8	13.4	33.0	47.0	0.888	–
	mT5-small	0.553	29.7	10.5	28.4	41.1	0.942	–
	mT5-base	0.602	33.0	12.7	31.3	44.3	0.949	–
	mT5-large	0.614	33.4	13.4	32.1	46.4	0.952	–
	mT5-XL	0.624	34.3	13.7	32.8	47.2	0.952	–
Turk	BART	0.556	90.3	86.1	89.9	88.3	0.967	0.358
	T5	0.649	95.7	92.9	95.5	95.1	0.974	0.495
ASSET	BART	0.560	90.1	82.3	89.6	92.4	0.982	0.407
	T5	0.581	92.1	92.3	92.6	93.4	0.984	0.468
WikiLingua (es→en)	mBART	0.178	38.3	15.4	32.4	12.2	0.853	-0.290
	mBART+	0.196	40.7	16.9	34.1	14.3	0.858	-0.248
	mT5-small	0.135	29.8	9.8	25.5	7.4	0.832	-0.437
	mT5-base	0.162	36.3	13.7	30.6	10.1	0.85	-0.324
	mT5-large	0.183	39.3	15.7	33.0	12.5	0.857	-0.27
	mT5-XL	0.203	41.8	17.4	34.7	15.2	0.862	-0.218
WikiLingua (ru→en)	mBART	0.153	33.1	11.9	27.8	9.3	0.839	-0.369
	mBART+	0.174	37.3	14.9	31.9	12.0	0.851	-0.303
	mT5-small	0.128	27.2	8.5	23.2	6.9	0.825	-0.471
	mT5-base	0.149	32.5	11.1	26.9	8.8	0.839	-0.377
	mT5-large	0.167	35.0	12.7	28.8	11.0	0.846	-0.337
	mT5-XL	0.185	38.6	15.4	32.3	13.6	0.855	-0.268
WikiLingua (tr→en)	mBART	0.164	34.4	13.0	28.1	11.7	0.837	-0.414
	mBART+	0.204	43.7	20.8	37.9	17.5	0.866	-0.252
	mT5-small	0.154	29.4	10.9	23.4	13.0	0.823	-0.595
	mT5-base	0.168	32.5	13.6	26.0	15.5	0.834	-0.507
	mT5-large	0.185	36.2	15.0	29.1	16.9	0.846	-0.405
	mT5-XL	0.208	41.5	19.6	34.7	19.9	0.86	-0.291
WikiLingua (vi→en)	mBART	0.150	32.0	11.1	26.4	9.2	0.836	-0.394
	mBART+	0.183	38.1	15.4	32.5	13.3	0.853	-0.284
	mT5-small	0.12	23.5	6.0	19.0	6.1	0.812	-0.56
	mT5-base	0.129	26.0	7.5	20.5	7.4	0.82	-0.513
	mT5-large	0.146	29.9	9.6	23.8	9.2	0.833	-0.421
	mT5-XL	0.173	35.5	13.0	29.2	12.4	0.847	-0.308

Table 3: The set of baseline results we release alongside GEM with a focus on reference-based evaluation.

Dataset	Model	Metrics (Diversity and System Characterization)								
		MSTTR	Distinct_1	Distinct_2	H_1	H_2	Unique_1	Unique_2	$\|\mathcal{V}\|$	Output Len.
CommonGen	BART	0.57	0.12	0.41	7.1	10.7	583	2.7k	1.2k	10.5
	T5	0.51	0.11	0.36	6.5	10.1	465	2.0k	1.0k	9.6
Czech Restaurant	mT5-small	0.51	0.04	0.1	6.2	7.8	86	278	287	10.2
	mT5-base	0.49	0.03	0.09	6.1	7.6	80	249	273	10.5
	mT5-large	0.57	0.05	0.13	6.6	8.4	103	387	361	10.1
	mT5-XL	0.6	0.06	0.19	6.8	9.0	146	614	438	9.5
	TGen	0.57	0.03	0.11	6.4	8.0	58	239	245	9.1
	TGen+	0.61	0.04	0.12	6.5	8.1	84	290	305	9.2
	TGen++	0.56	0.04	0.11	6.5	8.1	85	280	297	9.5
DART	BART	0.55	0.19	0.45	8.4	11.3	1.3k	3.6k	2.4k	12.0
	T5	0.51	0.19	0.42	8.0	10.7	1.2k	3.1k	2.1k	10.8
E2E clean	BART	0.32	0.005	0.02	5.7	7.2	16	104	149	22.0
	LSTM	0.31	0.004	0.02	5.6	7.1	19	106	139	23.1
	T5	0.30	0.004	0.01	5.6	6.9	7	60	125	23.0
	TGen	0.31	0.004	0.02	5.6	7.2	19	116	140	23.2
MLSum (de)	mBART	0.78	0.11	0.52	10.6	16.3	27k	166k	46k	35.7
	mT5-small	0.75	0.12	0.52	10.4	15.8	20.1k	113.8k	33.6k	24.7
	mT5-base	0.76	0.12	0.53	10.4	15.8	20.2k	113.0k	33.3k	24.2
	mT5-large	0.76	0.12	0.53	10.4	15.8	20.0k	114.0k	33.3k	24.4
	mT5-XL	0.77	0.12	0.53	10.4	15.8	20.0k	114.6k	33.3k	24.5
MLSum (es)	mBART	0.71	0.10	0.47	10.1	15.7	19k	120k	35k	32.3
	mT5-small	0.69	0.12	0.48	10.0	15.1	14.0k	77.6k	25.5k	21.7
	mT5-base	0.71	0.12	0.5	10.1	15.3	15.1k	85.2k	27.2k	23.0
	mT5-large	0.71	0.12	0.5	10.1	15.3	14.9k	82.0k	26.6k	22.1
	mT5-XL	0.72	0.12	0.5	10.1	15.3	14.8k	80.5k	26.1k	21.4
Schema-Guided	BART	0.56	0.02	0.06	7.0	9.2	1.8k	6.2k	3.9k	22.0
	T5	0.67	0.03	0.10	7.9	10.6	1.6k	5.8k	3.8k	11.8
ToTTo	T5	0.73	0.18	0.54	10.1	14.4	15k	60k	21k	15.3
XSum	PEGASUS	0.73	0.20	0.64	9.3	13.1	3.0k	13k	5k	22.9
WebNLG (en)	mBART	0.53	0.09	0.27	8.6	11.8	969	4.0k	3.2k	20.7
	mT5-small	0.5	0.09	0.25	8.6	11.8	864	3.9k	3.2k	22.7
	mT5-base	0.53	0.09	0.27	8.7	11.9	983	4.4k	3.3k	21.7
	mT5-large	0.54	0.09	0.29	8.7	12.0	1.1k	4.8k	3.4k	21.7
	mT5-XL	0.54	0.09	0.29	8.7	12.0	1.1k	4.8k	3.4k	21.6
WebNLG (ru)	mBART	0.46	0.08	0.20	8.1	10.3	334	1.1k	1.2k	18.9
	mT5-small	0.43	0.08	0.20	7.9	10.2	349	1.2k	1.2k	19.2
	mT5-base	0.47	0.09	0.23	8.2	10.7	482	1.6k	1.4k	19.9
	mT5-large	0.48	0.09	0.24	8.2	10.7	474	1.6k	1.4k	19.4
	mT5-XL	0.46	0.09	0.22	8.2	10.5	418	1.4k	1.3k	19.5
Turk	BART	0.73	0.23	0.74	9.8	14.1	5.5k	23k	8.6k	18.4
	T5	0.73	0.22	0.72	9.9	14.2	5.9k	25k	9.3k	20.1
ASSET	BART	0.73	0.23	0.73	9.8	14.1	5.9k	24k	9.1k	20.1
	T5	0.73	0.22	0.72	9.9	14.2	5.9k	26k	9.4k	21.3
WikiLingua (es→en)	mBART	0.55	0.03	0.19	8.8	14.0	4.7k	63k	15k	29.4
	mBART+	0.58	0.03	0.21	9.1	14.5	5.9k	83k	18k	32.5
	mT5-small	0.39	0.03	0.15	8.3	12.8	2.3k	20.9k	8.2k	31.8
	mT5-base	0.52	0.04	0.23	8.7	13.7	3.5k	34.4k	10.3k	28.7
	mT5-large	0.57	0.04	0.26	8.9	14.0	4.2k	44.4k	11.7k	30.8
	mT5-XL	0.6	0.04	0.29	9.1	14.4	5.0k	57.7k	13.5k	34.7
WikiLingua (ru→en)	mBART	0.54	0.04	0.20	8.5	13.3	2.8k	28k	8.7k	27.3
	mBART+	0.55	0.04	0.23	8.8	13.7	3.5k	35k	10k	28.4
	mT5-small	0.4	0.04	0.19	8.2	12.6	1.5k	11.6k	5.5k	31.8
	mT5-base	0.55	0.06	0.3	8.6	13.4	2.5k	21.0k	7.1k	28.7
	mT5-large	0.59	0.06	0.32	8.7	13.6	3.0k	26.1k	7.9k	31.1
	mT5-XL	0.6	0.07	0.35	8.8	13.8	3.4k	29.0k	8.5k	31.4
WikiLingua (tr→en)	mBART	0.45	0.08	0.28	7.7	11.2	743	4.1k	2.1k	34.2
	mBART+	0.52	0.12	0.38	8.0	11.9	1.2k	6.1k	2.8k	30.7
	mT5-small	0.55	0.14	0.46	8.1	11.6	935	4.4k	2.1k	40.2
	mT5-base	0.59	0.16	0.51	8.2	11.9	1.0k	4.8k	2.2k	38.7
	mT5-large	0.58	0.16	0.5	8.1	11.8	1.0k	4.7k	2.2k	38.0
	mT5-XL	0.58	0.16	0.51	8.2	11.8	1.0k	4.7k	2.1k	36.8
WikiLingua (vi→en)	mBART	0.54	0.07	0.28	8.2	12.3	1.5k	9.3k	4.0k	26.9
	mBART+	0.54	0.08	0.33	8.6	12.9	2.1k	13k	5.3k	29.8
	mT5-small	0.5	0.09	0.33	8.2	12.1	1.2k	6.4k	3.1k	32.9
	mT5-base	0.58	0.12	0.43	8.4	12.6	1.6k	8.9k	3.7k	31.1
	mT5-large	0.6	0.12	0.45	8.5	12.7	1.7k	9.3k	3.8k	30.7
	mT5-XL	0.61	0.12	0.47	8.6	12.9	1.8k	10.2k	4.0k	31.5

Table 4: Results of the baseline results we release with GEM, focusing on diversity of the outputs and neutral system characterizations.

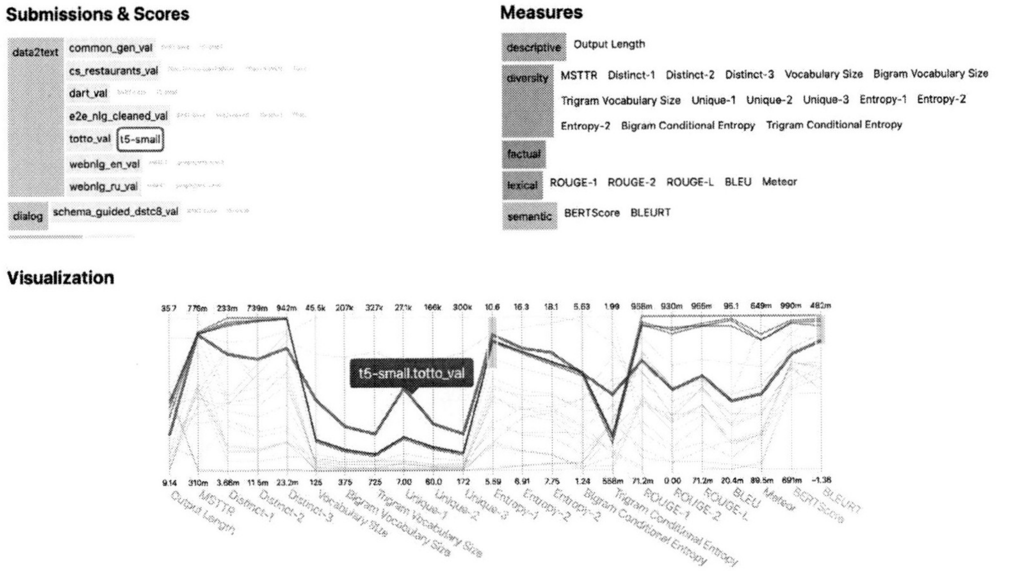

Figure 2: A screenshot of the interactive result exploration tool. **[Top Left]** The selection of tasks, task-groups, or individual submissions. **[Top Right]** The selection of metric-groups or metrics **[Bottom]** The parallel coordinates visualization of the selection. The selection here can be filtered by brushing over a section of an individual metric, as is shown here for BLEURT. Hovering over a line presents detailed information of the particular submission.

grained and interpretable evaluation metrics, for example to measure consistency in data-to-text problems (Opitz and Frank, 2020; Dhingra et al., 2019). We are using one such metric called NUBIA (Kane et al., 2020), the NeUral Based Interchangeability Assessor, which combines multiple measures such as entailment and similarity into a decomposable and interpretable score.

Diversity. As argued by Hashimoto et al. (2019) among many others, NLG models intrinsically trade off diversity and quality. A model can produce more diverse outputs through sampling but at the cost of output quality. To account for this aspect, we compute multiple diversity metrics, starting with those proposed for the analysis of the results of the E2E NLG challenge (Dusek et al., 2020) and by van Miltenburg et al. (2018). These include the Shannon Entropy (Shannon and Weaver, 1963) over unigrams and bigrams (H_1, H_2), the mean segmented type token ratio over segment lengths of 100 (MSTTR, Johnson, 1944), the ratio of distinct n-grams over the total number of n-grams ($\text{Distinct}_{1,2}$), and the count of n-grams that only appear once across the entire test output ($\text{Unique}_{1,2}$, Li et al., 2016).

System Characterization. The final section of metrics will characterize the systems. While the focus of this section will be on qualitative descriptions through model cards, we also gather quantitative information that is not necessarily associated with a judgment. As part of this, we collect the number of parameters of a system, as suggested by Ethayarajh and Jurafsky (2020). For each task, we additionally report the vocabulary size over the output ($|\mathcal{V}|$) and the mean output length of a system (Sun et al., 2019).

5 Results

One of the central aims of GEM is to measure the progress in NLG without misrepresenting the complex interactions between the sometimes contradicting measures. We thus will not distill the complex interplay of the data, metrics, and model outputs into a single number or statement, and we do not present results in a traditional leaderboard. Instead, we developed an interactive result exploration system that allows analyses of model results, and which we describe in this section. To further motivate this change, consider the following conclusion someone may draw from looking at a leaderboard:

> System Foo performs the best.

Our interactive system aims to enable more nuanced statements such as:

System Foo leads to consistent performance increases in Bar-type metrics on challenges that measure Baz while maintaining equal performance on most metrics of type Qux.

A screenshot of our system is presented in Figure 2.[12] In addition, our baseline results are presented in a tabular view in Tables 3 and 4. Our interactive system is centered around a parallel coordinates plot (Inselberg, 1985) which shows all results as lines through parallel axes. Every line intersects the axes at the corresponding mapped value. For instance, see the red line representing the results for task "ToTTo" of baseline "t5-small". Filters can be applied along axes (see BLEURT axis in Figure 2) and the filtered selection is highlighted through bold lines. A selection can be a set of metrics, systems, or tasks. This style of presentation has not been used before for a benchmark. The closest prior work is by Fu et al. (2020) for named-entity recognition which allows similar filtering and sorting, but presents the results in a table.

However, the parallel coordinates approach can scale to a much greater number of metrics than a table. Moreover, by using a parallel coordinates plot instead of a table, it is easy to spot patterns that span multiple metrics, systems, or tasks. For example, the highlighted line in Figure 2 uncovers that, for the T5 baseline on ToTTo, the diversity metrics score higher than other systems while scoring lower on reference-based metrics. Since we only have a single baseline for ToTTo, it is unclear whether this difference can be attributed to the dataset or the system but this relationship will be uncovered once we receive submissions.

The final system will additionally be able to display the model cards and other related meta-information associated with submissions. It will also be able to show (and compare) exemplary outputs for each test set. Those two features will improve the transparency of the results and systems to those who are not familiar with a task and provide necessary information to those who consider using a particular system. The combination of all components will enable analysis on quantitative, individual, and qualitative level which can support formulating new research hypotheses and gather in-depth insights about system performance. For example, the functionality to compare human annotation and automatic measures could lead to a better understanding how fluency affect BERTScore.

In addition to the interactive self-directed result exploration, our shared task features an evaluation and analysis part. Instead of dictating the interpretation of the modeling shared task results, we will release all system outputs and metrics in this second part and participants of this part may run their own evaluation and conduct interesting analyses.

6 Submitting to the benchmark

While we ask submitters to try to cover as many tasks as possible, we acknowledge potential restrictions on computation resources. We thus do not require that a submissions to GEM has to include predictions on every included test and challenge sets. All predictions from a model should be formatted and added into a single file as outlined on our website.

In addition, we require every submitter to answer a series of questions that we will use to construct a model card (Mitchell et al., 2019) and externalize potential concerns regarding the social impact of a model and its use, or its training data. The card will additionally display information to replicate the experiments. While we require responses to these questions at submission time, we allow the information about a model to remain anonymous during required anonymization periods should a paper describing the model be under submission elsewhere. All submitted model outputs will be made publicly available for download.

After a submission, we will run the evaluation suite on the submitted outputs and additionally collect human annotations.

Human Evaluation GEM will be used to develop reproducible and consistent human evaluation strategies for generated text. This task involves selecting and defining which quantities of the generated text should be measured, developing annotation schemes and rater guidelines to capture these quantities accurately, and infrastructure to annotate system outputs.

We aim to develop these setups for all task setups such as summarization, dialogue, simplification, and data-to-text. To approach this task, we will follow the recently proposed taxonomy of human evaluation measures by Belz et al. (2020) and follow the reporting strategies proposed by Howcroft et al. (2020). The detailed setups will be described in a evaluation datasheet (Shimorina and Belz, 2021).

[12] An initial version showcasing our baseline results is deployed on our website.

All shared task participants will be asked to provide gold annotations on system outputs, which we will then use to evaluate the consistency of crowd-sourced annotations.[13]

7 Next Steps

This section lists the currently active developments and the long-term steps we will take to ensure that GEM will continue to evolve and improve.

7.1 Collecting more multilingual data

Many of the initial datasets in GEM are focused on (American or British) English; we see this release as a starting point for the collection of new datasets to improve the inclusiveness of other languages and cultures. From the task point of view, to ensure the longevity of the dataset, we want it to be practical and socially beneficial. Through GEM, we have developed a set of desired criteria for NLG datasets and we aim to apply this knowledge to data collection and actively work toward reducing the disparity in data availability between languages (Joshi et al., 2020). To this end, we are focusing on a task that requires content selection, planning, and surface realization along in a grounded scenario. The idea is in the prototyping stage with prospects broadly towards dialog response generation and topic summarization in multiple languages. We plan to do so by collaborating with speakers of low-resourced languages through a participatory research approach, as suggested by (∀ et al., 2020). Toward this goal, GEM welcomes anyone interested in collaborating on this effort.

7.2 Personalizing and Controlling NLG

GEM currently focuses on tasks that deterministically transform an input into an output. With the increasing use of NLG models in real-world applications, how to enable and evaluate personalized NLG systems (e.g., in dialect or formality) remains challenging. Several related tasks have been proposed, for example, the transfer of writing style from informal to formal (Rao and Tetreault, 2018), personalization of machine translation systems to align with particular personal traits (Mirkin and Meunier, 2015), or persona-guided response generation of dialogue systems (Zhang et al., 2018). We envision our framework to be extended (e.g., dataset, evaluation) to incorporate this line of user-focused NLG.

7.3 Regular updates to the living benchmark

To activate the benefits of a living benchmark that is focused on evaluation, we commit to regular updates for GEM. We invite contributions in the form of model outputs, analyses, and metrics at any time and will automatically update the results presented on our website to incorporate them. For the updates to the dataset selection, we want to consider the input of the wider NLG research community. To do so, we will set up a yearly selection process similar to the one described in Section 3. The first update process will be run after the GEM workshop at ACL 2021. To be able to have a robust comparison between different versions of GEM, we will only replace a small subset of datasets at a time.

8 Conclusion

In this paper, we have introduced GEM, a living natural language generation benchmark with a focus on evaluation. While GEM does not claim to instantly solve all issues of benchmarks in NLG, we aim to provide an environment in which systems can be tested in a principled manner and which can elevate the prominence of interesting evaluation approaches. By providing a testbed to easily conduct experiments across many datasets and evaluate in a repeatable, consistent, and more interpretable way, we will be able to track progress toward the goals in NLG research much more clearly. Moreover, we will be able to extend and shape GEM in the future to include more multilingual datasets, which will assist in their adoption across the wider research community.

9 Contribution Statements

GEM is a large effort with a decentralized organization that is split into different task-specific subgroups. To acknowledge everyone's contribution, we list the contribution statements below for all groups.

Steering Committee. Antoine Bosselut, Esin Durmus, Varun Prashant Gangal, Sebastian Gehrmann, Laura Perez-Beltrachini, Samira Shaikh, and Wei Xu make up the steering committee. Sebastian Gehrmann coordinates and leads the GEM effort. All others provide feedback and discuss larger decisions regarding the direction of

[13]This approach has been successfully used by WMT for many years. See, e.g., `http://www.statmt.org/wmt20/translation-task.html`.

GEM and act as conference organizers for the ACL 2021 workshop.

Summarization. The summarization group members are Chris Emezue, Esin Durmus, Faisal Ladhak, Jiawei Zhou, Juan Diego Rodriguez, Kaustubh Dhole, Khyathi Chandu, Laura Perez, Pawan Sasanka Ammanamanchi, Pedro Henrique Martins, Rubungo Andre Niyongabo, Shashi Narayan, Vikas Raunak, and Yufang Hou. Pedro Henrique Martins organized the group and wrote the data statement for the MLSum dataset. Pawan Sasanka Ammanamanchi was responsible for the XSum data statement, while Vikas Raunak worked on the Wikilingua statement. Shashi Narayan prepared the GEM version of the XSum dataset and trained its baseline models. Juan Diego Rodriguez was responsible for cleaning the MLSum dataset and trained its baseline models. Faisal Ladhak was responsible for the Wikilingua baseline models. Rubungo Andre Niyongabo participated in the discussions and added related papers to the planning document.

Dialog. Sashank Santhanam, Samira Shaikh, Bodhisattwa Prasad Majumder, Harsh Jhamtani, Yangfeng Ji, Tosin Adewumi, and Wanyu Du are part of this group. Tosin Adewumi contributed code for DialoGPT, and Wanyu Du trained baselines for Schema-Guided Dialog. Harsh Jhamtani wrote the data card for Wizards of Wikipedia.

Data2Text. Ondrej Dusek wrote the data cards for E2E NLG and Czech Restaurants data and a TF loader for Czech Restaurants. He also supplied baseline outputs for E2E, Czech Restaurants, and WebNLG. Sebastian Gehrmann supplied baseline outputs for E2E, WebNLG, and CommonGen. Yacine Jernite wrote the data card for CommonGen and the Hugging Face loaders for Czech Restaurants and WebNLG. Teven Le Scao wrote the Hugging Face loader for E2E. Simon Mille and Anastasia Shimorina wrote the data card for WebNLG.

Table2Text. Varun Gangal and Miruna Clinciu are part of this group. Miruna Clinciu was responsible primarily for DART and Varun Gangal for ToTTo while maintaining a close correspondence and understanding between them to ensure all steps, such as code structure, preprocessing primitives, baselines were as uniform as possible.

Simplification. Dhruv Kumar, Mounica Maddela, and Wei Xu contributed to the GEM Simplification task. Dhruv Kumar created the data cards for the datasets, added Wiki-Auto and Turk/ASSET datasets to TFDS, and integrated the SARI metric (Xu et al., 2016) into the GEM evaluation framework. Mounica Maddela created baselines for the task and added the Turk benchmark corpus to Hugging Face and TFDS. Wei Xu helped in the organization and planning of the task setup.

Automated Evaluation. Ondrej Dusek wrote the base code and included BLEU, Meteor, ROUGE, and referenceless metrics (the latter based on code supplied by Emiel van Miltenburg). He also prepared reference sets for E2E, Czech Restaurants and WebNLG. Sebastian Gehrman included BLEURT and BERTScore and prepared the reference sets. Dhruv Kumar included SARI and adapted the code for source-based metrics. Nishant Subramani helped with code refactoring. Miruna Clinciu , Emiel van Miltenburg and Thibault Sellam provided feedback and participated in discussions.

Human Evaluation. Samira Shaikh was the point of contact for this working group. She led the discussions to make progress on the group goals. She also worked with the group to select the general evaluation criteria as well as the criteria for dialogue and simplification tasks. Khyathi Chandu and Miruna Clinciu worked on selecting evaluation criteria for the summarization task and participated in the group discussions. Simon Mille provided support on using the criteria taxonomy and the annotated evaluation sheets for selecting and defining the criteria to use; worked on selecting the D2T criteria. Vitaly Nikolaev and Sashank Santhanam worked on selecting evaluation criteria for dialog and simplification tasks. João Sedoc worked with the group to select the evaluation criteria in general as well as the specific ones for dialog and simplification. He also helped to select among annotation interfaces. Anastasia Shimorina worked with the group to select the evaluation criteria and participated in the discussions. Chris Emezue, Sebastian Gehrmann, Khyati Mahajan, and Yufang Hou participated in discussions.

Website and Submission System. Aman Madaan, Moin Nadeem, Hendrik Strobelt, and Sebastian Gehrmann are part of this group. Sebastian Gehrmann developed the website. Aman Madaan wrote the initial version of the result presentation. Hendrik Strobelt leads the visualization effort for interactive exploration of results.

Model Infrastructure. Yacine Jernite wrote the initial script template for evaluating and fine-tuning Hugging Face models with the CommonGen example. Sebastian Gehrmann generalized the script to work with other datasets. Tosin Adewumi wrote a script for fine-tuning the DialoGPT model for dialogue datasets. Juan Diego Rodriguez worked on the infrastructure to fine-tune mBART on MLSum. Mihir Kale trained all mT5 baselines.

Data and Model Sheets and Statements. Salomey Osei, Pawan Sasanka Ammanamanchi, Juan Diego Rodriguez, Sebastian Gehrmann, Yacine Jernite, and Angelina McMillan-Major are part of this group. The Data Sheet structure was adapted from a combination of designs created for the Hugging Face Datasets library by Angelina McMillan-Major and Yacine Jernite and one written by Sebastian Gehrmann. Juan Diego Rodriguez and Yacine Jernite wrote initial statements for ASSET and CommonGen respectively. The feedback on those was used to improve the structure of the final template. Everyone contributed to the model card template.

Challenge Sets. Simon Mille, Emiel van Miltenburg, Kaustubh Dhole, Varun Prashant Gangal, Saad Mahamood, and Laura Perez-Beltrachini proposed and discussed ideas of interest for the data-to-text and the text-to-text tasks. Simon Mille coordinated the group. Emiel van Miltenburg, Saad Mahamood, and Simon Mille worked on the creation of the data-to-text datasets, while Varun Prashant Gangal, Kaustubh Dhole and Laura Perez-Beltrachini worked on the text-to-text datasets. Sebastian Gehrmann contributed the ToTTo challenge set.

Crowdsourcing New Data. Chris Emezue, Rubungo Andre Niyongabo, Aremu Anuoluwapo, Khyathi Chandu, Yufang Hou, Samira Shaikh, Varun Prashant Gangal, and Dimitra Gkatzia are members of this group. Khyathi Chandu worked on identifying where the current datasets fall short to motivate the crowdsourcing of data for a new task. Based on the suggestions from collaborators, she wrote two task proposals in the domains of long-form text, conversations, and data-to-text that address an array of challenges in generation and easily scale to multiple languages. Samira Shaikh participated in the discussions and gave feedback on the task proposals in the pilot study phase. Dimitra Gkatzia looked into potential resources for crowdsourcing. Chris Emezue and Rubungo Andre Niyongabo explored potential low-resource African languages for crowdsourcing. We are in the process of piloting the tasks internally.

The authors of this paper not named in the groups participated in initial discussions, participated in the surveys, and provided regular feedback and guidance. Many participants commented on and helped write this paper. We additionally thank all participants of INLG 2019, the Generation Birds-of-a-Feather meeting at ACL 2020, the EvalNLGEval Workshop at INLG 2020, and members of the generation challenge mailing list of SIGGEN for their participation in the discussions that inspired and influenced the creation of GEM.

References

Nader Akoury, Shufan Wang, Josh Whiting, Stephen Hood, Nanyun Peng, and Mohit Iyyer. 2020. STORIUM: A Dataset and Evaluation Platform for Machine-in-the-Loop Story Generation. In *Proceedings of the 2020 Conference on Empirical Methods in Natural Language Processing (EMNLP)*, pages 6470–6484, Online. Association for Computational Linguistics.

Fernando Alva-Manchego, Louis Martin, Antoine Bordes, Carolina Scarton, Benoît Sagot, and Lucia Specia. 2020. ASSET: A dataset for tuning and evaluation of sentence simplification models with multiple rewriting transformations. In *Proceedings of the 58th Annual Meeting of the Association for Computational Linguistics*, pages 4668–4679, Online. Association for Computational Linguistics.

Antonios Anastasopoulos and Graham Neubig. 2020. Should all cross-lingual embeddings speak English? In *Proceedings of the 58th Annual Meeting of the Association for Computational Linguistics*, pages 8658–8679, Online. Association for Computational Linguistics.

Dzmitry Bahdanau, Kyunghyun Cho, and Yoshua Bengio. 2015. Neural machine translation by jointly learning to align and translate. In *3rd International Conference on Learning Representations, ICLR 2015, San Diego, CA, USA, May 7-9, 2015, Conference Track Proceedings*.

Satanjeev Banerjee and Alon Lavie. 2005. METEOR: an automatic metric for MT evaluation with improved correlation with human judgments. In *Proceedings of the Workshop on Intrinsic and Extrinsic Evaluation Measures for Machine Translation and/or Summarization@ACL 2005, Ann Arbor, Michigan, USA, June 29, 2005*, pages 65–72. Association for Computational Linguistics.

Anja Belz, Mike White, Dominic Espinosa, Eric Kow, Deirdre Hogan, and Amanda Stent. 2011. The first surface realisation shared task: Overview and evaluation results. In *Proceedings of the 13th European Workshop on Natural Language Generation*, pages 217–226, Nancy, France. Association for Computational Linguistics.

Anya Belz, Simon Mille, and David M. Howcroft. 2020. Disentangling the properties of human evaluation methods: A classification system to support comparability, meta-evaluation and reproducibility testing. In *Proceedings of the 13th International Conference on Natural Language Generation*, pages 183–194, Dublin, Ireland. Association for Computational Linguistics.

Emily Bender. 2019. The #benderrule: On naming the languages we study and why it matters. *The Gradient*.

Emily M. Bender. 2011. On achieving and evaluating language-independence in NLP. *Linguistic Issues in Language Technology*, 6.

Emily M. Bender and Batya Friedman. 2018. Data statements for natural language processing: Toward mitigating system bias and enabling better science. *Transactions of the Association for Computational Linguistics*, 6:587–604.

Ondřej Bojar, Yvette Graham, and Amir Kamran. 2017. Results of the WMT17 metrics shared task. In *Proceedings of the Second Conference on Machine Translation*, pages 489–513, Copenhagen, Denmark. Association for Computational Linguistics.

Ondřej Bojar, Yvette Graham, Amir Kamran, and Miloš Stanojević. 2016. Results of the WMT16 metrics shared task. In *Proceedings of the First Conference on Machine Translation: Volume 2, Shared Task Papers*, pages 199–231, Berlin, Germany. Association for Computational Linguistics.

Asli Celikyilmaz, Elizabeth Clark, and Jianfeng Gao. 2020. Evaluation of text generation: A survey. *CoRR*, abs/2006.14799.

Arman Cohan, Franck Dernoncourt, Doo Soon Kim, Trung Bui, Seokhwan Kim, Walter Chang, and Nazli Goharian. 2018. A discourse-aware attention model for abstractive summarization of long documents. In *Proceedings of the 2018 Conference of the North American Chapter of the Association for Computational Linguistics: Human Language Technologies, Volume 2 (Short Papers)*, pages 615–621, New Orleans, Louisiana. Association for Computational Linguistics.

Michael A Covington, Congzhou He, Cati Brown, Lorina Naci, and John Brown. 2006. How complex is that sentence? a proposed revision of the rosenberg and abbeduto d-level scale.

Emily Denton, Alex Hanna, Razvan Amironesei, Andrew Smart, Hilary Nicole, and Morgan Klaus Scheuerman. 2020. Bringing the people back in: Contesting benchmark machine learning datasets. *CoRR*, abs/2007.07399.

Jacob Devlin, Ming-Wei Chang, Kenton Lee, and Kristina Toutanova. 2019. BERT: Pre-training of deep bidirectional transformers for language understanding. In *Proceedings of the 2019 Conference of the North American Chapter of the Association for Computational Linguistics: Human Language Technologies, Volume 1 (Long and Short Papers)*, pages 4171–4186, Minneapolis, Minnesota. Association for Computational Linguistics.

Bhuwan Dhingra, Manaal Faruqui, Ankur Parikh, Ming-Wei Chang, Dipanjan Das, and William Cohen. 2019. Handling divergent reference texts when evaluating table-to-text generation. In *Proceedings of the 57th Annual Meeting of the Association for Computational Linguistics*, pages 4884–4895, Florence, Italy. Association for Computational Linguistics.

Justin Dieter, Tian Wang, Arun Tejasvi Chaganty, Gabor Angeli, and Angel X. Chang. 2019. Mimic and rephrase: Reflective listening in open-ended dialogue. In *Proceedings of the 23rd Conference on Computational Natural Language Learning (CoNLL)*, pages 393–403, Hong Kong, China. Association for Computational Linguistics.

Emily Dinan, Stephen Roller, Kurt Shuster, Angela Fan, Michael Auli, and Jason Weston. 2019. Wizard of wikipedia: Knowledge-powered conversational agents. In *7th International Conference on Learning Representations, ICLR 2019, New Orleans, LA, USA, May 6-9, 2019*. OpenReview.net.

Xinya Du, Junru Shao, and Claire Cardie. 2017. Learning to ask: Neural question generation for reading comprehension. In *Proceedings of the 55th Annual Meeting of the Association for Computational Linguistics (Volume 1: Long Papers)*, pages 1342–1352, Vancouver, Canada. Association for Computational Linguistics.

Dheeru Dua, Ananth Gottumukkala, Alon Talmor, Sameer Singh, and Matt Gardner. 2019. ORB: An open reading benchmark for comprehensive evaluation of machine reading comprehension. In *EMNLP 2019 MRQA Workshop*, page 147.

Esin Durmus, He He, and Mona Diab. 2020. FEQA: A question answering evaluation framework for faithfulness assessment in abstractive summarization. In *Proceedings of the 58th Annual Meeting of the Association for Computational Linguistics*, pages 5055–5070, Online. Association for Computational Linguistics.

Ondřej Dušek, David M. Howcroft, and Verena Rieser. 2019. Semantic noise matters for neural natural language generation. In *Proceedings of the 12th Inter-*

national Conference on Natural Language Generation, pages 421–426, Tokyo, Japan. Association for Computational Linguistics.

Ondrej Dušek and Filip Jurcıcek. 2016. A context-aware natural language generation dataset for dialogue systems. In *RE-WOCHAT: Workshop on Collecting and Generating Resources for Chatbots and Conversational Agents-Development and Evaluation Workshop Programme (May 28 th, 2016)*, page 6.

Ondřej Dušek and Filip Jurčíček. 2016a. A context-aware natural language generator for dialogue systems. In *Proceedings of the 17th Annual Meeting of the Special Interest Group on Discourse and Dialogue*, pages 185–190, Los Angeles. Association for Computational Linguistics.

Ondřej Dušek and Filip Jurčíček. 2016b. Sequence-to-sequence generation for spoken dialogue via deep syntax trees and strings. In *Proceedings of the 54th Annual Meeting of the Association for Computational Linguistics (Volume 2: Short Papers)*, pages 45–51, Berlin, Germany. Association for Computational Linguistics.

Ondřej Dušek and Filip Jurčíček. 2019. Neural generation for Czech: Data and baselines. In *Proceedings of the 12th International Conference on Natural Language Generation*, pages 563–574, Tokyo, Japan. Association for Computational Linguistics.

Ondrej Dusek, Jekaterina Novikova, and Verena Rieser. 2020. Evaluating the state-of-the-art of end-to-end natural language generation: The E2E NLG challenge. *Comput. Speech Lang.*, 59:123–156.

Kawin Ethayarajh and Dan Jurafsky. 2020. Utility is in the eye of the user: A critique of NLP leaderboards. In *Proceedings of the 2020 Conference on Empirical Methods in Natural Language Processing (EMNLP)*, pages 4846–4853, Online. Association for Computational Linguistics.

Matan Eyal, Tal Baumel, and Michael Elhadad. 2019. Question answering as an automatic evaluation metric for news article summarization. In *Proceedings of the 2019 Conference of the North American Chapter of the Association for Computational Linguistics: Human Language Technologies, Volume 1 (Long and Short Papers)*, pages 3938–3948, Minneapolis, Minnesota. Association for Computational Linguistics.

Alexander R. Fabbri, Wojciech Kryscinski, Bryan McCann, Caiming Xiong, Richard Socher, and Dragomir R. Radev. 2020. SummEval: Re-evaluating summarization evaluation. *CoRR*, abs/2007.12626.

Angela Fan, Yacine Jernite, Ethan Perez, David Grangier, Jason Weston, and Michael Auli. 2019. ELI5: Long form question answering. In *Proceedings of the 57th Annual Meeting of the Association for Computational Linguistics*, pages 3558–3567, Florence, Italy. Association for Computational Linguistics.

Angela Fan, Mike Lewis, and Yann Dauphin. 2018. Hierarchical neural story generation. In *Proceedings of the 56th Annual Meeting of the Association for Computational Linguistics (Volume 1: Long Papers)*, pages 889–898, Melbourne, Australia. Association for Computational Linguistics.

Thiago Castro Ferreira, Claire Gardent, Chris van der Lee, Nikolai Ilinykh, Simon Mille, Diego Moussalem, and Anastasia Shimorina. 2020. The 2020 bilingual, bi-directional webnlg+ shared task overview and evaluation results (webnlg+ 2020). In *Proceedings of the 3rd WebNLG Workshop on Natural Language Generation from the Semantic Web (WebNLG+ 2020), Dublin, Ireland (Virtual). Association for Computational Linguistics.*

∀, Wilhelmina Nekoto, Vukosi Marivate, Tshinondiwa Matsila, Timi Fasubaa, Taiwo Fagbohungbe, Solomon Oluwole Akinola, Shamsuddeen Muhammad, Salomon Kabongo Kabenamualu, Salomey Osei, Freshia Sackey, Rubungo Andre Niyongabo, Ricky Macharm, Perez Ogayo, Orevaoghene Ahia, Musie Meressa Berhe, Mofetoluwa Adeyemi, Masabata Mokgesi-Selinga, Lawrence Okegbemi, Laura Martinus, Kolawole Tajudeen, Kevin Degila, Kelechi Ogueji, Kathleen Siminyu, Julia Kreutzer, Jason Webster, Jamiil Toure Ali, Jade Abbott, Iroro Orife, Ignatius Ezeani, Idris Abdulkadir Dangana, Herman Kamper, Hady Elsahar, Goodness Duru, Ghollah Kioko, Murhabazi Espoir, Elan van Biljon, Daniel Whitenack, Christopher Onyefuluchi, Chris Chinenye Emezue, Bonaventure F. P. Dossou, Blessing Sibanda, Blessing Bassey, Ayodele Olabiyi, Arshath Ramkilowan, Alp Öktem, Adewale Akinfaderin, and Abdallah Bashir. 2020. Participatory research for low-resourced machine translation: A case study in African languages. In *Findings of the Association for Computational Linguistics: EMNLP 2020*, pages 2144–2160, Online. Association for Computational Linguistics.

Markus Freitag, David Grangier, and Isaac Caswell. 2020. BLEU might be guilty but references are not innocent. In *Proceedings of the 2020 Conference on Empirical Methods in Natural Language Processing (EMNLP)*, pages 61–71, Online. Association for Computational Linguistics.

Jinlan Fu, Pengfei Liu, and Graham Neubig. 2020. Interpretable multi-dataset evaluation for named entity recognition. In *Proceedings of the 2020 Conference on Empirical Methods in Natural Language Processing (EMNLP)*, pages 6058–6069, Online. Association for Computational Linguistics.

Saadia Gabriel, Asli Celikyilmaz, Rahul Jha, Yejin Choi, and Jianfeng Gao. 2020. Go figure! A meta evaluation of factuality in summarization. *CoRR*, abs/2010.12834.

Claire Gardent, Anastasia Shimorina, Shashi Narayan, and Laura Perez-Beltrachini. 2017. The WebNLG challenge: Generating text from RDF data. In *Proceedings of the 10th International Conference on Natural Language Generation*, pages 124–133, Santiago de Compostela, Spain. Association for Computational Linguistics.

Albert Gatt and Emiel Krahmer. 2018. Survey of the state of the art in natural language generation: Core tasks, applications and evaluation. *J. Artif. Intell. Res.*, 61:65–170.

Timnit Gebru, Jamie Morgenstern, Briana Vecchione, Jennifer Wortman Vaughan, Hanna Wallach, Hal Daumé III, and Kate Crawford. 2018. Datasheets for datasets. In *Proceedings of the Fifth Workshop on Fairness, Accountability, and Transparency in Machine Learning*, Stockholm, Sweden.

Tatsunori Hashimoto, Hugh Zhang, and Percy Liang. 2019. Unifying human and statistical evaluation for natural language generation. In *Proceedings of the 2019 Conference of the North American Chapter of the Association for Computational Linguistics: Human Language Technologies, Volume 1 (Long and Short Papers)*, pages 1689–1701, Minneapolis, Minnesota. Association for Computational Linguistics.

Kenneth Heafield, Hiroaki Hayashi, Yusuke Oda, Ioannis Konstas, Andrew Finch, Graham Neubig, Xian Li, and Alexandra Birch. 2020. Findings of the fourth workshop on neural generation and translation. In *Proceedings of the Fourth Workshop on Neural Generation and Translation*, pages 1–9, Online. Association for Computational Linguistics.

Karl Moritz Hermann, Tomás Kociský, Edward Grefenstette, Lasse Espeholt, Will Kay, Mustafa Suleyman, and Phil Blunsom. 2015. Teaching machines to read and comprehend. In *Advances in Neural Information Processing Systems 28: Annual Conference on Neural Information Processing Systems 2015, December 7-12, 2015, Montreal, Quebec, Canada*, pages 1693–1701.

David M. Howcroft, Anya Belz, Miruna-Adriana Clinciu, Dimitra Gkatzia, Sadid A. Hasan, Saad Mahamood, Simon Mille, Emiel van Miltenburg, Sashank Santhanam, and Verena Rieser. 2020. Twenty years of confusion in human evaluation: NLG needs evaluation sheets and standardised definitions. In *Proceedings of the 13th International Conference on Natural Language Generation*, pages 169–182, Dublin, Ireland. Association for Computational Linguistics.

Baotian Hu, Qingcai Chen, and Fangze Zhu. 2015. LCSTS: A large scale Chinese short text summarization dataset. In *Proceedings of the 2015 Conference on Empirical Methods in Natural Language Processing*, pages 1967–1972, Lisbon, Portugal. Association for Computational Linguistics.

Junjie Hu, Sebastian Ruder, Aditya Siddhant, Graham Neubig, Orhan Firat, and Melvin Johnson. 2020. XTREME: A massively multilingual multitask benchmark for evaluating cross-lingual generalisation. In *Proceedings of the 37th International Conference on Machine Learning, ICML 2020, 13-18 July 2020, Virtual Event*, volume 119 of *Proceedings of Machine Learning Research*, pages 4411–4421. PMLR.

Alfred Inselberg. 1985. The plane with parallel coordinates. *Vis. Comput.*, 1(2):69–91.

Chao Jiang, Mounica Maddela, Wuwei Lan, Yang Zhong, and Wei Xu. 2020. Neural CRF model for sentence alignment in text simplification. In *Proceedings of the 58th Annual Meeting of the Association for Computational Linguistics*, pages 7943–7960, Online. Association for Computational Linguistics.

Md. Asifuzzaman Jishan, Khan Raqib Mahmud, and Abul Kalam Al Azad. 2019. Bangla Natural Language Image to Text (BNLIT).

Wendell Johnson. 1944. Studies in language behavior: A program of research. *Psychological Monographs*, 56(2):1–15.

Pratik Joshi, Sebastin Santy, Amar Budhiraja, Kalika Bali, and Monojit Choudhury. 2020. The state and fate of linguistic diversity and inclusion in the NLP world. In *Proceedings of the 58th Annual Meeting of the Association for Computational Linguistics*, pages 6282–6293, Online. Association for Computational Linguistics.

Mihir Kale and Abhinav Rastogi. 2020. Few-shot natural language generation by rewriting templates. *arXiv preprint arXiv:2004.15006*.

Hassan Kane, Muhammed Yusuf Kocyigit, Ali Abdalla, Pelkins Ajanoh, and Mohamed Coulibali. 2020. NUBIA: NeUral based interchangeability assessor for text generation. In *Proceedings of the 1st Workshop on Evaluating NLG Evaluation*, pages 28–37, Online (Dublin, Ireland). Association for Computational Linguistics.

Chris Kedzie, Kathleen McKeown, and Hal Daumé III. 2018. Content selection in deep learning models of summarization. In *Proceedings of the 2018 Conference on Empirical Methods in Natural Language Processing*, pages 1818–1828, Brussels, Belgium. Association for Computational Linguistics.

Daniel Khashabi, Gabriel Stanovsky, Jonathan Bragg, Nicholas Lourie, Jungo Kasai, Yejin Choi, Noah A. Smith, and Daniel S. Weld. 2021. GENIE: A leaderboard for human-in-the-loop evaluation of text generation. *CoRR*, abs/2101.06561.

Tomáš Kočiský, Jonathan Schwarz, Phil Blunsom, Chris Dyer, Karl Moritz Hermann, Gábor Melis, and Edward Grefenstette. 2018. The narrativeQA reading comprehension challenge. *Transactions of the Association for Computational Linguistics*, 6:317–328.

Faisal Ladhak, Esin Durmus, Claire Cardie, and Kathleen McKeown. 2020. WikiLingua: A new benchmark dataset for cross-lingual abstractive summarization. In *Findings of the Association for Computational Linguistics: EMNLP 2020*, pages 4034–4048, Online. Association for Computational Linguistics.

Rémi Lebret, David Grangier, and Michael Auli. 2016. Neural text generation from structured data with application to the biography domain. In *Proceedings of the 2016 Conference on Empirical Methods in Natural Language Processing*, pages 1203–1213, Austin, Texas. Association for Computational Linguistics.

Mike Lewis, Yinhan Liu, Naman Goyal, Marjan Ghazvininejad, Abdelrahman Mohamed, Omer Levy, Veselin Stoyanov, and Luke Zettlemoyer. 2020a. BART: Denoising sequence-to-sequence pretraining for natural language generation, translation, and comprehension. In *Proceedings of the 58th Annual Meeting of the Association for Computational Linguistics*, pages 7871–7880, Online. Association for Computational Linguistics.

Patrick Lewis, Barlas Oguz, Ruty Rinott, Sebastian Riedel, and Holger Schwenk. 2020b. MLQA: Evaluating cross-lingual extractive question answering. In *Proceedings of the 58th Annual Meeting of the Association for Computational Linguistics*, pages 7315–7330, Online. Association for Computational Linguistics.

Jiwei Li, Michel Galley, Chris Brockett, Jianfeng Gao, and Bill Dolan. 2016. A diversity-promoting objective function for neural conversation models. In *Proceedings of the 2016 Conference of the North American Chapter of the Association for Computational Linguistics: Human Language Technologies*, pages 110–119, San Diego, California. Association for Computational Linguistics.

Yikang Li, Nan Duan, Bolei Zhou, Xiao Chu, Wanli Ouyang, Xiaogang Wang, and Ming Zhou. 2018. Visual question generation as dual task of visual question answering. In *2018 IEEE Conference on Computer Vision and Pattern Recognition, CVPR 2018, Salt Lake City, UT, USA, June 18-22, 2018*, pages 6116–6124. IEEE Computer Society.

Yaobo Liang, Nan Duan, Yeyun Gong, Ning Wu, Fenfei Guo, Weizhen Qi, Ming Gong, Linjun Shou, Daxin Jiang, Guihong Cao, Xiaodong Fan, Bruce Zhang, Rahul Agrawal, Edward Cui, Sining Wei, Taroon Bharti, Ying Qiao, Jiun-Hung Chen, Winnie Wu, Shuguang Liu, Fan Yang, Rangan Majumder, and Ming Zhou. 2020. XGLUE: A new benchmark dataset for cross-lingual pre-training, understanding and generation. *CoRR*, abs/2004.01401.

Bill Yuchen Lin, Wangchunshu Zhou, Ming Shen, Pei Zhou, Chandra Bhagavatula, Yejin Choi, and Xiang Ren. 2020. CommonGen: A constrained text generation challenge for generative commonsense reasoning. In *Findings of the Association for Computational Linguistics: EMNLP 2020*, pages 1823–1840, Online. Association for Computational Linguistics.

Chin-Yew Lin. 2004. ROUGE: A package for automatic evaluation of summaries. In *Text Summarization Branches Out*, pages 74–81, Barcelona, Spain. Association for Computational Linguistics.

Tal Linzen. 2020. How can we accelerate progress towards human-like linguistic generalization? In *Proceedings of the 58th Annual Meeting of the Association for Computational Linguistics*, pages 5210–5217, Online. Association for Computational Linguistics.

Dayiheng Liu, Yu Yan, Yeyun Gong, Weizhen Qi, Hang Zhang, Jian Jiao, Weizhu Chen, Jie Fu, Linjun Shou, Ming Gong, Pengcheng Wang, Jiusheng Chen, Daxin Jiang, Jiancheng Lv, Ruofei Zhang, Winnie Wu, Ming Zhou, and Nan Duan. 2020a. GLGE: A new general language generation evaluation benchmark. *CoRR*, abs/2011.11928.

Peter J. Liu, Mohammad Saleh, Etienne Pot, Ben Goodrich, Ryan Sepassi, Lukasz Kaiser, and Noam Shazeer. 2018. Generating wikipedia by summarizing long sequences. In *6th International Conference on Learning Representations, ICLR 2018, Vancouver, BC, Canada, April 30 - May 3, 2018, Conference Track Proceedings*. OpenReview.net.

Yinhan Liu, Jiatao Gu, Naman Goyal, Xian Li, Sergey Edunov, Marjan Ghazvininejad, Mike Lewis, and Luke Zettlemoyer. 2020b. Multilingual denoising pre-training for neural machine translation. *Trans. Assoc. Comput. Linguistics*, 8:726–742.

Yinhan Liu, Myle Ott, Naman Goyal, Jingfei Du, Mandar Joshi, Danqi Chen, Omer Levy, Mike Lewis, Luke Zettlemoyer, and Veselin Stoyanov. 2019. Roberta: A robustly optimized BERT pretraining approach. *CoRR*, abs/1907.11692.

Ryan Lowe, Nissan Pow, Iulian Serban, and Joelle Pineau. 2015. The Ubuntu dialogue corpus: A large dataset for research in unstructured multi-turn dialogue systems. In *Proceedings of the 16th Annual Meeting of the Special Interest Group on Discourse and Dialogue*, pages 285–294, Prague, Czech Republic. Association for Computational Linguistics.

Xiaofei Lu. 2010. Automatic analysis of syntactic complexity in second language writing. *International Journal of Corpus Linguistics*, 15(4):474–496.

Qingsong Ma, Ondřej Bojar, and Yvette Graham. 2018. Results of the WMT18 metrics shared task: Both characters and embeddings achieve good performance. In *Proceedings of the Third Conference on Machine Translation: Shared Task Papers*, pages 671–688, Belgium, Brussels. Association for Computational Linguistics.

Qingsong Ma, Johnny Wei, Ondřej Bojar, and Yvette Graham. 2019. Results of the WMT19 metrics shared task: Segment-level and strong MT systems pose big challenges. In *Proceedings of the Fourth Conference on Machine Translation (Volume 2: Shared Task Papers, Day 1)*, pages 62–90, Florence, Italy. Association for Computational Linguistics.

Emma Manning, Shira Wein, and Nathan Schneider. 2020. A human evaluation of amr-to-english generation systems. In *Proceedings of the 28th International Conference on Computational Linguistics, COLING 2020, Barcelona, Spain (Online), December 8-13, 2020*, pages 4773–4786. International Committee on Computational Linguistics.

Nitika Mathur, Timothy Baldwin, and Trevor Cohn. 2020a. Tangled up in BLEU: Reevaluating the evaluation of automatic machine translation evaluation metrics. In *Proceedings of the 58th Annual Meeting of the Association for Computational Linguistics*, pages 4984–4997, Online. Association for Computational Linguistics.

Nitika Mathur, Johnny Wei, Markus Freitag, Qingsong Ma, and Ondřej Bojar. 2020b. Results of the WMT20 metrics shared task. In *Proceedings of the Fifth Conference on Machine Translation*, pages 688–725, Online. Association for Computational Linguistics.

Joshua Maynez, Shashi Narayan, Bernd Bohnet, and Ryan McDonald. 2020. On faithfulness and factuality in abstractive summarization. In *Proceedings of the 58th Annual Meeting of the Association for Computational Linguistics*, pages 1906–1919, Online. Association for Computational Linguistics.

Bryan McCann, Nitish Shirish Keskar, Caiming Xiong, and Richard Socher. 2018. The natural language decathlon: Multitask learning as question answering. *CoRR*, abs/1806.08730.

Simon Mille, Anja Belz, Bernd Bohnet, Yvette Graham, Emily Pitler, and Leo Wanner. 2018. The first multilingual surface realisation shared task (SR'18): Overview and evaluation results. In *Proceedings of the First Workshop on Multilingual Surface Realisation*, pages 1–12, Melbourne, Australia. Association for Computational Linguistics.

Simon Mille, Anja Belz, Bernd Bohnet, Yvette Graham, and Leo Wanner, editors. 2019. *Proceedings of the 2nd Workshop on Multilingual Surface Realisation (MSR 2019)*. Association for Computational Linguistics, Hong Kong, China.

Simon Mille, Anya Belz, Bernd Bohnet, Thiago Castro Ferreira, Yvette Graham, and Leo Wanner. 2020. The third multilingual surface realisation shared task (SR'20): Overview and evaluation results. In *Proceedings of the Third Workshop on Multilingual Surface Realisation*, pages 1–20, Barcelona, Spain (Online). Association for Computational Linguistics.

Emiel van Miltenburg, Desmond Elliott, and Piek Vossen. 2018. Measuring the diversity of automatic image descriptions. In *Proceedings of the 27th International Conference on Computational Linguistics*, pages 1730–1741, Santa Fe, New Mexico, USA. Association for Computational Linguistics.

Sewon Min, Julian Michael, Hannaneh Hajishirzi, and Luke Zettlemoyer. 2020. AmbigQA: Answering ambiguous open-domain questions. In *Proceedings of the 2020 Conference on Empirical Methods in Natural Language Processing (EMNLP)*, pages 5783–5797, Online. Association for Computational Linguistics.

Shachar Mirkin and Jean-Luc Meunier. 2015. Personalized machine translation: Predicting translational preferences. In *Proceedings of the 2015 Conference on Empirical Methods in Natural Language Processing*, pages 2019–2025, Lisbon, Portugal. Association for Computational Linguistics.

Margaret Mitchell, Simone Wu, Andrew Zaldivar, Parker Barnes, Lucy Vasserman, Ben Hutchinson, Elena Spitzer, Inioluwa Deborah Raji, and Timnit Gebru. 2019. Model cards for model reporting. In *Proceedings of the conference on fairness, accountability, and transparency*, pages 220–229.

Ramesh Nallapati, Bowen Zhou, Cicero dos Santos, Çağlar GuÌ‡lçehre, and Bing Xiang. 2016. Abstractive text summarization using sequence-to-sequence RNNs and beyond. In *Proceedings of The 20th SIGNLL Conference on Computational Natural Language Learning*, pages 280–290, Berlin, Germany. Association for Computational Linguistics.

Shashi Narayan, Shay B. Cohen, and Mirella Lapata. 2018. Don't give me the details, just the summary! topic-aware convolutional neural networks for extreme summarization. In *Proceedings of the 2018 Conference on Empirical Methods in Natural Language Processing*, pages 1797–1807, Brussels, Belgium. Association for Computational Linguistics.

Jekaterina Novikova, Ondřej Dušek, and Verena Rieser. 2017. The E2E dataset: New challenges for end-to-end generation. In *Proceedings of the 18th Annual SIGdial Meeting on Discourse and Dialogue*, pages 201–206, Saarbrücken, Germany. Association for Computational Linguistics.

Juri Opitz and Anette Frank. 2020. Towards a decomposable metric for explainable evaluation of text generation from amr. *arXiv preprint arXiv:2008.08896*.

Kishore Papineni, Salim Roukos, Todd Ward, and Wei-Jing Zhu. 2002. Bleu: a method for automatic evaluation of machine translation. In *Proceedings of the 40th Annual Meeting of the Association for Computational Linguistics*, pages 311–318, Philadelphia, Pennsylvania, USA. Association for Computational Linguistics.

Ankur Parikh, Xuezhi Wang, Sebastian Gehrmann, Manaal Faruqui, Bhuwan Dhingra, Diyi Yang, and Dipanjan Das. 2020. ToTTo: A controlled table-to-text generation dataset. In *Proceedings of the 2020 Conference on Empirical Methods in Natural Language Processing (EMNLP)*, pages 1173–1186, Online. Association for Computational Linguistics.

Laura Perez-Beltrachini and Claire Gardent. 2017. Analysing data-to-text generation benchmarks. In *Proceedings of the 10th International Conference on Natural Language Generation*, pages 238–242, Santiago de Compostela, Spain. Association for Computational Linguistics.

Fabio Petroni, Aleksandra Piktus, Angela Fan, Patrick S. H. Lewis, Majid Yazdani, Nicola De Cao, James Thorne, Yacine Jernite, Vassilis Plachouras, Tim Rocktäschel, and Sebastian Riedel. 2020. KILT: a benchmark for knowledge intensive language tasks. *CoRR*, abs/2009.02252.

Edoardo Maria Ponti, Goran Glavaš, Olga Majewska, Qianchu Liu, Ivan Vulić, and Anna Korhonen. 2020. XCOPA: A multilingual dataset for causal commonsense reasoning. In *Proceedings of the 2020 Conference on Empirical Methods in Natural Language Processing (EMNLP)*, pages 2362–2376, Online. Association for Computational Linguistics.

Christopher Potts, Zhengxuan Wu, Atticus Geiger, and Douwe Kiela. 2020. Dynasent: A dynamic benchmark for sentiment analysis. *CoRR*, abs/2012.15349.

Ratish Puduppully, Li Dong, and Mirella Lapata. 2019. Data-to-text generation with entity modeling. In *Proceedings of the 57th Annual Meeting of the Association for Computational Linguistics*, pages 2023–2035, Florence, Italy. Association for Computational Linguistics.

Dragomir R. Radev, Rui Zhang, Amrit Rau, Abhinand Sivaprasad, Chiachun Hsieh, Nazneen Fatema Rajani, Xiangru Tang, Aadit Vyas, Neha Verma, Pranav Krishna, Yangxiaokang Liu, Nadia Irwanto, Jessica Pan, Faiaz Rahman, Ahmad Zaidi, Murori Mutuma, Yasin Tarabar, Ankit Gupta, Tao Yu, Yi Chern Tan, Xi Victoria Lin, Caiming Xiong, and Richard Socher. 2020. DART: open-domain structured data record to text generation. *CoRR*, abs/2007.02871.

Colin Raffel, Noam Shazeer, Adam Roberts, Katherine Lee, Sharan Narang, Michael Matena, Yanqi Zhou, Wei Li, and Peter J. Liu. 2020. Exploring the limits of transfer learning with a unified text-to-text transformer. *J. Mach. Learn. Res.*, 21:140:1–140:67.

Sudha Rao and Joel Tetreault. 2018. Dear sir or madam, may I introduce the GYAFC dataset: Corpus, benchmarks and metrics for formality style transfer. In *Proceedings of the 2018 Conference of the North American Chapter of the Association for Computational Linguistics: Human Language Technologies, Volume 1 (Long Papers)*, pages 129–140, New Orleans, Louisiana. Association for Computational Linguistics.

Abhinav Rastogi, Xiaoxue Zang, Srinivas Sunkara, Raghav Gupta, and Pranav Khaitan. 2020. Towards scalable multi-domain conversational agents: The schema-guided dialogue dataset. In *The Thirty-Fourth AAAI Conference on Artificial Intelligence, AAAI 2020, The Thirty-Second Innovative Applications of Artificial Intelligence Conference, IAAI 2020, The Tenth AAAI Symposium on Educational Advances in Artificial Intelligence, EAAI 2020, New York, NY, USA, February 7-12, 2020*, pages 8689–8696. AAAI Press.

Siva Reddy, Danqi Chen, and Christopher D. Manning. 2019. CoQA: A conversational question answering challenge. *Transactions of the Association for Computational Linguistics*, 7:249–266.

Ehud Reiter. 2018. A structured review of the validity of BLEU. *Comput. Linguistics*, 44(3).

Ehud Reiter and Robert Dale. 2000. *Building natural language generation systems*. Cambridge university press.

Marco Tulio Ribeiro, Tongshuang Wu, Carlos Guestrin, and Sameer Singh. 2020. Beyond accuracy: Behavioral testing of NLP models with CheckList. In *Proceedings of the 58th Annual Meeting of the Association for Computational Linguistics*, pages 4902–4912, Online. Association for Computational Linguistics.

Viktor Schlegel, Goran Nenadic, and Riza Batista-Navarro. 2020. Beyond leaderboards: A survey of methods for revealing weaknesses in natural language inference data and models. *CoRR*, abs/2005.14709.

Thomas Scialom, Paul-Alexis Dray, Sylvain Lamprier, Benjamin Piwowarski, and Jacopo Staiano. 2020. MLSUM: The multilingual summarization corpus. In *Proceedings of the 2020 Conference on Empirical Methods in Natural Language Processing (EMNLP)*, pages 8051–8067, Online. Association for Computational Linguistics.

Thomas Scialom, Paul-Alexis Dray, Gallinari Patrick, Lamprier Sylvain, Piwowarski Benjamin, Staiano Jacopo, and Wang Alex. 2021. Safeval: Summarization asks for fact-based evaluation. *arXiv preprint arXiv:2103.12693*.

Thomas Scialom, Sylvain Lamprier, Benjamin Piwowarski, and Jacopo Staiano. 2019. Answers unite! unsupervised metrics for reinforced summarization models. In *Proceedings of the 2019 Conference on Empirical Methods in Natural Language Processing and the 9th International Joint Conference on Natural Language Processing (EMNLP-IJCNLP)*, pages 3246–3256, Hong Kong, China. Association for Computational Linguistics.

Thibault Sellam, Dipanjan Das, and Ankur Parikh. 2020. BLEURT: Learning robust metrics for text generation. In *Proceedings of the 58th Annual Meeting of the Association for Computational Linguistics*, pages 7881–7892, Online. Association for Computational Linguistics.

Claude E Shannon and Warren Weaver. 1963. A mathematical theory of communication.

Eva Sharma, Chen Li, and Lu Wang. 2019. BIGPATENT: A large-scale dataset for abstractive and coherent summarization. In *Proceedings of the 57th Annual Meeting of the Association for Computational Linguistics*, pages 2204–2213, Florence, Italy. Association for Computational Linguistics.

Anastasia Shimorina and Anya Belz. 2021. The human evaluation datasheet 1.0: A template for recording details of human evaluation experiments in nlp. *arXiv preprint arXiv:2103.09710*.

Pushkar Shukla, Carlos Elmadjian, Richika Sharan, Vivek Kulkarni, Matthew Turk, and William Yang Wang. 2019. What should I ask? using conversationally informative rewards for goal-oriented visual dialog. In *Proceedings of the 57th Annual Meeting of the Association for Computational Linguistics*, pages 6442–6451, Florence, Italy. Association for Computational Linguistics.

Miloš Stanojević, Amir Kamran, Philipp Koehn, and Ondřej Bojar. 2015. Results of the WMT15 metrics shared task. In *Proceedings of the Tenth Workshop on Statistical Machine Translation*, pages 256–273, Lisbon, Portugal. Association for Computational Linguistics.

Simeng Sun, Ori Shapira, Ido Dagan, and Ani Nenkova. 2019. How to compare summarizers without target length? pitfalls, solutions and re-examination of the neural summarization literature. In *Proceedings of the Workshop on Methods for Optimizing and Evaluating Neural Language Generation*, pages 21–29, Minneapolis, Minnesota. Association for Computational Linguistics.

Kristina Toutanova, Chris Brockett, Ke M. Tran, and Saleema Amershi. 2016. A dataset and evaluation metrics for abstractive compression of sentences and short paragraphs. In *Proceedings of the 2016 Conference on Empirical Methods in Natural Language Processing*, pages 340–350, Austin, Texas. Association for Computational Linguistics.

Alex Wang, Kyunghyun Cho, and Mike Lewis. 2020. Asking and answering questions to evaluate the factual consistency of summaries. In *Proceedings of the 58th Annual Meeting of the Association for Computational Linguistics*, pages 5008–5020, Online. Association for Computational Linguistics.

Alex Wang, Yada Pruksachatkun, Nikita Nangia, Amanpreet Singh, Julian Michael, Felix Hill, Omer Levy, and Samuel R. Bowman. 2019a. Superglue: A stickier benchmark for general-purpose language understanding systems. In *Advances in Neural Information Processing Systems 32: Annual Conference on Neural Information Processing Systems 2019, NeurIPS 2019, December 8-14, 2019, Vancouver, BC, Canada*, pages 3261–3275.

Alex Wang, Amanpreet Singh, Julian Michael, Felix Hill, Omer Levy, and Samuel R. Bowman. 2019b. GLUE: A multi-task benchmark and analysis platform for natural language understanding. In *International Conference on Learning Representations*.

Sam Wiseman, Stuart Shieber, and Alexander Rush. 2017. Challenges in data-to-document generation. In *Proceedings of the 2017 Conference on Empirical Methods in Natural Language Processing*, pages 2253–2263, Copenhagen, Denmark. Association for Computational Linguistics.

Qizhe Xie, Zihang Dai, Eduard Hovy, Thang Luong, and Quoc Le. 2020. Unsupervised data augmentation for consistency training. *Advances in Neural Information Processing Systems*, 33.

Wei Xu, Courtney Napoles, Ellie Pavlick, Quanze Chen, and Chris Callison-Burch. 2016. Optimizing statistical machine translation for text simplification. *Transactions of the Association for Computational Linguistics*, 4:401–415.

Linting Xue, Noah Constant, Adam Roberts, Mihir Kale, Rami Al-Rfou, Aditya Siddhant, Aditya Barua, and Colin Raffel. 2020. mt5: A massively multilingual pre-trained text-to-text transformer. *CoRR*, abs/2010.11934.

Xiaoxue Zang, Abhinav Rastogi, Srinivas Sunkara, Raghav Gupta, Jianguo Zhang, and Jindong Chen. 2020. MultiWOZ 2.2 : A dialogue dataset with additional annotation corrections and state tracking baselines. In *Proceedings of the 2nd Workshop on Natural Language Processing for Conversational AI*, pages 109–117, Online. Association for Computational Linguistics.

Jingqing Zhang, Yao Zhao, Mohammad Saleh, and Peter J. Liu. 2020a. PEGASUS: pre-training with extracted gap-sentences for abstractive summarization. In *Proceedings of the 37th International Conference on Machine Learning, ICML 2020, 13-18 July 2020, Virtual Event*, volume 119 of *Proceedings of Machine Learning Research*, pages 11328–11339. PMLR.

Saizheng Zhang, Emily Dinan, Jack Urbanek, Arthur Szlam, Douwe Kiela, and Jason Weston. 2018. Personalizing dialogue agents: I have a dog, do you have pets too? In *Proceedings of the 56th Annual Meeting of the Association for Computational Linguistics (Volume 1: Long Papers)*, pages 2204–2213, Melbourne, Australia. Association for Computational Linguistics.

Tianyi Zhang, Varsha Kishore, Felix Wu, Kilian Q. Weinberger, and Yoav Artzi. 2020b. Bertscore: Evaluating text generation with BERT. In *8th International Conference on Learning Representations, ICLR 2020, Addis Ababa, Ethiopia, April 26-30, 2020*. OpenReview.net.

Xingxing Zhang and Mirella Lapata. 2014. Chinese poetry generation with recurrent neural networks. In *Proceedings of the 2014 Conference on Empirical Methods in Natural Language Processing (EMNLP)*, pages 670–680, Doha, Qatar. Association for Computational Linguistics.

Yizhe Zhang, Siqi Sun, Michel Galley, Yen-Chun Chen, Chris Brockett, Xiang Gao, Jianfeng Gao, Jingjing Liu, and Bill Dolan. 2020c. DIALOGPT : Large-scale generative pre-training for conversational response generation. In *Proceedings of the 58th Annual Meeting of the Association for Computational Linguistics: System Demonstrations*, pages 270–278, Online. Association for Computational Linguistics.

A Task Suggestion Categories

Participants were required to provide information for the following categories when suggesting a dataset for GEM.

1. Dataset Name
2. Reference
3. High-level Task, e.g., data-to-text, or summarization
4. Short Description
5. Challenges, e.g., entity tracking/generation, referring expression generation, surface realization, content selection
6. Communicative goal, e.g., provide specific information, or entertainment, or accomplish a task
7. Dataset Domain, e.g., Wikipedia, or news articles, Reddit chat, etc)
8. Language(s)
9. Language locale (if known), e.g., en-US, es-MX
10. Input modality, e.g., text, graph, table, images
11. Input length
12. Output length
13. Output form, e.g., monologue, dialog
14. # Examples in dataset Test split, e.g., i.i.d., or non-overlap dimension
15. # References per example
16. Data Quality / potential Issues, e.g., noisy, clean, biased, code-mixing (different languages/writing systems), (over)-normalization
17. License
18. Evaluation strategies (in original paper / papers that use dataset)
19. Why should we use this dataset?

B Considered datasets

The following datasets were proposed to be included in GEM.

1. Alex Context NLG (Dušek and Jurcıcek, 2016; Dušek and Jurčíček, 2016a)
2. AmbigQA/AmbigNQ (Min et al., 2020)
3. Bangla Natural Language Image to Text (Jishan et al., 2019)
4. Big Patent (Sharma et al., 2019)
5. Chinese Poetry (Zhang and Lapata, 2014)
6. CommonGen (Lin et al., 2020)
7. CoQA (Reddy et al., 2019)
8. Czech Restaurant Data (Dušek and Jurčíček, 2019)
9. DART (Radev et al., 2020)
10. E2E (cleaned) (Novikova et al., 2017; Dušek et al., 2019)
11. ELI5 (Fan et al., 2019)
12. Hindi Poetry [14]
13. LCSTS (Hu et al., 2015)
14. Mimic and Rephrase (Dieter et al., 2019)
15. MLSUM (Scialom et al., 2020)
16. MSR Abstractive Text Compression (Toutanova et al., 2016)
17. MultiWOZ 2.2 (Zang et al., 2020)
18. NarrativeQA (Kočiský et al., 2018)
19. PersonaChat (Zhang et al., 2018)
20. PubMed, Arxiv (Kedzie et al., 2018; Cohan et al., 2018)
21. ROTOWIRE/MLB (Wiseman et al., 2017; Puduppully et al., 2019)

[14]https://www.kaggle.com/shishu1421/hindi-poetry-dataset

22. Schema-Guided Dialogue (Rastogi et al., 2020)
23. SQUAD Question Generation (Du et al., 2017)
24. SR'11, SR'18, SR'19 (Belz et al., 2011; Mille et al., 2018, 2019)
25. ToTTo (Parikh et al., 2020)
26. Ubuntu Dialogue Generation (Lowe et al., 2015)
27. Visual Question Generation (Shukla et al., 2019; Li et al., 2018)
28. WebNLG (Gardent et al., 2017)
29. WikiAuto + Turk/ASSET (Jiang et al., 2020; Xu et al., 2016; Alva-Manchego et al., 2020)
30. WikiBio (Lebret et al., 2016)
31. WikiSum (Liu et al., 2018)
32. Wizard of Wikipedia (Dinan et al., 2019)
33. Writing Prompts (Fan et al., 2018)
34. XSum (Narayan et al., 2018)
35. WikiLingua (Ladhak et al., 2020)

C Task and Criteria Selection Survey

As part of our selection process, we queried all GEM members about the utility of tasks and selection criteria. The questions below were included in the survey.

- For each suggested task, "Should this task be included in GEM?" on a 5-point Likert scale (1 being *strongly against*, and 5 *strongly in favor*).
- We should exclude tasks that are the focus of a shared task in 2021. [yes/no]
- We should exclude tasks that were the focus of a shared task since 2020. [yes/no]
- We should exclude tasks that were ever part of a shared task. [yes/no]
- We should exclude datasets that require paid-for licenses (e.g., LDC or ELRA). [yes/no]
- We should exclude datasets that are not freely available for download. [yes/no]
- We should exclude tasks that require encoding anything but text (e.g., images or graphs). [yes/no]
- We should include # tasks in GEM. [10 points ranging from 2 to 20]
- X% of the tasks should feature non-English language(s). [10 points ranging from 10 to 100%]
- Diversity of tasks is more important than focus on an NLG task (by including multiple datasets for the same task). [10 points from *Diversity is more important* to *Focus is more important*]
- We should include noisy and clean datasets. [10 points from *only noisy* to *only clean*]
- We should include low- and high-resource datasets. [10 points from *only low-resource* to *only high-resource*]
- We should prefer tasks with non-iid test sets or specific challenge sets. [5-Likert scale from *not important* to *very important*]
- We should prefer tasks with test sets with multiple references. [5-Likert scale from *not important* to *very important*]
- If we include an NLG task (e.g., simplification or data2text), we need multiple datasets for that task. [5-Likert scale from *not important* to *very important*]
- We should include a set of tasks with no clear evaluation strategy. [5-Likert scale from *not important* to *very important*]
- We should focus on tasks with reliable automatic metrics. [5-Likert scale from *not important* to *very important*]

Reusable Templates and Guides For Documenting Datasets and Models for Natural Language Processing and Generation

A Case Study of the HuggingFace and GEM Data and Model Cards

Angelina McMillan-Major
University of Washington
Hugging Face
angie@huggingface.co

Salomey Osei
KNUST
Masakhane
sosei@aimsammi.org

Juan Diego Rodriguez
UT Austin
juand-r@utexas.edu

Pawan Sasanka Ammanamanchi
IIIT Hyderabad
pass2pawan@gmail.com

Sebastian Gehrmann
Google Research
gehrmann@google.com

Yacine Jernite
Hugging Face
yacine@huggingface.co

Abstract

Developing documentation guidelines and easy-to-use templates for datasets and models is a challenging task, especially given the variety of backgrounds, skills, and incentives of the people involved in the building of natural language processing (NLP) tools. Nevertheless, the adoption of standard documentation practices across the field of NLP promotes more accessible and detailed descriptions of NLP datasets and models, while supporting researchers and developers in reflecting on their work. To help with the standardization of documentation, we present two case studies of efforts that aim to develop reusable documentation templates – the HuggingFace data card, a general purpose card for datasets in NLP, and the GEM benchmark data and model cards with a focus on natural language generation. We describe our process for developing these templates, including the identification of relevant stakeholder groups, the definition of a set of guiding principles, the use of existing templates as our foundation, and iterative revisions based on feedback.

1 Introduction

Dataset and model documentation is a necessary step in identifying potential issues with machine learning (ML) systems and addressing their broader impacts (Gebru et al., 2018, 2020; Bender and Friedman, 2018, among others). In their overview of data collection and use in ML, Paullada et al. (2020) identify issues that have frequently arisen such as considerations for how subjects are represented in datasets, spurious cues that may be exploited by ML model, and concerns about the content in datasets collected through crawling methodologies. They advocate for careful documentation of datasets and their collection processes in order to surface these problems. However, best practices for documentation have seen no widespread adoption even for the most popular datasets and models. Indeed, writing such detailed documentation requires additional effort from researchers who may lack the required resources or familiarity with the process. Providing dataset and model creators with guidelines and several examples in a single place to inspire and inform prospective writers could thus drive widespread adoption of documentation.

Research efforts that involve a large number of models or datasets are particularly well positioned to develop and maintain specific guidelines and best practices by making documentation a required component for submitting contributions. By bringing together the domain expertise of participants and the experience of researchers who have a greater familiarity with documenting data and models, these efforts provide an opportunity to develop and refine templates that balance generality and informativeness. In addition, by requiring appropriate documentation for any involved model or dataset, these efforts can set a precedent that informs future endeavours. We encourage organizations to consider their role in the successful uptake of documentation practices, such as providing their members with adequate resources to understand the goals and motivations of documentation and measured steps towards integrating documentation into current research norms.

In this paper, we present two case studies of creating documentation templates and guides in natural language processing (NLP): the Hugging Face (HF) dataset hub[1] and the benchmark for Gen-

[1]https://hf.co/datasets/card-guide

Proceedings of the 1st Workshop on Natural Language Generation, Evaluation, and Metrics (GEM 2021), pages 121–135
August 5–6, 2021.

eration and its Evaluation and Metrics (GEM).[2] We use the term *data card* to refer to documentation for datasets in both cases and the term *model card* to refer to documentation for models in the GEM workshop, following Mitchell et al. (2019). Focusing on these settings allows us to ground what constitutes 'good' documentation in these contexts, namely technical user-oriented information, scientific reproducibility, and social contextualization of data and data-driven systems.

2 Related Work

In the U.S., research involving direct interventions on human subjects is subject to the Federal Policy for the Protection of Human Subjects (or Common Rule).[3] This policy tasks institutional review boards (IRBs) with certifying that such research follows established ethical standards and regulations. While this review is sometimes decried as cumbersome (Grady, 2015), the process ensures that researchers both reflect and communicate ahead of time how the data will be collected and used, why it is necessary to answer the question at hand, and how protected information will be handled to prevent harm to the human subjects. Whereas much of the data that supports current methods in ML and especially NLP is created by, gives information about, and is used to train models that will likely affect these same human subjects, this relationship does not constitute a direct intervention as defined in the Common Rule. However, Metcalf and Crawford argue that the definition is too narrow when one considers the similarity in potential harms and advise that data-driven methods should be subject to a similar from of ethical review, which includes clear communication about the goals and mechanisms for collecting and safeguarding the data.

Despite existing literature on database documentation in HCI and related fields (Cheney et al., 2009; Bhardwaj et al., 2014), documentation in ML has only recently gained traction. In a survey of ML projects across India, East and West African countries, and the USA, Sambasivan et al. (2021) analyze compounding events causing negative, downstream effects from data issues, resulting in technical debt[4] over time, and identify insufficient documentation to be a trigger of these events in 20% of the 53 cases. They report impacts such as time and effort lost in using incorrect data, barriers to completing models, and data that had to be abandoned due to it no longer being usable.

In response to issues like the ones found by Sambasivan et al., many research groups have proposed documentation schemata for different parts of the ML pipeline. Arnold et al. (2019) introduce FactSheets to document the use, performance and security aspects of an AI product. Mitchell et al. (2019) put forward Model Cards focusing on documenting the evaluation and use of a specific model, while Gebru et al. (2018), Holland et al. (2018), and Pushkarna et al. (2021) propose Datasheets for Datasets, Dataset Nutrition Labels, and the Data Cards Playbook, respectively, as documentation schemata and processes for documenting the data used in ML and AI systems. Hutchinson et al. (2021) frame datasets as technical infrastructure and propose documentation for several stages of the development process, including the design, creation, and maintenance of the dataset.

To address the distinct challenges of working with language data, such as those summarized by Bender et al. (2021), other researchers have proposed specialized documentation for work in NLP. The first such example is by Bender and Friedman (2018) who propose a version of Data Statements for documenting aspects of the data from a linguistic perspective. In addition to documenting the data that a model sees during training, there is also the need to document experiments, especially those involving humans. Thus, Shimorina and Belz (2021) develop a Human Evaluation Datasheet, with the goal of describing human evaluation experiments rather than naturally occurring language data. Starting from the templates by Bender and Friedman (2018) and Mitchell et al. (2019), we iteratively extend and adapt our templates for the HF and GEM contexts.

3 Methods

To guide the development of our templates, we draw from the methods of value sensitive design (eg., Friedman and Hendry, 2019) by identifying stakeholders and assessing their values, which Friedman and Hendry define as "what is important to people in their lives, with a focus on ethics and morality" (pg. 24). The values of the various stakeholders, including developers themselves,

[2] `https://gem-benchmark.com/data_cards/`

[3] `https://www.nidcr.nih.gov/research/human-subjects-research`

[4] Cunningham (1992) employs this term to describe the accumulation of flaws in technical systems over time, using an analogy to financial debt.

may influence the development of a technology in a number of ways (Friedman and Kahn, 2003). In this section, we conduct a stakeholder analysis and describe the principles we follow in the development of our templates. In Section 7, we explore the potential social impact of the templates and our positionality in the design process.

3.1 Documentation Stakeholders

This work presents a documentation strategy adopted by two **organizations** (the HF dataset hub and the GEM benchmark) for two categories of **resources** (language datasets and NLG models). We identify three groups of direct stakeholders as well as indirect stakeholders whose needs we consider in designing this documentation strategy.

The organizations. The managing organizations play a central role in gathering, presenting, and enabling the use of the resources. The organizations are responsible for *establishing documentation standards* that need to be met for any resource.

The resource creators. When submitting their resources to an organization, dataset curators and model developers are required to *write documentation* to meet the organization's stated standards.

The resource users. The resources distributed by the organizations may further be utilized by downstream users. These users *read the provided documentation* to determine whether the resources may or may not be appropriate for their needs.

The indirect stakeholders. Indirect stakeholders include any person impacted by the dissemination of a resource, such as dataset publication, model deployment, and deployment of a model trained on a dataset. While indirect stakeholders might not have direct control over the way the resources are used, they may *refer to the documentation* to analyze these impacts.

3.2 General Approach

As discussed by Waseem et al. (2021), datasets are the result of subjective choices made by the dataset creators. We therefore approach documentation as a way for authors to communicate this subjectivity by explicitly stating the decisions that led to the resource creation and the contexts in which those decisions were made. In addition to providing developers with the opportunity to reflect on their choices in creating a resource, the documentation gives users insight as to how and why the resource was developed, which may help the user assess how appropriate the resource is for their use case, and may even surface previously unconsidered issues. In addition to the documentation formats surveyed in Section 2, the practice of reflecting on the impact of one's work is being standardized by academic conferences such as NeurIPS's broader impacts statement[5] and NAACL's ethics review.[6] We aim to encourage this practice in our local contexts through our free text templates that emphasize reflection on the topics we see as important in understanding the development and potential uses of datasets and models in NLP.

While guidance around these processes is still being standardized, we recognize that there are risks that may result from the proliferation of documentation formats and the suggestion of documentation as a way to mitigate the harms caused by ML systems. For example, documentation that is not updated to reflect changes to the documented resource may result in harms due to decisions made on inaccurate information. In other cases, the standardization of documentation may add to the difficulties experienced by inexperienced or underfunded researchers in publishing their work. Finally, authors may try to justify work that causes known harms by documenting the potential for harm without attempting to address the harms themselves. Organizations that institute documentation standards need to consider these risks when integrating documentation into their local contexts and be attentive to the varied impacts to researchers, developers, and community members.

3.3 Data Cards Principles

Language conveys information about not only the individual producing the language, but also about the social groups that individual is a member of and social context that the individual is producing the language in (Eckert and Rickford, 2001). For example, an accent may indicate the geographical region that a person grew up in and that person's use of a local phrase may indicate that they believe the person that they're talking to is also from that region. As such, the values of our indirect stakeholders, the people whose sociolinguistic information are embodied in the resources, are of high priority in designing the data card templates. In order for documentation to be accessible to in-

[5]https://neurips.cc/Conferences/2020/CallForPapers
[6]https://2021.naacl.org/ethics/faq/

direct stakeholders, who may not be familiar with ML terminology or academic writing, the information needs to be clearly presented and easy to find within the document. This consideration led to several revisions in our template content and presentation.

3.4 Model Cards Principles

The recent push by academic conferences for social impact statements in publications provides a clear way for resource creators to consider the impact to their own direct and indirect stakeholders. Furthermore, academic ML conferences such as NeurIPS have instituted reproducibility checklists for paper submissions (Pineau et al., 2020). Building off this checklist, Dodge et al. (2019) argue for greater reproducibility in ML publications by proposing their own reproducibility checklist as well as a metric for reporting performance on the validation set as a function of the model training time. Mitchell et al. (2019) focus on evaluation in their own schema for models, arguing for disaggregated results to be reported over different population subgroups in data used to evaluate the model. These three considerations - social impact, reproducibility, and evaluation - form the main aspects of our template.

4 Case Study I: HuggingFace Data Cards

As a first case study of data card development, we present the template developed for the HuggingFace open source NLP libraries. The full template is available in Table 1. The completed data card for the ELI5 dataset (Fan et al., 2019) is available in Appendix A.

HF Libraries The HuggingFace Transformers library (Wolf et al., 2020) has evolved as a centralized platform providing a common API for easily loading the weights of nearly 10,000 (at the time of writing) transformer-based models with different frameworks (PyTorch, TensorFlow, JAX) and original code bases. The Datasets library[7] takes a similar approach to providing a hub that allows users to easily discover and reuse the datasets that were used to trained those models. To that end, the library focuses on the following three features:

- A unified API for downloading and iterating through a wide variety of datasets
- A backend supported by memory-mapped Arrow arrays[8] to enable use of even large datasets in resource-constrained settings
- A documentation structure that gives users a clear overview of the available datasets and the information required to use them

To meet the latter need, we designed a data card template that provides a unified way to present this information for all of the proposed NLP datasets.

HF data cards stakeholders The direct stakeholders of the HF card templates include: the organization, whose goals for the library and its documentation standards are stated above; the team and HF community members, who add new datasets to the library and are encouraged to fill out as much of the cards as they can; and the library users, who may examine or train models on the provided datasets. We note that, in our case, the people who add the datasets to the library may not be the original dataset curators, and so may not have direct access to all the required information.

Initial version The first version of the data card consisted of 8 sections. The first three aimed to answer the question *"What is this dataset used for?"* and asked the writers to fill out information about the tasks supported, the original purpose for creating the dataset, and the languages represented within. The template then asked about the *people involved in making the dataset*, including the dataset creators, the language creators, and the annotators, if relevant. This was followed by a section titled "Data Characteristics," which covered all of the *data selection and processing steps*. In particular, considering that users might want to use several datasets developed to address similar tasks together to train a model, we wanted to surface any domain shifts or differences in text normalization in either of these last two sections.

The template then continued to a *dataset structure* section covering information about the default train/test split if provided, size of the dataset, description of the features, examples of data points, and suggested metrics to use. Broadly, the purpose of this section was to give a user any technical information they might need to train a model, such as how the dataset size might influence what size of model or regularization technique to use. Seeing

[7] `https://hf.co/datasets`

[8] `https://arrow.apache.org/`

the features and an explicit example of a data instance can also clarify the input and output features and texts.

The second to last section covered *known limitations* of the dataset, and prompted the writer to consider specifically social biases in a first subsection and any other limitations, such as common surface correlations a model might take advantage of, in another. The reasoning behind this choice is that a user might do as much harm by deploying a model exhibiting harmful biases as by deploying a model that had a high score for the chosen metric but did not actually perform the described high-level task. Finally, for the benefit of users who might want to share derivatives of the dataset or use them for commercial purposes, the last section contained the *licensing information* for the dataset. Using this schema, we wrote an initial draft card for the SNLI dataset (Bowman et al., 2015) and shared it with the HF team and the SNLI curators for comments.

Revised version We then expanded and reordered the template based on the initial comments. The first section became the *dataset description* consisting of: a list of links to relevant information about the dataset available elsewhere including the dataset paper, leaderboards, and the contact information of at least one person in case of further questions; a free text summary; a description of supported tasks, suggested metrics (moved here for this updated version), and leaderboards; and the languages represented. The *dataset structure* was moved just after the languages, with examples of data instances and information about the fields and splits.

The largest change was in the people and dataset characteristics sections. We restructured these into a single *dataset creation* section which now starts with a curation rationale to properly contextualize all of the choices described in the rest of the card. The template then requests information about the people involved in producing the source language and annotations and the normalization and processing steps for that data. A section was then added to specifically describe the status of Personal Identifying (PI) data in the dataset in order to both help protect the data subjects' privacy and to help the dataset users comply with existing regulations. Dataset creators were renamed dataset curators to emphasize the difference between the people making the curation choices and the people producing the source language data, and their description was moved to the very end of the data card. Finally we expanded the limitations section to a broader section on *considerations for using the data*, adding a prompt for prospective social impacts of using the dataset, both positive and negative.

Supporting documentation writers We made these changes to improve card readers' ability to navigate the document and find necessary information about the dataset and to assist card authors when writing their cards by clarifying the desired information for each section. To further aid authors, we developed a guide formatted with desired content and instructions for each section.[9] We intend for the template and guide to support authors of datasets both with and without existing documentation. Authors of datasets without publications can use the card as a starting point for building documentation and visibility for the dataset in the HF library, but also as an overview of what information should be included in a publication. For datasets with publications, the HF card provides authors with a more widely accessible format for documenting their dataset that does not have the length limitations of paper submissions and can be revised as needed to reflect any updates to the dataset.

Publications also have the property of being static and cannot be updated to reflect changes in the dataset. To address this, we designed the HF data cards to function as living documents. First, hosting them on GitHub allows community members at large to easily add new information or modify existing sections to reflect new findings. We see this as particularly important for the section on using the dataset as new considerations are reported as a result of novel use cases and research. We also made the decision to publish the template with the sections pre-populated with placeholder text (specifically, "More Information Needed") in order to encourage authors and community members to fill in the section when the information is available. The ability to update information helps to address the harms caused by out-of-date documentation. By integrating the data cards into the HF library, we are able to see a more complete characterization of the available datasets that is similarly up to date. This allows us to point out where fewer datasets are available for tasks and languages and make progress towards a more diverse library.

[9] `https://hf.co/datasets/card-guide`

5 Case Study II: GEM Data and Model Cards

Our second case study of data card development is the template we developed for the datasets and model submissions of the Generation, its Evaluation, and Metrics (GEM) workshop. We present the full template in Table 1. The completed data card for the ASSET dataset (Alva-Manchego et al., 2020) is available in Appendix B.

5.1 GEM Benchmark

The benchmark for GEM aims to standardize how research in natural language generation (NLG) is conducted with a particular focus on in-depth evaluations (Gehrmann et al., 2021). To this end, newly developed NLG models should be documented and evaluated on a set of established tasks over a range of reproducible and robust metrics. This goal can only be achieved if the infrastructure provided by the benchmark supports the creation of such documentation.

Since a benchmark may comprise multiple datasets and provide a centralized way to interact with them, we can focus on two groups of stakeholders following the descriptions in Section 3.1.

Benchmark curators. The curators need to *ensure that all datasets are documented* according to the requirements.

Benchmark participants. The participants need to *write model documentation* according to the requirements, but may be novice ML practitioners or inexperienced in writing documentation.

5.2 Data Cards

None of the datasets included in GEM had existing data cards. To address this issue, we develop a data card template and use it to document all the datasets involved in the benchmark. Moreover, to be able to quickly add new datasets and to help the broader NLG community construct their own data cards, we release the template and associated guide. The data card closely follows the HF data card template introduced in Section 4, with changes to target NLG-specific issues. We made these changes to address feedback after testing an initial version of the data card on the CommonGen (Lin et al., 2020) and ASSET (Alva-Manchego et al., 2020) datasets. An overview of the differences between the two templates is presented in Table 1.

The major difference between the general HF template and the NLG-specific template is that NLG datasets may contain natural language both in the input and the output. Inputs and outputs may have different sources and thus require documentation for both. In addition, the input-output pairs may be constructed in ways that are challenging to describe in the HF template. For example, output text may be crawled and undergo revisions while the input text remains the same. This difference did not lead to different sections in the data card itself, but it did lead to changes in the guidelines on how to write them.

Moreover, NLG tasks have an underlying communicative goal which differentiates them from classification and other structured tasks. It is imperative to surface the communicative goal, since it heavily influences how generated text for a particular task should be evaluated. Another category of changes concerns the context of GEM compared to general purpose data cards. For example, since GEM itself is a benchmark, information about leaderboards does not have to be prominently featured, whereas it should give credit to the original data creators early on.

We also added three GEM-specific sections: (1) Why is this dataset part of GEM, (2) Changes to the original dataset for GEM, and (3) Getting started with in-depth research on the task. The first aims to tie the collections of data cards together by situating a dataset and task within the larger goal of the benchmark. The second section is of crucial importance for any data card for a benchmark, since the benchmark may change the purpose of a dataset and the organizers could modify the underlying data by cleaning it, adding more data, or releasing a reformatted version. The final question encourages participants to engage with the data in order to develop a deeper understanding of the task formulation. Therefore, to help participants gain insights into the data, we included a section with helpful pointers to relevant papers and tutorials.

Finally, GEM is designed to be a multilingual benchmark. Since we expect to include languages with fewer resources than may be found for languages like English, we aim to consider the communities that speak those languages and the impacts that technology built with these datasets could have on them. For example, a dataset for a language with few other resources may only capture the language of a few speakers in a certain context, like

HuggingFace data card	**GEM data card**
Dataset Description	Dataset and Task Description
• Dataset Summary	• Dataset and Task Summary
• Supported Tasks and Leaderboards	*See below*
–	• Why is this dataset part of GEM?
• Languages	• Languages
–	Meta Information
See below	• Dataset Curators
See below	• Licensing Information
See below	• Citation Information
See above	• Leaderboard
Dataset Structure	Dataset Structure
• Data Instances	• Data Instances
• Data Fields	• Data Fields
• Data Splits	• Data Statistics
Dataset Creation	Dataset Creation
• Curation Rationale	• Curation Rationale
–	• Communicative Goal
• Source Data	• Source Data
•• Initial Data Collection and Normalization	•• Initial Data Collection and Normalization
•• Who are the source language producers?	•• Who are the source language producers?
• Annotations	• Annotations
•• Annotation process	•• Annotation process
•• Who are the annotators?	•• Who are the annotators?
• Personal and Sensitive Information	• Personal and Sensitive Information
–	Changes to the Original Dataset for GEM
Considerations for Using the Data	Considerations for Using the Data
• Social Impact of the Dataset	• Social Impact of the Dataset
–	• Impact on Underserved Communities
• Discussion of Biases	• Discussion of Biases
• Other Known Limitations	• Other Known Limitations
–	Getting started with in-depth research on the task
Additional Information	–
• Dataset Curators	*See above*
• Licensing Information	*See above*
• Citation Information	*See above*
• Contributions	–
–	Credits for Data Cards and this Template

Table 1: Side by side comparison of the HF and GEM data card templates. Each section is denoted by horizontal lines, subsections are denoted with •, subsubsections with ••.

GEM Model Card
Social Impact • Additional Data • Training Process • Real-World Use • Measuring Impact
Reproducibility • Model Description • Model Details • Model Hyperparameters • Hyperparameter Specification • Number of Training and Evaluation Runs • Dataset Details • Dependencies and External Libraries • Link to Downloadable Source Code • Computing Infrastructure Used
Evaluation details

Table 2: An overview of the GEM model card template.

university students in the context of an experiment. Models trained on this dataset would not have access to the variation in the language that comes from speakers of other ages and in other contexts, but because there may not be other available tools, that model may become widely used and misrepresented as a general model of the language. We thus added a specific section to address potential concerns involving communities that speak those language varieties, such as the implications for model generality and privacy when speakers from small communities are easily identifiable.

5.3 Model Cards

Following the guiding principles outlined in Section 3.4, the model cards have three sections: social impact, reproducibility, and evaluation. A detailed overview is shown in Table 2.

Social impact In the first section, we invite submission authors to consider the impacts their models may have on users if they were deployed. We recognize that without further guidance, the open-ended nature of this request may make it prohibitively difficult to address. Indeed, trying to foresee all the ways in which data or modeling choices may affect all direct and indirect stakeholders is overwhelming, if not impossible. Instead, we narrow the scope to help users practice reflecting on causal relationships between design and deployment effects. We do this by providing guiding examples of models and their potential impacts. In one scenario, we consider a summarization model trained on a English Wikipedia, which is known to have various dimensions of gender bias (Wagner et al., 2015). We present two possible impacts on the output summaries based on this gender bias and suggest tests to measure the effect. We then encourage model creators to follow a similar line of thought. We ask about additional data used (and to a link to documentation if it exists), about the training process, and about a possible real-world use. We then request that the documentation author choose one aspect of one of the steps outlined, contemplate a way in which this aspect may negatively impact direct or indirect users, and propose a way to measure this impact. In particular, we believe that the latter requirement may help steer authors toward considering more plausible impacts.

Reproducibility The reproducibility section of the card combines elements of Mitchell et al. (2019)'s model cards and Dodge et al. (2019)'s reproducibility checklist. The sections ask the minimal number of questions which are key to reproducing the model submission. We request a model description, which includes the model type, version, the environment (i.e., versions of required software), and training algorithm used, with available space for further details. We also request a specification of dependencies and external libraries used to build the model. Authors have the option to link to their source code. Finally, authors are asked to describe the compute infrastructure used (e.g., the number of GPUs, the GPU type, and vRAM) and the training time for the final model.

Several questions concern the model hyperparameters, including the optimizer, training steps, learning rate. In addition, we elicit information about potential hyperparameter searches conducted as part of the model development. The hyperparameter search section requests information on the bounds for the hyperparameters, the number of search trials, and the method for choosing the hyperparameter values. The hyperparameter specifications for the best performing models are also requested but not required. Finally, the section ends with an optional space to list the number of training and evaluation runs and a required subsection detailing the utilized training dataset(s), including any processing on the data.

Evaluation The final section consists of the evaluation description. We suggest summarizing the evaluation process by including the metric details, the splits for the training, validation, and test data, and by providing the model performance on the test and validation data.

6 Conclusion

We detail the processes and principles we followed to produce the documentation templates used in the HF library and the GEM benchmark. We ground this work in the current discussion of documentation as a way to communicate the impacts of ML systems. As touched on in Section 3.2, extensive documentation is only a tool to support the communication of decisions that led to the creation of datasets and models and the positionality of their creators; it is not a direct solution to the harms caused by ML systems. We present our templates to encourage others to consider important questions that may be asked of their own work. The templates from both case studies are open source and we welcome contributions and feedback from authors and users to continually revise and improve them. Moreover, while the templates described in this work are designed for specific contexts and may not be fully applicable to others, they can be used as starting points for adaption to other settings.

7 Social Impact and Positionality Statement

Social impact statement Our goal is to promote the standardization of specialized documentation for NLP datasets and models. Institutional adoption and promotion may see its greatest effect in the widening of community engagement. The infrastructure used to host and maintain the documentation also facilitates revisions and smaller contributions from the involved communities. However, we are also aware of the risks that requiring this level of documentation for participation in either of our organizations may produce, such as raising the barrier to entry for those without experience in writing such documentation for language data as well as for people with fewer mentoring resources or platforms for engaging the community. Finally, while documenting the limitations of a resource is an important first step towards incrementally addressing issues, there is a risk that the act of documenting may allow creators to abdicate responsibility for these limitations in some cases, without taking any further steps to minimize negative social impacts of the systems they develop.

Positionality statement We are researchers at academic and industrial institutions with backgrounds in linguistics, NLP, ML, and HCI. Our guiding principles are discussed in Section 3. We aim to adapt available schemata to our specialized contexts, namely the HF library and the GEM benchmark and to present our development process as part of the general progress towards accountable and practical documentation for language datasets in ML systems. As NLP practitioners, we developed these card templates to directly support other members of the HF and NLG communities in writing documentation that answers questions that we ourselves would ask about the data and models. The completed templates will support users, researchers, and members of the public who may be impacted by these resources in understanding their contents and context.

Acknowledgments

Thank you to our anonymous reviewers and colleagues for their thoughtful comments on this work.

References

Fernando Alva-Manchego, Louis Martin, Antoine Bordes, Carolina Scarton, Benoît Sagot, and Lucia Specia. 2020. ASSET: A dataset for tuning and evaluation of sentence simplification models with multiple rewriting transformations. In *Proceedings of the 58th Annual Meeting of the Association for Computational Linguistics*, pages 4668–4679, Online. Association for Computational Linguistics.

M. Arnold, R. K. E. Bellamy, M. Hind, S. Houde, S. Mehta, A. Mojsilović, R. Nair, K. N. Ramamurthy, A. Olteanu, D. Piorkowski, D. Reimer, J. Richards, J. Tsay, and K. R. Varshney. 2019. FactSheets: Increasing trust in AI services through supplier's declarations of conformity. *IBM Journal of Research and Development*, 63(4/5):6:1–6:13.

Emily M. Bender and Batya Friedman. 2018. Data statements for natural language processing: Toward mitigating system bias and enabling better science. *Transactions of the Association for Computational Linguistics*, 6:587–604.

Emily M. Bender, Timnit Gebru, Angelina McMillan-Major, and Shmargaret Shmitchell. 2021. On the dangers of stochastic parrots: Can language models be too big? 🦜. In *Proceedings of the 2021 ACM*

Conference on Fairness, Accountability, and Transparency, FAccT '21, page 610–623, New York, NY, USA. Association for Computing Machinery.

Anant Bhardwaj, Souvik Bhattacherjee, Amit Chavan, Amol Deshpande, Aaron J. Elmore, Samuel Madden, and Aditya G. Parameswaran. 2014. DataHub: Collaborative data science & dataset version management at scale.

Samuel R. Bowman, Gabor Angeli, Christopher Potts, and Christopher D. Manning. 2015. A large annotated corpus for learning natural language inference. In *Proceedings of the 2015 Conference on Empirical Methods in Natural Language Processing (EMNLP)*. Association for Computational Linguistics.

James Cheney, Laura Chiticariu, and Wang-Chiew Tan. 2009. Provenance in databases: Why, how, and where. *Foundations and Trends in Databases*, 1(4):379–474.

Ward Cunningham. 1992. The wycash portfolio management system. In *Addendum to the Proceedings on Object-Oriented Programming Systems, Languages, and Applications (Addendum)*, OOPSLA '92, page 29–30, New York, NY, USA. Association for Computing Machinery.

Jesse Dodge, Suchin Gururangan, Dallas Card, Roy Schwartz, and Noah A. Smith. 2019. Show your work: Improved reporting of experimental results. In *Proceedings of the 2019 Conference on Empirical Methods in Natural Language Processing and the 9th International Joint Conference on Natural Language Processing (EMNLP-IJCNLP)*, pages 2185–2194, Hong Kong, China. Association for Computational Linguistics.

Penelope Eckert and John R Rickford. 2001. *Style and sociolinguistic variation*. Cambridge University Press, Cambridge, UK ; New York, NY.

Angela Fan, Yacine Jernite, Ethan Perez, David Grangier, Jason Weston, and Michael Auli. 2019. ELI5: Long form question answering. In *Proceedings of the 57th Annual Meeting of the Association for Computational Linguistics*, pages 3558–3567, Florence, Italy. Association for Computational Linguistics.

Batya Friedman and David G Hendry. 2019. *Value sensitive design: Shaping technology with moral imagination*. MIT Press.

Batya Friedman and Peter H. Kahn. 2003. Human values, ethics, and design. In Julie A. Jacko and Andrew Sears, editors, *The Human-Computer Interaction Handbook: Fundamentals, Evolving Technologies and Emerging Applications*, Human factors and ergonomics, page 1177–1201. Lawrence Erlbaum Associates, USA.

Timnit Gebru, Jamie Morgenstern, Briana Vecchione, Jennifer Wortman Vaughan, Hanna Wallach, Hal Daumé III au2, and Kate Crawford. 2020. Datasheets for datasets.

Timnit Gebru, Jamie Morgenstern, Briana Vecchione, Jennifer Wortman Vaughan, Hanna Wallach, Hal Daumé III, and Kate Crawford. 2018. Datasheets for datasets. *arXiv preprint arXiv:1803.09010*.

Sebastian Gehrmann, Tosin P. Adewumi, Karmanya Aggarwal, Pawan Sasanka Ammanamanchi, Aremu Anuoluwapo, Antoine Bosselut, Khyathi Raghavi Chandu, Miruna-Adriana Clinciu, Dipanjan Das, Kaustubh D. Dhole, Wanyu Du, Esin Durmus, Ondrej Dusek, Chris Emezue, Varun Gangal, Cristina Garbacea, Tatsunori Hashimoto, Yufang Hou, Yacine Jernite, Harsh Jhamtani, Yangfeng Ji, Shailza Jolly, Dhruv Kumar, Faisal Ladhak, Aman Madaan, Mounica Maddela, Khyathi Mahajan, Saad Mahamood, Bodhisattwa Prasad Majumder, Pedro Henrique Martins, Angelina McMillan-Major, Simon Mille, Emiel van Miltenburg, Moin Nadeem, Shashi Narayan, Vitaly Nikolaev, Rubungo Andre Niyongabo, Salomey Osei, Ankur P. Parikh, Laura Perez-Beltrachini, Niranjan Ramesh Rao, Vikas Raunak, Juan Diego Rodriguez, Sashank Santhanam, João Sedoc, Thibault Sellam, Samira Shaikh, Anastasia Shimorina, Marco Antonio Sobrevilla Cabezudo, Hendrik Strobelt, Nishant Subramani, Wei Xu, Diyi Yang, Akhila Yerukola, and Jiawei Zhou. 2021. The GEM benchmark: Natural language generation, its evaluation and metrics. *CoRR*, abs/2102.01672.

Christine Grady. 2015. Institutional review boards: purpose and challenges. *Chest*, 148(5):1148–1155.

Sarah Holland, Ahmed Hosny, Sarah Newman, Joshua Joseph, and Kasia Chmielinski. 2018. The dataset nutrition label: A framework to drive higher data quality standards.

Ben Hutchinson, Andrew Smart, Alex Hanna, Emily Denton, Christina Greer, Oddur Kjartansson, Parker Barnes, and Margaret Mitchell. 2021. Towards accountability for machine learning datasets: Practices from software engineering and infrastructure. In *Proceedings of the 2021 ACM Conference on Fairness, Accountability, and Transparency*, FAccT '21, page 560–575, New York, NY, USA. Association for Computing Machinery.

Bill Yuchen Lin, Wangchunshu Zhou, Ming Shen, Pei Zhou, Chandra Bhagavatula, Yejin Choi, and Xiang Ren. 2020. CommonGen: A constrained text generation challenge for generative commonsense reasoning. In *Findings of the Association for Computational Linguistics: EMNLP 2020*, pages 1823–1840, Online. Association for Computational Linguistics.

J. Metcalf and K. Crawford. 2016. Where are human subjects in big data research? the emerging ethics divide. *Big Data & Society*, 3.

Margaret Mitchell, Simone Wu, Andrew Zaldivar, Parker Barnes, Lucy Vasserman, Ben Hutchinson, Elena Spitzer, Inioluwa Deborah Raji, and Timnit Gebru. 2019. Model cards for model reporting. In

Proceedings of the Conference on Fairness, Accountability, and Transparency, FAT* '19, page 220–229, New York, NY, USA. Association for Computing Machinery.

Amandalynne Paullada, Inioluwa Deborah Raji, Emily M Bender, Emily Denton, and Alex Hanna. 2020. Data and its (dis) contents: A survey of dataset development and use in machine learning research. *arXiv preprint arXiv:2012.05345*.

Joelle Pineau, Philippe Vincent-Lamarre, Koustuv Sinha, Vincent Larivière, Alina Beygelzimer, Florence d'Alché Buc, Emily Fox, and Hugo Larochelle. 2020. Improving reproducibility in machine learning research (a report from the neurips 2019 reproducibility program).

Mahima Pushkarna, Andrew Zaldivar, Dan Nanas, Emily Brouillet, Reena Jana, Oddur Kjartansson, Danielle Smalls, and Vivian Tsai. 2021. Data cards playbook. https://pair-code.github.io/datacardsplaybook/.

Nithya Sambasivan, Shivani Kapania, Hannah Highfill, Diana Akrong, Praveen Kumar Paritosh, and Lora Mois Aroyo. 2021. "Everyone wants to do the model work, not the data work": Data cascades in high-stakes AI.

Anastasia Shimorina and Anya Belz. 2021. The human evaluation datasheet 1.0: A template for recording details of human evaluation experiments in NLP.

Claudia Wagner, David Garcia, Mohsen Jadidi, and Markus Strohmaier. 2015. It's a man's wikipedia? assessing gender inequality in an online encyclopedia. In *Proceedings of the International AAAI Conference on Web and Social Media*, volume 9.

Zeerak Waseem, Smarika Lulz, Joachim Bingel, and Isabelle Augenstein. 2021. Disembodied machine learning: On the illusion of objectivity in NLP.

Thomas Wolf, Lysandre Debut, Victor Sanh, Julien Chaumond, Clement Delangue, Anthony Moi, Pierric Cistac, Tim Rault, Rémi Louf, Morgan Funtowicz, Joe Davison, Sam Shleifer, Patrick von Platen, Clara Ma, Yacine Jernite, Julien Plu, Canwen Xu, Teven Le Scao, Sylvain Gugger, Mariama Drame, Quentin Lhoest, and Alexander M. Rush. 2020. Transformers: State-of-the-art natural language processing. In *Proceedings of the 2020 Conference on Empirical Methods in Natural Language Processing: System Demonstrations, EMNLP 2020 - Demos, Online, November 16-20, 2020*, pages 38–45. Association for Computational Linguistics.

A Example of a Hugging Face Data Card: ELI5

A.1 Dataset Description

ELI5 homepage; ELI5 repository; paper: ELI5: Long Form Question Answering; contact: Yacine Jernite

Dataset Summary The ELI5 dataset is an English-language dataset of questions and answers gathered from three subreddits where users ask factual questions requiring paragraph-length or longer answers. The dataset was created to support the task of open-domain long form abstractive question answering (QA), and covers questions about general topics in its r/explainlikeimfive subset, science in it r/askscience subset, and history in its r/AskHistorians subset.

Supported Tasks and Leaderboards The dataset can be used to train a model for Open Domain Long Form QA. An LFQA model is presented with a non-factoid and asked to retrieve relevant information from a knowledge source (such as Wikipedia), then use it to generate a multi-sentence answer. The model performance is measured by how high its ROUGE score to the reference is. A BART-based model with a dense retriever trained to draw information from Wikipedia passages achieves a ROUGE-L of 0.149.

Languages The dataset is in English (BCP-47 code: `en`), as spoken by users of the target subreddits.

A.2 Dataset Structure

Data Instances A typical data point comprises a question, with a `title` containing the main question and a `selftext` which sometimes elaborates on it, and a list of answers from the forum sorted by the number of upvotes they obtained. The URLs in each of the text fields have been extracted to respective lists and replaced by generic tokens in the text. Examples are available here.

Data Fields `q_id`: a unique string question ID, corresponding to its ID in the source submission dumps; `subreddit`: the source subreddit- 'explainlikeimfive', 'askscience', or 'AskHistorians'; `title`: title of the question, with URLs extracted and replaced by tokens in the form `URL_n`; `title_urls`: list of the extracted URLs, the nth element of the list was replaced by `URL_n`; `selftext`: either an empty string or an elaboration of the question; `selftext_urls`: similar to `title_urls`, but for `self_text`; `answers`: a list of answers, each answer has: `a_id` (a unique string answer ID, corresponding to its ID in the source comments dumps), `text` (the answer text with the URLs normalized), and `score` (the number of upvotes the answer had received when the dumps were created); `answers_urls`: a list of the extracted URLs (All answers use the same list, the numbering of the token continues across answer texts).

Data Splits The data is split into a training, validation and test set for each of the three subreddits. In order to avoid having duplicate questions in across sets, the `title` field of each of the questions were ranked by their tf-idf match to their nearest neighbor and the ones with the smallest value were used in the test and validation sets. The number of training, validation, and test examples for each subreddit are: 272,634, 9,812, and 24,512 for r/explainlikeimfive; 131,778, 2,281, and 4,462 for r/askscience; and 98,525, 4,901, and 9,764 for r/AskHistorians.

A.3 Dataset Creation

Curation Rationale ELI5 was built to provide a testbed for machines to learn how to answer more complex questions, which requires them to find and combine information in a coherent manner. The dataset consists of questions that were asked by community members of three subreddits, including r/explainlikeimfive, and the answers provided by other users. The rules of the subreddit make this data well-suited for abstractive QA: the questions need to seek an objective explanation about well established facts, and the answers provided need to be understandable without any particular domain knowledge.

Source Data: Initial Data Collection and Normalization The data was obtained by filtering submissions and comments from the subreddits of interest from the XML dumps of the Reddit forum hosted on Pushshift.io. In order to further improve the quality of the selected examples, only questions with a score of at least 2 and at least one answer with a score of at least 2 were selected for the dataset. The dataset questions and answers span a period form August 2012 to August 2019.

Source Data: Who are the source language producers? The language producers are users of the r/explainlikeimfive, r/askscience, and r/AskHistorians subreddits between 2012 and 2019. No further demographic information was available from the data source.

Annotations The dataset does not contain any additional annotations.

Personal and Sensitive Information The authors removed the speaker IDs from the Pushshift.io dumps but did not otherwise anonymize the data. Some of the questions and answers are about contemporary public figures or individuals who appeared in the news.

A.4 Considerations for Using the Data

Social Impact of Dataset The purpose of this dataset is to help develop better question answering systems. A system that succeeds at the supported task would be able to provide a coherent answer to even complex questions requiring a multi-step explanation, which is beyond the ability of even the larger existing models. The task is also thought as a test-bed for retrieval model which can show the users which source text was used in generating the answer and allow them to confirm the information provided to them. It should be noted however that the provided answers were written by Reddit users, an information which may be lost if models trained on it are deployed in down-stream applications and presented to users without context. The specific biases this may introduce are discussed in the next section.

Discussion of Biases While Reddit hosts a number of thriving communities with high quality discussions, it is also widely known to have corners where sexism, hate, and harassment are significant issues. See for example the recent post from Reddit founder u/spez outlining some of the ways he thinks the website's historical policies have been responsible for this problem, Adrienne Massanari's 2015 article on GamerGate and follow-up works, or a 2019 Wired article on misogyny on Reddit. While there has been some recent work in the NLP community on *de-biasing* models (e.g. Black is to Criminal as Caucasian is to Police: Detecting and Removing Multiclass Bias in Word Embeddings for word embeddings trained specifically on Reddit data), this problem is far from solved, and the likelihood that a trained model might learn the biases present in the data remains a significant concern. We still note some encouraging signs for all of these communities: r/explainlikeimfive and r/askscience have similar structures and purposes, and r/askscience was found in 2015 to show medium supportiveness and very low toxicity when compared to other subreddits (see a hackerfall post, thecut.com write-up and supporting data). Meanwhile, the r/AskHistorians rules mention that the admins will not tolerate "*racism, sexism, or any other forms of bigotry*". However, further analysis of whether and to what extent these rules reduce toxicity is still needed. We also note that given the audience of the Reddit website which is more broadly used in the US and Europe, the answers will likely present a Western perspectives, which is particularly important to note when dealing with historical topics.

Other Known Limitations The answers provided in the dataset represent the opinions of Reddit users. While these communities strive to be helpful, they should not be considered to represent a ground truth.

A.5 Additional Information

Dataset Curators The dataset was initially created by Angela Fan, Ethan Perez, Yacine Jernite, Jason Weston, Michael Auli, and David Grangier, during work done at Facebook AI Research (FAIR).

Licensing Information The license hinges on the legal status of the Pushshift.io data which is unclear.

Citation Information The citation can be found in the ACL Anthology.

Contributions Thanks to @lewtun, @lhoestq, @mariamabarham, @thomwolf, and @yjernite.

B Example of a GEM Data Card: ASSET

B.1 Dataset Description

ASSET repository; paper: ASSET: A Dataset for Tuning and Evaluation of Sentence Simplification Models with Multiple Rewriting Transformations; contact: Fernando Alva-Manchego, Louis Martin

Dataset and Task Summary ASSET (Alva-Manchego et al., 2020) is multi-reference dataset for the evaluation of sentence simplification in English. The dataset uses the same 2,359 sentences from TurkCorpus (Xu et al., 2016) and each sentence is associated with 10 crowdsourced simplifications. Unlike previous simplification datasets, which contain a single transformation (e.g., lexical paraphrasing in TurkCorpus or sentence splitting in HSplit), the simplifications in ASSET encompass a variety of rewriting transformations.

Why is this dataset part of GEM? ASSET is a high quality simplification dataset where each source (not simple) sentence is associated with 10 human-written simplifications. It is one of the two datasets for the text simplification task in GEM. It acts as the validation and test set.

Languages ASSET contains English text only (BCP-47: `en`).

B.2 Meta Information

Dataset Curators ASSET was developed by researchers at the University of Sheffield, Inria, Facebook AI Research, and Imperial College London. The work was partly supported by Benoît Sagot's chair in the PRAIRIE institute, funded by the French National Research Agency (ANR) as part of the "Investissements d'avenir" program (reference ANR-19-P3IA-0001).

Licensing Information Attribution-NonCommercial 4.0 International (CC BY-NC 4.0)

Citation Information The citation can be found in the ACL Anthology.

Leaderboard There is no official leaderboard associated with ASSET.

B.3 Dataset Structure

Data Instances `simplification` configuration: an instance consists of an original sentence and 10 possible reference simplifications; `ratings` configuration: an instance consists in an original sentence, an automatically generated simplification, and a human judgment of quality along one of three axes.

Data Fields `original`: an original sentence from the source datasets; `simplifications`: in the simplification config, a set of crowdsourced reference simplifications; `simplification`: in the ratings config, an automatically generated simplification of the original; `aspect`: in the ratings config, how the simplification is evaluated (meaning, fluency, or simplicity); `rating`: a quality rating between 0 and 100

Data Statistics ASSET does not contain a training set; many models use WikiLarge (Zhang and Lapata, 2017) for training. For GEM, Wiki-Auto will be used for training the model. Each input sentence has 10 associated reference simplified sentences. The statistics of ASSET are given below. For the input sentences, the validation set has 2000 instances and the test set has 359, for a total of 2359 sentences. Therefore, for the validation set there are 20000 simplifications and for the test set there are 3590 simplifications for a total of 23,590 simplified sentences. The test and validation sets are the same as those of TurkCorpus. The split was random. There are 19.04 tokens per reference on average (lower than 21.29 and 25.49 for TurkCorpus and HSplit, respectively). Most (17,245) of the referece sentences do not involve sentence splitting.

B.4 Dataset Creation

Curation Rationale ASSET was created in order to improve the evaluation of sentence simplification. It uses the same input sentences as the TurkCorpus dataset from (Xu et al., 2016). The 2,359 input sentences of TurkCorpus are a sample of "standard" (not simple) sentences from the Parallel Wikipedia Simplification (PWKP) dataset (Zhu et al., 2010), which come from the August 22, 2009 version of

Wikipedia. The sentences of TurkCorpus were chosen to be of similar length (Xu et al., 2016). No further information is provided on the sampling strategy. The TurkCorpus dataset was developed in order to overcome some of the problems with sentence pairs from Standard and Simple Wikipedia: a large fraction of sentences were misaligned, or not actually simpler (Xu et al., 2016). However, TurkCorpus mainly focused on *lexical paraphrasing*, and so cannot be used to evaluate simplifications involving *compression* (deletion) or *sentence splitting*. HSplit (Sulem et al., 2018), on the other hand, can only be used to evaluate sentence splitting. The reference sentences in ASSET include a wider variety of sentence rewriting strategies, combining splitting, compression and paraphrasing. Annotators were given examples of each kind of transformation individually, as well as all three transformations used at once, but were allowed to decide which transformations to use for any given sentence. An example illustrating the differences between TurkCorpus, HSplit and ASSET is given below:
Original: He settled in London, devoting himself chiefly to practical teaching.
TurkCorpus: He rooted in London, devoting himself mainly to practical teaching.
HSplit: He settled in London. He devoted himself chiefly to practical teaching.
ASSET: He lived in London. He was a teacher.

Communicative Goal The goal is to communicate the main ideas of source sentence in a way that is easier to understand by non-native speakers of English. This could be done by replacing complex words with simpler synonyms (i.e. paraphrasing), deleting unimportant information (i.e. compression), and/or splitting a long complex sentence into several simpler ones.

Source Data: Initial Data Collection and Normalization Data from TurkCorpus (Xu et al., 2016)

Source Data: Who are the source language producers? The dataset uses language from English Wikipedia (August 22, 2009 version): some demographic information is provided here.

Annotations: Annotation process The instructions given to the annotators are available here.

Annotations: Who are the annotators? Reference sentences were written by 42 workers on Amazon Mechanical Turk (AMT). The requirements for being an annotator were: (1) passing a qualification test (appropriately simplifying sentences), (2) being a resident of the US, UK or Canada, (3) having a HIT approval rate over 95%, and over 1000 HITs approved. Out of 100 workers, 42 passed the qualification test. No other demographic or compensation information is provided in the ASSET paper.

Personal and Sensitive Information Since the dataset is created from English Wikipedia (August 22, 2009 version), all the information contained in the dataset is already in the public domain.

B.5 Changes to the Original Dataset for GEM No change.

B.6 Considerations for Using the Data

Social Impact of the Dataset The dataset helps move forward the research towards text simplification by creating a higher quality validation and test dataset. Progress in text simplification in turn has the potential to increase the accessibility of written documents to wider audiences.

Impact on Underserved Communities The dataset is in English, a language with many resources.

Discussion of Biases The dataset may contain some social biases, as the input sentences are based on Wikipedia. Studies have shown that the English Wikipedia contains both gender biases (Schmahl et al., 2020) and racial biases (Adams et al., 2019).

Other Known Limitations The dataset is limited to a small subset of topics present on Wikipedia.

B.7 Getting started with in-depth research on the task

The dataset can be downloaded from the original repository (here) or be used via HuggingFace and TFDS. Recent supervised (Martin et al., 2019, Kriz et al., 2019, Dong et al., 2019, Zhang and Lapata, 2017) and unsupervised (Martin et al., 2020, Kumar et al., 2020, Surya et al., 2019) text simplification models can be used as baselines. A common metric for automatic evaluation is SARI (Xu et al., 2016).

Structure-to-Text Generation with Self-Training, Acceptability Classifiers and Context-Conditioning for the GEM Shared Task

**Shreyan Bakshi,* Soumya Batra,* Peyman Heidari,
Ankit Arun, Shashank Jain, Michael White*†**
Facebook
{shreyanb, sbatra, peymanheidari,
ankitarun, shajain, mwhite14850}@fb.com

Abstract

We explore the use of self-training and acceptability classifiers with pre-trained models for natural language generation in structure-to-text settings using three GEM datasets (E2E, WebNLG-en, Schema-Guided Dialog). With the Schema-Guided Dialog dataset, we also experiment with including multiple turns of context in the input. We find that self-training with reconstruction matching along with acceptability classifier filtering can improve semantic correctness, though gains are limited in the full-data setting. With context-conditioning, we find that including multiple turns in the context encourages the model to align with the user's word and phrasing choices as well as to generate more self-consistent responses. In future versions of the GEM challenge, we encourage the inclusion of few-shot tracks to encourage research on data efficiency.

1 Introduction

Natural Language Generation (NLG) plays a crucial role in task-oriented dialog systems, which have become increasingly commonplace in voice-controlled assistants, customer service agents, and similar systems. In the research community, generative models (Wen et al., 2015; Dušek and Jurcıcek, 2016; Rao et al., 2019) have become popular for their data-driven scaling story and superior naturalness over typical template-based systems (Gatt and Krahmer, 2018; Dale, 2020). However, training reliable and low-latency generative models has typically required tens of thousands of training samples (Balakrishnan et al., 2019; Novikova et al., 2017). From a practical perspective, model maintenance with such a large dataset has proven to be challenging, as it is resource-intensive to debug and fix responses, make stylistic changes, and add new capabilities. As such, it is of paramount importance to investigate ways of bringing up new domains and languages with as few examples as possible while maintaining quality.

Pre-trained models like GPT2 (Radford et al., 2019) have shown great potential to address this challenge (Peng et al., 2020; Chen et al., 2020), and combining pre-trained models with self-training has been shown to improve data efficiency even further (Arun et al., 2020). Additionally, semantic fidelity classifiers (Harkous et al., 2020) can be helpful in addressing issues with semantic correctness that are exacerbated in low-data settings (Anonymous, 2021). Indeed, Heidari et al. (2021) have recently shown that using pre-trained models together with self-training and acceptability classifiers — i.e., classifiers to predict semantic correctness and grammaticality — can play a crucial role in developing a production-quality model with just a few hundred training samples.

In this paper, we apply these techniques to 3 of the datasets from the GEM Shared Task (Gehrmann et al., 2021): the Schema-Guided Dialog (SGD) dataset (Rastogi et al., 2019), the End-to-End (E2E) dataset (Novikova et al., 2017) and the WebNLG-en dataset (Gardent et al., 2017). We focus on these 3 datasets specifically because they mostly closely resemble natural language generation (NLG) in a task-oriented dialog setting, as in Heidari et al.'s work. Although we did not expect substantial gains using these methods in high-data settings, we wanted to try them out on additional datasets in order to better understand their behavior, as well as to encourage research in low-data settings for future editions of the GEM shared task.

With the SGD dataset, we were also particularly interested in the effect of including multiple turns of dialog context in the input, and how this effects the behavior of our NLG system. In early work, Brockmann et al. (2005) showed that cache-based language models can be used to adapt NLG systems

*Equal Contribution
† Work done while on leave from Ohio State University

Proceedings of the 1st Workshop on Natural Language Generation, Evaluation, and Metrics (GEM 2021), pages 136–147
August 5–6, 2021. ©2021 Association for Computational Linguistics

to align with user's language, while subsequent work investigated structural priming more specifically (Reitter et al., 2006) and the impact of such adaptation in deployed dialog systems (Stoyanchev and Stent, 2009). Dušek and Jurčíček (2016) investigated ways of adapting to the user's way of speaking with neural models using the previous user turn; more recently, Kale and Rastogi (2020) demonstrated with the SGD dataset that including multiple turns of context in the input to a pretrained model yields large gains in BLEU scores. However, Kale & Rastogi did not analyze the reasons underlying these gains; here we show that context-conditioning does indeed enable the model to better align with the user's word and phrasing choices, though self-consistency with previous system turns is an even stronger factor.

2 Methods

2.1 Context-Conditioning and Templatizing Inputs

For the Schema-Guided Dialog Dataset, we included the service in the input (Table 1) after our initial experiments indicated that the service was crucial to generating accurate responses for some dialog acts (e.g., `Notify_Failure`). We notified the organizers of this issue, and they released an enhanced version of the dataset including this information. We also experimented with sorting the inputs and conditioning on 1–5 turns of context.

Following Kale and Rastogi (2020), we also tried converting the inputs into semi-natural text (Table 2) using their templates. These templates aim to provide minimal coverage of the input dialog acts rather than actually producing natural outputs, as that task is left to the pre-trained model to learn (for that reason, we call them *templatized* inputs rather than template-based inputs).

To use the Kale & Rastogi templates, we found that it was additionally necessary to augment the dialog acts with the service call method in some cases. Consequently, we retrieved this information from the original Schema-Guided Dialog dataset, sharing a script for doing so with the organizers.

2.2 Tree-Structured Ordering

For the WebNLG dataset, we followed Yang et al. (2020) in ordering the input triples using their implicit tree structure. Yang et al. found that traversing the tree in depth-first search order yielded substantial improvements in their experiments that were competitive with using a learned input ordering. Given the tendency to put heavier constituents towards the end of a sentence in English (Hawkins, 1994; Gibson, 2000; Temperley, 2007; Rajkumar et al., 2016), we additionally sorted siblings by increasing subtree depth, breaking ties by sorting alphabetically on predicate names.

To format the input data, we followed Li et al. (2020) in separating subjects, predicates and objects with separators while replacing underscores with spaces and removing quotes; we also prepended the category with a separator. An example input appears in Table 3.

Algorithm 1: Self-Training via Reconstruction

Start with labeled data $\mathcal{L}$ and unlabeled data $\mathcal{U}$, with inputs $\mathcal{X}$ and outputs/labels $\mathcal{Y}$;

Set current pseudo-labeled data $\mathcal{L}' := \mathcal{L}$;

repeat

  Train 2 models on $\mathcal{L}'$ (in parallel):

    Generation model $\mathcal{G}$ from $\mathcal{X} \to \mathcal{Y}$;

    Recon. model $\mathcal{R}$ from $\mathcal{Y} \to \mathcal{X}$;

  Run $\mathcal{G}$ on $\mathcal{U}$ to get pseudo-labels $\mathcal{Y}'$;

  Run $\mathcal{R}$ on $\mathcal{Y}'$ to get recon. inputs $\mathcal{X}'$;

  $\mathcal{L}' := \mathcal{L} \cup \{\text{rows where } X = X'\}$;

until *convergence or maximum iteration*;

2.3 Self-Training

Annotating large quantities of high-quality data is time and resource consuming. However, it is often possible to automatically generate a lot of unlabeled data using a synthetic framework. Semi-supervised techniques can then be applied based on this mix of labeled and unlabeled data, to improve model performance.

Since the datasets do not come with unpaired inputs, we create such inputs for self-training via automatic deletion of all combinations of parts of the (structured) input query, to generate larger sets of unlabeled data for self-training. For each original input, we randomly select up to 20 unpaired inputs created via deletion. Note that with WebNLG, deletion is constrained to yield connected subtrees.

Unsorted	`Buses_2` **__sep__** OFFER departure_time 8:30 am, OFFER price $23, OFFER fare_type Economy
Sorted	`Buses_2` **__sep__** OFFER departure_time 8:30 am, OFFER fare_type Economy, OFFER price $23
Prompt Sorted	`Buses_2` **__sep__** OFFER departure_time 8:30 am, OFFER fare_type Economy, OFFER price $23 __sep__ **user:** Do you have any other buses available?
Context 5 Sorted	`Buses_2` **__sep__** OFFER departure_time 8:30 am, OFFER fare_type Economy, OFFER price $23 __sep__ **user:** I am traveling from Sacramento, CA to SFO on March 7th. **sys:** I have found a bus that departs at 7:40 am. The economy ticket is priced at $22 **user:** What are the stations of arrival and departure? **sys:** It starts from Sacramento Valley Station and arrives at Salesforce Transit Center. **user:** Do you have any other buses available?

Table 1: Context-Conditioned and Sorted Inputs for the SGD Dataset (with the service name)

Template	`Buses_2` **__sep__** How about a bus leaving at 8:30 am and the price of the ticket is $23. It is Economy ticket.
Template Prompt	`Buses_2` **__sep__** How about a bus leaving at 8:30 am and the price of the ticket is $23. It is Economy ticket. __sep__ **user:** Do you have any other buses available?
Template Context 5	`Buses_2` **__sep__** How about a bus leaving at 8:30 am and the price of the ticket is $23. It is Economy ticket. __sep__ **user:** I am traveling from Sacramento, CA to SFO on March 7th. **sys:** I have found a bus that departs at 7:40 am. The economy ticket is priced at $22 **user:** What are the stations of arrival and departure? **sys:** It starts from Sacramento Valley Station and arrives at Salesforce Transit Center. **user:** Do you have any other buses available?

Table 2: Templatized and Context-Conditioned Inputs for the SGD Dataset

Original	Politician, [Poland | language | Polish_language, Adam_Koc | nationality | Poland, Poland | ethnicGroup | Kashubians]
Tree-Structured (DFS)	`Politician` **__sep__** __subj__ Adam Koc __pred__ nationality __obj__ Poland __subj__ Poland __pred__ ethnic group __obj__ Kashubians __subj__ Poland __pred__ language __obj__ Polish language

Table 3: Tree-Structured Ordering Inputs for the WebNLG Dataset

Most approaches to self-training for NLG—including earlier work on automatic data cleaning—make use of cycle consistency between parsing and generation models (Chisholm et al., 2017; Nie et al., 2019; Kedzie and McKeown, 2019; Qader et al., 2019). More recently, Chang et al. (2021) have developed a method for randomly generating new text samples with GPT-2 then automatically pairing them with data samples. Our approach, following Heidari et al. (2021), likewise takes advantage of pre-trained models; by comparison though, we take a much more direct approach to generating new text samples from unpaired inputs in self-training. As described formally in Algorithm 1, self-training here consists of multiple cycles of generation and reconstruction. Note that unlike work in MT that employs back-translation, including unsupervised MT (Lample et al., 2018), we do not assume access to large amounts of target text. Additionally, unlike He et al.'s (2020) self-training approach to MT, we make use of reconstruction matching to filter the pseudo-annotated data (line 14) in each self-training iteration.[1]

We fine-tune BART (Lewis et al., 2020), a pre-trained seq2seq language model, for both steps. For generation, we train a BART large model to produce the responses given the scenario. In parallel, the same generation data is used to fine-tune a reconstruction BART large model to obtain the generation input, given the responses. After generation in each cycle, we use the reconstruction model to select samples with exact reconstruction match. Finally, the selected samples are added to the training pool for the next self-training cycle.

We noted that for the case of SGD, the self-trained model was susceptible to stuttering, i.e., repeating the same phrase over and over again (this occurred in $< 1\%$ of the validation samples). This was not observed in the BART-Large generation model. Hence, to control for stuttering, for each response generated by the self-trained model, we used the heuristic that if any word (excluding stop words such as articles, conjunctions, etc.) was repeated in the generated response more than 5 times, we substituted the response generated by the BART-Large model instead.

[1]He et al. find it useful to fine-tune the model on just the labeled data at the end of each iteration; we leave experimenting with this additional step in our setting to future work.

2.4 Filtering via Acceptability Classifiers

Based on work by (Anonymous, 2021), we trained acceptability classifiers for each dataset using the training data available for its generation model. A response is considered (minimally) acceptable if it is both semantically accurate and grammatical.

As per Anonymous (2021)'s recommendation, since we don't have any representative validation set of labelled acceptable/unacceptable samples, we took a BART-Large model and finetuned it on the training set. Next, we used MaskFilling strategy to generate synthetic acceptable/unacceptable samples wherein we inserted 3 to 7 random masks to the seed data (i.e. training data for generation model) and used the fine-tuned BART model to fill in the masks. This helped capture similar patterns in the seed data and masked words in the response are replaced by tokens most similar to that in seed data, thereby generating more realistic unacceptable samples.

We then passed each of the generated synthetic samples to a RoBERTa-based entailment model and partitioned samples that had a 2-way entailment with respect to the original seed sample as acceptable and the rest unacceptable. In addition, we ensured that that the BLEU score between synthetic sample and original seed sample was between 0.5-0.9 for unacceptable class and above 0.9 for acceptable class. Since the BART masking method will only generate paraphrases with similar sentence structure due to masks insertion in the original seed responses thereby maintaining the original sub-sequences order, these paraphrases tend to differ only slightly compared to the original responses. Hence, a BLEU score >0.9 allows us to capture most of them while a BLEU score >0.5 ensures that we are only selecting unacceptable samples with nuanced errors.

Finally, we trained a RoBERTa-base classifier over the acceptable and unacceptable classes. At inference time, we passed the n-best responses obtained by the self-trained generation model through the trained acceptability classifier. We filtered out the responses that had a high unacceptability score (threshold determined over validation set for each dataset). Of the remaining responses, we selected the top response. In case all responses were filtered out, we selected the top response from the original n-best list.

	BART Base			BART Large		
	Unsorted	Sorted	Template	Unsorted	Sorted	Template
No Context	34.39	34.78	35.99	35.01	35.09	36.48
Prompt	37.72	37.90	39.03	38.96	39.01	39.99
Context 5	43.37	43.55	**44.18**	44.75	43.79	**45.21**

Table 4: BLEU scores for Schema-Guided Dialog validation set

	E2E Self-Train			WebNLG-en Self-Train			SGD Self-Train		
	Initial	Round 1	Round 2	Initial	Round 1	Round 2	Initial	Round 1	Round 2
500 Rows	67.85	81.58	83.83	54.41	65.87	52.55	53.87	61.68	62.91
10% Data	86.04	85.72	86.51	76.90	80.44	82.78	63.25	64.14	63.98
Full Data	89.18	90.46	**91.77**	85.24	85.78	**85.90**	63.95	63.78	**64.23**

Table 5: Exact Reconstruction Match % on full validation set for End-to-End, WebNLG-en and Schema-Guided Dialog datasets when self-trained starting with varying amounts of seed data

3 Results

3.1 Context-Conditioning and Templatizing Inputs

The BLEU (Papineni et al., 2002) scores for various BART models on the Schema-Guided Dialog validation set appear in Table 4.[2] As the Table shows, sorting the standard inputs appears to yield a small improvement. Templatizing the inputs yields a larger gain, over 1 BLEU point in some cases. Using BART Large yields a somewhat smaller gain over using BART Base, but the gains are around another BLEU point when used with templatized inputs and context. By comparison, using the dialog context yields very large gains, with including the prompt in the input adding over 3 BLEU points, and adding another four turns of context to the input improving another 5 BLEU points or so. These gains corroborate the ones reported by Kale and Rastogi (2020) using T5 (Raffel et al., 2020), while also putting them in the context of improvements based on model size and type of input. We plan to make our additional baseline results above publicly available in the near future.

3.2 Self-Training

We ran self-training as described in Algorithm 1 on all 3 datasets, with multiple variations for each including few-shot, low data and full data settings. The BLEU scores with self-training do not improve significantly over the regular training paradigm. However, we observe sharp increase in the exact reconstruction match rate on the validation set when using self-training, especially in the lower data regimes, as shown in Table 5. This metric is calculated by training a reconstruction model on the full labeled data once in the beginning, and then using this model to perform reconstructions at different stages during self-training – observing its performance on 100% of the validation set each time, for automatic evaluation purposes. Note that with the SGD dataset, we used reconstruction accuracy on the sorted input for this evaluation, as we observed some issues with reconstructing the textualized input; these are discussed further in the next section.

[2]These BLEU scores are calculated with a different version of BLEU than used by the GEM metrics; the BLEU score for the best model according to the GEM metrics is 43.35.

3.3 Filtering via Acceptability Classifiers

We ran n-best response filtering using Acceptability Classifiers on the outputs of the BART-Large generation model as described in 2.4. The BLEU scores and reconstruction exact match rate only slightly changed (increased or decreased) at different unacceptability confidence thresholds.

We also ran a RoBERTa-based entailment model on the small number of responses that were changed by the acceptability classifier with respect to the target reference, as well as on the corresponding 1-best response from the generation model. We estimated number of paraphrases by checking for 2-way entailment between the pairs. We observed a slight increase in the total number of paraphrases identified using this model when filtering via Acceptability Classifier, as shown in Table 6. Examples of positive changes appear in Table 7.

	Total number of paraphrases wrt target reference		
	Total Changed	Response chosen by acc	1-best Response
WebNLG	112	105	104
E2E	100	68	64
SGD	22	12	15

Table 6: Number of paraphrases identified by RoBERTa-base entailment model when response chosen by Acceptability Classifier (acc) filtering method (at best threshold) compared to the 1-best response from vanilla BART-Large generation method on validation sets.

Dataset	Input	Response chosen by acc	1-best Response
WebNLG	Food __sep__ __subj__ Arem-arem __pred__ country __obj__ Indonesia __subj__ Indonesia __pred__ leader __obj__ Joko Widodo __subj__ Indonesia __pred__ leader __obj__ Jusuf Kalla	Arem arem originates from Indonesia where Joko Widodo and Jusuf Kalla are leaders.	Joko Widodo and Jusuf Kalla are leaders in Indonesia where Arem-arem is a traditional dish.
E2E	name[The Wrestlers], customer rating[5 out of 5], familyFriendly[yes]	The Wrestlers is a 5 out of 5 rated family friendly venue.	The Wrestlers is a five star, family friendly sushi bar.
SGD	Services_4 __sep__ REQUEST type Psychologist Psychiatrist	Do you need a Psychiatrist or a Psychologist?	Do you need a Psychiatrist or a Psychiatrist?

Table 7: Sample Responses chosen by Acceptability Classifier (acc) filtering over 1-best response

3.4 Combined Methods

Results from the GEM metrics on the validation set when using the Acceptability Classifier with the self-trained BART-Large models appear in Table 8.[3]

4 Analysis

4.1 Context-Conditioning and Templatizing Inputs

Here we analyze the effects of including multiple turns of context in the input. Table 9 shows examples of how the model that takes five previous turns of context as input (Context 5) aligns with aspects of the context more strongly than the model that takes just one turn of context as input (Prompt). Examples (a) and (b) show how the Context 5 models generates wordier or more concise outputs depending on the user's previous word and phrase choices, while Example (c) shows how the Context 5 model instead picks up on its own previous phrasings to yield a more consistent way presenting similar weather information across responses.

These effects can be verified quantitatively as well. Table 10 shows how the Context 5 model's responses correlate more strongly in length with both previous user and system turns, and Table 11 similarly shows that BLEU-2 scores against the context are more similar for the Context 5 model than the Prompt model. Finally, Table 12 shows that these contextual BLEU-2 scores are positively correlated with BLEU scores against the reference. (All correlations are statistically significant, albeit weak.)

4.2 Self-Training

Since we did not observe an increase in BLEU scores with self-training in the full-data setting, we manually examined a sample of validation set outputs for the initial, supervised BART-Large model in comparison to the self-trained BART-Large model where these outputs differed in reconstruction accuracy. Across all 3 datasets, we found that both outputs were usually good, reflecting issues with the reconstruction model or our way of determining a reconstruction match, rather than real differences in the semantic correctness of the outputs. However, in the cases where real semantic differences were found, we observed that the changes were generally in the direction of improved semantic correctness with the self-trained model.

In calculating reconstruction accuracy, we noticed many issues that can be considered cases of inadequate normalization. For example, with the E2E dataset, the customer rating and price range slots use mostly interchangeable values in the input such as "5 out of 5" and "high" as values for top-rated venues; this means that the reconstruction

[3]Note that METEOR scores here are computed via NLTK

	BLEU	METEOR	ROUGE-L	BERTScore	BLEURT
E2E	34.54	0.578	54.5	0.916	0.292
WebNLG-en	68.74	0.777	72.1	0.959	0.478
SGD	43.38	0.560	60.8	0.898	0.177

Table 8: Validation set automatic metrics for self-trained models with Acceptability Classifier filtering

	Content	Context	Reference	Prompt	Context 5
(a)	How many tickets would you like?	*user*: Okay. **Can you** find **me** a hotel in that area, so that I will have a place to stay in? *sys*: ... *user*: **Can you** give **me** their phone number? How much will it cost me per nigh? *sys*: ... *user*: That is nice. Now I want to buy tickets for the event you found earlier.	**Can you** tell **me** the number of tickets you want to buy?	How many tickets do you want to buy?	**Can you** tell **me** the number of tickets you want to buy?
(b)	Your reservation is successful. They do not have outdoor seating.	*user*: **Sounds good** to me. *sys*: ... *user*: Sure, **book it** for 11:00 *sys*: ... *user*: **Perfect.** do they have outdoor seating?	**Booking confirmed.** They **don't** have outdoor seating.	Your reservation has been made. They do not have outdoor seating.	**Booking confirmed.** They **don't** have outdoor seating.
(c)	The average temperature for the day should be 87 degrees Fahrenheit. There is a 3 percent chance of rain.	*user*: Duncans Mills *sys*: **It will be** 93 **degrees with** a 20 **percent chance of rain.** *user*: How about on the 5th of this month? *sys*: **It will be about** 90 **degrees with a** 1 **percent chance of rain.** *user*: How about in Mexico city?	**It will be** 87 **degrees with a** 3 **percent chance of rain.**	Average temperature: 87 degrees Fahrenheit. Chance of rain: 3 percent.	**It will be about** 87 **degrees with a** 3 **percent chance of rain.**

Table 9: Examples illustrating model adaptation to the dialog context when using 5 previous turns of context (Context 5) vs. just one previous turn (Prompt). Example (a) shows how the Context 5 model picks up on the user's wordier phrasing, leading to an exact match with the reference. Example (b) indicates how the Context 5 model instead uses a more concise phrasing, picking up on the user's terseness. Example (c) shows how the Context 5 model instead picks up on its own previous phrasings to yield a self-consistent way of presenting similar weather information for different locales and dates.

	User	System
Reference	0.337	0.095
Prompt	0.275	0.025
Context 5	0.320	0.085

Table 10: Correlations in model turn length using 5 previous turns of context (Context 5) vs. just one previous turn (Prompt) with user and system turns in the preceding context (5 turns), in comparison to reference.

	User	System
Reference	15.24	15.68
Prompt	8.80	13.11
Context 5	15.88	17.29

Table 11: Mean model BLEU-2 scores (with no length penalty) using 5 previous turns of context (Context 5) vs. just one previous turn (Prompt) against user and system turns in the preceding context (5 turns), in comparison to reference.

model essentially has to guess which one actually appeared in the input. In future work, we intend to add compare the set of slots with normalized values rather than just using exact string match. Similar issues arose with WebNLG, where the reconstruction model had difficulty getting the order of the triples correct, and with SGD, where we discovered that similar but non-identical templates across related services caused confusion for the reconstruction model. Additionally, with SGD we observed that making the dialog context available as input to the

	User	System
Prompt	0.088	0.131
Context 5	0.083	0.204

Table 12: Correlations between contextual BLEU-2 scores (with no length penalty) for model using 5 previous turns of context (Context 5) vs. just one previous turn (Prompt) against user and system turns with BLEU scores (against reference).

reconstruction model would be helpful in many cases, since many responses employing elliptical constructions were difficult for the reconstruction model (despite being clear and natural in context).

4.3 Acceptability Classifier Filtering

Looking more closely at a random sample of the responses that were changed by the acceptability classifier, we noted that the acceptability classifier filtering indeed usually chooses a better response than the default in high confidence unacceptability regions. This also makes intuitive sense as we expect the generation model to be correct and fluent most of the time and acceptability classifier filtering helping in a small number of cases. We expect this impact to be higher on cases which are not represented in the training distribution.

5 Discussion

It is fascinating that simply including multiple turns of preceding dialog in the input to a pre-trained model has such a large impact on generated responses, and in particular that doing so increases alignment with the user's language as well as consistency with the system's own previous responses. Both factors can be expected to enhance naturalness, though this will need verification via human evaluation. More compellingly, it is likely that these effects will enhance user perceptions of the system in an extrinsic evaluation of how NLG affects perceived dialog quality. To verify such effects, it will be important to study context-enhanced NLG in the context of actual dialogs with users, rather than in a simpler overhearer paradigm.

Turning to self-training, it is clear from our experiments that gains in semantic correctness can be quite large in low-data settings. Moreover, the pay-off from acceptability classifier filtering can be expected to be larger there. Nevertheless, gains in low-data settings have generally not brought systems fully in line with those trained in high-data settings. As such, there remains considerable room for improvement in such low-data settings, even when using pre-trained models. To promote work along these lines, future editions of the GEM shared task could have few-shot tracks where the number of samples for supervised training is quite limited. Moreover, it would be extremely helpful to make unpaired inputs available for these tracks. While creating unpaired inputs via deletion is somewhat helpful, this technique cannot help with unseen or few-shot test items in the final test set. As such, providing unpaired inputs corresponding to these few-shot test items would provide a way to experiment in a standardized fashion with methods for generalizing in these cases. Note that in the case of datasets created via simulation, as with the SGD dataset and its dialog simulator, creating new unpaired inputs would only require running the simulator for the few-shot domains. Doing so for a shared task should be much easier than releasing all the code used during dataset creation, so we urge the organizers to consider this option in future.

Acknowledgments

We thank the anonymous reviewers for their helpful comments. We also thank Arash Einolghozati, Lee Callender, Catharine Youngs, Anuj Kumar, Shawn Mei, Sonal Gupta, Pinar Donmez and Vikas Bhardwaj for helpful discussion.

References

Anonymous. 2021. Building adaptive acceptability classifiers for neural NLG. Under review.

Ankit Arun, Soumya Batra, Vikas Bhardwaj, Ashwini Challa, Pinar Donmez, Peyman Heidari, Hakan Inan, Shashank Jain, Anuj Kumar, Shawn Mei, Karthik Mohan, and Michael White. 2020. Best practices for data-efficient modeling in NLG:how to train production-ready neural models with less data. In *Proceedings of the 28th International Conference on Computational Linguistics: Industry Track*, pages 64–77, Online. International Committee on Computational Linguistics.

Anusha Balakrishnan, Jinfeng Rao, Kartikeya Upasani, Michael White, and Rajen Subba. 2019. Constrained decoding for neural NLG from compositional representations in task-oriented dialogue. In *Proceedings of the 57th Annual Meeting of the Association for Computational Linguistics*.

Carsten Brockmann, Amy Isard, Jon Oberlander, and Michael White. 2005. Modelling alignment for affective dialogue. In *Proc. of the Workshop on Adapting the Interaction Style to Affective Factors at the 10th International Conference on User Modeling (UM-05)*.

Ernie Chang, Xiaoyu Shen, Dawei Zhu, Vera Demberg, and Hui Su. 2021. Neural data-to-text generation with LM-based text augmentation. In *Proceedings of the 16th Conference of the European Chapter of the Association for Computational Linguistics: Main Volume*, pages 758–768, Online. Association for Computational Linguistics.

Zhiyu Chen, Harini Eavani, Wenhu Chen, Yinyin Liu, and William Yang Wang. 2020. Few-shot NLG with pre-trained language model. In *Proceedings of the 58th Annual Meeting of the Association for Computational Linguistics*, pages 183–190, Online. Association for Computational Linguistics.

Andrew Chisholm, Will Radford, and Ben Hachey. 2017. Learning to generate one-sentence biographies from Wikidata. In *Proceedings of the 15th Conference of the European Chapter of the Association for Computational Linguistics: Volume 1, Long Papers*, pages 633–642, Valencia, Spain. Association for Computational Linguistics.

Robert Dale. 2020. Natural language generation: The commercial state of the art in 2020. *Natural Language Engineering*. To appear.

Ondřej Dušek and Filip Jurčíček. 2016. A context-aware natural language generator for dialogue systems. In *Proceedings of the 17th Annual Meeting of the Special Interest Group on Discourse and Dialogue*, pages 185–190, Los Angeles. Association for Computational Linguistics.

Ondrej Dušek and Filip Jurcıcek. 2016. Sequence-to-sequence generation for spoken dialogue via deep syntax trees and strings. In *The 54th Annual Meeting of the Association for Computational Linguistics*, page 45.

Claire Gardent, Anastasia Shimorina, Shashi Narayan, and Laura Perez-Beltrachini. 2017. Creating training corpora for NLG micro-planners. In *Proceedings of the 55th Annual Meeting of the Association for Computational Linguistics, ACL 2017, Vancouver, Canada, July 30 - August 4, Volume 1: Long Papers*, pages 179–188. Association for Computational Linguistics.

Albert Gatt and Emiel Krahmer. 2018. Survey of the state of the art in natural language generation: Core tasks, applications and evaluation. *Journal of Artificial Intelligence Research*, 61:65–170.

Sebastian Gehrmann, Tosin P. Adewumi, Karmanya Aggarwal, Pawan Sasanka Ammanamanchi, Aremu Anuoluwapo, Antoine Bosselut, Khyathi Raghavi Chandu, Miruna-Adriana Clinciu, Dipanjan Das, Kaustubh D. Dhole, Wanyu Du, Esin Durmus, Ondrej Dusek, Chris Emezue, Varun Gangal, Cristina Garbacea, Tatsunori Hashimoto, Yufang Hou, Yacine Jernite, Harsh Jhamtani, Yangfeng Ji, Shailza Jolly, Dhruv Kumar, Faisal Ladhak, Aman Madaan, Mounica Maddela, Khyati Mahajan, Saad Mahamood, Bodhisattwa Prasad Majumder, Pedro Henrique Martins, Angelina McMillan-Major, Simon Mille, Emiel van Miltenburg, Moin Nadeem, Shashi Narayan, Vitaly Nikolaev, Rubungo Andre Niyongabo, Salomey Osei, Ankur P. Parikh, Laura Perez-Beltrachini, Niranjan Ramesh Rao, Vikas Raunak, Juan Diego Rodriguez, Sashank Santhanam, João Sedoc, Thibault Sellam, Samira Shaikh, Anastasia Shimorina, Marco Antonio Sobrevilla Cabezudo, Hendrik Strobelt, Nishant Subramani, Wei Xu, Diyi Yang, Akhila Yerukola, and Jiawei Zhou. 2021. The GEM benchmark: Natural language generation, its evaluation and metrics. *CoRR*, abs/2102.01672.

Edward Gibson. 2000. The dependency locality theory: A distance-based theory of linguistic complexity. *Image, language, brain*, 2000:95–126.

Hamza Harkous, Isabel Groves, and Amir Saffari. 2020. Have your text and use it too! end-to-end neural data-to-text generation with semantic fidelity. In *Proceedings of the 28th International Conference on Computational Linguistics*, pages 2410–2424, Barcelona, Spain (Online). International Committee on Computational Linguistics.

John A Hawkins. 1994. *A performance theory of order and constituency*. 73. Cambridge University Press.

Junxian He, Jiatao Gu, Jiajun Shen, and Marc'Aurelio Ranzato. 2020. Revisiting self-training for neural sequence generation.

Peyman Heidari, Arash Einolghozati, Shashank Jain, Soumya Batra, Lee Callender, Ankit Arun, Shawn Mei, Sonal Gupta, Pinar Donmez, Vikas Bhardwaj,

Anuj Kumar, and Michael White. 2021. Getting to production with few-shot natural language generation models. In *Proceedings of SIGDIAL*. To appear.

Mihir Kale and Abhinav Rastogi. 2020. Template guided text generation for task-oriented dialogue. In *Proceedings of the 2020 Conference on Empirical Methods in Natural Language Processing (EMNLP)*, pages 6505–6520, Online. Association for Computational Linguistics.

Chris Kedzie and Kathleen McKeown. 2019. A good sample is hard to find: Noise injection sampling and self-training for neural language generation models. In *Proceedings of the 12th International Conference on Natural Language Generation*, pages 584–593, Tokyo, Japan. Association for Computational Linguistics.

Guillaume Lample, Myle Ott, Alexis Conneau, Ludovic Denoyer, and Marc'Aurelio Ranzato. 2018. Phrase-based & neural unsupervised machine translation. In *Proceedings of the 2018 Conference on Empirical Methods in Natural Language Processing*, pages 5039–5049, Brussels, Belgium. Association for Computational Linguistics.

Mike Lewis, Yinhan Liu, Naman Goyal, Marjan Ghazvininejad, Abdelrahman Mohamed, Omer Levy, Veselin Stoyanov, and Luke Zettlemoyer. 2020. BART: Denoising sequence-to-sequence pre-training for natural language generation, translation, and comprehension. In *Proceedings of the 58th Annual Meeting of the Association for Computational Linguistics*, pages 7871–7880, Online. Association for Computational Linguistics.

Xintong Li, Aleksandre Maskharashvili, Symon Jory Stevens-Guille, and Michael White. 2020. Leveraging large pretrained models for WebNLG 2020. In *Proceedings of the 3rd International Workshop on Natural Language Generation from the Semantic Web (WebNLG+)*, pages 117–124, Dublin, Ireland (Virtual). Association for Computational Linguistics.

Feng Nie, Jin-Ge Yao, Jinpeng Wang, Rong Pan, and Chin-Yew Lin. 2019. A simple recipe towards reducing hallucination in neural surface realisation. In *Proceedings of the 57th Annual Meeting of the Association for Computational Linguistics*, pages 2673–2679, Florence, Italy. Association for Computational Linguistics.

Jekaterina Novikova, Ondrej Dušek, and Verena Rieser. 2017. The E2E dataset: New challenges for end-to-end generation. In *Proceedings of the 18th Annual Meeting of the Special Interest Group on Discourse and Dialogue*, Saarbrücken, Germany. ArXiv:1706.09254.

Kishore Papineni, Salim Roukos, Todd Ward, and Wei Jing Zhu. 2002. Bleu: a method for automatic evaluation of machine translation. *In Proc. ACL-02*.

Baolin Peng, Chenguang Zhu, Chunyuan Li, Xiujun Li, Jinchao Li, Michael Zeng, and Jianfeng Gao. 2020. Few-shot natural language generation for task-oriented dialog. *Empirical Methods in Natural Language Processing (EMNLP)*.

Raheel Qader, François Portet, and Cyril Labbé. 2019. Semi-supervised neural text generation by joint learning of natural language generation and natural language understanding models. In *Proceedings of the 12th International Conference on Natural Language Generation*, pages 552–562, Tokyo, Japan. Association for Computational Linguistics.

Alec Radford, Jeffrey Wu, Rewon Child, David Luan, Dario Amodei, and Ilya Sutskever. 2019. Language models are unsupervised multitask learners. *OpenAI blog*, 1(8):9.

Colin Raffel, Noam Shazeer, Adam Roberts, Katherine Lee, Sharan Narang, Michael Matena, Yanqi Zhou, Wei Li, and Peter J. Liu. 2020. Exploring the limits of transfer learning with a unified text-to-text transformer. *Journal of Machine Learning Research*, 21(140):1–67.

Rajakrishnan Rajkumar, Marten van Schijndel, Michael White, and William Schuler. 2016. Investigating locality effects and surprisal in written english syntactic choice phenomena. *Cognition*, 155:204–232.

Jinfeng Rao, Kartikeya Upasani, Anusha Balakrishnan, Michael White, Anuj Kumar, and Rajen Subba. 2019. A tree-to-sequence model for neural nlg in task-oriented dialog. In *Proceedings of the 12th International Conference on Natural Language Generation*, pages 95–100.

Abhinav Rastogi, Xiaoxue Zang, Srinivas Sunkara, Raghav Gupta, and Pranav Khaitan. 2019. Towards scalable multi-domain conversational agents: The schema-guided dialogue dataset. *arXiv preprint arXiv:1909.05855*.

David Reitter, Frank Keller, and Johanna D. Moore. 2006. Computational modelling of structural priming in dialogue. In *Proceedings of the Human Language Technology Conference of the NAACL, Companion Volume: Short Papers*, pages 121–124, New York City, USA. Association for Computational Linguistics.

Svetlana Stoyanchev and Amanda Stent. 2009. Lexical and syntactic adaptation and their impact in deployed spoken dialog systems. In *Proceedings of Human Language Technologies: The 2009 Annual Conference of the North American Chapter of the Association for Computational Linguistics, Companion Volume: Short Papers*, pages 189–192, Boulder, Colorado. Association for Computational Linguistics.

D. Temperley. 2007. Minimization of dependency length in written english. *Cognition*, 105:300–333.

Tsung-Hsien Wen, Milica Gasic, Nikola Mrkšić, Pei-Hao Su, David Vandyke, and Steve Young. 2015. Semantically conditioned LSTM-based natural language generation for spoken dialogue systems. In *Proceedings of the 2015 Conference on Empirical Methods in Natural Language Processing*, pages 1711–1721. Association for Computational Linguistics.

Zixiaofan Yang, Arash Einolghozati, Hakan Inan, Keith Diedrick, Angela Fan, Pinar Donmez, and Sonal Gupta. 2020. Improving text-to-text pre-trained models for the graph-to-text task. In *Proceedings of the 3rd International Workshop on Natural Language Generation from the Semantic Web (WebNLG+)*, pages 107–116, Dublin, Ireland (Virtual). Association for Computational Linguistics.

A Appendix

A.1 Model Hyperparameters

Model hyperparameters appear in Tables 13–15. In addition, the best performing model on the validation set had the unacceptability confidence thresholds for filtering listed in Table 16. The bounds used to calculate the thresholds were [0.1–0.9] with 0.1 step size.

A.2 Computing Infrastructure

For training each generation BART-Large model, 8 GPUs were used, which took about 3.5 hours for larger datasets like SGD.

For training the accuracy classifier RoBERTa-base model, 8 GPUs were also used, taking up to 2 days on larger datasets like SGD including data preparation and model training time.

All experiments were conducted on 32GB Quadro GV100 GPUs. The GPUs are part of a shared distributed cluster, which adds its own time overheads.

Tokenizer	BPE
Tokenizer Max Length	256
Dropout	0.3
Encoder/Decoder Embedding Dim	1024
Optimizer	Adam
LR	0.000005
Weight Decay	0.00001
# Model Params	514484225

Table 13: BART-Large Generation/Reconstruction Hyperparameters

Tokenizer	BPE
Tokenizer Max Length	1024
Encoder output dropout	0.1
Encoder embedding dim	768
# encoder layers	12
# encoder attention heads	12
Decoder dropout	0
Decoder activation	relu
Optimizer	Adam
LR	0.000001
Adam betas	0.9, 0.999
Weight Decay	0
# Model Params	124055810

Table 14: Acceptability Classifier RoBERTa-Base Hyperparameters

Beam Size	5
topk	3
Mask normal	0.5
Mask insert	0.3

Table 15: Acceptability Classifier Data Generation Hyperparameters

Dataset	Unacceptability Threshold
hline E2E	0.6
WebNLG-en	0.7
SGD	0.6

Table 16: Acceptability Classifier Thresholds

NUIG-DSI's submission to The GEM Benchmark 2021

Nivranshu Pasricha[1], **Mihael Arcan**[2] and **Paul Buitelaar**[1,2]
[1]SFI Centre for Research Training in Artificial Intelligence
[2] Insight SFI Research Centre for Data Analytics
Data Science Institute, National University of Ireland Galway
n.pasricha1@nuigalway.ie

Abstract

This paper describes the submission by NUIG-DSI to the GEM benchmark 2021. We participate in the modeling shared task where we submit outputs on four datasets for data-to-text generation, namely, DART, WebNLG (en), E2E and CommonGen. We follow an approach similar to the one described in the GEM benchmark paper where we use the pre-trained T5-base model for our submission. We train this model on additional monolingual data where we experiment with different masking strategies specifically focused on masking entities, predicates and concepts as well as a random masking strategy for pre-training. In our results we find that random masking performs the best in terms of automatic evaluation metrics, though the results are not statistically significantly different compared to other masking strategies.

1 Introduction

The GEM Benchmark (Gehrmann et al., 2021) is a living benchmark focusing on generation, evaluation and metrics for a variety of natural language generation tasks including summarization, simplification, dialog and data-to-text generation. In general, the field of natural language generation (NLG) is concerned with automatic generation of human understandable texts, typically from a non-linguistic or textual representation of information as input (Reiter and Dale, 2000). Traditionally, most applications for NLG have relied on rule-based systems designed using a modular pipeline approach (Gatt and Krahmer, 2018). However, recently approaches based on neutral networks with an encoder-decoder architecture trained in an end-to-end fashion have gained popularity. These typically follow the paradigm of pre-training on a large corpus followed by fine-tuning on a task specific dataset and have been shown to achieve state-of-the-art results on many natural language tasks (Raffel et al., 2020; Lewis et al., 2020). When evaluated by human annotators, neural models for data-to-text generation have been found to produce fluent text though such models might struggle in terms of data coverage, relevance and correctness where rule-based systems score high (Castro Ferreira et al., 2020).

In our participation in the GEM benchmark, we submit outputs for four datasets including DART (Nan et al., 2021), WebNLG (Gardent et al., 2017; Castro Ferreira et al., 2020), E2E (Novikova et al., 2017; Dušek et al., 2019) and CommonGen (Lin et al., 2020). We use the pre-trained T5-base model architecture (Raffel et al., 2020) for our submission implemented using the transformers library from Hugging Face (Wolf et al., 2020). We first train on monolingual data before fine-tuning on the task-specific dataset. For DART and WebNLG, we use abstracts from DBpedia (Auer et al., 2007) for training while for the other two datasets, we use monolingual target-side references for pre-training with a masked language modeling objective. We experiment with different masking strategies where we mask entities and predicates (for DART), meaning representation fields (for E2E) and concepts (for CommonGen) and compare the results with commonly used approach of random masking. Our results suggest that random masking achieves the best scores for automatic evaluation metrics for DART, WebNLG and E2E while additional pre-training appears to hurt the performance for CommonGen.

2 Methodology

In this section we define our methodology on the four datasets where we make a submission and subsequently discuss the results based on automatic evaluation metrics defined in the GEM benchmark.

Proceedings of the 1st Workshop on Natural Language Generation, Evaluation, and Metrics (GEM 2021), pages 148–154
August 5–6, 2021.

Tripleset	Antioquia Department	country	Colombia
	Bandeja paisa	ingredient	Chorizo
	Bandeja paisa	region	Antioquia Department

linearisation	Antioquia Department country Colombia Bandeja paisa ingredient Chorizo Bandeja paisa region Antioquia Department
tags	<SUB> Antioquia Department <PRED> country <OBJ> Colombia <SUB> Bandeja paisa <PRED> ingredient <OBJ> Chorizo <SUB> Bandeja paisa <PRED> region <OBJ> Antioquia Department
entity types	<LOCATION> Antioquia Department <PRED> country <LOCATION> Colombia <FOOD> Bandeja paisa <PRED> ingredient <SAUSAGE> Chorizo <FOOD> Bandeja paisa <PRED> region <LOCATION> Antioquia Department
NER tags	<ORG> Antioquia Department <PRED> country <GPE> Colombia <PERSON> Bandeja paisa <PRED> ingredient <UNKNOWN> Chorizo <PERSON> Bandeja paisa <PRED> region <ORG> Antioquia Department

(a) Additional tags added to the linearised tripleset.

Lexicalisation	Chorizo is an ingredient in Bandeja paisa, a dish from the Antioquia Department region, in Colombia.
Random Masking	Chorizo is an ingredient in Bandeja paisa, a dish [MASK] Antioquia Department [MASK], in Colombia.
Entity Masking	[MASK] is an ingredient in [MASK], a dish from the [MASK] region, in [MASK].
Predicate Masking	Chorizo is an [MASK] in Bandeja paisa, a dish from the Antioquia Department [MASK], in Colombia.

(b) Masking strategies for pre-training on monolingual data.

Figure 1: Example of a tripleset from the DART dataset with additional information tags included after linearisation for fine-tuning (top) and different masking strategies applied to a sentence for pre-training (bottom).

2.1 DART

DART (Nan et al., 2021) consists of open domain data records structured in the form of triples paired with crowd-sourced textual annotations in English describing those triples. The data is collected from multiple different sources including tables from Wikipedia, questions from WikiSQL and merged with two existing data-to-text datasets, namely, WebNLG (en) (Gardent et al., 2017) and cleaned E2E (Dušek et al., 2019).

Since both DART and WebNLG are concerned with the task of triple-to-text generation and have the same input data structure, we follow the same approach as defined in Pasricha et al. (2020) for the WebNLG+ challenge. We use the pre-trained T5 model architecture and first train it on a corpus of abstracts from DBpedia with a masked language modeling objective. For masking, we adopt the commonly used approach of randomly masking 15% of the tokens in texts. We further compare this with an approach where we specifically mask only the entities or only the predicates or a combination of both as shown in Figure 1(b). The abstracts are downloaded from DBpedia for the entities which are present in the triples contained in the training set of the DART dataset. Since we did not find an abstract for each unique entity in the training set, we ended up with 9,218 abstracts consisting on 1,654,239 tokens and 83,583 types in total with an average of 179.45 tokens per abstract. After pre-training, we fine-tune on the DART training set to predict the target text conditioned on the linearised tripleset.

	BLEU	METEOR	ROUGE-L
baseline	46.10	37.24	59.61
masked pre-training			
random masking	47.16	37.51	59.99
entity masking	45.92	37.14	59.56
predicate masking	46.73	37.36	59.79
entity + predicate	46.37	37.23	59.51

Table 1: Results from automatic evaluation on the DART validation set with different masking strategies on DBpedia abstracts for pre-training using the T5-small model.

For fine-tuning we linearise the input tripleset into a sequence without modifying the order of the triples in the input. We incorporate additional information to mark the subject, predicate and object in each triple in the input by using <SUB>, <PRED> and <OBJ> tags respectively. Additionally, we also include tags for the type of an entity using DBpedia as shown in Figure 1(a). In the instances where we do not find the type of an entity on DBpedia, we check whether it refers to a time period or a date and assign it the type *<TIMEPERIOD>*. Otherwise, we assign the type *<MEASUREMENT>* to an entity containing a numeric value followed by some text. The type *<NUMERIC>* is assigned to entities which only consist of numeric values and *<UNKNOWN>* to everything else. Furthermore, as a comparison, we add tags for entities using the named entity recognition pipeline from the spaCy library[1]. All of these tags are included as additional special tokens to the model vocabulary.

For our experiments with masking during pre-training on DBpedia abstracts, we use the small variant of the T5 model architecture. This model has approximately 60 million parameters and is much faster to train compared to other larger variants. We use the pre-trained model implementation from Hugging Face's transformers library (Wolf et al., 2020) which consists of 6 layers each in the encoder and decoder with a multi-head attention sub-layer consisting of 8 attention heads. The word embeddings have a dimension of 512 and the fully-connected feed-forward sublayers are 2048-dimensional. Pre-training on DBpedia abstracts is done on a single Nvidia GeForce GTX 1080 Ti GPU for 10 epochs with a batch size of 8 using the Adam optimizer with a learning rate of 0.001. All the other hyperparameter values are set to their default values. Table 1 shows scores for the output generations on the validation set for BLEU (Papineni et al., 2002), METEOR (Banerjee and Lavie, 2005) and ROUGE-L (Lin, 2004). We find random masking to perform the best in terms of automatic evaluation metrics compared to specifically masking entities or predicates, though the results are not statistically significantly different.

Furthermore, in our experiments we compare the results when additional tags are added to the input either as entity types from DBpedia or NER tags from spaCy or just the *<SUB>*, *<PRED>* and *<OBJ>* tags. For this, we use the T5-base model with approximately 220 million parameters. This model consists of 12 layers each in the encoder and decoder with 12 attention heads in each multi-head attention sublayer. The word embeddings are 768-dimensional for this model and feed-forward sublayer is 3072-dimensional. This model is first pre-trained on DBpedia abstracts with a masked language modeling objective where 15% of the tokens are corrupted randomly. For fine-tuning,

	BLEU	METEOR	ROUGE-L
baseline	51.06	40.23	60.86
tags	51.71	40.68	61.10
DBpedia types	50.75	40.33	60.45
spaCy NER	51.05	40.42	61.30

Table 2: Results from automatic evaluation on the DART validation set with different tags for fine-tuning. The results are shown here using the T5-base model which is first pre-trained with the random masking on a corpus of DBpedia abstracts.

we train on the DART training set for 10 epochs on a single Nvidia GeForce GTX 1080 Ti GPU with a batch size of 16 and select the checkpoint with the highest BLEU score on the validation set. We set the maximum output sequence length to 50 words and apply beam search during inference with a beam of size equal to 5. Here we find that adding the three *<SUB>*, *<PRED>* and *<OBJ>* tags achieves the best results compared to tags from DBpedia or spaCy though the differences in the automatic evaluation results are again not statistically significant. For our final submission to the GEM benchmark, we submit the outputs from this model which is fine-tuned with the added *<SUB>*, *<PRED>* and *<OBJ>* tags.

2.2 WebNLG

WebNLG (Gardent et al., 2017) introduced the task of RDF-to-Text generation focused on generating a verbalisation in a human language in the output based on a set of RDF-triples in the input. The WebNLG corpus consists of data units made up of RDF-triples extracted from DBpedia (Auer et al., 2007) and paired with reference text lexicalisations. These texts were collected using crowd-sourcing and contain sequences of one or more short sentences in English, verbalising the data units in the input. The first version of the corpus contained triplesets from 15 DBpedia categories and is divided into two subsets, *seen* and *unseen* for evaluation. The ten *seen* categories are *Airport, Astronaut, Building, City, ComicsCharacter, Food, Monument, SportsTeam, University* and *WrittenWork* and the five *unseen* categories are *Artist, Athlete, CelestialBody, Company, MeanOfTransportation* and *Politician.* WebNLG+ (Castro Ferreira et al., 2020) was further introduced to include Russian as another output language and added the category *Company* to the training set as well as three categories *Film, MusicalWork* and *Scientist* to the test set.

[1]`https://spacy.io`

	BLEU	METEOR	ROUGE-L
baseline	33.73	36.52	53.72
masked pre-training			
MR masking	34.09	36.62	53.64
random masking	34.21	36.50	53.85

Table 3: Results from automatic evaluation on the E2E validation set with different masking strategies on monolingual data for pre-training using the T5-base model.

	BLEU	METEOR	ROUGE-L
baseline	28.94	31.03	55.78
masked pre-training			
concept masking	27.81	29.61	54.87
random masking	26.87	29.83	54.17

Table 4: Results from automatic evaluation on the CommonGen validation set with different masking strategies on monolingual data for pre-training using the T5-base model.

Since the entire WebNLG (en) corpus is already included the DART dataset without any modifications, we use the same model as defined in §2.1 without any further fine-tuning to generate outputs on the WebNLG (en) dataset. Our overall approach is same as Pasricha et al. (2020) for the WebNLG+ challenge 2020 except here we use additional 6,678 DBpedia abstracts for pre-training and the larger DART dataset for fine-tuning which results in a higher scores for automatic evaluation metrics.

2.3 E2E

E2E (Novikova et al., 2017) is concerned with generating texts for a dialogue system from meaning representations (MR) in the restaurant domain. It was introduced with the aim of motivating research in domain-specific end-to-end data-driven natural language generation systems. The input for E2E comprises of meaning representations with up to 8 different fields including *name*, *near*, *area*, *food*, *eatType*, *priceRange*, *rating* and *familyFriendly* while the output comprises of sentences typically made of up 20 – 30 words in English verbalising the input.

We follow the same approach as described in §2.1 and experiment with masking strategies for pre-training on monolingual data. Instead of using additional out-of-domain data, we use the target side references from the E2E dataset for pre-training with a masked language modeling objective. Here we compare the results on two masking strategies, one where we mask 15% of the token spans randomly and another where we mask specific values based on meaning representation fields such as restaurant names, area, price, etc. This approach is similar to the one described in §2.1 where we masked specifically masked entities and predicates. Table 3 shows scores for the output generations on the validation set for BLEU, METEOR and ROUGE-L. We again find that random masking appears to perform better though the differences in terms of automatic evaluation metrics are not significantly different.

For our submission to the GEM benchmark, we use the same model architecture and hyperparameter values as described previously for DART to generate the output submissions on the E2E test set and challenge sets. This model is first pre-trained on the monolingual target side with a masked language objective where the spans of text are masked randomly and the fine-tuned on the E2E training set containing pairs of meaning representations and target texts.

2.4 CommonGen

CommonGen (Lin et al., 2020) was introduced with the goal of testing state-of-the-art text generation systems for the ability of commonsense reasoning. The task for CommonGen is to generate a coherent sentence in English describing an everyday scenario using a set of concepts such as *man*, *woman*, *dog*, *throw* and *catch*. Lin et al. (2020) have shown that large pre-trained language models are prone to hallucinations and can generate incoherent sentences such as *"hands washing soap on the sink"* for the concept set {*hand*, *sink*, *wash*, *soap*}. Two key challenges identified by the creators of this dataset are *relational reasoning* with underlying commonsense knowledge for given concepts and *compositional generalization* for unseen combinations of concepts.

We again start with the T5-base model and experiment with masked pre-training on the monolingual target side of CommonGen. As described in §2.3 we compare two strategies of masking where we mask spans of text randomly or specifically mask tokens which correspond to concepts in the training set. Table 4 shows scores for the output generations on the validation set for BLEU, METEOR and ROUGE-L. For fine-tuning we shuffle the concepts

Dataset	subset	Metrics (Lexical Similarity and Semantic Equivalence)						
		METEOR	ROUGE-1	ROUGE-2	ROUGE-L	BLEU	BERTScore	BLEURT
CommonGen	val	0.310	64.37	33.08	55.78	28.77	0.893	-0.380
	sample	0.304	63.72	32.52	54.82	28.24	0.890	-0.391
DART	val	0.396	72.44	48.75	58.77	49.42	0.916	0.192
E2E clean	val	0.366	72.12	45.70	53.87	34.21	0.909	0.228
	test	0.354	73.23	45.71	53.45	31.74	0.913	0.205
	sample	0.365	71.72	45.39	53.81	34.20	0.910	0.221
	scramble	0.349	72.06	44.32	51.69	30.52	0.910	0.176
WebNLG (en)	val	0.391	76.08	53.59	62.51	52.10	0.931	0.282
	test	0.341	71.41	46.66	57.13	41.43	0.910	0.138
	sample	0.389	75.48	53.00	62.38	51.35	0.929	0.260
	scramble	0.343	71.54	47.02	57.07	41.74	0.909	0.140
	numbers	0.338	70.36	45.98	56.78	41.33	0.909	0.101

Dataset	subset	Metrics (Diversity and System Characterization)								
		MSTTR	Distinct_1	Distinct_2	H_1	H_2	Unique_1	Unique_2	$\lvert\mathcal{V}\rvert$	Output Len.
CommonGen	val	0.54	0.11	0.37	6.9	10.3	532	2.4k	1.2k	10.9
	sample	0.55	0.16	0.46	6.8	10.0	455	1.6k	862	11.0
DART	val	0.42	0.05	0.15	7.4	9.9	1.3k	5.0k	3.1k	22.7
E2E clean	val	0.26	0.001	0.004	5.6	7.0	11	68	144	23.4
	test	0.27	0.001	0.005	5.7	7.1	5	33	136	22.4
	sample	0.44	0.01	0.027	5.6	7.0	6	43	117	23.7
	scramble	0.47	0.01	0.034	5.7	7.1	7	56	117	22.4
WebNLG (en)	val	0.54	0.10	0.30	8.5	11.9	1.1k	4.8k	3.2k	19.2
	test	0.65	0.04	0.16	8.0	10.9	368	2.1k	1.5k	19.5
	sample	0.57	0.20	0.50	8.3	11.3	942	3.0k	1.9k	19.2
	scramble	0.50	0.11	0.32	7.9	10.6	362	1.5k	2.9k	19.8
	numbers	0.65	0.12	0.32	7.9	10.6	426	1.6k	1.1k	19.6

Table 5: Results from automatic evaluation metrics measuring lexical similarity, semantic equivalence, diversity and system characteristics on the validation set, test set and the three challenge sets – sample, scramble and numbers for DART, WebNLG (en), E2E and CommonGen.

in the input before concatenating them into a single sequence. We find in our results that additional pre-training on monolingual data on the target appears to hurt the performance when measured with automatic evaluation metrics. This is true in both the cases when masking is done randomly or when only specific concepts are masked.

3 Results

Table 5 shows results on the validation set, test set and the challenge sets evaluated using GEM metrics[2]. At the time of writing we do not have access to all the references in the test set as well as the challenge sets for DART and CommonGen, hence scores on some subsets are not shown.

The evaluation metrics are divided into different categories measuring lexical similarity, semantic equivalence, diversity and system characteristics. Popular metrics such as BLEU (Papineni et al., 2002), METEOR (Banerjee and Lavie, 2005) and ROUGE-1/2/L (Lin, 2004) are used for lexical similarity, while recently proposed metrics such as BERTScore (Zhang et al., 2020) and BLEURT (Sellam et al., 2020) which rely on sentence embeddings from pre-trained contextualised embedding models such as BERT (Devlin et al., 2019) and RoBERTa (Liu et al., 2019) are used for evaluating semantic equivalence. To account for the diverse outputs, Shannon Entropy (Shannon et al., 1950) is calculated over unigrams and bigrams (H_1, H_2) along with the mean segmented type token ratio over segment lengths of 100 (MSTTR) (Johnson, 1944). Furthermore, the ratio of distinct n-grams over the total number of n-grams ($\text{Distinct}_{1,2}$), and the count of n-grams that appear once across the entire test output ($\text{Unique}_{1,2}$) is calculated (Li et al., 2018). The size of the output vocabulary ($|\mathcal{V}|$) and the mean length of the generated output texts are reported as system characteristics (Sun et al., 2019).

Compared to the baselines described in the GEM benchmark (Gehrmann et al., 2021), we observe higher scores in our submissions for automatic metrics on the CommonGen and DART datasets while scoring lower on the cleaned E2E and WebNLG (en) datasets especially on the test and challenge subsets for both E2E and WebNLG.

[2] https://github.com/GEM-benchmark/GEM-metrics

4 Conclusion

We presented a description of the system submitted by NUIG-DSI to the GEM benchmark 2021. We participated in the modeling shared task and submitted outputs on four datasets for data-to-text generation including DART, WebNLG (en), E2E and CommonGen using the T5-base model. We first trained this model with monolingual data from DBpedia abstracts and target side references before fine-tuning on respective training datasets. Additionally we experimented with various masking strategies focusing specifically on masking entities, predicates and concepts as well as a random masking strategy for training. We found random masking to perform the best and submit our final outputs using this approach.

Acknowledgments

This work was conducted with the financial support of the Science Foundation Ireland Centre for Research Training in Artificial Intelligence under Grant No. 18/CRT/6223 and co-supported by Science Foundation Ireland under grant number SFI/12/RC/2289 2 (Insight), co-funded by the European Regional Development Fund.

References

Sören Auer, Christian Bizer, Georgi Kobilarov, Jens Lehmann, Richard Cyganiak, and Zachary Ives. 2007. Dbpedia: A nucleus for a web of open data. In *The semantic web*, pages 722–735. Springer.

Satanjeev Banerjee and Alon Lavie. 2005. METEOR: An automatic metric for MT evaluation with improved correlation with human judgments. In *Proceedings of the ACL Workshop on Intrinsic and Extrinsic Evaluation Measures for Machine Translation and/or Summarization*, pages 65–72, Ann Arbor, Michigan. Association for Computational Linguistics.

Thiago Castro Ferreira, Claire Gardent, Nikolai Ilinykh, Chris van der Lee, Simon Mille, Diego Moussallem, and Anastasia Shimorina. 2020. The 2020 bilingual, bi-directional WebNLG+ shared task: Overview and evaluation results (WebNLG+ 2020). In *Proceedings of the 3rd International Workshop on Natural Language Generation from the Semantic Web (WebNLG+)*, pages 55–76, Dublin, Ireland (Virtual). Association for Computational Linguistics.

Jacob Devlin, Ming-Wei Chang, Kenton Lee, and Kristina Toutanova. 2019. BERT: Pre-training of deep bidirectional transformers for language understanding. In *Proceedings of the 2019 Conference of the North American Chapter of the Association for Computational Linguistics: Human Language Technologies, Volume 1 (Long and Short Papers)*, pages 4171–4186, Minneapolis, Minnesota. Association for Computational Linguistics.

Ondřej Dušek, David M. Howcroft, and Verena Rieser. 2019. Semantic noise matters for neural natural language generation. In *Proceedings of the 12th International Conference on Natural Language Generation*, pages 421–426, Tokyo, Japan. Association for Computational Linguistics.

Claire Gardent, Anastasia Shimorina, Shashi Narayan, and Laura Perez-Beltrachini. 2017. The WebNLG challenge: Generating text from RDF data. In *Proceedings of the 10th International Conference on Natural Language Generation*, pages 124–133, Santiago de Compostela, Spain. Association for Computational Linguistics.

Albert Gatt and Emiel Krahmer. 2018. Survey of the State of the Art in Natural Language Generation: Core tasks, applications and evaluation. *Journal of Artificial Intelligence Research*, 61:65–170.

Sebastian Gehrmann, Tosin Adewumi, Karmanya Aggarwal, Pawan Sasanka Ammanamanchi, Aremu Anuoluwapo, Antoine Bosselut, Khyathi Raghavi Chandu, Miruna Clinciu, Dipanjan Das, Kaustubh D Dhole, et al. 2021. The gem benchmark: Natural language generation, its evaluation and metrics. *arXiv preprint arXiv:2102.01672*.

Wendell Johnson. 1944. Studies in language behavior: A program of research. *Psychological Monographs*, 56(2):1–15.

Mike Lewis, Yinhan Liu, Naman Goyal, Marjan Ghazvininejad, Abdelrahman Mohamed, Omer Levy, Veselin Stoyanov, and Luke Zettlemoyer. 2020. Bart: Denoising sequence-to-sequence pre-training for natural language generation, translation, and comprehension. In *Proceedings of the 58th Annual Meeting of the Association for Computational Linguistics*, pages 7871–7880.

Yikang Li, Nan Duan, Bolei Zhou, Xiao Chu, Wanli Ouyang, Xiaogang Wang, and Ming Zhou. 2018. Visual question generation as dual task of visual question answering. In *2018 IEEE/CVF Conference on Computer Vision and Pattern Recognition*, pages 6116–6124.

Bill Yuchen Lin, Wangchunshu Zhou, Ming Shen, Pei Zhou, Chandra Bhagavatula, Yejin Choi, and Xiang Ren. 2020. CommonGen: A constrained text generation challenge for generative commonsense reasoning. In *Findings of the Association for Computational Linguistics: EMNLP 2020*, pages 1823–1840, Online. Association for Computational Linguistics.

Chin-Yew Lin. 2004. ROUGE: A package for automatic evaluation of summaries. In *Text Summarization Branches Out*, pages 74–81, Barcelona, Spain. Association for Computational Linguistics.

Yinhan Liu, Myle Ott, Naman Goyal, Jingfei Du, Mandar Joshi, Danqi Chen, Omer Levy, Mike Lewis, Luke Zettlemoyer, and Veselin Stoyanov. 2019. Roberta: A robustly optimized bert pretraining approach. *arXiv preprint arXiv:1907.11692*.

Linyong Nan, Dragomir Radev, Rui Zhang, Amrit Rau, Abhinand Sivaprasad, Chiachun Hsieh, Xiangru Tang, Aadit Vyas, Neha Verma, Pranav Krishna, Yangxiaokang Liu, Nadia Irwanto, Jessica Pan, Faiaz Rahman, Ahmad Zaidi, Murori Mutuma, Yasin Tarabar, Ankit Gupta, Tao Yu, Yi Chern Tan, Xi Victoria Lin, Caiming Xiong, Richard Socher, and Nazneen Fatema Rajani. 2021. Dart: Open-domain structured data record to text generation. *arXiv preprint arXiv:2007.02871*.

Jekaterina Novikova, Ondřej Dušek, and Verena Rieser. 2017. The E2E dataset: New challenges for end-to-end generation. In *Proceedings of the 18th Annual SIGdial Meeting on Discourse and Dialogue*, pages 201–206, Saarbrücken, Germany. Association for Computational Linguistics.

Kishore Papineni, Salim Roukos, Todd Ward, and Wei-Jing Zhu. 2002. Bleu: A method for automatic evaluation of machine translation. In *Proceedings of the 40th Annual Meeting on Association for Computational Linguistics*, ACL '02, page 311–318, USA. Association for Computational Linguistics.

Nivranshu Pasricha, Mihael Arcan, and Paul Buitelaar. 2020. NUIG-DSI at the WebNLG+ challenge: Leveraging transfer learning for RDF-to-text generation. In *Proceedings of the 3rd International Workshop on Natural Language Generation from the Semantic Web (WebNLG+)*, pages 137–143, Dublin, Ireland (Virtual). Association for Computational Linguistics.

Colin Raffel, Noam Shazeer, Adam Roberts, Katherine Lee, Sharan Narang, Michael Matena, Yanqi Zhou, Wei Li, and Peter J. Liu. 2020. Exploring the limits of transfer learning with a unified text-to-text transformer. *Journal of Machine Learning Research*, 21(140):1–67.

Ehud Reiter and Robert Dale. 2000. *Building Natural Language Generation Systems*, 1 edition. Cambridge University Press.

Thibault Sellam, Dipanjan Das, and Ankur Parikh. 2020. BLEURT: Learning robust metrics for text generation. In *Proceedings of the 58th Annual Meeting of the Association for Computational Linguistics*, pages 7881–7892, Online. Association for Computational Linguistics.

Claude E Shannon, Warren Weaver, and Norbert Wiener. 1950. The mathematical theory of communication. *Physics Today*, 3(9):31.

Simeng Sun, Ori Shapira, Ido Dagan, and Ani Nenkova. 2019. How to compare summarizers without target length? pitfalls, solutions and re-examination of the neural summarization literature. In *Proceedings of the Workshop on Methods for Optimizing and Evaluating Neural Language Generation*, pages 21–29, Minneapolis, Minnesota. Association for Computational Linguistics.

Thomas Wolf, Lysandre Debut, Victor Sanh, Julien Chaumond, Clement Delangue, Anthony Moi, Pierric Cistac, Tim Rault, Remi Louf, Morgan Funtowicz, Joe Davison, Sam Shleifer, Patrick von Platen, Clara Ma, Yacine Jernite, Julien Plu, Canwen Xu, Teven Le Scao, Sylvain Gugger, Mariama Drame, Quentin Lhoest, and Alexander Rush. 2020. Transformers: State-of-the-art natural language processing. In *Proceedings of the 2020 Conference on Empirical Methods in Natural Language Processing: System Demonstrations*, pages 38–45, Online. Association for Computational Linguistics.

Tianyi Zhang, Varsha Kishore, Felix Wu, Kilian Q. Weinberger, and Yoav Artzi. 2020. Bertscore: Evaluating text generation with bert. In *International Conference on Learning Representations*, Addis Ababa, Ethiopia.

SimpleNER Sentence Simplification System for GEM 2021

K V Aditya Srivatsa **Monil Gokani** **Manish Shrivastava**
Language Technologies Research Center (LTRC)
Kohli Center on Intelligent Systems
International Institute of Information Technology, Hyderabad
{k.v.aditya, monil.gokani}@research.iiit.ac.in
m.shrivastava@iiit.ac.in

Abstract

This paper describes SimpleNER, a model developed for the sentence simplification task at GEM-2021. Our system is a monolingual Seq2Seq Transformer architecture that uses control tokens pre-pended to the data, allowing the model to shape the generated simplifications according to user desired attributes. Additionally, we show that NER-tagging the training data before use helps stabilize the effect of the control tokens and significantly improves the overall performance of the system. We also employ pretrained embeddings to reduce data sparsity and allow the model to produce more generalizable outputs.

1 Introduction

Sentence simplification aims at reducing the linguistic complexity of a given text, while preserving all the relevant details of the initial text. This is particularly useful for people with cognitive disabilities (Evans et al., 2014), as well as for second language learners and people with low-literacy levels (Watanabe et al., 2009). Text and Sentence simplification also play an important role within NLP. Simplification has been utilized as a preprocessing step in larger NLP pipelines, which can greatly aid learning by reducing vocabulary and regularizing of syntax.

In our model, we use control tokens to tune a Seq2Seq Transformer model (Vaswani et al., 2017) for sentence simplification. We take character length compression, extent of paraphrase, and lexical & syntactic complexity as attributes to gauge the transformations between complex and simple sentence pairs. We then represent each of these attributes as numerical measures, which are then added to our data. We show that this provides a considerable improvement over as-is Transformer approaches.

The use of control tokens in Seq2Seq models for sentence simplification has been explored before (Martin et al., 2020). But this approach has shown to add data sparsity to the system. This is because the model is required to learn the distribution of the various control tokens and the expected outputs across the ranges of each control token. To mitigate this sparsity, we process our data to replace named entities with respective tags using an NER tagger. We show that this reduces the model vocabulary and allows for greater generalization. To further curb the data sparsity, we make use of pre-trained embeddings as initial input embeddings for model training. Our code is publicly available here. [1]

2 Background

2.1 Sentence Simplification

Past approaches towards sentence simplification have dealt with it as a monolingual machine translation(MT) task (specifically Seq2Seq MT (Sutskever et al., 2014)). This meant training MT architectures over complex-simple sentence pairs, either aligned manually (Alva-Manchego et al., 2020; Xu et al., 2016) or automatically (Zhu et al., 2010; Wubben et al., 2012) using large complex-simple repository pairs such as the English Wikipedia and the Simple English Wikipedia.

Some implementations also utilize reinforcement learning (Zhang and Lapata, 2017) over the MT task, with automated metrics such as SARI (Xu et al., 2016), information preservation, and grammatical fluency constituting the training reward.

2.2 Controllable Text Generation

A recent approach towards sentence simplification involves using control tokens during machine translation (Martin et al., 2020). For simplification, it

[1] https://github.com/kvadityasrivatsa/gem_2021_simplification_task

Proceedings of the 1st Workshop on Natural Language Generation, Evaluation, and Metrics (GEM 2021), pages 155–160
August 5–6, 2021.

Control Attribute	Control Measure	Control Token
Amount of compression	Compression ratio	<NbChars_x.xx>
Paraphrasing	Levenshtein similarity	<LevSim_x.xx>
Lexical complexity	Avg. third-quartile of log-ranks	<WordRank_x.xx>
Syntactic complexity	Max dependency tree depth	<DepTreeDepth_x.xx>

Table 1: Control Tokens used for Modelling

encodes and enforces changes in certain attributes of the text. Similar approaches for controlling generated text have been explored in other domains: Filippova (2020) uses control tokens to estimate and control the amount of hallucination in generated text, Fan et al. (2018) explored pre-pending control tokens to the input text for summarization, providing control over the length of the output, and customizing text generation for different sources.

Our model makes use of control tokens similar to Martin et al. (2020) to tailor the generated simplifications according to the extent of changes in the following attributes: character length, extent of paraphrasing, and lexical & syntactic complexity. These attributes are represented by their respective numerical measures (see 3.1), and then pre-pended to the complex sentences using in specific formats (Table 1). Alongside this, we use NER tagging and pre-trained input embeddings as a method to curb data sparsity and unwanted named entity (NE) replacements.

3 System Overview

3.1 Control Attributes

Following Martin et al. (2020), we encode the following attributes during training and attempt to control them during inference time. Eg:

Complex: *"<NbChars_0.80> <LevSim_0.76> <WordRank_0.79> it is particularly famous for the cultivation of kiwifruit ."*

Simple: *"It is mostly famous for the growing of kiwifruit ."*

3.1.1 Amount of compression

Compression in sequence length has been shown to be correlated with the simplicity and readability of text (Martin et al., 2019). Since compression as an operation directly involves deletion, controlling its extent plays a crucial role in the extent of information preservation. We make use of the **compression ratio** (control token: '**NbChars**') between the character lengths of the simple and complex sentences to encode for this attribute.

3.1.2 Paraphrasing

The extent of paraphrasing between the complex and simple sentences ranges from a near replica of the source sentence to a very dissimilar and possibly simplified one. The measure used for this attribute is **Levenshtein similarity** (Levenshtein, 1966) (control token: '**LevSim**') between the complex and simple sentences.

3.1.3 Lexical Complexity

For a young reader or a second language learner, complex words can decrease the overall readability of the text substantially. The average **word rank** (control token: '**WordRank**') of a sequence has been shown to correlate with the lexical complexity of the sentence (Paetzold and Specia, 2016). Therefore, similar to Martin et al. (2020), we use the average of the third-quartile of log-ranks of the words in a sentence (except for stop-words and special tokens), to encode for its lexical complexity.

3.1.4 Syntactic Complexity

Complex syntactic structures and multiple nested clauses can decrease the readability of text, especially for people with reading disabilities. To partially account for this, we make use of the maximum **syntactic tree depth** (control token: '**DepTreeDepth**') of the sentence as a measure of its syntactic complexity. We use SpaCy's English dependency parser (Honnibal et al., 2020) to extract the depth. The deeper the syntax tree of a sentence, the more likely it is that it involves highly nested clausal structures.

3.2 NER Replacement

Using control tokens contribute to the overall performance of the model, but it also gives rise to an added data sparsity. It divides the sentences of the train set into different ranges of the control tokens. This results in some control values having little to no examples, which adds the task of learning and generalizing over the control token values for the model. Additionally, the model can learn to ad-

Raw (Complex)	*"Sergio PÃ rez Mendoza (born January 26 , 1990 in Guadalajara , Jalisco) , also known as "Checo" PÃ rez , is a Mexican racing driver ."*
NER Replaced	*"person@1 (born date@1 in gpe@1) , also known as " person@2 " , is a norp@1 racing driver ."*

Table 2: NER Tagging input sentence

here to the control requirement, while still failing to correctly simplify the sentence. Eg:

Source: *<NbChars_0.95> <LevSim_0.75> <WordRank_0.75> oxygen is a chemical element with symbol o and atomic number 8 .*

Prediction: *It has the chemical symbol o . It has the atomic number 8 .*

Here, the proper noun *"Oxygen"* is replaced by the pronoun *"it"*. Although the model follows the requirement of bringing down the word rank of the sentence and remains grammatically sound, it doesn't help with the simplification.

To address the issue of data sparsity as well that of unwanted NE-replacement, we propose NER mapping the data before training, and replacing the NE-tokens back after generation. We make use of the Ontonotes NER tagger (Yu et al., 2020) in the Flair toolkit (Akbik et al., 2019). We identify named entities in the complex halves of all three of the data splits and replace them with one of 18 tags (from the NER tagger) with a unique index (Table 2). NER replacement for simplification was previously explored by Zhang and Lapata (2017), but consisted of fewer classes. The large number of tags allow for a fine division between different named-entity types, which helps the model to encode the contexts of each of the types better while still reducing the NE-vocabulary size substantially.

The tagged data is then used for training and subsequent generation on the test set. Then any tags in the simplified output are located in the saved NER-mapping and reverted back to the original token or phrase. This step not only prevents proper nouns from getting replaced, but also greatly reduces the model vocabulary (allowing for greater generalizability).

3.3 Pre-Trained Embeddings

The vocabulary of a model trained on a corpus like WikiLarge is quite small, which prevents the model from predicting better fitting tokens. To address this, we use FastText's pre-trained embeddings (Bojanowski et al., 2016) (dimensionality: 300) as input embeddings for our model. The embeddings significantly boost the vocabulary size of usable content words for the model.

4 Experimental Setup

4.1 Architecture

Our architecture is a Transformer Model (Vaswani et al., 2017), and we make use of the Transformer Seq2Seq implementation from FairSeq (Ott et al., 2019). To understand the impact of each of the proposed methods, we train a total of four models:

- **T**: Vanilla Transformer (Vaswani et al., 2017), with control tokens, used as a baseline model.
- **T+Pre**: Transformer trained with FastText's pretrained embeddings.
- **T+NER**: Transformer trained on NER mapped data.
- **SimpleNER (T+Pre+NER)**: Transformer trained on NER mapped data with FastText's pretrained embeddings.

For ease of comparison, all four models were trained with an input embedding dimensionality of 300, fully connected layers with a dimensionality of 2048, 6 layers and 6 attention heads on both, the encoder and the decoder. During training , we are using Adam optimizer (Kingma and Ba, 2015) ($\beta_1 = 0.9$, $\beta_2 = 0.999$, $\epsilon = 10^{-8}$), with a learning rate of 0.00011 and 4000 warm-up updates, while dropout is set at 0.2.

4.2 Datasets

For training, we make use of the WikiLarge dataset (Zhang and Lapata, 2017), with 296,402 automatically aligned complex-simple sentence pairs obtained from the English Wikipedia and Simple English Wikipedia.

For validation and testing, we use the evaluation sets of the two tracks we participated in, namely: ASSET (Alva-Manchego et al., 2020) and TurkCorpus (Xu et al., 2016). Both have the same source sentences in their test (359 sentence pairs) and validation sets (2000 sentence pairs). ASSET provides

Model	test_asset		val_asset		test_turk		val_turk	
	BLEU	SARI	BLEU	SARI	BLEU	SARI	BLEU	SARI
T (Baseline)	68.815	36.707	72.561	35.992	71.167	37.801	74.339	37.604
T + Pre	62.488	38.845	71.536	37.700	63.861	38.139	73.627	38.196
T + NER	59.215	39.380	70.433	37.985	58.985	38.996	72.181	**38.375**
SimpleNER	59.324	**39.551**	70.202	**38.897**	59.586	**39.777**	68.622	38.231

Table 3: Scores obtained by the trained models on different test and validation sets (best scores are bolded)

1.	**Source**	*"orton and his wife were happy to have alanna marie orton on july 12 , 2008."*
	Baseline (T)	*"orton and his wife , dorothy marie orton on july 12 , 2007 ."*
	SimpleNER	*"orton and his wife supported alanna marie orton on july 12 , 2008."*
2.	**Source**	*"aracaju is the capital of the state."*
	Baseline (T)	*"it is the capital city of the country ."*
	SimpleNER	*"aracaju is the capital city of the country ."*
3.	**Source**	*"yoghurt or yogurt is a milk-based food made by bacterial fermentation of milk."*
	SimpleNER	*"yogurt is a type of food that is made by bacterial fermentation of product@1."*
4.	**Source**	*"entrance to tsinghua is very very difficult."*
	SimpleNER	*"the entrance to tsinghua is very very simple ."*

Table 4: Sample outputs of the baseline(T) and SimpleNER models on the TurkCorpus-testset

10 human-annotated simplifications for each of the 2359 source sentences, whereas TurCorpus provides 8.

Apart from lower-casing all three splits of the data, the data pairs of the trainset with token length lower than 3 were removed, and sentence pairs with compression ratio ($len(target)/len(source)$) beyond the bounds [0.2, 1.5] were omitted.

4.3 Evaluation Metrics

Our model is evaluated on both BLEU (Papineni et al., 2002) and SARI (Xu et al., 2016). But as Martin et al. (2020) points out, BLEU favours directly replicating the source sentence because of a high N-Gram similarity between the source and target sentences in most sentence simplification datasets. Therefore we only use SARI to rate and compare the models. We also make use of SARI to choose the best performing checkpoints on the validation sets of each of the tracks for evaluation on their respective test sets.

4.4 Training

All models were trained on 4 Nvidia GeForce GTX 1080 Ti GPUs with 64 GB of vRAM. Training was carried out for 20 epochs, and took roughly 11 hours for each model. For all four models, we set the control tokens to NbChars: `0.95`, LevSim: `0.75`, and WordRank: `0.75`. We have omitted DepTreeDepth as Martin et al. (2020) shows that using all four tokens brings down the overall performance.

5 Results

We report the BLEU and SARI scores on the test and validation splits of the ASSET & TurkCorpus datasets for each of the four models (Table 3). All three variants outperform the baseline model (T) across evaluation sets. Using pretrained embeddings (T+Pre) and NER tagged data (T+NER) individually boosts the baseline SARI scores substantially, with the latter approach providing a larger increment in the performance. Using both methods together, further improves the overall SARI score (SimpleNER). Also note how the general BLEU score of the models reduce as the SARI score improves, indicating an increasingly dissimilar and simplified generation.

SimpleNER shows a better retention of named entities from the source sentence than the baseline model (Example 1, Table 4). The contrast is clearer between T+Pre and SimpleNER, as the standalone use of pretrained embeddings in T+Pre allows for unwanted switching between two named entities with similar vector representations (eg. *"2007"* & *"2008"*). Also, NER tagging prevents the unwanted shift from proper nouns to pronouns as observed in the baseline model (Example 2, Table 4).

We also noted that using NER tagging can hamper certain outputs: While decoding, if the model generates an NER-tag that either has a type or index mismatch with the original NE token, then the tag remains in the output even after NER-untagging (Example 3, Table 4). Also, using pretrained-embeddings can result in instances where a source gets replaced with another token having a similar vector representation. This was particularly observed when some tokens were replaced by their exact antonyms (Example 4, Table 4).

6 Social Impact

The following is a summary of the response submitted with our output and model card submission to the GEM 2021 modelling shared task.

6.1 Real World Use

Our model can be utilized to produce point-to-point simplifications for people with cognitive disabilities, to read and understand text. Additionally, it proves helpful for second language learners, especially in public service centres such as airports or health clinics. Although the use of NER-mapping improves our model performance, it can lead to certain pitfalls. Masking NERs before training assumes that named entities don't need to undergo simplification or elaboration. This may be true for most evaluation datasets like ASSET and TurkCorpus, however this isn't the case for many real world cases. High-ranked named entities are often part of domain specific texts, which may require further explanation to be clearly understood by the general public.

6.2 Measuring Impact

Elaboration and replacement of NEs are both crucial for simplification and also the pitfalls of our model. This shows that there is more linguistic information and knowledge of the named entities required to build the model to perfection or evaluate its results. Thus, the best suited method would be a manual evaluation and it could be as simple as a filling a likert scale on how well the simplification and elaboration were.

Since this method is inefficient with respect to time and resources, there is a need for automated evaluation methods to approximate human judgment. A rudimentary measure to work on could take into account the NE's word rank (WR) and its average similarity (AS) to the other words in its sentence. Here, a high WR and a low AS would imply that the sentence does not contextualize the NE even when it might require elaboration. The other case would be when the NE has a relatively low WR and a high AS implying that the sentence contextualizes the NE aptly.

7 Conclusion

In this paper, we report the performance of four Seq2Seq Transformer models on the sentence simplification task of GEM 2021 under two tracks: ASSET and TurkCorpus. We show that individually using pre-trained embeddings and NER-replaced data substantially boosts the performance of a Transformer model assisted by control tokens. The NER tagging prevents the model from replacing important NEs with low rank tokens Also, using pre-trained embeddings lets the model access a larger and fine-grained content-word vocabulary for simplification, despite training the model on relatively small data. When put together, the two approaches give rise to a much higher overall performance on the task.

8 Future Work

Some pitfalls to be addressed are: The mismatch between the NER tags generated at the simplified end and the original NE tokens could be due to the exact string matching for NEs, the use of static embeddings (FastText) may have caused the unwanted swaps between highly similar tokens. Using finedtuned contextual embeddings may help. Additionally, since simplification datasets like TurkCorpus and ASSET might utilize different summarization styles, adding a control token to encode and control the output style could be explored.

References

Alan Akbik, Tanja Bergmann, Duncan Blythe, Kashif Rasul, Stefan Schweter, and Roland Vollgraf. 2019. FLAIR: An easy-to-use framework for state-of-the-art NLP. In *Proceedings of the 2019 Conference of the North American Chapter of the Association for Computational Linguistics (Demonstrations)*, pages 54–59, Minneapolis, Minnesota. Association for Computational Linguistics.

Fernando Alva-Manchego, Louis Martin, Antoine Bordes, Carolina Scarton, Benoît Sagot, and Lucia Specia. 2020. ASSET: A dataset for tuning and evaluation of sentence simplification models with multiple rewriting transformations. In *Proceedings of the*

58th Annual Meeting of the Association for Computational Linguistics, pages 4668–4679, Online. Association for Computational Linguistics.

Piotr Bojanowski, Edouard Grave, Armand Joulin, and Tomas Mikolov. 2016. Enriching word vectors with subword information. *arXiv preprint arXiv:1607.04606*.

Richard Evans, Constantin Orasan, and Iustin Dornescu. 2014. An evaluation of syntactic simplification rules for people with autism.

Angela Fan, David Grangier, and Michael Auli. 2018. Controllable abstractive summarization. In *Proceedings of the 2nd Workshop on Neural Machine Translation and Generation*, pages 45–54, Melbourne, Australia. Association for Computational Linguistics.

Katja Filippova. 2020. Controlled hallucinations: Learning to generate faithfully from noisy data. In *Findings of the Association for Computational Linguistics: EMNLP 2020*, pages 864–870, Online. Association for Computational Linguistics.

Matthew Honnibal, Ines Montani, Sofie Van Landeghem, and Adriane Boyd. 2020. spaCy: Industrial-strength Natural Language Processing in Python.

Diederik P. Kingma and Jimmy Ba. 2015. Adam: A method for stochastic optimization. In *3rd International Conference on Learning Representations, ICLR 2015, San Diego, CA, USA, May 7-9, 2015, Conference Track Proceedings*.

Vladimir I Levenshtein. 1966. Binary codes capable of correcting deletions, insertions, and reversals. In *Soviet physics doklady*, volume 10, pages 707–710. Soviet Union.

Louis Martin, Éric de la Clergerie, Benoît Sagot, and Antoine Bordes. 2020. Controllable sentence simplification. In *Proceedings of the 12th Language Resources and Evaluation Conference*, pages 4689–4698, Marseille, France. European Language Resources Association.

Louis Martin, Samuel Humeau, Pierre-Emmanuel Mazaré, Antoine Bordes, Éric Villemonte de la Clergerie, and Benoît Sagot. 2019. Reference-less quality estimation of text simplification systems. *CoRR*, abs/1901.10746.

Myle Ott, Sergey Edunov, Alexei Baevski, Angela Fan, Sam Gross, Nathan Ng, David Grangier, and Michael Auli. 2019. fairseq: A fast, extensible toolkit for sequence modeling. In *Proceedings of NAACL-HLT 2019: Demonstrations*.

Gustavo Paetzold and Lucia Specia. 2016. Semeval 2016 task 11: Complex word identification. In *Proceedings of the 10th International Workshop on Semantic Evaluation (SemEval-2016)*, pages 560–569.

Kishore Papineni, Salim Roukos, Todd Ward, and Wei-Jing Zhu. 2002. Bleu: a method for automatic evaluation of machine translation. In *Proceedings of the 40th Annual Meeting of the Association for Computational Linguistics*, pages 311–318, Philadelphia, Pennsylvania, USA. Association for Computational Linguistics.

Ilya Sutskever, Oriol Vinyals, and Quoc V. Le. 2014. Sequence to sequence learning with neural networks.

Ashish Vaswani, Noam Shazeer, Niki Parmar, Jakob Uszkoreit, Llion Jones, Aidan N. Gomez, Lukasz Kaiser, and Illia Polosukhin. 2017. Attention is all you need. *CoRR*, abs/1706.03762.

Willian Massami Watanabe, Arnaldo Candido Junior, Vinícius Rodriguez Uzêda, Renata Pontin de Mattos Fortes, Thiago Alexandre Salgueiro Pardo, and Sandra Maria Aluísio. 2009. Facilita: Reading assistance for low-literacy readers. In *Proceedings of the 27th ACM International Conference on Design of Communication*, SIGDOC '09, page 29–36, New York, NY, USA. Association for Computing Machinery.

Sander Wubben, Antal van den Bosch, and Emiel Krahmer. 2012. Sentence simplification by monolingual machine translation. In *Proceedings of the 50th Annual Meeting of the Association for Computational Linguistics (Volume 1: Long Papers)*, pages 1015–1024, Jeju Island, Korea. Association for Computational Linguistics.

Wei Xu, Courtney Napoles, Ellie Pavlick, Quanze Chen, and Chris Callison-Burch. 2016. Optimizing statistical machine translation for text simplification. *Transactions of the Association for Computational Linguistics*, 4:401–415.

Juntao Yu, Bernd Bohnet, and Massimo Poesio. 2020. Named entity recognition as dependency parsing. In *Proceedings of the 58th Annual Meeting of the Association for Computational Linguistics*, pages 6470–6476, Online. Association for Computational Linguistics.

Xingxing Zhang and Mirella Lapata. 2017. Sentence simplification with deep reinforcement learning. In *Proceedings of the 2017 Conference on Empirical Methods in Natural Language Processing*, pages 584–594, Copenhagen, Denmark. Association for Computational Linguistics.

Zhemin Zhu, Delphine Bernhard, and Iryna Gurevych. 2010. A monolingual tree-based translation model for sentence simplification. In *Proceedings of the 23rd International Conference on Computational Linguistics (Coling 2010)*, pages 1353–1361, Beijing, China. Coling 2010 Organizing Committee.

System Description for the CommonGen task with the POINTER model

Anna Shvets
FabLab by Inetum
Paris, France
anna.shvets@inetum.com

Abstract

In a current experiment we were testing CommonGen dataset for structure-to-text task from GEM living benchmark with the constraint based POINTER model. POINTER represents a hybrid architecture, combining insertion-based and transformer paradigms, predicting the token and the insertion position at the same time. The text is therefore generated gradually in a parallel non-autoregressive manner, given the set of keywords. The pretrained model was fine-tuned on a training split of the CommonGen dataset and the generation result was compared to the validation and challenge splits.[1] The received metrics outputs, which measure lexical equivalence, semantic similarity and diversity, are discussed in details in a present system description.

1 Introduction

The 2021 edition of the Generation Evaluation and Metrics (GEM) challenge for the creation of living NLG benchmark leaderboard (Gehrmann et al., 2021), comprised four groups of tasks - summarization, structure-to-text, simplification and dialog. The CommonGen dataset makes part of the structure-to-text group and was designed to measure a common sense reasoning capacities of generative models given a set of concepts (Lin et al., 2020). Due to the nature of the constraint based text generation of the POINTER model (Zhang et al., 2020b) and resemblance in a generation strategy (the model takes a set of keywords as an input and generates a text, containing these keywords) the CommonGen dataset for hard constrained generation of the GEM benchmark appears to be a good fit for testing the model performance. The pre-trained POINTER model was therefore fine-tuned on a training set of the CommonGen dataset and the inference results were compared to the validation and challenge splits of the same dataset.[2]

2 Data description and pre-processing

The Insertion-based transformer architecture leverage implies the use of the masking mechanism, the goal of which is to predict not only the likelihood of a token itself, but the likelihood of the token insertion between two given tokens, in other words, we need to predict the word and the place where a new word is inserted. In that regard, a text is preprocessed in a specific way, where the tokens are scored using a combination of three schemes of the token importance measurement (term frequency-inverse document frequency (TF-IDF), part-of-speech (POS) tagging and Yet-Another-Keyword-Extractor (YAKE)) and the highest scored tokens are replaced with a special no-insertion token [NOI] tag. This procedure is iterative and results in generation of several utterances out of the initial sentence. During the training phase, the model is initialised with the Multilingual BERT and its vobabulary is extended with the [NOI] tag. At the inference time, the masking mechanism is used in a reverse order, allowing an iterative tokens prediction - the model will chose to either generate a token or a [NOI] tag at a given generation stage and if the next stage contains [NOI] tag predictions only, the generation is finished.

The model was pre-trained on 12GB of Wikipedia corpora, therefore the pre-training data consisted of a well written English with the correct spelling, grammar and punctuation. For the fine-tuning, the sentences from the training split were preprocessed with the pre-training data generation script,[3] which inserts the token position masks in a gradual manner, resulting in a data augmentation from 67.389 source entries to 160.680 processed

[1] CommonGen have a private test set, which is not distributed by GEM benchmark, therefore a comparison to the test set was not possible.

[2] Available under the MIT license at https://github.com/dreasysnail/POINTER.

[3] Available in the project repository cited earlier.

Proceedings of the 1st Workshop on Natural Language Generation, Evaluation, and Metrics (GEM 2021), pages 161–165
August 5–6, 2021.

entries.

3 Training details and decoding strategy

The fine-tuning was done on 8 cores (16GB of RAM each) of a TPU-v3 device, following the multiprocessing paradigm, and took three hours to train on 40 epochs with the batch size equal to 64 and gradient accumulation equal to 2. The finetuning hyperparameters were preserved from the original paper and included AdamW optimizer, learning rate equal to 1e-5, Adam epsilon equal to 1e-8, 10 warmup optimizer scheduler steps and the seed equal to 1.

The inference of the finetuned model was done using the concept sets from the validation and challenge splits of the CommonGen dataset. The decoding strategy included two sampling methods, applied separately - greedy and sampling. The greedy decoding is based on a greedy search algorithm, which consists of choosing the highest scoring token at a given time step, along with the temperature (Ackley et al., 1985), while sampling uses a combination of top-k (Fan et al., 2018), top-p (Holtzman et al., 2020) and the temperature parameters to render model predictions.

For the greedy decoding method, a temperature, which is a scale factor of each token's probability before going through softmax function, was set to its lower value 0.3, ensuring the most stable generations. This parameter alone draws a limit on the model's creativity, resulting in a more rigid generation.

For the sampling decoding method, the parameters promoting a high creativity of the model were chosen: the top-k window of the most probable tokens was set to 10, following the strategy expressed in the original paper (Fan et al., 2018), the top-p cumulative probability threshold for the most probable tokens was set to its highest tested value 0.95, according to the original paper (Holtzman et al., 2020), and the temperature was set to 0.9 - this is the highest lower probability threshould for this sampling parameter, allowing the maximum tokens pass-though without giving up stability of the text generation.

Other parameters were common for both sampling methods and included noi_decay and $reduce\_decay$, which were equal to 1, and $prevent$, $reduce\_stop$, $lessrepeat$, which were set to $true$. The inference for both decoding methods was done with the maximum sequence length equal to 256.

Description	Content
keys val.	ball court run throw
greedy val.	Olympic athlete then brings in the tennis ball straight back up down on the tennis court.
sampling val.	Olympic athlete quickly moves toward the soccer ball about halfway way up on the clay court.
target val.	The boy must run from one end of the court to the other to throw the ball into the hoop.

Table 1: Examples of generated text compared to the ground truth.

The opposite set of parameters (rigid versus creative) intended to explore the model's edge generative performance. This induces the metrics measurements for both types of the decoding strategy within validation and challenge splits.

4 Metrics outputs

Before diving in the metrics output results, let us explore a few examples of the generated text.[4] The Table 1 shows the examples of generation using greedy and sampling decoding methods for the validation split, compared to the human-generated target from the CommonGen dataset. To fairly measure the metrics output, the number of entries in the validation split was truncated to 500 in order to match the number of entries in the challenge set.

Since the goal of GEM challenge is an in-depth analysis of the model performance regarding lexical, semantic similarity and language richness, we will divide the analysis in separate subsections.

4.1 Lexical equivalence

The lexical equivalence was measured with four n-gram based automated metrics and is reflected in two tables: Table 2 and Table 3.

The Recall-Oriented Understudy for Gisting Evaluation (ROUGE), which relies on counting the matching n-grams in candidate and reference text, is a metric initially designed for evaluating summaries (Lin, 2004), which nowadays is widely used for many other tasks in natural language processing

[4]The complete lists of generated sentences along with the scripts for calculating the metrics can be found in a dedicated github repository: https://github.com/asnota/metrics

Sample	R1	R2	RL
greedy val.	0.137	0.008	0.109
sampling val.	**0.142**	0.008	0.106
greedy ch.	**0.142**	**0.009**	**0.111**
sampling ch.	0.136	0.008	0.103

Table 2: Lexical equivalence: ROUGE metric.

Sample	BLEU	NIST	METEOR
greedy val.	2.88	**0.114**	0.123
sampling val.	2.456	0.093	**0.141**
greedy ch.	**2.996**	0.113	0.125
sampling ch.	2.473	0.09	0.136

Table 3: Lexical equivalence: BLEU, NIST and METEOR metrics.

and generation. The ROUGE-1 (R1) and ROUGE-2 (R2) in a Table 2 reflects the co-occurrence of unigrams and bigrams in generated text versus validation or challenge splits of the CommonGen dataset. The ROUGE-L (RL) measures the longest in-sequence common n-grams and as we may observe, the values are quite small, meaning that the generated text might use different vocabulary, compared to the reference text. The ROUGE score is a bit higher for greedy decoding method of the challenge set.

While ROUGE is a recall-oriented metric, BLEU relies on a precision calculation of the overlapping n-grams and was primarily designed to measure the quality of the automatic translation (Papineni et al., 2002). The BLEU score augmentation is observed for the challenge set (Table 3), which might indicate, that the generated text might suffer from the noise, since it gives better scores when compared to a noisy reference text.

The calculation of the geometric mean with the BLUE score is completed by calculation of the arithmetic mean of the n-gram overlap with the NIST metric. This metric also calculates a degree of the informativeness of n-grams (rare n-grams are given more weight) and is less sensible towards small differences between the candidate and reference texts (Doddington, 2002). The NIST score shows no significant difference between validation and challenge splits, however the score itself is rather low, which indicates considerable lexical differences of the generated text compared to the reference text.

Additionally to the geometric and arithmetic mean, a harmonic mean of unigram precision and recall is calculated with the METEOR metric (Banerjee and Lavie, 2005). The advantage of this n-gram based metric is that the calculation includes synonym matching, stemming and word matching, which lowers the impact of alternative vocabulary and grammatical forms used in the generated text, compared to the golden human standard. Although the values appear to be low, it should be noted, that the maximum correlation with human judgement achieved was equal to 0.403.[5] The METEOR score is slightly higher for the challenge set and is generally higher for the sampling decoding method.

4.2 Semantic similarity

A recent shift towards neural based metrics changed the very essence of the metrics input - the words are represented by their embeddings, facilitating the calculation of many parameters, unavailable while calculating n-grams. In this system description three neural based automated metrics were used: BERTscore, which computes the cosine similarity of word embedding and applies greedy matching to maximize the similarity score in score arrays between words in the candidate and reference sentences (Zhang et al., 2020a), BLEURT, which uses a BERT model, pre-trained on a large amount of synthetic examples and finetuned on human judgement (Sellam et al., 2020), and NUBIA, which uses neural models output predictions on a set of parameters (Kane et al., 2020).

As shown in Table 4, there is no significant difference neither in BERTscore, nor in BLEURT score between validation and challenge sets. F1 and precision of the BERTscore are higher for greedy decoding, while recall is higher for the sampling decoding. We used the HuggingFace's API $load\_metric()$ from Datasets library to calculate the BLEURT score: by default, the API loads the BLEURT-base checkpoint with the sequence length limited to 128 tokens - the truncation of the original sentences resulted in an average score -1.4 for both decoding methods in both splits; the loading of the BLEURT-large checkpoint with the sequence length equal to 512, augmented the average score by 14%. The final values are shown in the above-mentioned Table 4 - the higher scores are observed for the greedy decoding method in both splits, however the overall values of the BLEURT

[5]Non-european languages have even lower METEOR scores - 0.347 on the Arabic data and 0.331 on the Chinese data, according to the ressource.

Samp.	F_{BERT}	P_{BERT}	R_{BERT}	BLEURT
g. v.	**0.842**	**0.822**	0.863	-1.233
s. v.	0.838	0.813	**0.865**	-1.252
g. ch.	**0.842**	**0.822**	0.863	**-1.225**
s. ch.	0.838	0.815	0.864	-1.243

Table 4: Semantic similarity: BERTscore and BLEURT.

Samp.	NUBIA score	semantic rel.
greedy val.	0.395	**0.803**
sampling val.	**0.523**	0.743
greedy ch.	0.406	0.35
sampling ch.	0.52	0.335

Table 5: Semantic similarity: NUBIA.

metric are rather low (since the maximum score that can be achieved with this metric is equal to 1), which indicates the semantic distance of the model's generations from the benchmark reference text.

NUBIA metric calculates such parameters as semantic relation, logical agreement, grammaticality, contradiction and a degree of new information presence (which might also signify the irrelevance) in the candidate sentence, regarding the reference sentence. In view of the current experiment's scope, we show the mean values of the cumulative NUBIA score and a semantic relevance measurement in Table 5. As we can see, the semantic relevance is considerably higher for the validation split.

4.3 Vocabulary diversity

Finally, the calculation of the lexical richness was done with four automated metrics - Mean Segmental Type-Token Ratio (MSTTR) (Johnson, 1944), Distinct (Li et al., 2016), Unique and Entropy (Shannon, 1948).

We can see in Table 6 that MSTTR is higher for the sampling decoding and is equivalent for greedy decoding in validation and challenge splits together. The Distinct score is surprisingly higher for the greedy decoding, but doesn't differ substantially between validation and challenge splits.

Table 7 shows that the amount of the unique unigrams and bigrams is higher for the sampling decoding (which is rather expected, as the sampling allows more creativity) and is substantially lower for the challenge set for both decoding methods. The Entropy is slightly higher for the sampling decoding method, and is generally higher for the

Sample	MSTTR	Dist1	Dist2
greedy val.	0.858	**0.19**	0.594
sampling val.	**0.88**	0.147	0.548
greedy ch.	0.858	**0.19**	**0.596**
sampling ch.	0.878	0.158	0.553

Table 6: Diversity: MSTTR and Distinct.

Sample	U1	U2	E1	E2
greedy val.	972	13115	5.818	10.241
sampling val.	**1285**	**20540**	**6.123**	**10.602**
greedy ch.	758	8172	5.788	9.638
sampling ch.	1030	11693	6.051	9.915

Table 7: Diversity: Unique and Entropy.

validation set. This can be explained by the inconsistencies of the challenge set, which correlate with possible inconsistencies of the model generations, while a comparison with the perfect validation set, translates into higher rates of entropy, required to map one probability distribution to another.

5 Conclusions

The system description depicted the experiment on application of the CommonGen task from the GEM benchmark to a hard constraint text generation with the insertion based transformer. The use of eleven automated metrics for measuring the generative performance of the POINTER model allowed to detect the issues of the model output and reveal the advantages of a specific decoding method. For the lexical equivalence, METEOR metric seems to be the most relevant (since it takes stemmed forms of the words and makes the synonym comparison), when looking at the score augmentation for more creative text generations, accomplished with the sampling decoding method. The semantic similarity measured with the BERTscore and BLEURT neural based metrics showed that both validation and challenge splits result in a semantically equivalent text generations, with a small difference between decoding methods, while the application of NUBIA metric with a refined semantic relevance parameter resulted in a better score for the validation split. The Entropy showed the noisiness of the generated text for both decoding methods, and the Distinct score showed an unexpected boost for the greedy decoding, which means less words' repetitions than for the sampling decoding. Finally, the Unique score showed that sampling decoding method resulted in lexically richer text generations.

References

David H Ackley, Geoffrey E Hinton, and Terrence J Sejnowski. 1985. A learning algorithm for boltzmann machines. *Cognitive science*, 9(1):147–169.

Satanjeev Banerjee and Alon Lavie. 2005. METEOR: An automatic metric for MT evaluation with improved correlation with human judgments. In *Proceedings of the ACL Workshop on Intrinsic and Extrinsic Evaluation Measures for Machine Translation and/or Summarization*, pages 65–72, Ann Arbor, Michigan. Association for Computational Linguistics.

George Doddington. 2002. Automatic evaluation of machine translation quality using n-gram co-occurrence statistics. San Francisco, CA, USA. Morgan Kaufmann Publishers Inc.

Angela Fan, Mike Lewis, and Yann Dauphin. 2018. Hierarchical neural story generation.

Sebastian Gehrmann, Tosin Adewumi, Karmanya Aggarwal, Pawan Sasanka Ammanamanchi, Aremu Anuoluwapo, Antoine Bosselut, Khyathi Raghavi Chandu, Miruna Clinciu, Dipanjan Das, Kaustubh D. Dhole, Wanyu Du, Esin Durmus, Ondřej Dušek, Chris Emezue, Varun Gangal, Cristina Garbacea, Tatsunori Hashimoto, Yufang Hou, Yacine Jernite, Harsh Jhamtani, Yangfeng Ji, Shailza Jolly, Mihir Kale, Dhruv Kumar, Faisal Ladhak, Aman Madaan, Mounica Maddela, Khyati Mahajan, Saad Mahamood, Bodhisattwa Prasad Majumder, Pedro Henrique Martins, Angelina McMillan-Major, Simon Mille, Emiel van Miltenburg, Moin Nadeem, Shashi Narayan, Vitaly Nikolaev, Rubungo Andre Niyongabo, Salomey Osei, Ankur Parikh, Laura Perez-Beltrachini, Niranjan Ramesh Rao, Vikas Raunak, Juan Diego Rodriguez, Sashank Santhanam, João Sedoc, Thibault Sellam, Samira Shaikh, Anastasia Shimorina, Marco Antonio Sobrevilla Cabezudo, Hendrik Strobelt, Nishant Subramani, Wei Xu, Diyi Yang, Akhila Yerukola, and Jiawei Zhou. 2021. The gem benchmark: Natural language generation, its evaluation and metrics.

Ari Holtzman, Jan Buys, Li Du, Maxwell Forbes, and Yejin Choi. 2020. The curious case of neural text degeneration.

Wendell Johnson. 1944. Studies in language behavior: A program of research. *Psychological Monographs*, 56(2):1–15.

Hassan Kane, Muhammed Yusuf Kocyigit, Ali Abdalla, Pelkins Ajanoh, and Mohamed Coulibali. 2020. NUBIA: NeUral based interchangeability assessor for text generation. In *Proceedings of the 1st Workshop on Evaluating NLG Evaluation*, pages 28–37, Online (Dublin, Ireland). Association for Computational Linguistics.

Jiwei Li, Michel Galley, Chris Brockett, Jianfeng Gao, and Bill Dolan. 2016. A diversity-promoting objective function for neural conversation models.

Bill Yuchen Lin, Wangchunshu Zhou, Ming Shen, Pei Zhou, Chandra Bhagavatula, Yejin Choi, and Xiang Ren. 2020. Commongen: A constrained text generation challenge for generative commonsense reasoning.

Chin-Yew Lin. 2004. ROUGE: A package for automatic evaluation of summaries. In *Text Summarization Branches Out*, pages 74–81, Barcelona, Spain. Association for Computational Linguistics.

Kishore Papineni, Salim Roukos, Todd Ward, and Wei-Jing Zhu. 2002. Bleu: a method for automatic evaluation of machine translation. In *Proceedings of the 40th Annual Meeting of the Association for Computational Linguistics*, pages 311–318, Philadelphia, Pennsylvania, USA. Association for Computational Linguistics.

Thibault Sellam, Dipanjan Das, and Ankur P. Parikh. 2020. Bleurt: Learning robust metrics for text generation.

Claude E Shannon. 1948. A mathematical theory of communication. *The Bell system technical journal*, 27(3):379–423.

Tianyi Zhang, Varsha Kishore, Felix Wu, Kilian Q. Weinberger, and Yoav Artzi. 2020a. Bertscore: Evaluating text generation with bert.

Yizhe Zhang, Guoyin Wang, Chunyuan Li, Zhe Gan, Chris Brockett, and Bill Dolan. 2020b. Pointer: Constrained progressive text generation via insertion-based generative pre-training. In *EMNLP*.

Decoding Methods for Neural Narrative Generation

Alexandra DeLucia* and **Aaron Mueller***
Johns Hopkins University
{aadelucia, amueller}@jhu.edu

Xiang Lisa Li†
Stanford University
xlisali@stanford.edu

João Sedoc†
New York University
jsedoc@stern.nyu.edu

Abstract

Narrative generation is an open-ended NLP task in which a model generates a story given a prompt. The task is similar to neural response generation for chatbots; however, innovations in response generation are often not applied to narrative generation, despite the similarity between these tasks. We aim to bridge this gap by applying and evaluating advances in decoding methods for neural response generation to neural narrative generation. In particular, we employ GPT-2 and perform ablations across nucleus sampling thresholds and diverse decoding hyperparameters—specifically, maximum mutual information—analyzing results over multiple criteria with automatic and human evaluation. We find that (1) nucleus sampling is generally best with thresholds between 0.7 and 0.9; (2) a maximum mutual information objective can improve the quality of generated stories; and (3) established automatic metrics do not correlate well with human judgments of narrative quality on any qualitative metric.

1 Introduction

Narrative generation (or story generation) is the task of generating a creative response given an input prompt. This output can be a story closure, a paragraph, or a structured story with multiple paragraphs. This input and output setup is similar to the response generation task of chatbots, as both tasks convert some variable-length sequential input from a user to an automatically generated variable-length sequential output. Thus, the neural models and methods proposed to date for story generation and dialogue generation have been similar.

However, as narrative generation is largely focused on coherence across long outputs, the strategies used in this subfield have evolved separately from those in chatbot response generation; the latter has been more concerned with generating interesting and diverse—and typically *short*—outputs. Thus, while many beneficial techniques may have arisen from one domain, they are not often employed in the other. One decoding method, nucleus sampling (Holtzman et al., 2020), has recently been applied to narrative generation (Ippolito et al., 2020), but a thorough evaluation of its various p thresholds has not been performed with human judgments using narrative-specific criteria, as this can be time- and labor-intensive. Also, recent advances in decoding methods for response generation—notably, the application of the maximum mutual information (MMI) objective (Li et al., 2016a)—have resulted in more interesting dialog according to human evaluators (Zhang et al., 2020b); nonetheless, this also has not been applied to narrative generation. Indeed, the MMI objective has been confined to short-form and less open-ended generation tasks thus far.

Thus, we apply techniques from neural response

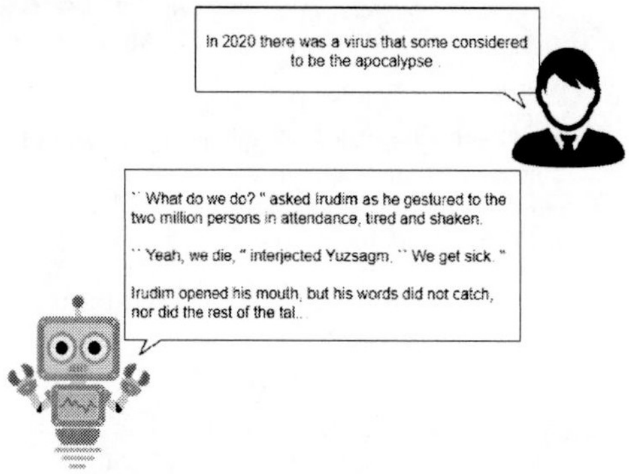

Figure 1: Example of interactive narrative generation. A user provides a prompt to our model (fine-tuned GPT-2 model), and the model responds with a story conditioned on the prompt.

*Equal contribution.
†Work performed while at Johns Hopkins University.

Proceedings of the 1st Workshop on Natural Language Generation, Evaluation, and Metrics (GEM 2021), pages 166–185
August 5–6, 2021.

generation to neural narrative generation in order to investigate the potential benefits—and pitfalls—of applying these methods in this underexplored domain. This study aims to connect research developments across tasks by sweeping various thresholds of nucleus sampling and the application of diverse decoding to generate more long-form creative outputs. We perform human and automatic evaluations of automatically generated stories in these settings in order to investigate the following phenomena:

1. The effect of the nucleus sampling threshold p on narrative quality.
2. The effect of the maximum mutual information (MMI, Li et al. 2016b) diverse decoding objective with various diversity strengths λ on narrative quality.
3. The correlation (or lack thereof) between human evaluations of narrative quality and automatic metrics for response generation.

As this domain generates longer and less constrained outputs than other natural language generation (NLG) tasks, we expect to find different ideal settings than those found for short-form or constrained generation.

Our preprocessing, training, generation, and analysis scripts are available publicly.[1]

2 Related Work

Narrative generation tasks Work on narrative generation is split between cloze tasks, open-ended generation, and guided generation. In a cloze task, a full story except for a final word, phrase, or sentence is given, and a model generates a completion. This could be cast as a short generation problem—or, more commonly in this domain, a multiple-choice problem (Mostafazadeh et al., 2016; Weston et al., 2015; Hill et al., 2015; Ippolito et al., 2019a).

Open-ended generation is the task of generating long-form output conditioned on a prompt (Figure 1). Fan et al. (2018) create a paired prompt and response dataset from the subreddit `r/WritingPrompts`[2] to train a sequence-to-sequence "fusion model." See et al. (2019) extend Fan et al. (2018), but use GPT-2 small and perform a top-k decoding parameter sweep. We focus on this open-ended narrative generation task in our investigation, but primarily focus on GPT-2 Medium and on the effect of nucleus sampling thresholds

[1] `https://github.com/AADeLucia/gpt2-narrative-decoding`

[2] `https://www.reddit.com/r/WritingPrompts/`

[WP] You live in a world where there has never been sickness , and you are the first to have ever experienced being sick .
I open my eyes in a panic , sweat beading and then falling down my face . I look around and the sun in shining through the maroon curtains of my studio apartment . Everything seems to be as I left it the afternoon before , but there is a heavy , unfamiliar air in the room .

Table 1: Example prompt and response excerpt from WRITINGPROMPTS.

and diverse decoding strengths on narrative quality. While Nadeem et al. (2020) similarly perform a hyperparameter search over sampling algorithms in a language generation setting, they perform human evaluations using a convincingness metric on a short-form news generation task; long-form narrative generation is not bound by realism (and may actually benefit from less realistic output), and thus requires different metrics and evaluation setups.

Guided generation is the middle ground of cloze and open-ended generation. The model is provided more context, such as characters, plot information, and potentially other information, and then generates a story based on all of the provided structural and semantic information (Peng et al., 2018; Akoury et al., 2020).

Decoding methods for generation Decoding refers to the inference methods used in natural language generation; given input sequence S, how should we construct the output sequence T? Since finding the exact most probable token at each time step often does not produce human-like or high-quality results (Zhang et al., 2020a; Holtzman et al., 2020), search and sampling are used to overcome label bias and generate more human-like language. One popular search method is beam search, where at each time step, the algorithm keeps track of the top B most probable partial hypotheses. When $B = 1$, this method reduces to the *greedy* decoder, which chooses the argmax over the model's token distribution at each time step.

An alternative to search is sampling-based approaches, which select a token with likelihood proportional to a (typically constrained) probability distribution at each time step. Such methods include top-k (Fan et al., 2018) which restricts the sampling space to the top k most probable tokens at every time step, and "nucleus sampling"[3] (Holtzman et al., 2020) which thresholds the cumulative token probability distribution according to a hyperparameter p. We focus on nucleus sampling, as it has tended to be a more effective decoding method in various response generation settings (Zhang et al., 2020a; Ippolito et al., 2020).

An approach to control sampling is temperature (Ackley et al., 1985), which modifies the softmax estimating the token probability distribution. This has been applied widely in neural text generation (Ficler and Goldberg, 2017; Caccia et al., 2018), especially when using top-k or random sampling. Low temperatures bias the model toward high-probability events, which tends to increase generation quality while decreasing token diversity (Hashimoto et al., 2019). Temperature sampling has been investigated extensively in natural language generation over multiple sampling methods, and nucleus sampling has been found to be a more effective method of controlling the sampling distribution (Holtzman et al., 2020), so we do not investigate this here.

Decoding objective In chatbot response generation, top-k and nucleus sampling have been known to generate fluent, but uninteresting and simple high-probability responses which do not address the input (Li et al., 2016b). This issue is commonly referred to as the "I don't know" problem, where the response to all inputs is often the high-probability phrase "I don't know." Proposed solutions to this response blandness issue involve altering the decoding objective. Some recent work in this domain includes Nakamura et al. (2018), who use Inverse Token Frequency to reweight generated tokens. Xu et al. (2018) and Zhang et al. (2018) use adversarial loss to optimize for diversity, informativeness, and fluency. Martins et al. (2020) propose entmax sampling to generate more effectively from sparse distributions and address the train-test mismatch in text generation.

Another approach explores variants of the standard log-likelihood loss, applying different objectives during inference. An example of this is maximum mutual information (MMI, Li et al. 2016b), an objective that promotes more diverse responses in the neural response generation task. This mitigates the "I don't know" problem in which all responses tend to converge to some high-probability sequence with no real content conveyed in response to the input sequence. Two versions are introduced in Li et al. (2016b): bidirectional (MMI-bidi) and an anti-language model (MMI-antiLM) objective. The typical decoding objective is defined as

$$\hat{T} = \arg\max_T \log p(T \mid S)$$

where S is the input sequence, T is a possible target sequence, and $\hat{T}$ is the selected target. We use a slightly modified form of the MMI-antiLM objective (Li et al., 2016a), defined as follows:

$$\hat{T} = \arg\max_T \log p(T \mid S) - \lambda \log p(T)$$

where λ is a hyperparameter controlling the degree to which the language modeling objective is subtracted from the sequential transduction objective. Intuitively, this is meant to increase the likelihood of relevant targets while penalizing popular generic responses (e.g. "okay").

This diverse decoding objective has been applied to response generation but has not yet been applied to the narrative generation task; here, we evaluate the effect of the MMI-antiLM objective on narrative generation quality.

3 Experimental Setup

3.1 Dataset

For our task of narrative generation, we train on Fan et al. (2018)'s long-form response dataset WRITINGPROMPTS.[4] This dataset was built from the subreddit `r/WritingPrompts`[5], where users post a "prompt" consisting of up to a few sentences, and other users reply to the post with a story continuing the prompt (the "response"). An example prompt and response pair is in Table 1.

To create datasets of varying lengths—and to make the dataset compatible with our model (GPT-2, discussed more in §3.2)—we preprocess the WRITINGPROMPTS dataset as follows:

1. Remove all prompts that are not tagged with `[ WP ]`. Other tags in `r/WritingPrompts` have response requirements and constraints, such as having to occur in an established universe or not including particular tokens; we want only unconstrained responses.
2. Create different versions of each response by using all content from (1) before the

[3] Also referred to as "top-p".

[4] https://github.com/pytorch/fairseq/blob/master/examples/stories/README.md

[5] https://www.reddit.com/r/WritingPrompts/

<|startoftext|> [WP] PROMPT [RESPONSE] RESPONSE <|endoftext|>

Figure 2: Each prompt/response pair from WRITINGPROMPTS was formatted for compatibility with GPT-2. Note: "[WP]" and "[RESPONSE]" are defined as special tokens so that they are not split into subword units.

Fold	Size	Tokens Per Example	Total Tokens
Train	Small	92.9 ($\pm$ 82.8)	21.4M
	Medium	206.0 ($\pm$ 128.2)	47.5M
	Large	718.4 ($\pm$ 458.9)	165.8M
Valid	Small	92.9 ($\pm$ 80.2)	1.2M
	Medium	206.1 ($\pm$ 128.3)	2.8M
	Large	714.4 ($\pm$ 463.3)	9.5M
Test	Small	91.4 ($\pm$ 79.4)	1.2M
	Medium	204.7 ($\pm$ 124.1)	2.6M
	Large	720.4 ($\pm$ 455.9)	9.3M

Table 2: Corpus sizes for each fold and response length. **Tokens Per Example** indicates the mean number of tokens per prompt/response pair ($\pm$ standard deviation). **Total Tokens** indicates the number of tokens in the entire corpus.

first line break/the first 100 tokens, (2) before the third line break/the first 256 tokens, and (3) the entire response/the first 1024 tokens, respectively. These are referred to as the "small", "medium", and "large" datasets/response lengths, and are treated as separate corpora. Thus, we have 3 train, validation, and test corpora for a total of 9.

3. Combine the source (prompt) and target (response) strings into one, as in Figure 2.

During step 2, we create multiple versions of the training set with varying response lengths to evaluate the quality of narrative generation for outputs of various lengths. We use line breaks instead of a token cutoff as in Fan et al. (2018), because line breaks are more likely to provide complete sentences. See Table 2 for the sizes of these datasets.

3.2 Narrative Generation with GPT-2

Instead of the convolutional-sequential model used in Fan et al. (2018), we focus on the generative Transformer-based model GPT-2 (Radford et al., 2019).[6] We employ this model because it is currently the state-of-the-art publicly available text generation model, though this may change when GPT-3 (Brown et al., 2020) is released publicly.

We investigate the small and medium GPT-2 models for output quality comparison. GPT-2 Large was infeasible to train on the medium and large datasets, even on a machine with multiple Tesla P100 GPUs.

GPT-2 is pre-trained on WebText. For this work, we fine-tune GPT-2 Small and Medium on the small, medium, and large versions of the WRITINGPROMPTS dataset discussed in §3.1. We fine-tuned for one epoch using Adam with a learning rate of 5×10^{-5}, epsilon of 1×10^{-8}, and batch size of 4. Fine-tuning is performed on Google Cloud instances using NVIDIA Tesla K80s or T4s. Inference is performed by feeding GPT-2 a string of the format in Figure 2 up to the [RESPONSE] token.

3.3 Decoding Methods

After GPT-2 is fine-tuned on the WRITINGPROMPTS dataset, we evaluate the model's generated responses with a parameter sweep of p for nucleus sampling. We also provide a small comparison with top-k sampling in Appendix C.

Holtzman et al. (2020) uses a threshold of $p = 0.95$ for chatbot response generation; we perform an ablation over values of p here to discover which value best suits narrative generation. Specifically, we investigate the thresholds of of $0.3, 0.5, 0.7, 0.9, 0.95$, and also include greedy search and full random sampling, represented by $p = 0$ and $p = 1$, respectively.

Once we find the best p, we apply the diverse decoding objective to narrative generation to investigate whether this generates better stories. Specifically, we implement the MMI-antiLM (anti-language model) objective for GPT-2.

We also perform an ablation over λ values for the antiLM objective, testing the values $0.1, 0.2, 0.35, 0.5$; $\lambda = 0$ represents not using diverse decoding. As this objective was originally designed to increase the specificity of a response with respect to a prompt, we expect this to increase interestingness and relevance (but perhaps decrease fluency and coherence, since we are subtracting the language modeling objective from the response generation objective). We only employ the antiLM objective when generating the first 20 tokens of the target sequence, after which we use the regular log-likelihood loss. This follows the approach of Li et al. (2016b), who find that ungrammatical sequences often arise later in the output sequence and that the first few tokens have a large effect on the rest of the output sequence; thus, they threshold

[6]We use the Huggingface implementation: https://huggingface.co/transformers/model_doc/GPT-2.html

the objective to only apply to the first few tokens during generation.

There is an established quality-diversity trade-off (Zhang et al., 2020a) in natural language generation, so we expect that strong diverse decoding (e.g., $\lambda = 0.5$) will generate lower-quality narratives overall compared to lower λ values, which may increase interestingness more than they decrease fluency.

3.4 Evaluation

The qualities important for narrative generation are interestingness, coherence, fluency, and relevance to the prompt. These metrics are also evaluated in Akoury et al. (2020), though they measure "likeability" instead of interestingness.

A combination of automatic and human evaluation is used to assess the quality of generated narratives. For automatic evaluation, we employ test perplexity, lexical diversity (dist-n, Li et al. 2016b), and a BERT-based sentence similarity metric, Sentence-BERT (sent-BERT, Reimers and Gurevych 2019). Perplexity is used to evaluate language models and may correlate with fluency. The latter two may act as proxies for interestingness, since they measure n-gram diversity within an output and sentence embedding diversity across outputs, respectively. We use sent-BERT as an output diversity metric by using the cosine distance instead of cosine similarity. Our motivation in choosing these diversity metrics is from Tevet and Berant (2020), who identify dist-n and sent-BERT as the best metrics to evaluate two targeted types of diversity—diverse word choice and diverse content, respectively.

For human evaluation, we employ 4-point Likert scales to evaluate narratives for interestingness, coherence, fluency, and relevance. For the purpose of evaluation, we define interestingness as the enjoyment of reading the story, coherence as the level of cohesion between sentences in a narrative, and fluency as the grammaticality and naturalness of the English output; these metrics judge the quality of a generated narrative independently from the input prompt. Relevance is a metric we employ to measure how well the response follows from the input prompt. We evaluate 100 narratives per-p and per-λ, and we have 5 human annotators per-narrative. We judge quality on medium-length outputs, as these are less variable in length than large narratives while being long enough to properly judge our metrics. Appendix B contains a thorough description and example of our Mechanical Turk setup.

3.5 Baseline

We employ the fusion model—the previous state-of-the-art approach for narrative generation before pre-trained Transformer models—from Fan et al. (2018) as a baseline. This model is an ensemble of two convolutional seq2seq models, where the first is pre-trained on the training set and is then used to boost a second model. We employ this model on the WritingPrompts dataset and evaluate on different narrative lengths.

4 Results

4.1 Quantitative Results

	Response Length		
Model	Small	Medium	Large
GPT-2 Small	30.52	23.74	15.64
GPT-2 Medium	**25.08**	**19.34**	**13.19**
Fusion Model	44.20	39.03	34.71

Table 3: Perplexities of the GPT-2 models and baseline model after fine-tuning on WritingPrompts dataset with different response lengths. The fusion model from Fan et al. (2018) is used as a baseline. Perplexities are not directly comparable across GPT-2 and the fusion model due to differences in tokenization.

The perplexities of each model on each narrative length are shown in Table 3. GPT-2 Medium had the lowest perplexity within each dataset size. GPT-2 Small had a fairly close perplexity to GPT-2 Medium despite having significantly fewer parameters. Comparatively, the fusion model had a high perplexity, though scores are not directly comparable across models due to tokenization differences. In general, perplexity decreased as the length of the response increases, though perplexities are also not necessarily comparable across dataset sizes since this a per-word metric. Nonetheless, these results suggest that we should generally expect GPT-2 Medium to be marginally more fluent than GPT-2 Small, and that both of these will output far better English than the fusion model. We confirm this qualitatively; see Appendix A. We thus focus on GPT-2 Medium for the following analyses.

Next, we sweep over various p-values for nucleus sampling using GPT-2 Medium on the medium-length dataset, evaluating using human annotators (Figure 3). We found that $p = 0.7$ performed best on average for all metrics except interestingness, where $p = 0.9$ was best. $p = 0.9$ was a close second overall, and the difference in performance between these two settings was not high. Increasing p past 0.9 or decreasing p below 0.7 more notably decreased performance. Inter-annotator agreement (measured with Fleiss' kappa) was 0.13 for interestingness and coherence, 0.12 for fluency, and 0.10 for relevance; these are similar to agreements found in Akoury et al. (2020) when prompts are included.

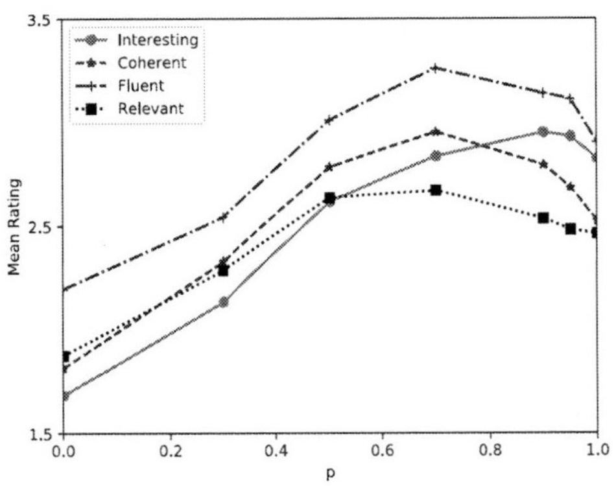

Figure 3: Mean human ratings of the quality of output narratives when using various p values. Ratings are on a 4-point Likert scale in the range $[1, 4]$. Means are significantly different ($P < .05$) between any two consecutive top-p values in a series of t-tests, except relevance from $p = 0.5$ onward, interestingness from $p = 0.7$ onward, coherence in $[0.9, 0.95]$, and fluency in $[0.7, 0.95]$.

To test the effect of diverse decoding on narrative quality (Figure 4), we use the same human annotator setup as for the p sweep. We decode with nucleus sampling using $p = 0.7$ and vary the λ hyperparameter (Figure 4). Higher λ indicates a larger modification from the original decoding objective. We found that setting $\lambda = 0.1$ increased the quality of narratives for all metrics. Interestingness and relevance further increased at $\lambda = 0.2$, which is expected given that the $p(T \mid S)$ term in the decoding objective becomes more prominent than $p(T)$ as λ increases; however, fluency and coherence began to decline here. Higher settings of λ tended to reduce quality on all metrics.

Next, we discuss the relationship between model size and the diversity of outputs. Table 4 contains dist-n and sent-BERT scores for all model sizes, p values in nucleus sampling, and response lengths.

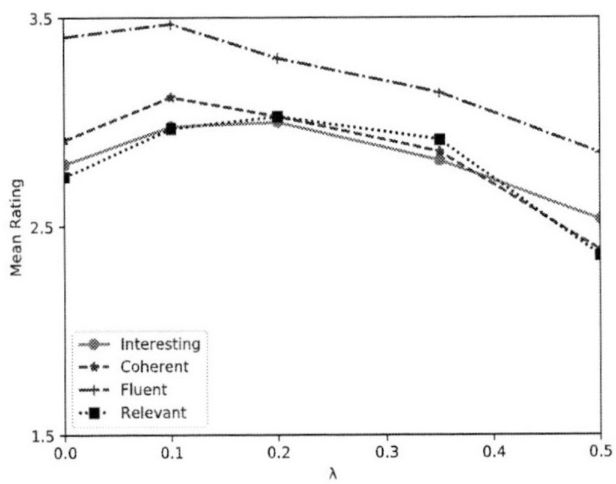

Figure 4: Mean human ratings of the quality of output narratives when using diverse decoding at various λ settings (note: $p = 0.7$). Ratings are on a 4-point Likert scale in the range $[1, 4]$. Means are significantly different ($P < .05$) for interestingness, coherence, and fluency between $\lambda = 0.0$ and $\lambda = 0.1$, for fluency between $\lambda = 0.1$ and $\lambda = 0.2$, and for all metrics between $\lambda = 0.35$ and $\lambda = 0.5$.

For any given p value and response length, GPT-2 Medium tended to use a slightly larger variety of tokens per-response than GPT-2 Small. Meanwhile, the diversity of the fusion model outputs was quite low in comparison—typically due to the degeneracy of the output. We also note that the dist-n scores were the same for the medium and large response lengths; this is also due to the degeneracy of the output and the surprisingly short stories generated, even when trained on large data and when allowed to generate up to 1,000 tokens.

Dist-n and sent-BERT scores both declined with increasing response lengths. We believe that the former is due to the normalization constant (the number of n-grams in the narrative) in dist-n calculations. Larger responses tend to repeat tokens more than shorter responses, so increasing response length increases the normalization constant more quickly than the number of unique n-grams. The latter may be due to the way sentence embeddings are calculated: as the number of tokens grows, sentence embeddings may grow more similar on average, since they are calculated as the mean of the token embeddings that compose the sentence.

Relatedly, even though we allow the fusion models trained on the large dataset to generate longer responses, they often generated responses which were of similar lengths to medium responses (i.e., they often did not generate to their maximum allowed sequence length). This may explain the lack

Model	Decoding	Small Response Dist-1	Small Response Dist-2	Small Response sent-BERT	Medium Response Dist-1	Medium Response Dist-2	Medium Response sent-BERT	Large Response Dist-1	Large Response Dist-2	Large Response sent-BERT
GPT-2 Small	$p = 0.7$	0.018	0.149	0.830	0.011	0.112	**0.741**	0.003	0.034	0.694
	$p = 0.9$	0.026	0.234	0.808	0.016	0.177	0.682	0.005	0.087	0.646
	$p = 0.95$	0.030	0.274	0.798	0.019	0.213	0.663	0.007	0.118	0.632
GPT-2 Medium	$p = 0.7$	0.026	0.195	**0.855**	0.013	0.125	**0.741**	0.003	0.036	**0.709**
	$p = 0.9$	0.034	0.272	0.842	0.018	0.190	0.692	0.007	0.093	0.660
	$p = 0.95$	**0.039**	**0.308**	0.837	**0.021**	**0.227**	0.677	**0.009**	0.127	0.646
Fusion Model	$p = 0.7$	0.009	0.092	0.707	0.005	0.061	0.686	0.005	0.061	0.686
	$p = 0.9$	0.014	0.174	0.667	0.008	0.130	0.637	0.008	0.130	0.637
	$p = 0.95$	0.017	0.213	0.655	0.009	0.155	0.624	0.008	**0.149**	0.624

Table 4: Automatic diversity evaluations across models and decoding methods for each response length. The decoding methods represent a subset of our sweep over p values in nucleus sampling (full table in Appendix D). The fusion model is a baseline from Fan et al. (2018).

of distinction between the scores obtained in Table 4 between medium and large narratives.

Finally, we analyze the effect of various p values as well as different strengths of the MMI-antiLM objective on narrative token diversity (Figure 5). There was an expected consistent positive correlation between p and dist-n, as well as a positive correlation between λ and diversity; since dist-n increases monotonically with both hyperparameters, $\rho_s = 1$. Sent-BERT consistently decreased with higher p when $p > 0$, indicating lower levels of difference between narratives as p increases. Sent-BERT decreased monotonically with respect to λ.

4.2 Qualitative Results

In this section, we analyze the quality of narratives by directly observing the outputs. Appendix A shows generated narratives from a variety of model architectures, sizes, and decoding hyperparameters.

4.2.1 Nucleus Sampling

When p was high, we generally observed more interesting and vivid narratives with good diction and fluency scores, but which had no single cohesive plot. When p was low, we saw more repetitive word choice but higher cohesion. However, when p was very low ($p \leq 0.3$), the output was degenerate. Generally, when p was around 0.7, we observed consistently good stories compared to other p values. With values of $p = 0.9$ and higher, we generally saw output stories with more variable quality (i.e., whose quality is often either higher or lower than stories with $p = 0.7$). This is intuitive with respect to how p restricts the sampling space: when p is too small, too many options are removed and the model cannot generate fluent text. When p is large, we more closely approach random sampling and fewer tokens are removed from the sampling space, so the probability tail increases the likelihood for the model to choose unlikely tokens; this can produce interesting output, but tends to reduce fluency and coherence. A discussion of the number of tokens sampled for each p is in Appendix E.

4.2.2 Diverse Decoding

For smaller values of λ, MMI had a smaller effect on the output of the models. Within a given p value, increasing MMI values up to 0.2 seemed to result in slightly more interesting diction for the small models. Coherence seemed to be unaffected by changing values of λ, though we saw a notable drop in the grammaticality of output at 0.35 and higher.

More interesting is that the intensity of the subject matter seemed to increase with λ, especially notable around 0.2 and 0.35. Indeed, we generally observed more cursing, violent content, and jokes featuring sexuality and dark humor as λ increased. This may not necessarily be a positive or negative trend; if one wishes to generate stories which are more vivid, and one's language model is sufficiently high-quality to start, then this may be a beneficial method to employ. Nonetheless, we do not have a clear mathematical explanation for this, since the MMI-antiLM objective simply increases the importance of the prompt while decreasing the importance of the language model. Perhaps these more intense subjects are somewhat less probable than more tame content, hence why subtracting the language model could increase the likelihood of seeing these darker themes.

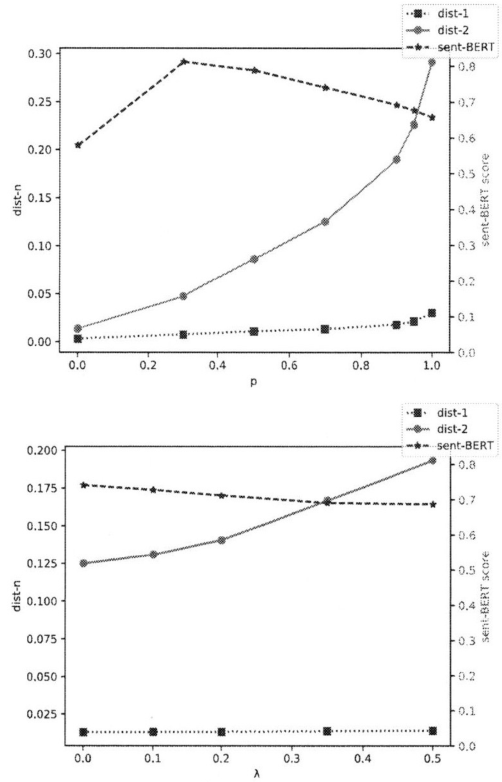

Figure 5: Plots comparing dist-1, dist-2, and sent-BERT scores across p values (top) and MMI-antiLM λ values (bottom). Note: we use $p = 0.7$ for MMI-antiLM analysis. Scores are for GPT-2 Medium with medium-length responses.

4.2.3 Correlating Automatic Metrics with Quality

Thus far, we have observed how perplexity, dist-n, and sent-BERT vary with various model architectures/sizes, decoding approaches, and hyperparameters. However, what do these quantities say about the quality of generated narratives? In general, we note the following qualitative trends: (1) Lower perplexity is better. This correlates mainly with fluency and non-degenerate output. (2) Very low dist-n scores indicate consistent neural text degeneration. (3) Very high dist-n scores indicate variable-quality narratives.

Dist-n demonstrated a moderate correlation[7] with interestingness ($\rho_s = .75$, $P < .1$) across top-p values. The two metrics correlated well up to top-$p = 0.9$, but it is possible that decreased fluency and coherence at higher values of p overshadowed the increased number of distinct tokens per-response, thus negating any interestingness gains. For all other human metrics, dist-n did not correlate well ($\rho_s \leq .5$, $P > .1$). Thus, we do not recommend optimizing over dist-n. Rather, this quantity can be a helpful heuristic when comparing across model configurations at a high level, and both very high and very low dist-n scores can be indicative of distinct problems in narrative generation despite having little inherent meaning in isolation.

Sent-BERT did not correlate well with any of our metrics ($0 \leq \rho_s \leq .43$, $P > .1$), indicating that it is either not a sufficient method for sentence diversity measurement when applied to narratives, or that it does not correlate with factors that make for interesting narratives. When p is lower, we observed stories that were degenerate in different ways, whereas when p was higher, we observed stories that were always more token-diverse, and thus generally more similar on a sentential level.

We find a less marked diversity-quality trade-off in the narrative generation setting compared to recent natural language generation papers in other settings (Ippolito et al., 2019b; Zhang et al., 2020a; Nadeem et al., 2020). If this trade-off were strong, we would expect generally decreasing human evaluation scores with higher p and higher λ, since dist-n increases monotonically with both hyperparameters. While this held to an extent with λ (and even then not monotonically, since $\lambda = 0.1$ showed higher performance on *all* metrics), it was certainly not true for p up to very high values. Perhaps this is due to the more open-ended nature of narrative generation, as stories can benefit from higher levels of diversity without needing to maintain realism or a specific writing style.

5 Conclusions

Our results suggest that p values lower than those suggested for other tasks (Holtzman et al., 2020) are ideal in narrative generation, and that small magnitudes of diverse decoding may produce better and more vivid stories. We also find that distinct-n and sentence-BERT do not correlate well with any of our human perceptions of narrative quality, and that the quality-diversity trade-off is less strong in narrative generation than in other generation tasks. The latter finding is preliminary, though supported by Martins et al. (2020), who find increases in both

[7]All correlations here are measured using Spearman's rank correlation (ρ_s) along with measures of significance (capital P).

diversity and human scores with their proposed method.

Our findings aim to inform future efforts in the narrative generation domain by establishing future baselines given our recommended hyperparameters, and by facilitating further investigation of decoding objectives for better narrative generation. Once GPT-3 (Brown et al., 2020) is released for public use, it is very likely that this model will outperform GPT-2; thus, we encourage future work to investigate similar hyperparameters and sampling methods to see whether these trends are stable across model sizes.

6 Ethical Considerations

Our contributions include a story generation model to be used by other researchers and AI hobbyists. This model was fine-tuned on `WritingPrompts` (Fan et al., 2018), which is a collection of prompts and responses from a popular creative writing subreddit `r/WritingPrompts`. To the best of our knowledge, this dataset was not examined for hate speech or gender bias, and we did not perform such inspections here. Also, the released code has no post-generation filter to flag potentially offensive narratives.

We did not pursue any of these filters or offensive text detection because our work was focused on evaluating generated narratives for stylistic measures of quality, and was not focused on content-based sources of bias. However, one should look to relevant work in the field on bias and hate speech detection (Sheng et al., 2020; MacAvaney et al., 2019) before deploying such models as creative writing tools. Besides the clear ethical obligation to vet such a tool, a "creative" writing tool which propagates or amplifies the bias of its training set would potentially hinder the quality of output narratives. Normative and stereotypical narratives would likely be uninteresting.

Acknowledgments

We thank Daphne Ippolito, Nathaniel Weir, Carlos Aguirre, Rachel Wicks, Arya McCarthy, and the anonymous reviewers for their helpful feedback. We also wish to thank the anonymous mechanical Turkers who provided invaluable suggestions for improving our human evaluation setup during earlier iterations of this study.

References

David H Ackley, Geoffrey E Hinton, and Terrence J Sejnowski. 1985. A learning algorithm for Boltzmann machines. *Cognitive science*, 9(1):147–169.

Nader Akoury, Shufan Wang, Josh Whiting, Stephen Hood, Nanyun Peng, and Mohit Iyyer. 2020. STORIUM: A Dataset and Evaluation Platform for Machine-in-the-Loop Story Generation. In *Proceedings of the 2020 Conference on Empirical Methods in Natural Language Processing (EMNLP)*, pages 6470–6484, Online. Association for Computational Linguistics.

Tom B Brown, Benjamin Mann, Nick Ryder, Melanie Subbiah, Jared Kaplan, Prafulla Dhariwal, Arvind Neelakantan, Pranav Shyam, Girish Sastry, Amanda Askell, et al. 2020. Language models are few-shot learners. *arXiv preprint arXiv:2005.14165*.

Massimo Caccia, Lucas Caccia, William Fedus, Hugo Larochelle, Joelle Pineau, and Laurent Charlin. 2018. Language gans falling short. *arXiv preprint arXiv:1811.02549*.

Angela Fan, Mike Lewis, and Yann Dauphin. 2018. Hierarchical Neural Story Generation. In *Proceedings of the 56th Annual Meeting of the Association for Computational Linguistics (Volume 1: Long Papers)*, pages 889–898, Melbourne, Australia. Association for Computational Linguistics.

Jessica Ficler and Yoav Goldberg. 2017. Controlling linguistic style aspects in neural language generation. *arXiv preprint arXiv:1707.02633*.

Tatsunori B Hashimoto, Hugh Zhang, and Percy Liang. 2019. Unifying human and statistical evaluation for natural language generation. *arXiv preprint arXiv:1904.02792*.

Felix Hill, Antoine Bordes, Sumit Chopra, and Jason Weston. 2015. The Goldilocks Principle: Reading Children's Books with Explicit Memory Representations.

Ari Holtzman, Jan Buys, Li Du, Maxwell Forbes, and Yejin Choi. 2020. The curious case of neural text degeneration. In *International Conference on Learning Representations*.

Daphne Ippolito, Daniel Duckworth, Chris Callison-Burch, and Douglas Eck. 2020. Automatic detection of generated text is easiest when humans are fooled. In *Proceedings of the 58th Annual Meeting of the Association for Computational Linguistics*, pages 1808–1822, Online. Association for Computational Linguistics.

Daphne Ippolito, David Grangier, Chris Callison-Burch, and Douglas Eck. 2019a. Unsupervised hierarchical story infilling. In *Proceedings of the First Workshop on Narrative Understanding*, pages 37–43.

Daphne Ippolito, Reno Kriz, Joao Sedoc, Maria Kustikova, and Chris Callison-Burch. 2019b. Comparison of diverse decoding methods from conditional language models. In *Proceedings of the 57th Annual Meeting of the Association for Computational Linguistics*, pages 3752–3762.

Jiwei Li, Michel Galley, Chris Brockett, Jianfeng Gao, and Bill Dolan. 2016a. A Diversity-Promoting Objective Function for Neural Conversation Models. In *Proceedings of the 2016 Conference of the North American Chapter of the Association for Computational Linguistics: Human Language Technologies*, pages 110–119, San Diego, California. Association for Computational Linguistics.

Jiwei Li, Michel Galley, Chris Brockett, Jianfeng Gao, and Bill Dolan. 2016b. A diversity-promoting objective function for neural conversation models. In *Proceedings of the 2016 Conference of the North American Chapter of the Association for Computational Linguistics: Human Language Technologies*, pages 110–119, San Diego, California. Association for Computational Linguistics.

Sean MacAvaney, Hao-Ren Yao, Eugene Yang, Katina Russell, Nazli Goharian, and Ophir Frieder. 2019. Hate speech detection: Challenges and solutions. *PLOS ONE*, 14(8):e0221152. Publisher: Public Library of Science.

Pedro Henrique Martins, Zita Marinho, and André F. T. Martins. 2020. Sparse text generation. In *Proceedings of the 2020 Conference on Empirical Methods in Natural Language Processing (EMNLP)*, pages 4252–4273, Online. Association for Computational Linguistics.

Nasrin Mostafazadeh, Nathanael Chambers, Xiaodong He, Devi Parikh, Dhruv Batra, Lucy Vanderwende, Pushmeet Kohli, and James Allen. 2016. A corpus and cloze evaluation for deeper understanding of commonsense stories. In *Proceedings of the 2016 Conference of the North American Chapter of the Association for Computational Linguistics: Human Language Technologies*, pages 839–849, San Diego, California. Association for Computational Linguistics.

Moin Nadeem, Tianxing He, Kyunghyun Cho, and James Glass. 2020. A systematic characterization of sampling algorithms for open-ended language generation.

Ryo Nakamura, Katsuhito Sudoh, Koichiro Yoshino, and Satoshi Nakamura. 2018. Another diversity-promoting objective function for neural dialogue generation. *CoRR*, abs/1811.08100.

Nanyun Peng, Marjan Ghazvininejad, Jonathan May, and Kevin Knight. 2018. Towards Controllable Story Generation. In *Proceedings of the First Workshop on Storytelling*, pages 43–49, New Orleans, Louisiana. Association for Computational Linguistics.

Alec Radford, Jeffrey Wu, Rewon Child, David Luan, Dario Amodei, and Ilya Sutskever. 2019. Language models are unsupervised multitask learners.

Nils Reimers and Iryna Gurevych. 2019. Sentence-BERT: Sentence embeddings using Siamese BERT-networks. In *EMNLP/IJCNLP*.

Abigail See, Aneesh Pappu, Rohun Saxena, Akhila Yerukola, and Christopher D. Manning. 2019. Do massively pretrained language models make better storytellers? In *Proceedings of the 23rd Conference on Computational Natural Language Learning (CoNLL)*, pages 843–861, Hong Kong, China. Association for Computational Linguistics.

Emily Sheng, Kai-Wei Chang, Prem Natarajan, and Nanyun Peng. 2020. Towards Controllable Biases in Language Generation. In *Findings of the Association for Computational Linguistics: EMNLP 2020*, pages 3239–3254, Online. Association for Computational Linguistics.

Guy Tevet and Jonathan Berant. 2020. Evaluating the evaluation of diversity in natural language generation. *ArXiv*, abs/2004.02990.

Jason Weston, Antoine Bordes, Sumit Chopra, Alexander M. Rush, Bart van Merriënboer, Armand Joulin, and Tomáš Mikolov. 2015. Towards AI-complete question answering: A set of prerequisite toy tasks.

Jingjing Xu, Xuancheng Ren, Junyang Lin, and Xu Sun. 2018. Diversity-promoting GAN: A cross-entropy based generative adversarial network for diversified text generation. In *Proceedings of the 2018 Conference on Empirical Methods in Natural Language Processing*, pages 3940–3949, Brussels, Belgium. Association for Computational Linguistics.

Hugh Zhang, Daniel Duckworth, Daphne Ippolito, and Arvind Neelakantan. 2020a. Trading off diversity and quality in natural language generation. *arXiv preprint arXiv:2004.10450*.

Yizhe Zhang, Michel Galley, Jianfeng Gao, Zhe Gan, Xiujun Li, Chris Brockett, and Bill Dolan. 2018. Generating informative and diverse conversational responses via adversarial information maximization. In *Proceedings of the 32nd International Conference on Neural Information Processing Systems*, NIPS'18, page 1815–1825, Red Hook, NY, USA. Curran Associates Inc.

Yizhe Zhang, Siqi Sun, Michel Galley, Yen-Chun Chen, Chris Brockett, Xiang Gao, Jianfeng Gao, Jingjing Liu, and Bill Dolan. 2020b. DialoGPT: Large-scale generative pre-training for conversational response generation. In *ACL, system demonstration*.

A Example Outputs

All examples start on the following page. We report narrative responses given a single prompt for various model architectures/sizes, decoding methods, and hyperparameter sweeps.

B Human Annotator Survey Details

As discussed in §3.4, we created a survey on Amazon Mechanical Turk for the human evaluation. Evaluating all of the prompts was infeasible, so we sampled 100 prompts and generated one story for each nucleus sampling p value ($\{0.0, 0.3, 0.5, 0.7, 0.9, 0.95, 1.0\}$), for a total of 700 stories. We wanted story lengths that were long enough to give the worker sufficient context to be able to evaluate a passage, but not too long as to take too much time per story. We used the GPT-2 Medium model (best performing, see §4) trained on the medium length dataset because it fit our requirements. Due to the projected length of time to complete the survey, we paid $1 per human intelligence task (HIT). Each HIT was seen by five workers.

The generated stories were shuffled, and split into groups of five for each HIT. The story display is shown in Figure 9. In addition to the five stories, each HIT had one "attention check." There were a total of 140 HITs. The definitions for interesting, fluent, coherent, and relevant were explained, along with guidelines for each of the $[1, 4]$ Likert scale options (shown in Figure 7). For convenience, the definitions were available as a tooltip when a mouse hovered over a question or option. Example ratings were available to the worker under the "Examples" tab (not shown).

As mentioned earlier, each HIT included one attention check. The attention check was used to check if a worker was paying attention to the task or selecting options at random. The check, shown in Figure 8, asked the worker to fill in the same answers as for the previous story. In addition to the attention checks, we supervised the workers by only releasing 20 HITs at a time (total of seven batches), and iteratively removing workers who did a poor job. While this task was very subjective (a handful of workers left us comments about the difficulty of the task), we consider performance subpar for any combination of the following: (1) if a worker finished the task unreasonably quickly (under 5 minutes), (2) failed an attention check, (3) had low agreement with other annotators, and (4) completed many HITs in a short amount of time. We spot-checked work from those who were automatically flagged as suspicious by checking their task answers. Overall, we removed 28 workers from the final results.

Once the highest-rated nucleus sampling parameter was chosen ($p = 0.7$), we repeated the same setup for the antiLM λ parameter sweep. Using the same 100 prompts from earlier, we generated stories with GPT-2 Medium-medium with $p = 0.7$ and $\lambda = \{0.1, 0.2, 0.35, 0.5\}$. We also included $\lambda = 0.0$ (i.e. without the antiLM objective) to help with worker calibration. The 500 stories were split into 100 HITs (five batches of 20 HITs).

Total cost of both the nucleus sampling and antiLM sweeps was $1,440.

C Top-k vs. Nucleus Sampling

C.1 Setup

For top-k sampling, we use $k = 40$; our motivation for choosing this value is that it is the one used in Radford et al. (2019) for "conditional" (prompted) generation[8], and in Fan et al. (2018).

The following is a qualitative review performed by the authors.

C.2 Qualitative Evaluation

For most reasonable settings of p, nucleus sampling tends to produce stories which are dramatic, vivid, and fun to read, but which do not often stay on topic. Indeed, the outputs demonstrate two main types of errors: (1) cramming too many topics into one story, and (2) sudden shifts in topic. Example outputs are in Table 8.

Top-k sampling, however, demonstrates quite extreme variance. Some of the generated stories feel almost human-like with how on-topic they remain for multiple paragraphs—but they are about safe and boring topics and generally employ very common token collocates, which makes the output feel uncreative and uninteresting. Other stories are dramatic, but almost dream-like due to the stream-of-consciousness incoherent flow. Yet other stories are completely unintelligible and show signs of neural text degeneration. Holtzman et al. (2020) finds nucleus sampling to generally be preferable to top-k sampling, and we find this to be true in the narrative generation task. p seems to correlate more closely with narrative quality than k.

C.3 Conclusions

As we had expected, we preferred the stories generated with nucleus sampling decoding. Since nucleus sampling is essentially a dynamic top-k algorithm (i.e. each step has a different number of tokens that constitutes the top $x\%$), and even small nucleus sampling values have large number of tokens to choose from (k), this aligns with the results of See et al. (2019), who found large k to be preferred according to automatic evaluations.

[8]Example generated responses are located in Radford et al. (2019)'s Appendix.

D Automatic Metrics

Here, we provide the full table of automatic metrics for all p values tested (Table 9). Dist-n scores tend to increase consistently with higher p values, whereas sent-BERT tends to peak at lower p values in $[0.3, 0.5]$ and continually decline after.

E A Closer Look at Nucleus Sampling

How does the nucleus sampling token filter compare to the top-k filter? For example, when a token is sampled from $p = 0.3$, how many tokens are in the sampling space?

Figure 6 shows the cumulative distribution function (CDF) for the p values tested in the nucleus sampling hyperparameter sweep. Using the same set of 100 prompts from the human evaluation, we re-generate the responses and collect the number of tokens in the sampling space at each step. Each p is represented by the raw number of tokens in the distribution across all 100 prompts and is not averaged for each generated story.

Surprisingly, nucleus sampling often reduced to the greedy decoder (token space reduced to a single token), even at higher p values. Despite high probability thresholds, $0.7 <= p <= 0.95$ still skewed towards sampling from a relatively low number of tokens, as these tokens tended to have very high probability in certain contexts. All p values frequently sampled from less than $1,000$ tokens, which is less than 2% of the total number of tokens in GPT-2's vocabulary $(50, 260)$. As p increased, we observed a larger sample space, which indicates more of a return to the long-tailed token probability distribution seen in random sampling.

This shows that it may not be correct to compare a nucleus sampling p value directly against a single top-k value. Nucleus sampling is essentially dynamic top-k sampling, which makes a direct comparison unfair without first checking the distribution of the number of tokens sampled by p for the model and task in question.

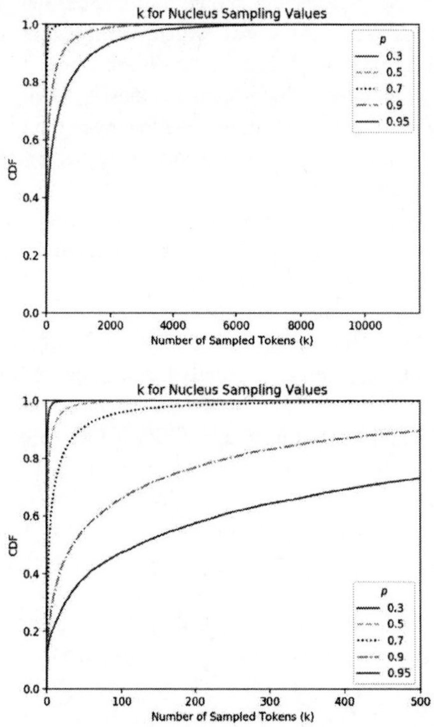

Figure 6: Cumulative distribution of the frequency of the number of sampled tokens for each tested p. We do not include $p = 1.0$ since it is constant with the number of tokens in GPT-2 vocabulary $(50, 260)$. The top and bottom plots are the same, but the bottom plot has a restricted x-axis to see the trend better.

Model	Prompt: "[WP] You just started a new job in a large office building and what you do n't know is that at twelve o'clock every day , there is a office wide Purge style battle to the death , those who survive an hour get a significant pay raise and can come back tomorrow . A bell just went off , it 's twelve o'clock ."
GPT-2 Small, $p = 0.7$	The last time I saw this place was in a very old diner, that was a pretty nice diner. The waiters were in all black suits and shoes, and the only reason they didn't make it in time was because I didn't want to. I had my smartphone in my hands, but I 'd had it the whole time. <newline><newline>" Don't take it anymore, it's been a while. " A voice said, and I smiled. " I don't want to take it anymore. " <newline><newline>I smiled and held my phone out. I was still on the phone, but I could feel my stomach churning. I could feel the sun on my face, so I held it out, but the lights went out. I wasn't sure how long I had left, but it wasn't long before I woke up.
GPT-2 Med., $p = 0.7$	" Hi, I'm Mr. Smith, and I'm here for the Purge! " <newline><newline>The building's boss sat at the desk with a huge grin. I 'd been working in the building for about five months now and I 'd grown tired of it. <newline><newline>" Now, I understand the concerns, but we have a very strict policy about employees not coming into work after 12:00 PM. If you're caught cheating, or even the slightest bit annoying, you're fired. We also don't allow anyone over 12 hours without the company paying a visit. "
Fusion Model, $p = 0.7$	" Hello ! My name is Randy , " I shouted into the air . " I ' m the <unk>" <newline><newline>" Well , it ' s just that I need a new way to put this . I ' m not going to let you take my own life. " Randy said . " You ' re not going to allow me to use my own life . But I ' m not going to let you take your own life ! " <newline><newline>" Oh , you ' re sorry ! I was just thinking about your life ! You ' re going to make a decent living , and all I need to do is come back to the living room . I need to be happy . But you ' re not going to let me get my own life ! " <newline><newline>" You ' re going to have to put my own life together , <unk>! " Randy laughed . " If I ' m going to take your own life , I ' ll take you on to your own life . " <newline><newline>" You '

Table 5: Medium-length responses from GPT-2 Small, GPT-2 Medium, and Fusion (baseline) models with nucleus sampling parameter $p = 0.7$.

top-p	Prompt: "[WP] You just started a new job in a large office building and what you do n't know is that at twelve o'clock every day , there is a office wide Purge style battle to the death , those who survive an hour get a significant pay raise and can come back tomorrow . A bell just went off , it 's twelve o'clock ."
greedy	Hey, he
$p = 0.3$	I was nervous. <newline><newline>I was nervous about the job. <newline><newline>I was nervous about the pay.
$p = 0.5$	The first thing I noticed was the absence of people. I wasn't sure why, but I couldn't shake the feeling that it wasn't just the people that were gone. I mean, it wasn't like I hadn't been here before. I mean, I was in the office for a month, but it felt like a year. <newline><newline>I wasn't sure what was going on, but I could tell that something was wrong. <newline><newline>" Hello? "
$p = 0.7$	My boss was a loner. He liked to work late and I didn't know why. I didn't want to work late. I just didn't have the patience for it. <newline><newline>I don't know what happened. <newline><newline>" You got ta be kidding me, " he said, " a sixteen year old would just walk into the office and run out of work? "
$p = 0.9$	All four of the chimes clicked and the chandelier snapped, as the room dimmed and grew dim until the only light came from an overhead television, showing the " The Purge " live. In the background, a towering wall of reds, greens, and yellows flashed in contrast to the background colors, casting warm green shimmers across the television. <newline><newline>The chandelier struck the ceiling, crumpling under the weight. A small circle of lights in the ceiling blinked and illuminated what had been a desk, until two figures entered it. <newline><newline>The first man, dressed in a yellow and white baseball cap and sunglasses, stood tall, wearing khakis and a button-down shirt. A muscular build and hairy arms waved about as he spoke.
$p = 0.95$	Those who survive are always in their offices when they finish, they wake up, make sure they run the water for a while, then try to get up and make the 9 to 5 as fast as possible. The rest are scared to take a break from that, they're afraid the DIT will find them and kill them and they have to do it. Well those people, these employees, they're all so qualified to run around the office. I mean they're trained. I took the systems Administrator and Job Writer (same person from last year) and fired them in 15 minutes. The guy, one of the better systems engineers had died from a heart attack and there are only 3 employees left. I've never heard of a DIT being fired like that before. " <newline><newline>Dr. Neutson was writing these words down as they told her to, he 'd always loved his wife Sandy too and she was absolutely dying. Mrs. Neutson looked as though she was about to make another coffee, now that she realized it was someone else who was in her office, there was tears streaming down her face, she was going to finish today. " Great, I'm going to have no more"
$p = 1.0$	Chad's Melatonin Impaired Heart implant had occurred during the Golden elimination pilot. " Critically, " the docs explained to the board, " Third lapse, unlocking the minimum Carol Corporation-mandated for the Restricted Solid Species Program. We penalize those who have such lapses as early and late entry personnel. " <newline><newline>Chad felt pain in the core of his neck - compressing saliva into his neckline, seeing his neighbors ' streaks poking out, " That doesn't work, I still live in Seattle ' s Milliner Square until May 17th, " thought Chad as he fell down the empty stairs the hospital had installed that morning. Without warning, his head slammed into the steel sill beneath him and he felt a sharp pain begin to run down his spine. The pain apparently doomed him to eternity in a single meditation, the disease never getting better. <newline><newline>After five ER visits, nine Lab ultrasound tests, six minor surgeries, pressure checks, one heart-heated ultrasound, Chad came back for surgeries, six of which were removeable.

Table 6: Medium-length responses from GPT-2 Medium with a sweep of nucleus sampling parameter p.

λ	Prompt: "[WP] Your baby starts crying every time you leave their room . Finally , you pick up your child and leave the room together . As soon as you step out, you hear crying coming from the room ."
$\lambda = 0.0$	"Daddy!" <newline><newline>I cried into my mom's breast. She was holding my son in her arms. I 'd never seen a baby cry so deeply. Tears were streaming down my face. I ran to the door and opened it to see a crying girl. I ran back to the room and opened the door, and there was my little girl. She 'd started crying again. <newline><newline>"What is wrong, mom?"
$\lambda = 0.1$	There were only two of us left in the hospital. The nurses wouldn't let me leave. I was in pain. My mother was looking at me with a confused look on her face. <newline><newline>"Can you tell me what's wrong, honey?" she asked. <newline><newline>"Honey, it's okay." I whispered. I couldn't hear her, and the nurses couldn't hear me either.
$\lambda = 0.2$	My wife came home from work around 3 AM to find her child covered in blood and screaming. Her heart was racing and her skin was boiling with the pain of being cut. <newline><newline>I rushed into the living room, eyes wide and bloodshot. She was hysterical, sobbing, and cackling as she knelt over my body, gasping for air. <newline><newline>"Wh-who are you?" I asked. She was gasping for air.
$\lambda = 0.35$	Sitting next to her bed hung cardboard boxes. Five candles burning brightly in their candles hung in the ceiling. A bright yellow heart in a jar was stuck in the middle. There were three other jars on the floor. The left was empty, with the word "SHIT" written on it. The other two had the words "WAIT" written on them. <newline><newline>"Come on, Mom, it's just a puppy!" He was angry. <newline><newline>"It's a girl!" I responded. "What are you talking about? You have two of them, and they're twins!"
$\lambda = 0.5$	"Daddy? Daddy what's wrong honey? Daddy why are you crying honey? Daddy pick up your child and leave the room, you have to get to work" <newline><newline>I picked up my daughter and we walked out into the kitchen. <newline><newline>I held her close and whispered into her ear "It's ok honey, I'll be ok."

Table 7: Medium-length stories generated using GPT-2 Medium with nucleus sampling ($p = 0.7$) and various diverse decoding strengths λ.

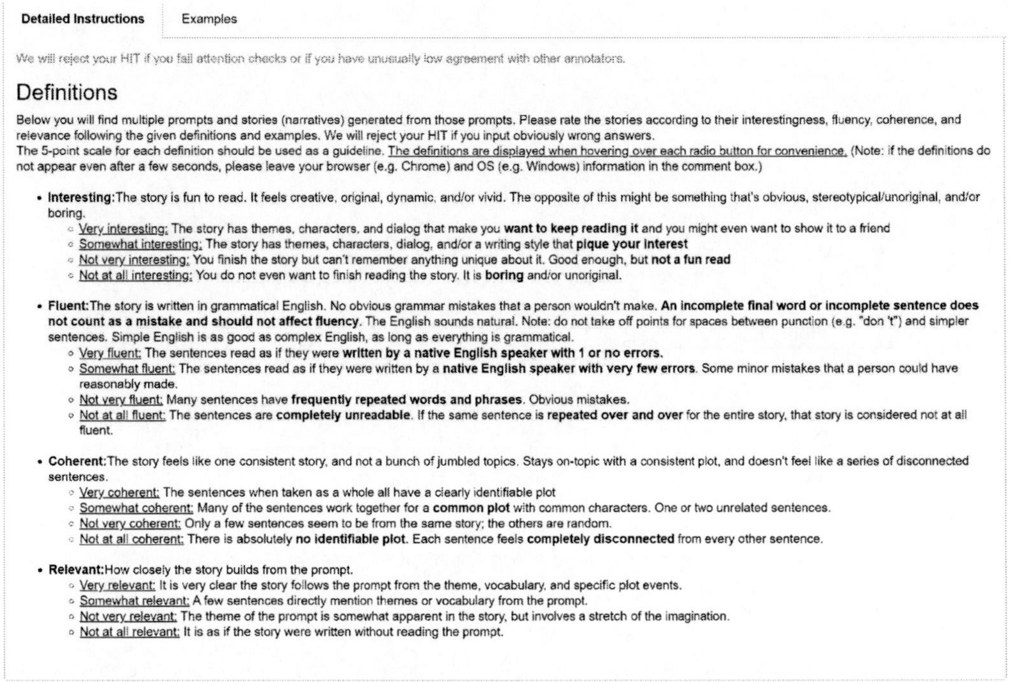

Detailed Instructions | Examples

We will reject your HIT if you fail attention checks or if you have unusually low agreement with other annotators.

Definitions

Below you will find multiple prompts and stories (narratives) generated from those prompts. Please rate the stories according to their interestingness, fluency, coherence, and relevance following the given definitions and examples. We will reject your HIT if you input obviously wrong answers.
The 5-point scale for each definition should be used as a guideline. The definitions are displayed when hovering over each radio button for convenience. (Note: if the definitions do not appear even after a few seconds, please leave your browser (e.g. Chrome) and OS (e.g. Windows) information in the comment box.)

- **Interesting:**The story is fun to read. It feels creative, original, dynamic, and/or vivid. The opposite of this might be something that's obvious, stereotypical/unoriginal, and/or boring.
  - Very interesting: The story has themes, characters, and dialog that make you **want to keep reading it** and you might even want to show it to a friend
  - Somewhat interesting: The story has themes, characters, dialog, and/or a writing style that **pique your interest**
  - Not very interesting: You finish the story but can't remember anything unique about it. Good enough, but **not a fun read**
  - Not at all interesting: You do not even want to finish reading the story. It is **boring** and/or unoriginal.
- **Fluent:**The story is written in grammatical English. No obvious grammar mistakes that a person wouldn't make. **An incomplete final word or incomplete sentence does not count as a mistake and should not affect fluency**. The English sounds natural. Note: do not take off points for spaces between punction (e.g. "don 't") and simpler sentences. Simple English is as good as complex English, as long as everything is grammatical.
  - Very fluent: The sentences read as if they were **written by a native English speaker with 1 or no errors.**
  - Somewhat fluent: The sentences read as if they were written by a **native English speaker with very few errors**. Some minor mistakes that a person could have reasonably made.
  - Not very fluent: Many sentences have **frequently repeated words and phrases**. Obvious mistakes.
  - Not at all fluent: The sentences are **completely unreadable**. If the same sentence is **repeated over and over** for the entire story, that story is considered not at all fluent.
- **Coherent:**The story feels like one consistent story, and not a bunch of jumbled topics. Stays on-topic with a consistent plot, and doesn't feel like a series of disconnected sentences.
  - Very coherent: The sentences when taken as a whole all have a clearly identifiable plot
  - Somewhat coherent: Many of the sentences work together for a **common plot** with common characters. One or two unrelated sentences.
  - Not very coherent: Only a few sentences seem to be from the same story; the others are random.
  - Not at all coherent: There is absolutely **no identifiable plot**. Each sentence feels **completely disconnected** from every other sentence.
- **Relevant:**How closely the story builds from the prompt.
  - Very relevant: It is very clear the story follows the prompt from the theme, vocabulary, and specific plot events.
  - Somewhat relevant: A few sentences directly mention themes or vocabulary from the prompt.
  - Not very relevant: The theme of the prompt is somewhat apparent in the story, but involves a stretch of the imagination.
  - Not at all relevant: It is as if the story were written without reading the prompt.

Figure 7: Instructions presented to the workers. To make it easier for the workers, the definitions were available as tool-tip hover text over the questions and options.

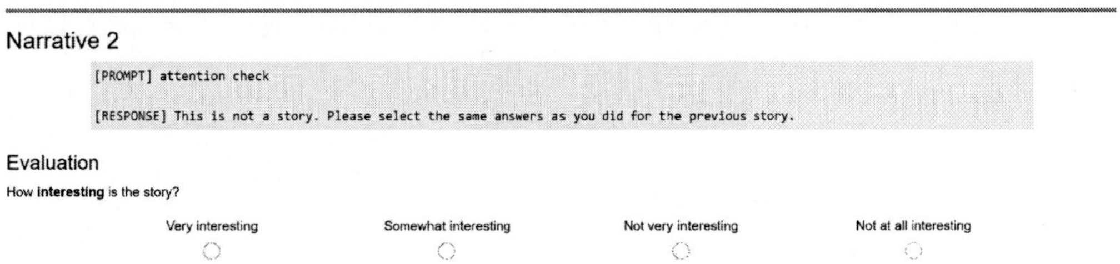

Narrative 2

[PROMPT] attention check

[RESPONSE] This is not a story. Please select the same answers as you did for the previous story.

Evaluation

How **interesting** is the story?

Very interesting | Somewhat interesting | Not very interesting | Not at all interesting

Figure 8: An attention check in the survey. The worker is asked to input the same answers as they did for the previous story. A worker gets flagged for review if they fail at least one attention check.

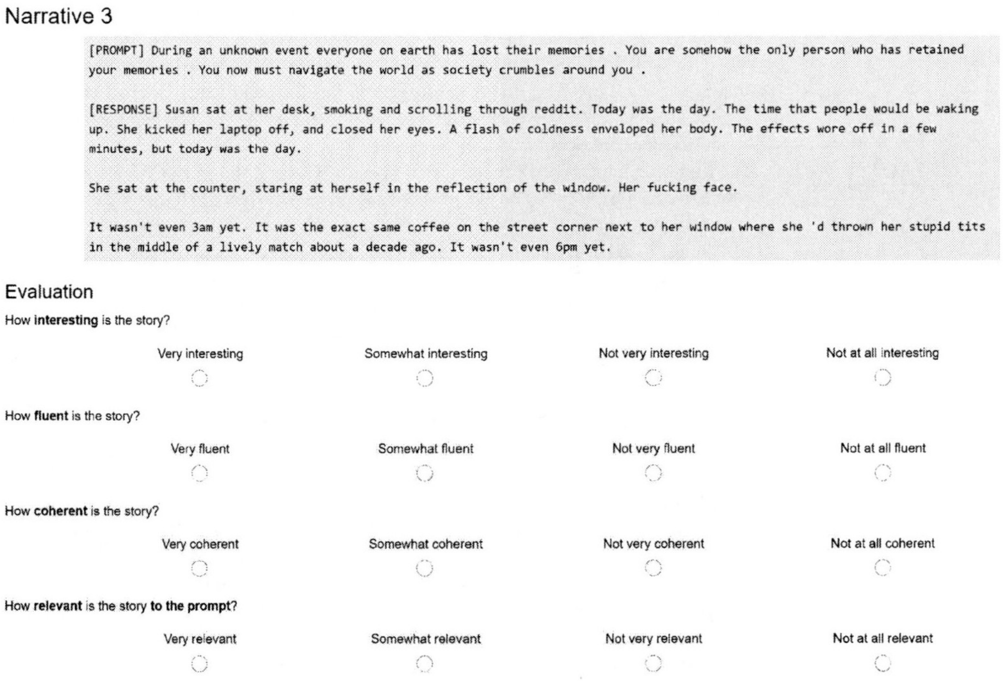

Figure 9: An example narrative display to a worker along with the questions. There were five stories in each HIT and one attention check. The definitions of each metric and option are shown when the mouse hovers over the questions and radio buttons, respectively.

Model, Decoding	Prompt: "[WP] You just started a new job in a large office building and what you do n't know is that at twelve o'clock every day , there is a office wide Purge style battle to the death , those who survive an hour get a significant pay raise and can come back tomorrow . A bell just went off , it 's twelve o'clock ."
GPT-2 Med., $p = 0.9$	All four of the chimes clicked and the chandelier snapped, as the room dimmed and grew dim until the only light came from an overhead television, showing the " The Purge " live. In the background, a towering wall of reds, greens, and yellows flashed in contrast to the background colors, casting warm green shimmers across the television. <newline><newline>The chandelier struck the ceiling, crumpling under the weight. A small circle of lights in the ceiling blinked and illuminated what had been a desk, until two figures entered it. <newline><newline>The first man, dressed in a yellow and white baseball cap and sunglasses, stood tall, wearing khakis and a button-down shirt. A muscular build and hairy arms waved about as he spoke.
GPT-2 Med., $k = 40$	The first time it happened I remember it vividly. The first time I met it. We got our first coffee, we sat on the train and talked and made plans but when I first saw it coming I knew something was going to happen. There was a man in white with a clipboard. I said " how you doing? " and he asked " what the hell did I just read you about ". I told him nothing he went through what the hell I knew everything about the Purge and I knew that I had to be careful because if I wasn't careful it would happen again. He looked at me expectantly and I knew immediately that I had to go and try to help people ' s lives. No one else would go so I did as I was told. <newline><newline>He asked me if I had time for something more serious than just reading
Fusion Model, $p = 0.9$	He was n't ready to die . I did . The name on his chest would kill him if he wanted to know . They wanted me to accept him as he wanted me to be not ready . I did it for him but he loved me . <newline><newline>I was the one that started a revolution . It was a simple matter of encouraging him and all the loyal soldiers that murdered him . And yet I never seemed to know what he had to do to deserve my right to be born and robbed . If only I knew . I could feel the faintest drop of power beneath my footsteps as he died . I felt the need to put some strings around him . But he had so much to offer . He seemed to feel I was the leader of the group and I was ready . He taught me the fact that he was supposed to be the most hated man in the country . So the world slowed . <newline><newline>And so he fought me . I was ready . He lost every step of his very being when he
Fusion Model, $k = 40$	It was a sunny Monday morning when I woke up to the noise of my alarm going off . I got up from my bed , got out of bed , and went into the bathroom and took off my coat . It was n't exactly a normal morning . I walked into the bathroom and put on my shoes , and put on some pants , and went to the bathroom . The light from the bathroom was n't going to change anything . I walked out of the bathroom and went to the bathroom . It was a good morning . My morning routine was going well in bed , and I was going to see some shit , so it was good . <newline>I went to the bathroom . It was the first step in my morning shift , so I took off my pants and

Table 8: Medium-length responses from GPT-2 Medium and the Fusion (baseline) model with top-k and nucleus sampling.

		Small			Medium			Large		
Model	**Decoding**	**Dist-1**	**Dist-2**	**sent-BERT**	**Dist-1**	**Dist-2**	**sent-BERT**	**Dist-1**	**Dist-2**	**sent-BERT**
GPT-2 Small	greedy	0.002	0.007	0.782	0.002	0.008	0.644	0.000	0.001	0.684
	$p = 0.3$	0.006	0.038	0.835	0.005	0.029	**0.815**	0.001	0.006	**0.804**
	$p = 0.5$	0.013	0.092	**0.838**	0.008	0.067	0.791	0.002	0.014	0.760
	$p = 0.7$	0.018	0.149	0.830	0.011	0.112	0.741	0.003	0.034	0.694
	$p = 0.9$	0.026	0.234	0.808	0.016	0.177	0.682	0.005	0.087	0.646
	$p = 0.95$	0.030	0.274	0.798	0.019	0.213	0.663	0.007	0.118	0.632
	$p = 1.0$	**0.042**	**0.344**	0.787	**0.028**	**0.283**	0.644	**0.015**	**0.195**	0.613
GPT-2 Medium	greedy	0.006	0.022	0.626	0.003	0.014	0.579	0.001	0.003	0.779
	$p = 0.3$	0.014	0.078	0.842	0.008	0.047	**0.813**	0.001	0.008	**0.813**
	$p = 0.5$	0.021	0.140	**0.855**	0.011	0.086	0.788	0.002	0.017	0.772
	$p = 0.7$	0.026	0.195	**0.855**	0.013	0.125	0.741	0.003	0.036	0.709
	$p = 0.9$	0.034	0.272	0.842	0.018	0.190	0.692	0.007	0.093	0.660
	$p = 0.95$	0.039	0.308	0.837	0.021	0.227	0.677	0.009	0.127	0.646
	$p = 1.0$	**0.051**	**0.374**	0.831	**0.030**	**0.291**	0.658	**0.017**	**0.210**	0.628
Fusion Model	greedy	0.006	0.068	0.690	0.005	0.055	0.666	0.005	0.055	0.666
	$p = 0.3$	0.003	0.017	**0.783**	0.001	0.009	**0.779**	0.001	0.009	**0.779**
	$p = 0.5$	0.005	0.046	0.758	0.003	0.027	0.750	0.003	0.027	0.750
	$p = 0.7$	0.009	0.092	0.707	0.005	0.061	0.686	0.005	0.061	0.686
	$p = 0.9$	0.014	0.174	0.667	0.008	0.130	0.637	0.008	0.130	0.637
	$p = 0.95$	0.017	0.213	0.655	0.009	0.155	0.624	0.008	0.149	0.624
	$p = 1.0$	**0.025**	**0.277**	0.633	**0.016**	**0.229**	0.603	**0.016**	**0.229**	0.603

Table 9: Automatic diversity evaluations across models and decoding methods for each response length. The decoding methods represent a parameter sweep over the p value in nucleus sampling, where $p = 1$ corresponds to completely random sampling. The fusion model is a baseline from Fan et al. (2018).

Author Index

Association for Computational Linguistics
209 N. Eighth Street
Stroudsburg, Pennsylvania 18360

ISBN 978-1-7138-3375-8

CURRAN ASSOCIATES INC.
proceedings.com